T0208964

"God Bless Daddy, Mother,
Bill, Ron, Jerry,
Carol Ann, Linda Jane,
Dick, and Little Tom"

"God Bless Daddy, Mother, Bill, Ron, Jerry, Carol Ann, Linda Jane, Dick, and Little Tom"

By

Richard L. Kramer

ISBN: 978-1-5882-0389-2 (sc)

Print information available on the last page.

This book is printed on acid-free paper.

1stBooks – rev. 8/15/00

Acknowledgments

It has taken three years for me to write these stories. Various family members have read them and have remembered things differently. In response to their differing memory, I have simply said, "write your own account." Because of their comments, I have remembered many other events that deserve recording and I am currently in the process of doing so.

I wish to acknowledge the suggestions and the thorough, critical reading of these stories by my sister, Carol Taylor and by two good friends, Nancy Crowder and Cathy Spencer. Acknowledgements also to my good friend Terri Ritz who typed rough drafts.

In addition, I want to acknowledge the editorial expertise of my son, Dane and his computer skills. I also would like to thank my daughter, Cass for her warm, complimentary introduction.

Dedicated to:

- **God**, who gave me life through my wonderful parents **Arthur William Kramer (Art)** and **Cecilia Frances (Ringle) Kramer (Ceal)**,

- My wife, **Margaret (Fane) Kramer (Peg)** who is incessantly supportive and tolerant,

- Our son, **Dane Edward Kramer (Dane)** who edited this book and brought it together,

- Our daughter, **Casady Lynn Kramer (Cass)** who wrote the complimentary introduction,

- My six brothers and sisters:
  William Leo Kramer (Bill) who will save me,
  Ronald Joseph Kramer (Ron) who gives me courage,
  Gerald Francis Kramer (Jerry) who fosters simplicity, health, and the pursuit of common sense,
  Carol Ann Taylor (Carol) who continually nourishes family and the love of family history,
  Linda Jane VanTreese (Linda) who is a model of commitment and strength, and
  Thomas Edward Kramer (Tom) who was a perfect childhood playmate and completes Bill's logical, definitive approach.

- **Lastly, to my** Grandma Kramer **and** Aunt Gene Kramer.

Contents

Introduction

by Casady Lynn Kramer

"I love the rain." The most common reaction I receive after making this statement is the simple question: "Why?" To me the answer is just as simple: "Dad." Everything about the rain reminds me of my childhood and the special kind of magic that it seemed to evoke in my father. I remember when the smell of rain was in the air and we were frantically gathering toys scattered in the yard from a hard day of playing. My brother and I would enjoy a nice hot dinner with Mom and Dad, but when night fell and the rain was beating on the rooftops, Dane and I would join Dad on the front porch. Dad would sit in the middle of the white wicker swing and, like bookends, we would sit on either side and snuggle up close under the blankets we had brought to the porch. We would watch the rain pouring down, feel the mist on our faces and listen to the music it beat out all around us. As Dad rocked the swing with his long, sturdy legs, each arm wrapped around one of his children, we would talk lightly of the day's events. Then, it would begin. Sometimes we had to ask but more often, as I remember, Dad would simply begin, "Once upon a time…."

It didn't take long for the magic of Dad's stories to envelop us as we lay safe at his side. He could weave a tale. Sometimes scary, sometimes weird, sometimes fantasy, but always good. His stories often had a moral. I remember one in particular of a young man who, in an effort to be included in his rich Grandmother's will, always complimented her on a hideous, life-size painting of a cowboy. The young man got into her will all right, he got the painting. As he was cursing his misfortune, the cowboy came to life and said, "Be careful what you wish for 'cause you just might get it!"

Some of Dad's stories were explanatory: "Why the weeping willow tree weeps," or "Why clouds are sometimes flat on the bottom." Whatever they were, Dad's stories were always fun. He has a wonderful imagination. Nevertheless, my favorites, (and most of the ones I remember) are the true stories he would tell about his childhood. Just picturing my father as a little kid, running around with his brothers and sisters, causing all kinds of mischief still puts a smile on my face. As far as I am concerned, no one can tell a story like my Dad. I hope you will agree.

Section 1

Personal Development

Unhappy, and Didn't Know Why

When I was very young, two or three at the most, I was sent to Lanesville, Indiana for a period of time one summer. I was very unhappy being sent away from home and I do not remember anyone explaining to me why I had to go. Aunt Till arrived and before I knew it, we were on the train to New Albany and from there we went to Lanesville. The only thing I remember about the train trip was passing through the deep gorges and tunnels of the knobs, Floyd Knobs. I must have slept most of the way. The northern portion of Indiana is flat but in the south, where Lanesville is located, there are hills and the knobs.

I spent an eternity in Lanesville that summer. I didn't know what to do with myself. There was nothing to do, no one else to play with, and I missed my older sisters and brothers. I also missed, most of all, my Mother. I slept in the childhood home of my Mother, Aunt Till and Aunt Olive's home. There was also a man there called Uncle John. He passed the hours of the day sitting on the roofed porch between the house and the smokehouse. For some reason, he had a collection of comic books. He would doze, snoring on occasion, while I thumbed through the books. I couldn't read the stories, but I looked at the pictures while sitting on the cool floor of the porch.

Cousin John and Dick
(smokehouse in background)

Various people came to visit to try to cheer me up but I persisted in my foul mood for as long as I was there. On one 'big occasion,' I was sent across the creek to spend the night at Uncle George and Aunt Hilda's home. Wading in the creek was fun, but beyond that there was little difference for me. Their home sat above the creek on the side of a hill. They were tenants in half of the house that belonged to an old lady that they insisted I address as "Aunt Lou." She was a large lady who was always sitting in a chair. On the following morning, after breakfast, I decided it might be entertaining to lie on my side and roll down the hill toward the creek. Aunt Hilda would not have this, but I insisted on doing it anyway. After several admonitions to stop from Aunt Hilda, I stuck my tongue out at her thinking she did not have the authority to tell me to do anything; she was not Mother. When I stuck my tongue out at her, she slapped me across the face and told me never to do that again. I never stuck my tongue out at her again and I stopped rolling down the hill. However, I did stick my tongue out for pictures, never cooperating with the adults taking the picture. I don't know why I couldn't have been happier with the situation. After all, people were going out of their way to entertain me.

I was taken by hand into town, two blocks away, for ice cream. Aunt Till always had a supply of the soft mint candies I really liked in her two-door cupboard that sat in the kitchen. If she ran out, we would make a special trip to the grocery store to buy more of them. The store always had wieners made of pork, which I really liked with mustard after they were boiled. My aunts were nice to me when they put me to bed. I should have felt like royalty and made the most of it, but something just did not fit.

Uncle John Ringle and Dick
(St. Mary's steeple in background)

It seemed to me I was there too long and I was beginning to think that I was not wanted at home any more. I was really down on the whole situation. I couldn't stand to listen to Uncle John snoring by the cistern on the porch, I was tired of exploring the smokehouse and the root cellar, tired of playing in the creek, tired of walking up the hill to the church and the graveyard, and bored with the comic books and the walks into town. Then it happened. The telephone rang. The telephone hung on the wall in the kitchen. Everyone in Lanesville had the same ring, a double "ring, ring." Aunt Till answered the phone and almost before I was told that I had a new baby brother in Indianapolis, the whole of Lanesville knew that my Mother, Cecilia, had given birth. The local operator, who connected the calls, always listened in and proceeded to spread the word to the entire town. Word spread like a grass fire with a healthy wind to its back. As for me, I was amazed that there was another person in the family. I hadn't noticed any difference in my Mother's shape. If I did, I had no idea what was happening. She must have been pregnant right before my eyes, but I still had no idea why I was sent away. I endured the separation from family in Indianapolis for about two months with an alien family in Lanesville; a family that treated me well, loved me, but who I didn't understand or want to be with.

Just as suddenly as my bag was packed and I was taken from Indianapolis to Lanesville, my bag was packed and I was taken from Lanesville back to Indianapolis. The return home was gratifying, and I was glad to be there. The smell of the home was the same as I remembered, and the feel of the bed was the same. My older sisters were the same as ever, but they made over a new arrival, my little brother, Tommy. I still don't know why I had to be sent away.

Lent

You might get the idea by the title that this is a short story about a person who has loaned something to someone else. It's not. It is about a period in the yearly calendar of the Catholic Church. The four weeks of Lent arrive in the early spring (sometimes very late winter and into early spring because of the calendar which dictates these events). It is a period that is akin to 'forever' when you are a child who has given up candy for the duration of lent. Family custom followed church custom and you were expected to "give something up for lent" as a penance in atonement for your sins. Lent ended on the Easter Sunday following Good Friday. I cannot, for the life of me, understand why the Friday on which we remember the crucifixion and death of Jesus is referred to as "Good." "Bad" seemed more appropriate, or maybe "Sad."

The children always gave up candy. At least I know that Tommy and I did. We stuck to it too. Mother helped. However, giving up the consumption of candy didn't stop us from collecting all that we could during the four weeks of lent.

At play, in the back yard, we would hear the back door of our neighbors' house open and we would instinctively stand up so that we could see over the hedge. We were hoping it was Mrs. Fultz so that we could say, "Hello Mrs. Fultz," in as nice a tone as we could muster.

Tommy at the hedge

If it were she, she would wave and say hello and then tell us to, "Wait there a minute." She would go back into the house and Tommy and I would look at each other knowingly. She would soon come out again and cross her drive to the hedgerow. Handing a couple of candy bars, usually Hershey bars, across the hedge, she would say something like, "Here, take these. You boys are so nice." Tommy and I would thank her in a voice that conveyed surprise, like we really didn't expect to be given candy bars.

"Why thank you Mrs. Fultz! Thank you very much!"

The transaction complete, we were tempted to sneak behind our garage and eat them on the spot. During lent, Mother kept a watchful eye. She would soon appear at the back door, call and wave hello to Mrs. Fultz who was making her way toward the back of their property to do who knows what, and then she would say to us, "OK, Dick and Tom, bring those in here." She would call out a "Thank you." to Mrs. Fultz as we approached the back door with the candy bars in hand.

"Well, you know this is Lent and we need to put those in the tin until Lent is over." Mother would then go to the kitchen pantry and retrieve a large, round cookie tin and pry it open. She would extend it to us for the deposit. By the end of Lent the tin was nearly filled with confiscated candy.

We knew Lent was nearing an end when we boiled and colored several dozen eggs. On the first nice day, we gathered weathered grass and fashioned nests all about the yard in plain view but also under bushes and in stands of tulips. Mother would then want a tour of the yard to see the nests we had made. On Easter morning, after mass and while we were changing clothes, Mother or Daddy would go out into the yard and run from nest to nest and put in the very eggs we had colored. While we were still in the process of changing, Daddy would come to the base of the stairs and call to us that he had seen the Easter Bunny and that we had better hurry. Of course, we never got down in time to see the bunny because "he had just left." "Oh, there he goes," Daddy would say while looking out a window that was too high for us to see out of, usually the kitchen window toward the back of the lot. We scrambled with our baskets out the back door and collected the eggs from the nests. They didn't let us miss any either, suggesting we look here or there. We were none the wiser simply thinking we were collecting eggs left by the bunny and that we would add to the ones we had colored.

The same stuff went on with the idea of Santa Claus only that went on for a much longer period of time, prompting us to be better than "good."

Oh, if we could have seen out the window.

The One and Only First Grade Event

St. Francis de Sales Grade School was a large one. The old, two-story brick building with four rooms downstairs and four rooms upstairs couldn't accommodate the eight grades neatly quartered in one building as it once did.

The first grade was taught by a slight nun, Sister Ernesta, in a large room located directly behind the priests' house and off the hallway that led from their home to the sacristy of the church. The second grade was taught across the playground in the convent, the sisters' home. The church, the school and the convent all had Avondale Street addresses and faced west. My Father and all his brothers and sisters had attended grade school at St. Francis, a German-speaking parish, except maybe for Dolores, my Daddy's youngest sister, one of Grandma Mary and Grandpa Joseph's daughters.

Tom, Sister Ernesta,
and Dick

I never knew Grandpa Joseph. After he died, Grandma sent Dolores to live with some relatives in Texas, because she had too many mouths to feed on a railroad man's pension or whatever income she had, if not from her other children, sent to work before their time.

Anyway, they had all attended St. Francis de Sales Grade School. The summer I turned six, I knew I would be starting school in the fall. Going never bothered me much, because it seemed like our family school. We had history there. Besides, my Father and all my Kramer aunts and uncles, I was preceded by three older brothers and two older sisters. I don't know if they all attended the first grade in the room off the sacristy of the church, but that's where I went.

Sister Ernesta had taught my oldest brother, Bill, and all the rest, and now here I was. I felt connected.

Besides, for years, and before I attended grade school, we had cut up sheets of letters and numbers and placed a set of each in little cloth pouches for Sister Ernesta's new first graders. So, I already knew the nuns.

The nuns had a convivial relationship with the Kramer household. They would often walk the tracks from Sherman Drive and pick blackberries or black raspberries with Mother, always in their habits, only with their sleeves rolled up. Some of them had hair on their arms. Once, they were back picking berries, and a rain shower suddenly came up. The starched parts collapsed, and the bibs rolled up. Mother and the two nuns raced to the house and could hardly stop laughing. One would pull the bib down and let it go. It would roll right back up like a window shade and set them all laughing again amidst speculation about what their Mother Superior would think.

Sisters of St. Francis
(Sister Ernesta in
center)

We seemed to be a class of about fifty, but Sister Ernesta, who towered over us at all of five feet, wore the black robes of power and mystery, her face surrounded with the same stiff, cardboard-like white frame of starched cloth and long, squared stiff bib of the Sisters of Saint Francis.

She was quietly talking and we were quietly listening to her instructions. We were all in our seats and there was a moment when Sister Ernesta stopped talking and the room was filled with silence.

Then everyone heard it, even those who were furthest away, the splattering of water on the wooden floor.

One of the students, one of my classmates, too afraid to ask to leave the room, had "lost her water." We knew she had peed. She was quickly approached by Sister Ernesta and escorted from the room. There was a whisper but nothing more from the class. That's all I remember of my first grade experience at St. Francis de Sales, and that was the first day of my formal education.

Prayers

Teeth were brushed and the face was washed with a cloth and then came time to get out of your clothes and into pajamas. Before getting into bed we were asked to kneel beside it and say our night prayers. Mother was the culprit. She insisted that we say our night prayers and many prayers for that matter, before and after meals, during storms, for the conversion of Russia, morning prayers, the Angelus and the rosary.

Night prayers included the Our Father, the Hail Mary, the Glory Be, and the blessing for the family. The blessing was said in two or three seconds. "God bless Daddy, Mother, Bill, Ron, Jerry, Carol Ann, Linda Jane, Dick and Little Tom." That accomplished, we were able to get under the covers, adjusting the pant legs of our pajamas so that they were not twisted and we were off to sleep.

Another prayer we were encouraged to say after we were tucked in was, "And now I lay me down to sleep, I pray the Lord my soul to keep. If I should die before I wake, I pray the Lord my soul to take." I sort of cringed at the line, "If I should die before I wake," and often lay awake wondering what it would be like if I really should die before I awoke. I came to the realization that if the event of death should occur before I awoke then I wouldn't know it would I? Pondering the mystery of death, I was asleep before I knew it and was awake when I did know it.

Well, morning prayers were very similar to night prayers. The Our Father, the Hail Mary, and the Glory Be. I included a prayer of my own which echoes the "Now I lay me down." It goes, "Good morning Lord, I'm awake, and my soul You did not take. Thank You for a good night's sleep. Throughout this day my soul please keep!"

Morning prayers were muttered while showering, brushing your teeth or dressing so that when you got to the breakfast table you could answer in the affirmative to Mother's query, "Did you say your morning prayers?"

Under the threat of nuclear destruction and the news of the Children of Fatima and their "sealed messages" which only the Pope in Rome was allowed to read, we were encouraged through the Catholic Church to pray the rosary for the conversion of Russia and because the family that prays together, stays together. Each evening, after the supper dishes were finished and the kitchen floor was swept clear of debris, Mother would invite us to her bedroom to light a candle in front of a statue of the Blessed Virgin and to pray the rosary. Daddy most often ignored the invitation, continuing to read the evening paper or to watch the television. We would often set the bedroom door to near closure to shut out the sound of the television. The monotonous rhythm of the rosary would begin; the Apostles Creed, a Glory Be, three Hail Mary's and another Glory Be. Then the meat of the thing ensued; five decades, each introduced by one of five glorious mysteries, one of five sorrowful mysteries, or one of five joyful mysteries. The set of mysteries used

Daddy ignoring the rosary

depended on the week or the season or calendar of the church, if not all three. Someone kept track of all this and published a guide of which Mother had a copy for our use. She would often ask one of the older children to lead the rosary and provide them with the guide. Five decades, each introduced by the Our Father followed by ten Hail Mary's and a Glory Be to the Father.

During these evening interruptions for prayer, I always thanked God for the bed around which we were kneeling for it was possible to lift yourself off your knees for relief by pressing your elbows into the mattress.

"Holy Mary, Mother of God, pray for us sinners now and at the hour of our death. Amen!"

"Holy Mary, Mother of God, pray for us sinners now and at the hour of our death. Amen!"

"Holy Mary, Mother of God..." Ten times five equals fifty. There were fifty-three Hail Mary's, six Our Father's, six Glory Be to The Father's, one Apostles Creed and, as though that wasn't enough, there was a prayer to be said at the close of the rosary that started with "Remember O most Gracious Virgin Mary that never was it known, that anyone who fled to thy protection, implored thy help, or sought thy intercession, was left unaided. Inspired by this confidence I fly unto thee........ etc., etc."

When the rosary was finished and the candle blown out, we would lift ourselves off aching knees and emerge from the bedroom into brighter light.

On many occasions, when traveling home from the cottage, someone would suggest that we say the rosary sometime after passing the Ten O'clock line. It was usually Mother or Jerry. Well, who could refuse? On these occasions, Daddy was a captive participant. In the darkness of the car, we would fumble among the contents of our pockets for the rosary we always carried and we would begin the countdown. For entertainment, I would often ignore the counting of the beads and see if I could simply predict when the last Hail Mary of a decade would be said.

There was also a period of time when we would be called to say the Angelus. I have no recollection of how this prayer begins. While working in the garden on Saturday's, we could hear the bells of St. Francis de Sales Church tolling the noon call to prayer. Mother would have us gather and say the Angelus. This was a European custom and the Catholic Church here was making an attempt at domesticating it. It failed.

Prayer was a part of my life, prayer is a part of my life and I suppose, prayer will be a part of my life until my death. While prayer was a part of my life as a child as much because it was expected and accomplished by rote as it was demanded, prayer is now a part of my life because I do believe in a Supreme Being and do desire to give praise and thanks for a multitude of gifts, not the least of which is the family into which I was born and the parents who nurtured me.

Aunt Lottie

Charlotte was my grandmother's sister. That made her my great-aunt, but I always knew her as Aunt Lottie. When Charlotte was a little girl of eight or nine years of age, she had an accident while roller-skating near the family home on Massachusetts Avenue. My Grandmother always related that Charlotte was skating and fell backwards onto a broken gate and one of the rusty nails pierced the back of her skull and she later developed meningitis. The illness left her deaf and deranged. Her parents (my great-grandparents) cared for her until their deaths. Then her care fell to the siblings. Since Grandma was the only one of her siblings in Indianapolis, the burden of care fell to her. From the age of twenty-one or so, Charlotte spent her time living with Grandma and living at Central State Hospital on West Washington Street in Indianapolis. She spent more time at Central State, Seven Steeples, than she did at Grandma's home next door to us on East 21st Street.

Aunt Lottie was all of five feet and ten inches tall. She weighed no more than 110 pounds, very thin. She dressed in long sleeved black dresses that reached her ankles, dresses that her mother might have worn in the late eighteen hundreds. She was accomplished at crocheting. She never sat to crochet but carried her current piece with her and performed her miracles with thread and needle while she walked about. Charlotte also prayed incessantly from a little black book that she always carried with her in one of the pockets of her long skirt.

When Aunt Lottie was with Grandma, it was for brief periods of time, maybe three months, and then she would be returned to Central State. My Grandmother's patience with her would be exhausted. Grandmother was determined to cure her with her own methods through reasoning and arguing. When Aunt Lottie was with Grandma, she would often come next door to our home and help my Mother with housework. Mostly she would do the ironing. She wouldn't speak but she was exceedingly gentle with everything and with anyone she encountered, silently appearing and silently leaving. She often presented my Mother with a piece of her handiwork from her crochet needle. Her eyes were downcast and we paid little attention to her comings and goings. She was just there from time to time. I think she enjoyed helping Mother with the chores of our home because Mother placed no demands on her whatsoever. The work she did was always just fine and appreciated.

On the other hand, this was Grandma's younger sister and she was determined to have Aunt Lottie behave as normal as possible.

I only heard Aunt Lottie's voice on a couple of occasions. On one of those occasions Charlotte was simply screaming. While playing in the back yard on a hot summer's day, I heard this shrill screaming coming from the other side of Grandma's house. I ran over to their drive and saw Aunt Lottie sticking out the window in the stairwell, her arms flailing in the air. Grandma was inside, behind her, holding the sash against her back and pushing down. Grandma was saying something but I couldn't understand what was going on. By the time I got into the house through the back door, the incident had ended and Aunt Lottie had disappeared into her upstairs bedroom. Grandma was muttering something about her sister and how she intended to make her behave. I thought it best to leave. Mother advised me to forget it after I told her what I had seen.

It was an odd sensation. I mean, here was this loving Grandmother with whom I spent countless hours, behaving in, what appeared to be, a cruel manner toward another human being. It just didn't fit.

There were other occasions when Grandma's treatment of her sister seemed amusing and somewhat appropriate and more acceptable. Aunt Lottie, praying if not crocheting, often stood in front of the huge bush in front of Grandma's house. Between prayers, she would admonish the travelers on 21st Street for going too fast. She pressed back into the branches of the bush that towered above the first floor of the house as though she were the Madonna at Fatima, praying and intermittently yelling at the motorists. "Slow down! Don't go so fast." Grandma would put up with this until she had enough. Aunt Lottie's admonitions would draw me toward the front of Grandma's house from play in our back yard. I would encounter Grandma unwinding the hose from the side of her house. She would signal to me to be quiet but there seemed to be little need for Charlotte was deaf. The signal to be silent indicated to me that maybe Grandma knew that Aunt Lottie wasn't as deaf as she behaved. I never learned the truth of that matter.

Grandma would pull the hose up the side steps of her porch and out to the front rail behind the towering bush. Having already turned on the spigot, she would turn the nozzle open and spray toward Aunt Lottie through the bush. Aunt Lottie would run toward the street and continue her prayers. Grandma would come off the porch, trailing the hose, and run toward her out the drive. Aunt Lottie would retreat to the other side of the street while grandma struggled with the nozzle of the hose to get the best force available. She would hold the nozzle as high as she could, sending an arch of water across 21st street in an attempt to get her sister to stop her behavior. Aunt Lottie simply stepped backwards out of reach of the water. I have to admit that it was fun to participate in this activity and I had to laugh. Grandma was trying to tame the beast in Aunt Lottie the only way she knew. She thought that if she got her wet enough, she would cease her public and embarrassing display and come into the house to change clothes.

Who knows what went on in the mind of my great Aunt Lottie? There were times when she was obviously lucid but most of the time she was a mystery. Hearing her yell at the motorists on 21st Street was only the second time I ever heard her voice and it was clear.

While Aunt Lottie was confined at Central State, Grandma and Aunt Gene would visit her at least once a month. For them, it was an entire day of the weekend for they had to take the bus. These visits occurred on Saturdays and I was allowed to go with them from time to time. We would arrive at Central State Hospital and walk to the main building. Eventually, Aunt Lottie would appear, escorted by an aide. We usually sat in a swing, a two-seater, with the seats facing each other. To make it move you had to pump the deck with your feet. There were long periods of silence. Aunt Lottie would just sit and stare and listen while Grandma and Aunt Gene talked to one another and to her. Mostly, it was as if she were not there at all. They would give her a jar of peanut butter and she seemed appreciative but there was little other interaction. I remember most the long trip back on the bus to the East side and home and what a long exhausting day it had been.

I don't remember when Aunt Lottie died or why she died but she passed from my childhood. Trying to remember without the help of Grandma or Aunt Gene is impossible. The best I can think of is that it is like walking into an unknown and realizing that you have stepped into a cobweb. The webbing is all over your face and your immediate reaction is to step back and brush it off as quickly as possible, hoping that the spider is not somewhere in your hair or on your clothes.

She was there in my life, she was strange and different, she was quiet and gentle, she wove intricate patterns and she was patient, waiting and praying.

The Lump

Before the bathroom was installed at our house, it was not a simple matter to take a bath. Preparations were made beyond what I realized were required for as I was at play, unaware. Sunday was the day to go to Mass at St. Francis de Sales Church near Brightwood and, in preparation, Saturday night was bath night. Mother would heat water in buckets and kettles on the stove. The blue flames aglow under the containers seemed warm in the darkened kitchen in spite of their color. While the water was heating, the round galvanized tub, placed on the kitchen floor, was surrounded on three sides with kitchen table chairs draped with towels. Surrounded so, there was some privacy and the draped chairs created a windbreak and held in some of the precious heat.

Mother decided who was bathed and when. I suppose, from week to week, she tried to change the order in which she called us so that occasionally we would be bathed in unused water. No one wanted to be called. The older ones were allowed complete privacy. They would go into the darkened kitchen, close the door and after a time, emerge robed with their hair in a towel. My brother, Tommy, and I were still being bathed.

I don't have any recollection of Mother or Daddy bathing or how they did it. I didn't wonder about it then but I wonder about it now.

With clean underwear and pajamas at the ready, Tommy or I would be called to the bath. Daddy would urge us on our way by just being there. We didn't dare to be called the second time. When called, our response was immediate for he took note of that with a glance. Entering the kitchen, we were told, "Close the door and get your clothes off." Sitting on the cold linoleum floor, the untied shoes were pulled off, then the socks. That was a mistake. Taking off the shoes was smart because you couldn't get the pants off over them, but we should have left the socks on until the long legged pants were removed. I still sometimes forget that today. I suppose we removed the socks because it was easier to do it while still sitting on the floor. Standing then to remove the pants over hot, sweaty feet almost killed us on occasion and made a lot of noise as we fell. While holding onto the doorknob, the back of a chair of the kitchen table, we struggled to remove the pants. The sweaty feet stuck to the linoleum and stuck to the inside of the pant leg. I did not like to walk to the tub across the linoleum floor with sweaty feet. I wonder why we weren't advised to take off our socks at tub side. We were allowed to wait to remove our underwear at tub side just before we stepped in. Then Mother would pull the T-shirt off over our head as we raised our arms at her command. Naked we sat in the tepid, sometimes used, scummy water. Mother was always aware of water temperature, checking it from time to time with her elbow. If it seemed to cool to her she would add hot water from the large, spouted, hot water kettle that kept heating on the stove. She would carefully direct the flow so as not to scald us. The added warmth would induce a shiver and we would fight the urge to pee. You never wanted to admit to Mother that you made pee in the water but if it happened you were obliged to tell her. If you did pee in the water it probably guaranteed that the next to bathe would have fresh water.

It was my call. "Dick, time for your bath."

After I was sitting in the tub, Mother started at the top. Using a soaped washrag, she washed my face with that awful ivory soap, rinsed it, and re-soaped the rag. She said little, only speaking to instruct me to cooperate so I wouldn't get soap in my eyes. The chest was scrubbed, the arms raised and the pits swabbed. Each of the arms, top and bottom, front and back, were washed. The hands, between each finger, were washed and then the back. The washing of the back was the best; it was soothing. To feel the water lifted in a cupped hand and poured at the nape of the neck felt good. Soaped and rinsed, the back was finished and all was well.

Mother's hands were soft but Aunt Gene's hands were the softest of all. She had the softest hands of any I can remember. She occasionally wiped our faces and necks at her kitchen sink in the summertime. Her hands were soft.

Then came the dreaded, "Okay, stand up. Let's wash your behind and the rest of you." Soaped rag in hand, Mother went to work. I turned to face front and supported myself, right hand on her left shoulder, left hand on the back of a towel draped chair, and, in the dim light, she quietly exclaimed, "What is that lump?"

"Where?" I asked.

"Here," she said as she pointed without touching.

I looked down and saw the lump. On the left side and above the convenience, there was a protruding lump.

"When did that happen?" I was asked.

"I don't know," I said.

"Art! . . . . Art! Come in here!" Mother shouted. Her call created a commotion of sorts and the news spread quickly, "Dickie has a hernia!"

"Oh my God, I have a hernia! What's that?" I thought.

A doctor's appointment was made, first with Doctor Gick and then with some other doctor downtown in the Hume Manser Building. All the doctors in the world were housed in the Hume Manser Building. It was confirmed. I had a hernia. However, it was determined that it was too soon to operate and that we should try to treat the hernia with a truss. This truss was a painful device I was supposed to wear daily. Upon hugging me good-bye on a school day, Mother would often deftly check to see if the truss was in place before I left.

"Do you have a handkerchief?" she would ask while patting my backside checking to see if she could feel the hard, plastic band of the truss around my waist. The truss had an oval, half-egg protrusion that was to be placed directly over the lump to push the hernia back into my body. The lump never disappeared, but then the truss was seldom in place in spite of its grip on an active child. It probably more often pressed the lump out rather than in by sliding above or below the assigned spot.

I wish I had one of the trusses today that I was supposed to have used in the hope of support or in the hope of correcting this deformity, so I could burn it! Whatever happened to those instruments? I don't know. I can see the first one today as clearly as I saw it then.

In the mornings I put on the truss as part of preparation for school. After being hugged I would announce that I had forgotten something. Rushing upstairs, I hurriedly removed the device and hid it for the day under the stack of my underwear in the bottom drawer. Was Mother ever the wiser?

Bathing was hard work in the dimly lit kitchen. Only one bath was really scary, the bath the night the lump was found.

Games

Around dusk, someone would suggest, "let's play hide and seek." The grimy sweaty kids would be gathered and all would join in. "So, who is 'it?' " Usually, a smaller one was selected and they had to hide their eyes at the designated home base and count very slowly to ten. While 'it' counted, we scrambled to be the best concealed but nearest home base so as to get home free. This was truly agonizing, trying to decide where to hide and not to have decided as you heard "six, seven, eight ...." Almost frantic to find a place, as you watched others conceal themselves, you would fling yourself into half lit places, like under bushes you wouldn't crawl into in full daylight because of the bugs. Somehow the dusk hid things as though they weren't there and you were at liberty to lie on the ground under a bush without fear. The greater fear was being seen by 'it' and hearing your name called out, having no chance to beat 'it' to home base. If you didn't beat 'it' to home base then you became 'it' and had to do the seeking. I think the rules changed from time to time. Sometimes you were just out - sometimes you became 'it'.

It was that way with most of the games we played like "king of the mountain," "redrover, redrover, send so and so over," or "mother may I," with it's baby steps, giant steps, scissor steps and free steps, which were always in dispute as to their execution. There was also "freeze," "rock school" on the front steps of the house, "drop the handkerchief," which always seemed silly to me, "crack the whip," "follow the leader," and some game we played as a variation on "redrover" by throwing a ball over the old frame garage to a team on the other side, a game I never understood.

The most favorite game of all for me was "tin can alley." Though it was often very confusing, it was a variation on "hide and seek." This game was also played at dusk and required 'it' not only to find those hiding, but also to protect home base (a tin can) from being kicked. Any tin can would do. It would be placed somewhere in the open yard or driveway, and 'it' would place a foot on the can and count to a specified number slowly while hiding the eyes. Every one who was 'it' peeked to see where hiders were going. As in "hide and seek," depending on the rules set down at the start, you, the seeker, might find someone and beat them back to the can and place your foot on the can before them, and then they had to help you capture others. Of course, there were variations here also. Even if your foot were on the can, it had to have enough pressure on it to prevent your opponent from kicking the can out from under your foot. If those sought beat the seeker to the can and kicked the can away 'it' had to retrieve the can, replace it in its assigned spot, and start again. Another of anyone hiding could also burst from concealment and try to beat 'it' to the can and kick it if 'it' strayed too far a field while searching for those hiding. Also, while 'it' was racing for the can, having found a hider, another hider could race to the can, kick the can and save the found hider from 'it.'

Why don't you read that last paragraph again?

Tin can alley was rough. Shins were kicked around the can, people were shoved into bushes followed by threats of "I'm gonna tell." In spite of the roughness of this game, I don't recall any serious injuries, only bruises and hurt feelings.

My younger brother, Tommy, and I had a game of our own. Armed with one of Grandma's old iron cow stakes, used in the garden as row markers, we pretended we were exceedingly strong and would take turns swinging the iron rod through the rusted upright wires of the fence along the garden path. The fence separated our garden area from the neighbors. This was a forbidden activity, but it was exceedingly entertaining. We didn't do a lot of fence cutting at one time but only a few uprights on each occasion, just enough to satisfy our need to feel we were powerful conquerors. Tommy had taken his turn, and I took the rod, gripping it like a baseball bat, Tommy at my left and behind me. I swung at the fence and five or six wire strands gave way like butter. I swung much harder than necessary and the momentum carried the rod right past my left shoulder and struck Tommy in the forehead just above his left eye. I can still feel the rebound in the iron rod and hear the dull thud.

He immediately began to run for the house, clutching his left eye. He started to cry and I ran after him.

"No, Tommy, no! Don't go in," I said as I pulled him behind a bush by the neighbor's garage.

15

"It hurts," he said.

"Let me see," I said.

Seeing it convinced me that it hurt, but I was panicking. They would find out we were doing wrong, and we would be punished.

"It will be all right. Just wait," I said. But it got worse. The swelling increased and bulged beneath his eyebrow. It was getting dark in color.

"Oh, Tommy," I exclaimed. "We'll tell them it was a baseball bat, that I accidentally hit you with a baseball bat while practicing my swing."

Tommy marched to the back door, climbed the steps and went in. I can't for the life of me remember the outcome.

No one was ever injured so seriously at "tin can alley" when they, by rights, should have been.

School Is Out / Boredom Sets In

The last day of school for the summer was always cause for celebration. Everyone was always promoted to the next grade and big plans were made in our minds for all the time off during the summer. Within a week, boredom set in and we were at the tails of Mother's dress asking her what there was to do. She would suggest we play with the dominoes or the checkerboard but none of her suggestions piqued our interest. Tinker toys was a favorite pastime but there never seemed to be enough parts to make the elaborate designs we had in mind, let alone those on the paper that came inside the Quaker Oats style box. Often, the parts didn't fit together tightly enough and the contraption would collapse before it was finished.

She might suggest we play with the clay and make something with it. Clay came at Christmas and was usually saved until summer. The box had six sticks of clay, each wrapped with a thin sheet of clear paper. There were sticks of red, green, yellow, blue, gray and brown. It was always a thrill to open the clay sticks and to promise yourself that, "no matter what I make, I will separate the colors when I finish." All of the clay eventually ended up brown. Even though we would play with the clay in the basement where it was cooler, the pieces would stick together and would finally be folded into one. Instead of making the layout of a country cottage with a garden with corn stalks and tomato plants, we found ourselves making a fort from the old West or a log cabin in Kentucky. It was easier to work with brown. Sometimes it would be so hot, even in the basement, that we would cool the clay in the refrigerator so we could continue to form it into logs.

Mother's suggestions were endless. "Make a telephone out of tin cans and a string," she suggested. Though we tried, it didn't really work. Then she came up with the best idea of all, recalling her own childhood. "Make some mud pies and bake them in the sun," she said.

"How do we do that?" we asked.

Her instructions were simple and short. "Get a bucket from the basement and put some water in it. Then, take it outside and find some dirt from the garden. Mix some of the water with the dirt in another container. Here use this." She handed us an old kettle and a spoon. "Then mix it up and pat the pies out in your hands and lay them on something to dry in the sun."

We went right to work. We learned a lot about adding water to dirt so that it wasn't too runny or too thick to handle. Most of the first mud pies crumbled as we tried to remove them from the board on which they were drying. We learned that a painted board was better for drying than an unpainted one but that a piece of metal was the best. Mother may have loaned us a cookie sheet on which to dry the pies. We also found that the deeper we dug into the ground for the dirt, the better the pies held together. We turned out stacks of pies in the following days, intent on finding the right mix and the right drying surface and the right drying time. We had found clay in our own back yard and using the sun to do the finish work was a lot easier than waiting on the refrigerator to cool the Christmas clay.

All of the pies wound up back on the garden plot but the making and the baking and finding the right mix occupied a lot of our time. We never again asked what there was to do that summer because we always knew we could make and perfect mud pies. We added pieces of shredded grass clippings to the mixture of mud and water to hold them together as they dried, but breaking one in half was not at all appetizing. Mother, in her wisdom, knew how to get us off the tails of her dress. We went from pies to cookies that we decorated with dandelion and violet blossoms found in the yard, sticking them into the 'cookie' before they began to dry. The cookies were sold for a penny apiece to Grandma and Aunt Gene, to Mother and Daddy and to other members of the family. They would pretend to eat them by breaking off pieces and throwing them into the yard exclaiming how good they were to our delight. We all had a good laugh over the mud pies and cookies.

We also entertained ourselves by making braids of long stemmed clover blossoms and wearing them as crowns. Carol Ann and Linda Jane were best at braiding.

Making hollyhock ladies was fun but you had to work fast because the open blossom would begin to wilt fairly soon after it was picked. We always started with preparing the head before we picked the dress. Have you ever made these?

We collected cottonwood grapes and kept them in a container until they dried and burst open, creating a mound of white fluff. The bunches of seedpods were especially plentiful after a summer storm. The fluff would be released into the air as we lifted it in our hands to the wind much as the blossom of the dandelion. Snapdragon blooms were plucked and were entertaining for a brief period of time as we squeezed the sides to open the "mouth." We made "ink" from all sorts of wild plant fruit that was collected, crushed, and mixed with water. Catalpa fingertips were fun but also short lived. It was difficult to cover all ten fingers without help. Though we looked incessantly, I never found the four-leaf clover that I must have overlooked.

Mud pies were the best.

At The End of His Rope

I knew he wouldn't do what I was afraid of, but I was certain he might. I wished I was the younger and could stand and watch, like Tommy. The water was colder than usual, and I was scared to death to let go and do what he was telling me to do. I never saw him swim, yet he was determined that we should know how to swim and he intended for us to learn that very day in ten minutes or less.

Mother dipping lake water off of the first dock

Mother was really concerned about one of us drowning at Graybrook Lake, and I suspect she shared her concern frequently with Daddy. Her worry probably influenced her disposition and caused her to be tense the whole time we were at the cottage. We didn't worry much about drowning when we went out in the boat and rocked it from side to side or moved from stem to stern, stepping over the oars and oarsman; or when we beat the water with oars trying to splash each other. All of this activity occurred around the bend in the lake, out of Mother's sight. We didn't worry about falling in off the end of the dock while fishing or chasing each other. We didn't fear drowning until Daddy became as determined to teach us to swim as he was determined to allay Mother's fear.

As I said, I never saw Daddy swim so it's safe to assume he didn't know how. I don't suppose he ever knew how because swimming is like a lot of other things, once you learn, you never forget. That surprises me a little, what with his ease at being on or around the water, deep water, and his childhood on 21st Street near Pogue's Run and the swimming holes. Of course, it's possible the swimming holes were not over his head, and he simply stood up to get out after jumping in.

Tom, Dick, Carol Ann, And Linda Jane

Also, I suspected he didn't really know how to swim because of his chosen method of instruction. He didn't get into the water with us, but used a more direct approach. He tied a large towing hemp rope around our skinny waists and instructed us to climb down the ladder and let go. Yep, that was it, tied the rope around our waist, had us climb down into the water and told us to let go.

When you think about it, you can imagine it working, and you get this image of a concerned man who is calmly explaining to his two little shivering boys that he is sure he knows what he is doing. He believes this will work and he wants to teach them how to swim because he doesn't want them to drown. He is encouraging; he is talking reassuringly in a confident voice. Well, that approach certainly would have been a positive addition to being treated like a tea bag and being cursed at for not producing.

I must say that he did take the time to wrap the end of the harsh hemp rope in a white rag, which he taped with black electrical tape. This cushioned it against the skin. That did demonstrate some concern for us on his part, but that was about it. I know today that he was confident then, and he would not let us drown.

The lesson went something like this.

"Daddy, I don't want to do this," as he tied the rope around my waist.

No response.

"Is that too tight?" Daddy asked.

"No, I don't think so." I responded.

"Okay, now I'm going to hold you up with this rope so you won't go under, and you are going to learn to swim," he encouraged.

I had to pee and said nothing.

"Climb down the ladder," Daddy instructed.

"But what if . . . ," I stammered.

He cut me off saying, "I've got the rope. Climb down the ladder."

"The water's cold," I complained.

"God damn it, climb down the ladder," he exclaimed.

"Oooooooo, it's cold!" I complained further.

"Get in the water . . . . Do it faster and it won't be so cold," he shouted.

"It's cold," I said for the very last time.

As I slowly lowered myself, the cold line of water marched up the ankles, around the calves, rising as I slowly lowered myself, kind of almost tickling as it rose to the trunks and the crotch. The water changed temperature and became even colder than it was, becoming the coldest ever on the back. So there I was, the water ringing my neck.

"Now, let go and swim," Daddy demanded

"Nooooooo . . . .!" I answered.

"'God damn it, let go of the dock and swim!" he insisted.

The underside of the dock was absolutely full of spider webs and spiders. They were long legged, skinny bodied, water spiders. The light brown, crunchy shells of the Katy-did bugs were hanging all over, like the ornaments on the bottom side of a Christmas tree. The undersides of the boards on the deck were spotted with a kind of white mold. The pilings, which had been driven into the muddy lake bottom through holes cut in the ice, were still covered with their bark. Oh, what a vivid scene . . . then the toe of a shoe was pushing at my shoulder and a voice booming.

"Let go of the God damn dock, go on, I got you, get out there, you won't drown."

The whole lake knew of my plight and the folks across the lake must have been watching. I imagine they stopped whatever they were doing, wherever they were doing it, to watch Art Kramer teach his boys to swim and to listen to his method.

None of his yelling and pulling or his nudging with his foot, being watched, or the sight of the underside of the dock motivated me to take the plunge and let go, as much as the realization that my feet were so deep in the dark green water, that they were colder than the top of me, and I couldn't see them. I was sure something was rising to have a sample.

In that instant, I tried to swim.

I don't know how many attempts it took or how many times he let us sink before he pulled us up, but both Tommy and I learned to swim. Our Daddy taught us off the end of our dock on the end of a rope. City pool swimming at Longacre hadn't prepared us as much for the deep water as we thought it had. We were blue lipped, red waisted but proud.

Mysterious Frank

Spring arrived and new life presented itself in the form of tulips, hyacinths, budding trees and hedgerows. People came outdoors and cleaned up their yards. We had cleaned them up in the fall but there was always the winter refuse to clean out of the hedgerow. Our hedge row was a long one running from the front yard all the way back to the neighbors' garage on the West side of our home. Sometimes the hedgerow would get too tall and in the early spring we would cut it completely back and the new growth would break out at the base of the plants. When we cut the hedgerow back there was a lot to burn, so much so that it could not be burned all at once. Clearing the hedgerow fully exposed our neighbors to the West, the Fultz's. The adults could see them and talk to them above the hedge when it was tall and children would be picked up and held or stood on a tree stump that was in the row so that Mrs. Fultz could see us. Mrs. Fultz lived in a very small two-bedroom house that sat well back on the lot so that her front door was about twenty feet behind the back door of our house. The original developers had intended to build a larger home in front of this 'temporary' one which would stand in line with the other homes on 21st Street. This was never accomplished. Also in the home were Rose, Art and Frank Fultz, the children of Mrs. Fultz. As long as I can remember, Mrs. Fultz was old. Even Rose seemed old and I never thought of her as a daughter but used to think that she was a sister of Mrs. Fultz. Art worked every day at the gas company. Rose took care of the home and her mother but Frank was a mystery.

Even during the winter months you would see Mrs. Fultz occasionally and Rose and Art regularly, coming and going. Art always had a cigar in his mouth and both he and Rose were very friendly people. So was their mother for that matter. Frank would never be seen.

In the spring, with the hedgerow cleared, a full view of the neighbors home was provided. Frank would come out of the front door of the house and begin to perform some of his own spring-cleaning. He never looked at us and never spoke to us. He was a thin, tall man, almost too thin for his height. He would close the storm door very quietly as if he were sneaking out of the house. There was no porch on the house, just two concrete steps down to the yard. He would stand for a while facing the steps and then remove a handkerchief from his right back pocket. He would unfold it and hold it by one of the corners and begin to clean the top step by snapping it at the step. He would do this for a long time. We would continue to play but we were intent on staying where we could watch his activity. After ten minutes of cleaning the step with the snap, snap, snap of his handkerchief, he would refold it, place it in his pocket, and sit on the step. He wouldn't sit there very long before he would get up and walk to the middle of their front yard. We had to reposition our play further into our back yard so that the corner of our house did not block our view of what was going on. Mother would sometimes quietly admonish us for she knew we were intent on watching. On some occasions she would simply call us in. If she did call us in, we would go to the upstairs bedroom and watch Frank from the West windows. We could see what he was doing because the huge Red-haw tree had not yet put on its leaves.

Frank would stand in the middle of their large front yard facing 21st Street. Suddenly, he would raise both arms above his head while pivoting sideways and execute a cartwheel. His cartwheels were not show material but I couldn't execute one half as well. In the process of turning the cartwheel, his comb from his shirt pocket and coins from his pants pockets would tumble out to the ground. He would then spend the next several minutes snapping his handkerchief at the grass in a meticulous process of locating each coin. This could go on longer than we could stand to watch. The strange thing is, once he was satisfied he had found all of the coins, which he placed back in his pockets as he found them one by one and, after he combed his hair and placed the comb in his shirt pocket, he would resume his stance, throw up his arms, pivot and do another cartwheel. The search for comb and coins would begin again with the snapping of the handkerchief.

There were also times when Frank, after his brief respite on the cleaned front step, would walk to a spot in the yard and begin snapping at it with his handkerchief. He would do this until the tip of the handkerchief had cleared all of the grass in that particular spot down to the dirt. I often wondered if he felt he was missing a coin and was determined to find it in that particular spot. I never saw him retrieve anything.

Mother must have done something right because we never made fun of Frank nor chided him. He never looked at us nor spoke to us though he must have known we were watching. Of course, we didn't speak to him either. Still, I was tempted to step over the hedgerow and walk to the step and just sit down beside him on the cleaned step. I thought about it but I never did follow through, probably out of fear of what I imagined might happen.

Parents' Night Out

Sometimes the only way to get the hard or semi-hard deposits out of your nose is to stick the index finger, or whichever finger you are accustomed to using, up your nose and scrape its insides with your fingernail. Opening the nasal passages was important and blowing your nose into a handkerchief didn't always work.

Clean handkerchiefs were always available in the top bureau drawer in Mother and Daddy's bedroom. That was the only source of supply. Ironed and neatly folded, the stack was always there. We never ran out. On occasion, when picking my nose, I would suddenly cause it to bleed!

I learned to put my head back, press on the bleeding side of the nose, breath through the other and place a damp, cold cloth at the back of my neck.

My nose seemed to bleed easily. Sometimes spontaneously and with out picking, a sneeze or a cough would start it. It bled if I was struck in the middle of the back with an open hand. What malady was this? Did others have nosebleeds so easily? I don't remember my last nosebleed as an adult, but I remember the gaiety with which my brothers and sisters sometimes caused my nose to bleed.

Every now and then it happened that Mother and Daddy would both be gone from our house, leaving Jerry and Carol Ann "in charge." Usually, it was on a Wednesday night when Daddy went bowling and Mother had a P.T.O. meeting or ladies club or whatever at St. Francis de Sales School and Church.

Daddy left shortly after dinner, and as she left, Mother would leave instructions to behave. We behaved all right! As we chose to behave, but not, I'm sure, as she would have had us behave. We played hide and seek. The clothes hamper in the bathroom was a favorite of the smaller ones. Closets, among smelly shoes and behind the hanging clothes, behind the couch, behind the floor length drapes, not daring to breath much, under the kitchen table among the chair legs, behind doors and under beds with carpeted floors were our hiding places. We didn't hide much under beds with linoleum floors because of all the dust balls; those light gray transparent puffs of dust always seemed to be there like clouds that settled on the floor. No one ever hid in the dark recesses of the basement! We had our rules.

Tiring of hide and seek, we would sometimes raid the kitchen cabinets for kettles, lids, and table knives and work up a marching band. It sometimes worked, but mostly we would make such a din that Art, our neighbor next door, must have easily heard us and wondered what was going on. As I look at that now, Jerry must have been quite proud at how he kept us entertained. We never washed the kettles, lids or knives that served as band instruments, but we did put them away, with sweaty hands, lest their use be discovered.

Another fantastic bit of adventure that Jerry showed us, I remember, was to turn on all the lights in the house and walk slowly, peering into a mirror held at our waist. The ceilings, identified as we went from room to room, gave you a slight dizzying feeling of imbalance and an exciting, different view of things. On occasion, we would do the same thing, entertaining ourselves, with all the house lights out and using a flashlight.

On one of these evenings, after Tom had gone to bed, my sisters convinced me, against my better judgment, to let them dress me up like a girl. Using their articles of clothing and their makeup, they had me dress in a skirt, blouse and scarf. The makeup was added after I was outfitted. Adding insult to injury, they took a picture.

Dick after "makeover"

I guess there was a limit to ideas. Without Mother or Daddy in the house, no one was interested in sedate games like tic-tac-toe or connect the dots. Besides, it took far too long to set up a game like connect the dots.

We were chasing each other through the house, and I think Jerry said with a devious giggle, "Let's make Dick's nose bleed." That was scary, to be singled out like that. Besides, there were many times, especially at school, when I didn't think it would stop bleeding after it started. Mother was called to St. Francis de Sales Grade School many a time to get it stopped or to bring a clean shirt or handkerchief. Mother wasn't at home now.

I ran but got caught on the stairway to the basement. Turning the corner, through the kitchen doorway, my right hand hit the light switch, and the light came on as I bounded down the stairs. Jerry's hand caught me flat in the middle of my upper back. I stopped on about the third step. Sure enough, the warm, slick, salty stuff ran out of my nose and over my lip.

"Ah! His nose is bleeding," Jerry said. They assisted me to the bathroom warning me not to tell Mother.

We were in bed before Mother came home. She always got home before Daddy. I wonder today if she knows how we behaved on parents' night out.

The Cure

A letter from my Mother to her sisters in Lanesville, Indiana:
(Note that parenthetical phrases are my comments.)

Dear Till, Olive and Hilda,

Hope you all are well. This has really been a busy spring. It seems like one of the kids are sick all of the time. (She really means that one kid is sick and then another, not that the same kid is sick and then the same kid is sick again.) I have been able to get some of the spring-cleaning finished between the illnesses. The bedrooms have been done but none of the closets have been cleaned. There are still all of the clothes to go through. Linda is tired of Carol Ann's hand-me-downs and I really ought to try to find a way to get Linda some of her own things. (Meaning new ones, but she didn't know how she could manage it financially.) I have been able to get the windows on the downstairs washed but there are still the upstairs ones to do. The windowsills all need to be painted but Art says it is dumb to do it every year. He'll do it though. (If he didn't he wouldn't hear the end of it.)

Linda was sick first and missed a few days of school. Then Carol Ann got it and she gave it back to Linda. I think it is because they are in such a small room that they give it to each other. They finally got over the sore throat and then little Tommy got it. They have a fever and a sore throat and that lasts about three days but they are so tired that I keep them home a few days more just to be sure they are over whatever it is. It's probably some sort of flu. If they complain and stay home or say they are sick, then I make them stay in for the day. I think sometimes they use the fact to get more sympathy so I don't allow them to go out to play in the afternoon or the evening when they say they are feeling better. (If you claim to be sick in the morning then there is no reason for you to go out in the evening for any reason. If you are sick, you need your rest.)

After Tommy was about over it, Dick got sick with a sore throat. He stayed home from school and I made sure he got plenty of liquids like the hot lemonade. Mom Kramer brought over some chicken soup. She is a dear person and always tries to help but she comes over and through the back door at the worst time yelling my name so loud that she scares me to death. I do love her for the way she tries to help me. And, I don't mean that she doesn't help me, she does.

Well, I will keep you posted but Dick is calling and I want to get this in the mail before the mailman comes so goodbye for now,

Love, Ceal   XX OO

Aunt Hilda's response to my Mother:
(Again, parenthetical phrases are mine)

Dear Ceal.

We are all fine. I do so wish we were closer so that we could help you with your children. It must be difficult with so many sick at once and then to have the same one get sick again. We have had the flu here as well. Alberta has been under the weather (here she means ill as we are all under the weather all of the time if you think about it) for more than a month. Till and George, and I have not had any of this flu and I sure hope we don't get it. I'm always afraid that George will bring it home from school and give it to the rest of us because he is in daily contact with so many children and many of them have been sick with the symptoms you describe.

Olive has not been feeling well. She comes home from the shirt factory and lies down on the couch and is just too tired to do anything. Till and I want her to go to the doctor but she says she doesn't have the time. (Or the money.)

This is a short letter just to let you know that we did receive your letter and to let you know that you and your family are always in our prayers. It's short also because I'm making all of the gowns for the Schellambager wedding and I still don't have all of the material. Some of them expect miracles.

Love, Hilda

P.S. Picnic plans are being made and we think we will make over $10,000.00 this year.
P.S. Oneda just stopped by and said to tell you all hello. She, Johnny, and family are fine.

Oh yes, my throat hurts and I wouldn't kid about that. Yeah, I stayed home from school today because my throat hurt so bad I didn't want to swallow my own spit. I broke out in a sweat thinking that I was going to have the same thing that Ron had had last year when he was sick for most of the spring and summer, scarlet fever! I knew "scarlet" meant red but he didn't look red from what I remember of that bittersweet spring and summer.

I remember that one morning Ronnie was ill and the routine of the household was sort of put on suspension. Daddy was home and he and Mother were waiting on the doctor to arrive. She diagnosed his ailment as a serious kind of flu called scarlet fever and she took the time to give elaborate instructions to my parents about how to contain the disease so as not to spread it to the rest of the family. After the doctor left, one of the first things Daddy did was to drive two nails into the walls or the woodwork at the top of the stairs and to hang a heavy bedspread over the doorway to sort of contain the air that Ronnie was breathing.

Then I remember some similar pounding on the front porch. When we were outside playing later that day, we saw the board that had been nailed to the front of our house. It had been nailed right through the asbestos redbrick like siding and it read, "Quarantine, Scarlet Fever, Do Not Enter." In a way this seemed like we were very special and it set us apart from the rest. We were able to continue our regular routines as a family but with the restriction that only a few members of the family could go upstairs to tend to Ronnie. I'm sure there were all kinds of precautions laid down for those who went upstairs during that long, long period of time like how to handle the wash, changing the bed, getting rid of the waste, and the washing of the hands before and after contact with anything that was connected to that area of the house. We went to bed in makeshift beds on the floor of the living room, the living room couch and the dining room daybed through all of this.

Ronnie was isolated from the rest of the family, save the caretakers, for an eternity. Daddy spent a lot of time upstairs with him. During that time, they built model airplanes out of balsa wood, glue, and very thin paper. The planes were shellacked when completed and stored in the attic. They were rediscovered several years later when Daddy turned the attic spaces into closets. It was the first time we saw them. The day Ronnie was declared 'safe' we were escorted upstairs to see him and to wish him well. Then, one day, he was allowed to come downstairs and there was a celebration that he had survived. Only then did I realize the seriousness of the situation and learned that he could have died. Died!

So, here I am with a sore throat wondering if I am the next to have the dreaded scarlet fever. Somewhere along the way, through all of these childhood illnesses my parents contended with, my Father decided that he could do as well as any M.D. at treating early symptoms. My Mother agreed and acted as the attendant nurse. I hated to have to admit that I had a sore throat because I knew that when Daddy got home from work at Chevrolet he would suggest that they had to "paint the throat." I hoped that maybe he would decide, as he looked into my throat, that my tonsils had to be removed. One summer, Carol Ann, Linda, and Ron had their tonsils removed, one after the other and they got to eat all of the ice and ice cream that they wanted. Unfortunately, that was not the case with me. I had a raw, red throat that simply needed painting. They always had a supply of Methiolate and long sticks with cotton on the end. Oh, I hated to hear the words, "let's paint his throat."

Where one nail would do, Daddy drove two. So it seemed the same with the painting of the throat. Where one coat was enough, he would apply two or three. The gagging was awful as he probed with the cotton tipped stick.

"Open up," he would command. "Put your head back and stick your tongue out."

Following this initial effort, if the illness persisted into the following day, the treatment would intensify. The throat would be painted and then they would debate the merits of the highly dreaded enema. They pretended not to make the decision in front of the patient but the discussion occurred within earshot and the sweating persisted.

"Where is the damn thing?" Daddy would ask as he looked for the device.

Mother would answer, "It's right in here Art, just a minute, I have to be sure it is clean. I'll scald it first."

The water could be heard to run in the kitchen and then in the bathroom and then they would appear, the two together. Mother would hold the orange, swollen, bladder-like reservoir high and the Vaseline coated tip of the four inch black nozzle would be inserted gently into the rectum. The nozzle was connected to the bladder by a long rubber tube. Once inserted, the black nozzle released the tepid water when the clip was released. The higher the bladder was held, the greater the flow.

At this point, instructions were given and encouragement to "hold it, don't let go." You felt as if you couldn't take another drop and they would say "this is almost enough." I felt as if we were well beyond enough and that I would make a mess. I always thought I would lose control when the probe was removed, that the stream would follow. I was then helped to the bathroom and was thankfully left alone to purge myself of the fluid. It was embarrassing because everyone in the house at the time knew what was going on, that the dreaded enema was being administered. Sympathy was in the air and you could see it in the eyes of the siblings who were hanging around in the dining room to catch a glimpse of you as you hurried from the bedroom to the bathroom.

My motto became, "don't report a sore throat until you can't eat." But as I reflect on the treatment of early symptoms that my parents conducted, I realize there may have been two things going on. One is that their early interventions really worked and prevented more serious illnesses. The other is that the threat of their early interventions was, in and of itself, a cure.

Tommy Was Good

I vaguely recall the work of busting up the basement floor. I didn't bust it up but Daddy and the older ones did. They carried it all out the back door and I helped by hauling it away in the wagon. I think the basement floor was lowered about 14 inches after we were hooked up to the sewers of the city. It was a mess. It must have been. It was more of an adventure for me; not real work, and yet another affirmation that no job was too big to tackle. If you wanted it done, you could do it yourself. It was from exposure to situations like these that taught me I could do anything. Never mind you've never done it before, just think about it, plan it (but don't plan too long), and just do it. Half the effort was in just getting started and when the job was done, you wondered why you were ever worried about whether you could do it in the first place and why it took so long to get started.

These projects also taught me no matter how much you plan, you can't anticipate everything you might run into and there would be delays and endless trips to the hardware store, Interstate Hardware.

I'll never forget the trips to Interstate Hardware on Sherman Drive. It was the same way we went to go to church. Turn right out of the driveway, go to Sherman Drive and turn right to Interstate, just before Massachusetts Avenue. Daddy would charge into the hardware store. The hardware was a lot like our mess in the basement. Everything was in disarray and the shelves, laden with dust, overwhelmed the inner space of the store. They practically met you at the door.

"Denny!" Daddy would shout as he entered the store. Denny was the proprietor, always standing behind the U-shaped counter amid his catalogues, an unlit cigar butt in his mouth, secure between his teeth. With his glasses on his forehead and the phone secure against his ear, propped by his shoulder, he would grunt some acknowledgement that we had arrived.

In spite of the fact he was obviously talking on the phone, Daddy would ask for whatever it was he needed in some foreign language.

Daddy and Denny had what seemed to me to be a rude relationship. I was usually embarrassed when I went with Daddy to Interstate, but I also found their bantering amusing. They would curse at each other while laughing, though they appeared angry. I don't know of any other situation in which Daddy used foul language except in anger. I was also attracted to the liberties we were given in the hardware store.

"God damn it, Art, I'm busy on the phone," Denny would growl.

"Well, just tell me where it is, and I'll find the Goddamn thing myself like I always do," Daddy would respond.

'Aisle three, near the paint," Denny directed, "bottom bin."

With that, we entered the maze of shelving and dusty bins. Daddy went on his search and I wandered freely, peering into the shelves and bins, wiping my hands on my pants after fondling oily pieces of pipe called elbows, nipples, female and male adapters, all of which were intriguing. My first suspicions about the anatomy of the human body were confirmed at Interstate Hardware.

Denny often did not have in stock what was needed, and the two would argue and improvise or argue and criticize.

"You never have what I need. I don't know why I bother to come here," Daddy would say laughing.

"Well, Goddamn, Art, I can't stock every Goddamn thing you need!" Denny retorted.

I wondered why. The place seemed full to me, dark, dirty and full of everything. I was amazed at the number of times Denny gave accurate directions to the bin or shelf, and Daddy came away with what was needed. When he did, Daddy complained about the price no matter who was around or behind the counter.

"Well, Goddamn it, Art, I have to make a living! Hell, you would complain about the sunset if you weren't ready for it!" Denny would say.

We always left on a friendly note, Daddy exclaiming that he would see him later. It never quite fit, but I think they really liked each other.

When the basement project was finished, we had an island that supported the hot water heater, furnace, and gun rack. The old monstrous coal furnace had been converted to a forced air oil furnace. It forced hot air up through its tentacles providing small patches of warmth in a cold house above. These registers were briefly occupied, while getting ready for school on cold winter mornings, letting warm air course up the pant legs or skirt. The favorite register, and most convenient to the breakfast table, was in the dining room.

The furnace occupied most of the island in the basement. The island created an oval, and the entire floor, tiled in brittle black squares, sloped to the drain outside the shower, next to the basement toilet. This oval and the slope of the floor created a whole new playground. Because of the basement project, we played in the basement as never before. The favorite sport was to sit on a metal roller skate with metal roller skates on your feet and propel yourself around the island again and again, pushing against the floor with your hands. The down side was past the hissing oil burner, while the up side began at the base of the stairway, under the clotheslines toward the south end.

The champion oval racer was Tommy. No one could beat his time, clocked with Daddy's stop watch, or more often, counted with "one, one thousand, two, one thousand, three, one thousand, four..." No one could beat his time. The metal wheels against the tiled concrete can still be recalled today. He was the youngest, and he was the best.

Years later, Tommy had a blue scooter, gas powered. I don't know who paid for all the gas he burned in that scooter, but he was the best in time on that as well. This oval was around the garden, and just as he spent hours sitting on a skate, he spent hours on that damn blue scooter, whizzing around the garden plot.

The garden plot was turned over each spring for years by an old man and a team of horses. I don't know where they appeared from, but it was always an exciting event for me to see that blade cut smoothly through the earth, laying it open for further preparation and planting. Our garden always generated some sense of pride and covered the back of the lots of our home and that of Grandma's and Aunt Gene's.

Planting was a joyous time, and the garden looked good. So why was Tommy allowed to create this unsightly path around it? It pissed me off. It made it hard to mow. I really think it pissed me off because he was so damn good on skates on our oval basement track, and he was so damn good on his scooter around the garden as well. I told myself he had more time to practice.

A Walk With Purpose

After the evening meal, Grandma would sometimes bolt from her back door and head back the driveway in her thin-soled, soiled shoes. She seemed intent on reaching some pre-determined point. She lifted her shoulders, right then left with her left-right stride, swiftly covering the distance from the back door to the grape arbor, past the huge maple tree.

The maple tree stood as testimony to her ability to grow things. It had happened one summer, after the construction of a two-car brick garage, that we wanted more trees on our property than we had at the time. So we harvested small, sapling maple trees from somewhere on North Sherman Drive or along White River. After we had planted the "best" of the lot, we had laughingly offered the "runt of the litter" to Grandma.

Complete optimism is a fault of mine inherited from my Grandma. She took the runt and stuck it into a hastily dug and ill-prepared hole in a bed of lily of the valley amidst currant bushes. The tree exploded into life, nourished by Grandma and surpassed all others planted in the front yards and back yards alike. She eventually moved the currant bushes, due to excessive shade, but the lily of the valley and spearmint flourished. She reminded us frequently how we had laughed when she planted her tree.

As she swiftly walked back the driveway, shoulders in opposing cadence with her stride, she would occasionally brush the back of her left hand against the back of her dress and across her buttocks. I would watch this swift march from our back porch and call, "Hi, Grandma."

She would continue swiftly, raise her right hand in a kind of regal, impersonal salute and continue her march.

I wasn't aware then of what was going on, although I do recall the putt, putt puttering as she walked swiftly back her driveway.

Now that I'm middle aged, I know that she wasn't so much in a hurry to go anywhere in particular, as she was in a hurry to escape the confines of her house, to relieve herself of gas and to brush herself clear of any odors, leaving them hurriedly behind.

Man's Best Friend

Big old dog! I can't tell you how big he was, because I was so small when we had Captain. His dog pen lay beyond the garage just before the garden plot. The cherry trees offered their shade in the morning and some other big old tree offered the same in the evening. A doghouse stood in the middle of the high fenced pen. Captain was some sort of retriever, I think. He got out of his pen only when Daddy let him out. We weren't allowed to let him out. When Captain's gate was opened he would tear around the home place and romp with Daddy, who complained he never really had time to train him as a good hunting dog. I don't know how often Captain got to show his stuff at the hunt, but he sure knew how to entertain his master and us kids. Daddy would fill a bucket with water. After showing a golf ball to Captain, Daddy would drop it in the bucket and it would sink to the bottom. Without hesitation, Captain would plunge his head into the pail and come up snorting with the ball in his mouth. I used to wonder what possessed him to do that. Did he open his eyes? How did he keep from drowning if he opened his mouth to get the ball?

Captain

Captain left one night. Sometime during the following day, when Mother discovered the pen was empty, she called Daddy at work. She seldom called him there. You were to call only in emergencies. This probably wasn't a real emergency, but I thought she did the right thing. After dinner that same evening, and in a drizzle, we got into the car and drove around the east side of town. It seemed to be as long a trip as from Indianapolis to Lanesville, Mother's birthplace. It finally got dark and was cold and damp. It was only 7:00 P.M., but it seemed like midnight to me. Daddy and Mother decided to give up looking for Captain. Daddy pulled into the service drive of the huge water tower at 10th and Arlington Streets to turn around to go home when two bright green eyes were reflected in the headlights. It was Captain! We took him home; he was thin and shivering. He died on the back porch the next day, releasing his runny brown bowels as he lay on his side, his back to the wall, head at the top of the basement stairs. His death prompted another call to Daddy at work.

We were sheltered from the labor of Captain's disposal. Someone came to pick him up. We didn't bury him like we did the pet parakeet, whose neck was broken in the pantry door. The parakeet belonged to my oldest brother Bill, who was away at GMI (General Motors Institute) in Flint, Michigan. With the bird on his shoulder, Tommy stepped into the dark kitchen pantry and closed the door to see what the bird would do. But, as he stepped in beside the trash can and pulled the door shut quickly, the bird scrambled through the air for the light and his neck was caught between the door and jamb. He plopped to the floor, jerked twice and was dead. Tommy felt really bad.

Anyway, after Captain, Spike appeared. Spike was a hound dog; a handsome, short, muscular, boxy-headed dog with long ears. He was a hunting dog, supposed to be good for tracking rabbit. I wasn't old enough to go hunting, but Daddy took the older ones. Daddy would go with Bill and Ron and sometimes with other folks. He always complained about Spike. Spike was considered a mean dog. Once, Grandma went with me to feed Spike in Captain's old pen, and he came at her. He didn't bite her, but she meant it when she called him a "sowmench." I think that's German for "son of a bitch."

Carol Ann, Linda Jane, Dick, and Spike

Spike was chained to the doghouse, and he would frequently hang himself by jumping over the fence from the top of his house. The chain wasn't long enough for his feet to reach the ground on the other side and, because the doghouse weighed more than he did, he would hang himself. Spike tried different sides of the pen, but since the doghouse was in the center of the pen, it made no difference. So, no matter how smart he was to try different sides, it always came out the same. Dumb! Whoever saw Spike hanging would throw him back over, and he would breath again. Usually, Mother was the one who saw him out the back kitchen window. She would tear outside and just throw him back over.

Tom, Dick, and Spike

Spike also bit Tommy's ear. Tommy liked to fold Spike's long ears between his thumb and the index finger and rub the pinched ear back and forth on itself. It felt as smooth as silk. On one of these occasions Spike nipped Tommy's ear.

Shortly after, on a hunting trip, Daddy came home without Spike or rabbits. He always said, "The dog ran a rabbit and never came back." Daddy claimed he called and looked for him for a long time. I think he shot Spike.

The following summer, Daddy came home from work and called me outside. As I stood nearby, he opened the back door of the car, picked up a rope and coaxed another hound dog out of the back seat floor. I was delighted, but I never forgot about Spike and my suspicion. Daddy told me how he bought the year old dog from some man at work who always kept the dog chained to a fence. The man described the area on the west side of Indianapolis as smoky. "That's it! We'll call him Smokey," I said.

Then, "Oh, can I name him?" I asked.

"Sure, he's yours," Daddy answered.

Smokey had quite a life at our house. He was well cared for. The routine was the same as for Spike; feed the dog and burn the trash. Table scraps were added to his can of food in moderation because after a dinner with five to seven kids at the table, there weren't many scraps left. The plates were scraped with a spoon into one as they were removed from the table and dog food added. I always enjoyed feeding the dog and burning the trash. You could dally and get out of the kitchen chores, a little while anyway.

The bag of trash was dumped into the fireplace and the dog fed and petted a little. Then the trash would be arranged a little until the various boxes and containers became a city. The match would be lit and strategically placed to represent a fire in an apartment, a fire in a factory, or a fire in an office building. The flame would slowly consume the city while sirens roared in the imagination and people screamed and raced to the outskirts (ants and spiders). The firemen never saved the city. It always burnt so fast, too fast, and the drama was over. Sometimes the brown grocery bag was placed in the chimney of the fireplace, open end down, and as the city was consumed, the bag would ignite, burn in a flash, and large chunks of ember lit shards of black paper were fired out of the flue by the heat of the updraft. The drama ended abruptly, often enough with, "Richard Louis, bring that plate in here now! We want to finish dishes!" It was frequently at the very height of the drama, but that was easily abandoned with the threat of reprisal in Carol Ann or Linda's voice calling from the back door.

Smokey was often unchained and allowed to run rabbits at the end of the lot. He ran rabbits well and frequently returned with blood all over his mouth, triumphant in the chase. I don't know if he just killed the rabbits he caught or actually ate his fill. I suspect he did both. Most probably, he only unearthed a litter and killed or ate the little helpless ones. I liked him anyway. He was my link to that wild side. I was secretly proud when he came back bloody and imagined he could provide for us both if need be.

Daddy took Smokey hunting only a few times, because, like Spike, he never performed like a hunting hound dog. Spike was his own dog and did as he pleased on a hunt, but from what I heard, Smokey was no good because he cowered in fear when the shotgun sounded. He soon began to cower on the ground in anticipation of the blast when anyone took aim. That was okay with me also. It didn't diminish his stature in my book. After all, I didn't like shotguns either. I understood.

Dick, Tom, and Smokey

When we went with Smokey to the end of the lot and Pogue's Run, he was glad we were with him, tail wagging, panting, nose to the ground. But, his nostrils soon tempted him away, and he was off on the chase. We almost always returned to the house without him, long bored with skipping stones or

34

launching a bottle into the creek and bombarding it with stones, while scrambling along the bank, until we hit and sank it.

During the summer, Smokey would pass the heat of the day dozing. I could lie in the grass in the sun and pat the ground next to me, calling him over, and he would stretch out on his side with his back next to me. He would doze while being petted or he was content to lay undisturbed.

He spent each winter outdoors until the temperature dropped and the wind howled and Mother felt that no amount of doghouse winterizing had been adequate. She would come to the foot of the stairs in the middle of the night, flip on the light and call quietly, "Dick, come and let the dog into the basement."

Smokey and Dick

Without hesitation, and thankful that she was so sympathetic; I would pull on my play clothes and bring him into the basement. A rug was spread on the concrete island next to the furnace and Smokey was content. He was tethered there so as to limit probable deposits in the laundry room area. Knowing he was warm and sound asleep made the return to my bed, after a "Thanks Mother," all the warmer.

During spring renovations to the yard, Smokey's doghouse was moved every few years because he destroyed the grass around his house to the extent that his chain allowed. He eventually wound up in front of the two-car brick garage daddy built out of the nine loads of brick he got at a dollar a load from the destruction of the old St. Francis de Sales School House. The school building was the traditional four rooms up, four rooms down, two story structure where my father, his sister, Aunt Gene, and other brothers and sisters had all gone to grade school as had all of us, except Tommy.

At sixteen, a sophomore in high school, I went to work at J.C. Penney's on the circle and worked every evening after school until 5:00 P.M. The bus to downtown was in front of Scecina and, books in hand; I caught it religiously each afternoon. I would arrive at 3:30 and go to work, picking up lay-aways throughout the three floors of the store, between "running packages" that customers finally paid off, some, 50 cents at a time. All new lay-aways would be shelved, hung or stored in Z - corner. The cards appropriately marked would be turned in to the office. The bell announcing the store's closure would sound, "bong, bong, bong, bong," and it was time to take the employee's cart of packages to the doors of the main floor. All the packages were sealed with a tag to be matched on exit by the employee. After delivering the cart of packages to the assigned department head on duty, I would return to the lay-away area on the second floor to relieve Mr. Williams, the store comptroller, my boss, at accepting the money bags. Exchanging each employees tag for their numbered moneybag, they were stored in stacks of tens in the money cart. The count of bags was reconciled and a tag yet on the board signaled a bag still out. When finally all were in, the heavy, money laden cart was shoved out of lay-away past the machines that clattered earlier, registering payments and the racks and racks of files holding cards with outstanding balances. The cart was left standing outside lay-away while I ran through the kitchen and into the employee's locker room to cut the lights on that part of the second floor. The cart was then pushed to the office area on the other side of the second floor, routing it past the elevators, and into the safe. The safe was secured, lights doused, and all left the store. I would hurry to Meridian Street to catch the East 21st Street bus in front of the Board of Trade Building. The ride home was quick enough and I looked forward to crossing 21st Street after the bus passed, and being greeted by the rattle of Smokey's chain as he came out of his doghouse to meet me on the gravel drive. I always went straight to him before I went in to the dinner that Mother kept warming on the stove.

One Saturday evening, I was walking up the gravel drive and reached the top of the little rise and realized I didn't hear Smokey's chain. I looked to the garage and the doghouse was gone.

"Oh, they've moved his doghouse again. I wonder where to?" I thought.

I went to the spot. It was raked clean and grass seed was already sprinkled about. I went around the West side of the garage and looked all about.

"Mother!" I called as I went bounding in the back door. Mother was re-warming dinner.

"Hi, Mother. Where's Smokey?" I asked.

She fumbled with the contents of the skillet and without looking at me she said, "You better ask your sister."

"Carol Ann?" I asked.

"Yes," she said

"Where is she?" I asked.

"In her bedroom," she answered.

"Carol Ann!" I called, and as she came out of her room I added, "Where's Smokey?"

She said, without hesitation, "I had him put to sleep."

"You what!! Why?!" I was dumbfounded.

"I took him to the pound and had him put to sleep. He was dribbling all over the place," she explained.

Smokey had lost bladder control and did drip. I suppose others said things in her defense or just said things. I don't know, I didn't hear them. I know Smokey had grown old, I just hadn't known when.

I did ask someone about his doghouse. It might have been Carol Ann, but I don't remember the exact answer she gave me. It was given to someone and I remember thinking how incredible this was that "they" were so thorough. Here I was at work at Penny's all day. I had gone out the front door to catch the bus that Saturday morning before anyone else was up, and while I was at work, Carol Ann and her accomplices had taken my dog to the pound, gotten rid of his house and cleaned up the site. At what point in the day did my wonderful friend die without being told good-bye?

I have forgiven Carol Ann and "them" inside, whoever they were, but I've never told them so. I think, though, until I tell them, I will not really have forgiven them. I don't think they even know they need my forgiveness. If they don't know it, then do they need it?

They were probably right in what they did in that Smokey needed merciful treatment, and it's with that reasoning I've forgiven. I haven't forgiven their failure to involve me in the decision or the lack of opportunity to face the truth and say good-bye to my friend.

Section 2

Family Ties

C.C.C.

There were a couple of rabbit hutches attached to the back of the wood frame garage. They were homemade and covered with chicken wire, top, sides, and bottom. The rabbits, stepping around on the chicken wire, must have hurt their feet; at least it seemed that way to me. They

were large rabbits and were seldom taken out to play. My oldest brother, Bill, raised rabbits to eat, not as pets. "Hasenpfeffer," Grandma said. Bill did have a hard time killing them. He would take one from the cages by the ears and carry it into the garage and close the door. He would sit in the garage and pet the rabbit for a long time before he could finally hit it in the back of the head with a club. Sometimes hitting it once wasn't enough. That must have been tough because you can imagine how you could become attached. Mother would pass sentence, so to speak, by asking him to kill a couple of rabbits for dinner- hasenpfeffer. He would decide which ones and then often could hardly eat. On occasion, the female rabbit would kill her newborn before Bill got them separated. I believe she couldn't imagine living in such a small space with eight other rabbits and self-preservation kicked in. We were never allowed to open the cages and play with them but we did feed them clover through the chicken wire and we did stick our fingers through the wire to touch their sides and feel the soft, cool fur. There was a pet store smell about the rabbit hutches, probably the food pellets.

Carol Ann, Bill, Jerry, and Linda Jane with rabbits

It wasn't at the same time, but my second oldest brother, Ron, decided to raise chickens. Grandma had chickens for the eggs but Ron raised chickens for the chicken meat. He purchased a factory made chicken coop from friends of the family. It looked like a piece of cake and ice cream roll because of the shape. It had a little door on one end and two, four-pane windows on either side. The rounded roof was removable. It was hinged so that it could be lifted and raised while sliding it to one side. That way a person could stand up and clean the coop. I don't know if raising rabbits or chickens had anything to do with the war or the depression that followed, but I've wondered what would motivate parents to allow their oldest boys to engage in these activities.

Ron received his live, golden little chicks in brown pasteboard boxes. The chicks would be released into the coop and a light bulb would often have to be left on all night for the warmth. The following day he would remove the dead chicks. Through the night, as they clamored for the warmth of the light bulb, some of those in the middle, nearest the bulb, would be crushed by the weight of the others. I'm not sure how successful Ron was at raising chickens but, ultimately, like the rabbit venture, the chicken raising came to an end. However, the big difference between the rabbits and the chickens was the coop. The hutches, one sunny afternoon, were unceremoniously dismantled. They were torn from

Carol Ann, Dick, Mother, Linda Jane, and Jerry with rabbits

the back of the frame garage and trashed but the coop underwent a transformation. Like Cinderella's pumpkin became her coach, the coop became our clubhouse. We worked several days cleaning it up. There was the sweeping, hosing, scrubbing, and splashing of bleach water that Mother had us do to make it safe and clean. It had to dry out forever before we were able to give it a fresh coat of white paint and finally seat ourselves inside of it, snug on throw rugs and old comforters. It was then that deliberations began on the name of the club.

Our club was finally named the "C.C.C." The three letters were painted above the little door in an arch and it stood for the "Catholic Children's' Club." The club was launched with five charter members and ended with the same membership. We had a president (Jerry), a vice president (Carol Ann) and a secretary (Linda Jane) although we did not keep minutes. We didn't recruit new members because we didn't want other members. It was our club. Besides, the coop wasn't big enough for a larger membership body. Five was just right!

We had no by-laws, but what we did have was a self-imposed system of merits and demerits. There were no written guidelines for how you could earn merits or have them taken away. We sort of made that up as we went along. For example, complimenting another person, not just club members, by saying "that's a nice shirt," or "that's a good color for you," or "I like the way your hair looks," or "you look good today," and so on, you could earn one merit. Doing something nice for another person like taking out the trash when it was their job but they forgot or by making their bed or picking up their laundry and taking it to the hamper, earned a couple of merits. Cursing, teasing or making fun of another person meant demerits!

Holy card of St. Ann

The number of merits earned or lost was somewhat arbitrarily applied. It depended on the value of the nicety extended to another person or the severity of the infraction. As an example of an infraction consider this. Suppose you threw a green apple at another person. Questions to be considered would be, "Was it tossed to tease or thrown with force? Did it miss, tossed or thrown or did it strike? If it struck, was it tossed or thrown? Did it hurt or not? If it hurt, how much? And, did the perpetrator laugh or apologize immediately?" You get the point. It was very complicated. Imagine the number of demerits you could receive if you threw the green apple with malice, intending to strike the person and do harm and you did, it hurt a lot, leaving a red mark or bruise and then you laughed at the "cry baby!" Ha! Name calling besides! It could add up. At weekly club meetings, all of these things were hashed out. Under scrutiny, however, lies were told and denials prevailed as well as false claims of good deeds.

Of course, someone had to keep the book in which were added merits earned and demerits deducted. These records were tallied weekly at our regular C.C.C. meeting. Changes were made at the meeting as the individuals recalled events not recorded. At the end of the tally some one of the membership was recognized for having earned the greatest number of merits for that week. After a few weeks, it became clear that the person who kept the book was always the winner, Carol Ann, the vice president. I've often wondered if she added merits to her column. I mean, she kept book on everybody and the book was with her all the time. Having the book, she could see, in an on-going way, where she stood. She might have emerged from her room with the knowledge of where she stood, said three nice things and go right back to her room to post the profits.

In recognition of being the week's first place earner of the most merits, a little something or another, like a holy card, was presented. The system went by the wayside soon enough because at least four members lost interest due to the lack of positive reinforcement (no prizes).

The chicken coop was eventually moved to the cottage at Graybrook Lake and used as a storage shed until it also went by the wayside due to a lack of paint. It fell to flames consuming termites and all - set afire where it stood. I thought we should have set it afire at home after the first meeting of the C.C.C.

Addendum to C.C.C.

Here is a copy of the original record of merits and demerits for the members of the Catholic Children's' Club. Carol Ann was the "grand prize" winner, her name boldly outlined in addition to her hand-scrawled announcement at the bottom of the first page of the record.

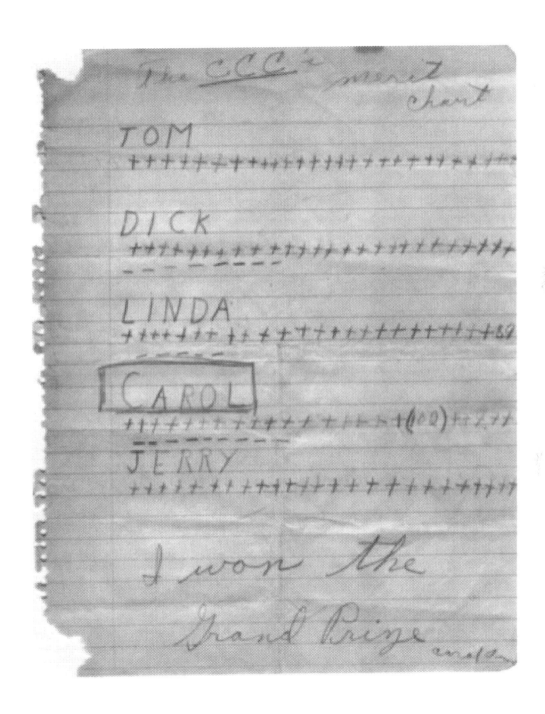

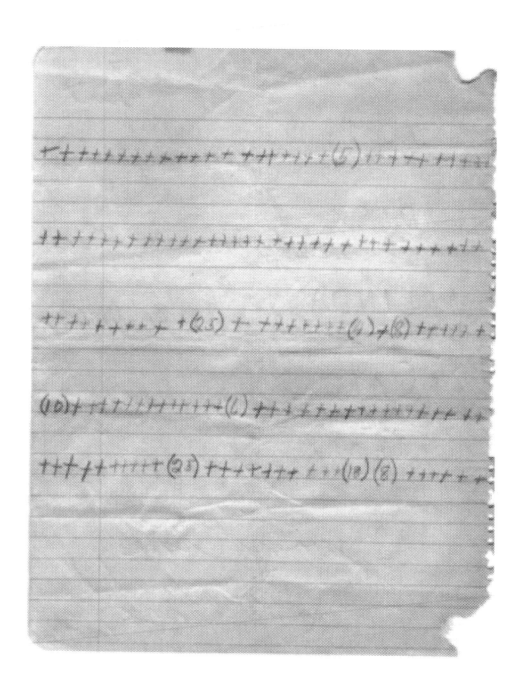

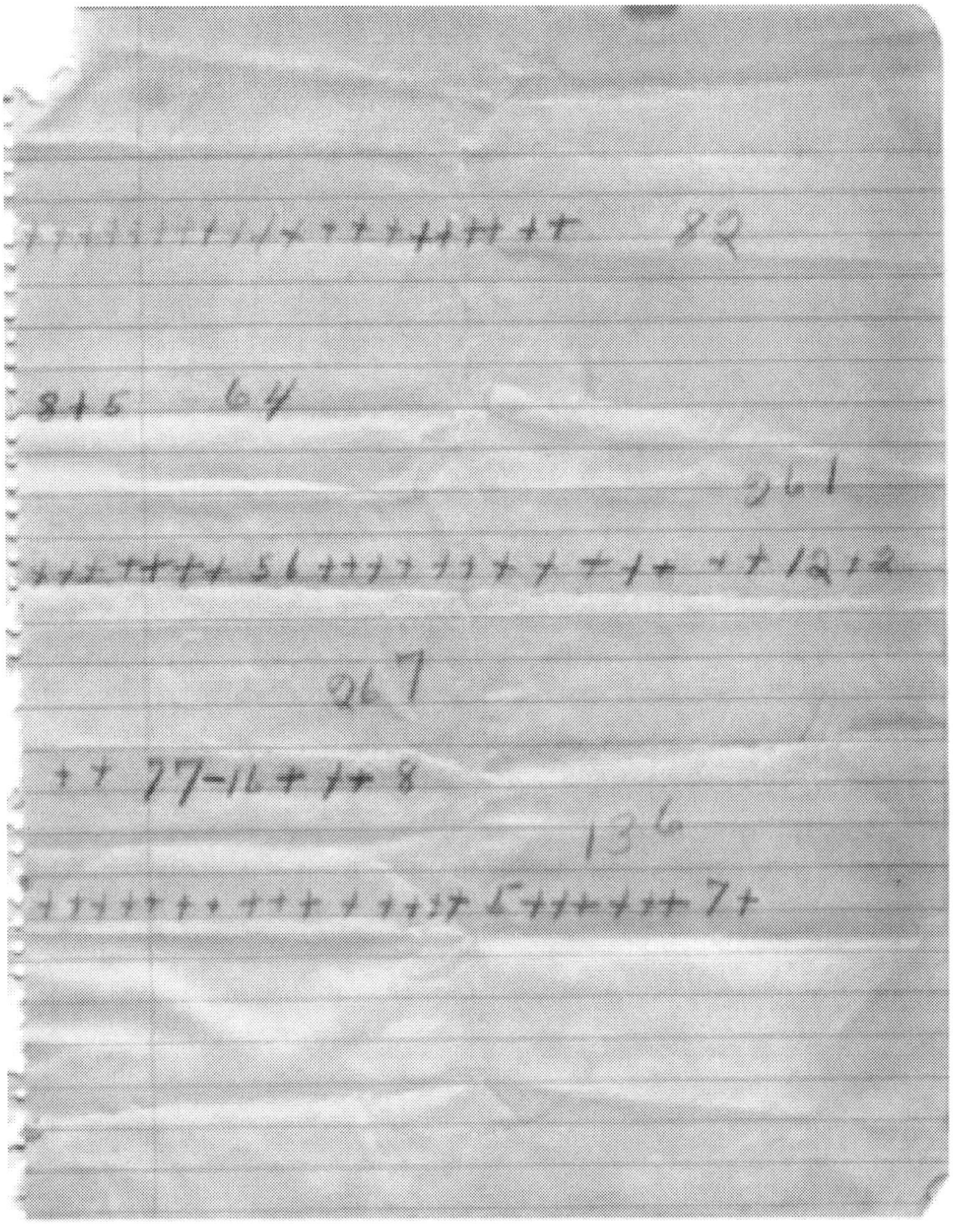

+++++++++++++++++++++ 82

8+5 64

361

+++++++ 56 +++++++++++++ 12+2

267

++ 77-16 +++ 8

136

+++++++++++++++37 5+++++7+

43

Tommy earned 82 merits over the four or five week period that the club existed and received no demerits - the numbers check out!

Linda Jane earned 266 merits less the 5 demerits for a total of 261 - the numbers check out!

Carol Ann earned 276 merits less the 9 demerits for a total of 267 - the numbers check out!

Jerry earned 136 merits and received no demerits - the numbers check out!

However, I only earned 69 merits over the four or five-week period the C.C.C. was active, less my eight demerits for a total of 61, yet the record shows 64.

I cannot figure out what might have generated the parenthetical figures in Tommy's, Linda Jane's, Carol Ann's, and Jerry's recorded line of merits. Some of them are extraordinarily large, i.e. "102" and "77" in Carol Ann's line; "89," "25" and "56" in Linda Jane's line; and "25" and "18" in Jerry's line of merits. These three all have other figures in their lines. Tommy has one "5" and I only have extra numbers of "8" and "5" tacked on the end. Even if my figure were accurately tallied, I still clearly came in last.

The order of first to last at the finish was Carol Ann, Linda Jane, Jerry, Tommy, and Dick. I have some questions!

Connections

In Indianapolis, as was true of everywhere else in the country, when telephones were introduced to the home, "party lines" were available. They were less expensive by the month than a private line. A party line meant that your telephone was on the same service as that of another home telephone line. The telephone company instructed the homeowner what to listen for in order to know that a call was meant for them. Our particular ring was two short rings and a long one while the other household on the same line was one short ring and one long. I never understood how the caller got the correct household when both had the same numbers until I grasped the concept of the operator. On a party line, you knew when the others were receiving a call because of the ring but you never knew when they were making a call and were using the line. Often times, if we wanted to make a call and picked up the receiver, there was conversation on the line meaning the other household on the party line was using the system. With a brief "Oh, sorry," the receiver would be hung up and the wait to use the phone would begin. The only way to find out if your line was free to place a call was to pick up the receiver and hope for a dial tone. Otherwise, the brief apology was in order. Party line members often got angry with their other party line members, though they never knew who they were or where they lived, for taking so much time on the phone. On the other hand, there was a great deal of cooperation because if you needed the line in an emergency, they would hang up and open the line for your use.

We did not have a party line as long as Aunt Gene and Grandma. We, soon, were the proud owners of the private line. There were nine people in our home, including five teenagers. The line was private until Mother called Lanesville, Indiana, her birthplace. About twice a year Mother would place a call to her home place in Lanesville to talk to her sisters, my Aunts, Bertilla and Olive. When she decided to place the call, she informed those in the house what she was about to do and called us to her skirt to stand by. We would fumble about on the linoleum of the kitchen floor and wait, bored.

Her conversation went something like this:

(Mother) "Oh darn, I got a busy signal." We began to scatter and Mother would say, "No, no. Come back here. I must have dialed wrong. I'll try again." She dialed again as we regrouped at her feet.

(Mother) "Hello, Virginia?,... Yes, this is Ceal in Indianapolis. Connect me with 1524,.....thank you....Yes,...no, everyone is fine....OK, yes, yes, I will....Thanks!" We waited while the telephone at 1524 rang.

(Mother) "Hello, Till, this is Ceal.....no, everyone is fine...no, everything is OK." They always assumed the worst, otherwise, why would anyone be making a long-distance call when sending a letter was so much less expensive? Mother continued, "I just wanted to call to let you know we are well and to see if everything and everyone was OK there.....Yes, we are doing fine......No, Art is in the other room.....What?.....Oh, hello Hilda, how is George.....Good!....Till!, I think Hilda is on the line....Yes, Virginia must have connected her...Yes....Well, whenever I call the word goes out.....Yes, it does. It's good to hear your voices! You sound so clear. I wish we were as close as.....What!?....Oh, hello, Cornelia!....Cornelia is on the line. Cornelia, how are you?.....Yes, we are all fine. I just decided to call home to say hello. How is Uncle Dominic?.....Oh, I see....OK. No, thanks, we are all fine....No they are all here, everyone is well, thank goodness! OK, Good-bye Cornelia. Yes, good-bye,....I love you too.....Till? Hilda?, are you still there?.....Oh, thank goodness! I didn't, know if you got cut off or not. Oh, Olive.....Till must have put you on while Cornelia was on the line.....Oh, you heard all of that?......No, they are all here and I want them to say hello......Yes.....Yes.....Everyone is fine.....What?....Oh, hello Germaine, and who else is on the line, is that you Oneda?....Yes, we are all OK. I hope everything is OK with you also?.....Good......Oh?.....Good......Oh, that's wonderful!....Good, I'm glad for you. Say hello to all your families for me....Yes, thank you.....thank you...yes, I love you too. I'll write soon.....Yes, I'll tell him.....OK, thanks and good-bye.....Yes, thanks.....Olive and Hilda, I want the kids to say hello.....No, it will just take a minute.....Its not costing too much. Here, wait, this is Tommy."

"Tommy, say hello to Aunt Hilda," Mother instructed as she handed the receiver to Tommy.

"Hello, Aunt Hilda....Yes, I'm fine......Oh? Hello Aunt Till." Tommy says.

"Speak louder," instructed Mother for she realized Aunt Till was again on the line and Aunt Till was very hard of hearing.

So Tommy would shout, "Hello Aunt Till."

The passing of the receiver went on like this on both ends for about five minutes, Virginia, the operator in Lanesville continuing to take it upon herself to plug other people into the conversation she just knew Mother would "want to say hello to."

After we finished our turn on the telephone, we were free to go and Mother was left to say her goodbyes. I could hear her from the dining room saying how much she missed them, how much she wished they lived closer, that she would write soon and that they should tell anyone who had not been on the phone with them that she sends her greetings and those of "Art as well." Art, Daddy, never got on the phone but continued to read the daily newspaper in the living room.

"Thank you.....thank you...yes, I love you too. I'll write soon.....Yes, I'll tell him...." Mother concluded.

These infrequent calls were important but draining on Mother. You could see both the joy and the sadness in her face as she finally hung up the receiver, sometimes a tear or two, while smiling, would spill from her eyes before she could catch them with the apron she took from her waist.

Sunday Relaxation

In my childhood, Sundays were a day of rest and relaxation. Sundays began with 9:00 a.m. Mass at St. Francis de Sales unless we were going to Lanesville then we went to the 6:00 A.M. Mass. After Mass and breakfast we would celebrate birthdays, have company or visit other families. We stayed in our good clothes longer on Sunday than on any other day and lined up in various groupings for pictures by the spiraea bushes in front of our home - Mother wielding the telescopic Kodak.

(Left to Right in back) Bill, Mother, Daddy, Ron
(Left to Right in front) Jerry, Linda Jane, Tom, Carol Ann, Dick

In the summer, our Sunday relaxation took several forms that often only involved our family. I remember the gatherings and visits and celebrations and pictures and so on, when the good clothes and shoes stayed on, but the fondest and warmest memories are of the Sundays spent with just the immediate family. A Sunday drive in the car was such an event. We would head east on 21st Street. The first site just up the street to be pointed out was Black's house, Mother and Daddy's first house, Harry's Grocery Store, Naval Avionics and then country.

Harry's Store was really small and sat at the corner of Drexel and 21st Street, about four blocks from our home. It seems to me we went to Harry Grassoff's Grocery at least once each day, sometimes twice, either because we forgot something or Mother forgot something. I can still see the store's interior clearly. The bell on the door tinkled when you went in. The floor was wooden and worn. It creaked in places. Harry cut the meat, weighed it and wrapped it in brown paper. He secured it with paper tape and marked the price on the paper with a grease pencil that he always tucked behind his ear, all in one motion. He stocked the shelves and helped us find the items we couldn't find. He reached those we couldn't reach, and he checked us out. If there were more than one customer, he was everywhere doing everything, but he always had time.

He also "carried" people. The money Mother sent went on the account; what we purchased went there also. Harry was a very nice man of some unknown nationality. He didn't seem American to me but more middle-eastern and mysterious. He was a small man. Some years later, he hired a neighbor, Josephine, as his check out clerk.

When the store "Walt's" opened at 21st and Linwood, only one block from home, we stopped going to Grassoff's Grocery with our wagon. That's too bad because Walt's didn't carry anyone for anything. Walt's was more like the Standard Store in Brightwood where we did our weekly, heavy shopping on Friday or Saturday evenings. When Walt's opened, Harry's soon closed. Even round shouldered Josephine left Harry's and took a checkout job at Walt's. At Walt's and Standard, you paid as you "goed."

We still had to go to the drugstore for Alophon pills for Daddy. The drugstore was just across the street from Harry's, and when I went there I always wondered about Harry and how he was doing.

I stared in awe at Naval Avionics as we passed and was sorry we lived so close. As I recall, they made bombing sights during the Second World War. I figured this place was marked for an atom bomb when we were attacked and we wouldn't stand a chance at home. Even in school at St. Francis, I thought it was ridiculous that we practiced the "duck and cover" method of survival practice when Naval Avionics was so close. Remember the drill? "When you see the flash, duck and cover." Duck and cover meant we were to crouch under our desk in a little ball and cover our heads and face with our hands and arms. If we were forewarned enough, we could go from the classrooms into the hallway and duck and cover there. What a joke! But it gave us the hope that we could survive the atom bomb, and hope was important. Anyway, on to the country to enjoy this day.

There were berries to look for, the old persimmon tree, paw paws and walnuts. We would visit Geist Reservoir. Parking the car, we walked to the dam and visited the spillway. What a sight: the blue-green, deep water behind the huge curved concrete top of the dam and the green, mossy, slimy face of the spillway with a steady curtain of water pouring over! I marveled at how "they" got the thing so level at such a span so that the water flowed over so evenly. This, to me, was the beginning of Fall Creek.

Dick and Jerry at Geist

I was amazed that we always found our way home from Geist. I never believed I could ever find my way to Geist and back. I know I couldn't then, and I'm not so sure today. Fall Creek Parkway, the bridge to cross and the embankment, was much like the cliff at our Pouge's Run, where people fired at targets into the dirt. I wonder how much lead from rifles and shotguns has been pumped into that hillside.

After several stops to do or see this or that, all familiar sights, and when we were on our way home, the notorious five in the back seat would put heads together and raise an agreed upon shout for watermelon or ice cream.

"Okay let's go, one, two, three ...." Jerry would conduct and the chorus was raised.

"We want ice cream, we want ice cream, we want ice cream. I scream, you scream, we all scream for ice cream," and so on.

We would laugh and roll about in the back seat, exaggerating our inability to stay upright at corners and continuing our chant, sometimes mistakenly chanting for watermelon too late in the summer season. If that were pointed out by Mother, we would readily switch to ice cream, knowing the power we wielded and that the Blue Ribbon on 10th Street always had ice cream no matter what the season.

Whatever the chant, Mother and Daddy would talk quietly to one another above the din and frolic in the back seat. While we chanted, we carefully watched this consultation, poking and congratulating each other, for, we always got our wish, seasonal or otherwise.

I suspect, when we went on these trips, Mother and Daddy had financially planned to be able to meet our "demands" else we didn't go for such drives, but we knew no better. We knew from the start, when a Sunday drive was suggested, that we would endure the scenes and raise a chant on the return trip. I don't know who knew we were near the home place to suggest we begin the chant to divert the driver, Daddy. I suspect it was Jerry and Carol Ann. It was a game.

And so we would wind up stopping at a roadside market for watermelon or at the Blue Ribbon Ice Cream Parlor for ice cream.

If we got a watermelon, we took it home, arriving about dusk, and invited Grandma and Aunt Gene to join us. Newspapers were spread on the back steps of our home and the watermelon was cut and passed out piece by piece. Seeds were spit in all directions but usually "accidentally" at each other, and friendly fights ensued with rind and watermelon juice and mosquitoes. Not to worry, as amid the laughter and chase, we could be hosed down along with the steps.

I remember once when fastidious Linda was particularly annoyed with Little Tom and warned him only once that if he did whatever it was he was doing "one more time," he would be sorry. He did. With the scooped out butt end of the watermelon in her right hand, she chased him down, and very quickly, I might add. She caught him with her left hand, and there, for all to see, whipped him to the ground. As he sat up, she plopped the watermelon bowl on top of his burr cut head and ground it back and forth as though she were grinding the juice from half an orange. Juice ran down all around and Grandma whooped and laughed, Daddy too, while Mother called out "Linda Jane!" as though she would stop. When Linda Jane decided to, she stopped and walked back and plopped the rind into the bucket and smacked her hands as if brushing them off, congratulating herself for having accomplished a difficult task so handily and easily.

If we got ice cream from Blue Ribbon, we took it home, and, after inviting Grandma and Aunt Gene to join us, it was taken into the kitchen and served in bowls. Mother and Daddy decided what to buy. Daddy's favorite was black walnut but that was more expensive. Vanilla was the standby. Neopolitan was often the choice for it was a layered combination of vanilla, strawberry and chocolate. They usually purchased two one quart blocks or one half gallon in the blue and white thick paper wrapping.

In our kitchen, the block laid open, would be sliced into squares with the same butcher knife used to dissect a watermelon. Ice cream was always served with ice water.

I remember the "pop" of the watermelon and the familiar rip of the paper wrapping under the knife. What wonderfully caring, responsive parents, the best in the world!

Other Sunday relaxation affairs were Fall Creek fishing trips. Preparations for these trips began Saturday evening as the sun went down. Daddy would begin to "water the lawn," or so it appeared to me. When I was sure the grass had enough, he would still sit on the steps at the back door and spray the yard, brown beer bottle in hand - Schlitz.

When enough water had been sprayed over the back yard, he would come in the house and wait awhile. Then he would get a flashlight and invite his children to the harvest. We were instructed to be quiet and to step lightly. We were going to harvest night crawlers.

I had seen robins do it after a rain. They were real good at it. We had turned over boards and stones and had discovered huge pink-banded worms that we picked up on sticks, hoes, or shovels and carried them to Grandma's chickens. The chickens were delighted and competed for the fat, cool, damp worms. We enjoyed watching them compete as we dangled the long, slimy things from the transporter. I was amazed at how long they could get before they snapped and curled about the hen's beak. The hens also seemed amazed that a squirming worm suddenly surrounded their beaks, but putting their beaks to the ground, they clawed the worm off and devoured them cleanly.

So we were going to catch night crawlers! I learned that the water filled their burrows and they came up for air to keep from drowning. Stepping lightly into the cool, glistening grass, the flashlight casting its beam, Daddy would suddenly thrust his hand into the grass and triumphantly say "Ah ha!" Pulling easily, the worm would slip from the hole in the ground and he would place it into a one pound coffee can that he had saved for the harvest.

If you approached heavily on foot, the vibration would drive the worm underground as if it were a stretched rubber band suddenly released. I came upon two huge worms at the same time. They were lying next to each other. I was going to get two at once! Training the light on them in my left hand, I slowly moved my right hand above them, secretly hoping a vibration of some sort would cause me to miss. I thrust my hand on the pair and lost them both in opposite directions but was left with the milky white, sticky residue all over my palm and fingers. I learned later they were "mating." This was enough for me. I couldn't wash my hands at the back porch sink fast enough.

Sunday morning, after church, we went fishing on Fall Creek with the harvested worms. Daddy, and whomever, would fish while Mother scoured the banks for berries. The younger children would be allowed to stay in the car and listen, much to our frightened delight, to such programs on the car radio as "The Creaking Door" and "The Shadow Knows."

"Who knows what evil lurks in the hearts of men? The Shadow Knows," a deep voice would say. The screams, shouts and hugs of delight at the mere introductions of those programs are vivid. Forget the stories, the intros were enough!

On occasion, with Daddy still fishing and baiting his hook with Saturday evening's night crawlers, Mother would drive home from the Fall Creek site and make fudge and popcorn for snacks and then return.

These were the relaxing but emotionally exhausting Sundays I remember most. Chanting for watermelon or ice cream or screaming at the intro of "The Creaking Door," all in a car that transported us as a family into our imaginations and the power we thought we held over our parents.

Jessie is Biting the Cherry Tree

We had cherry trees. There were three. Actually, we had only one and Grandma and Aunt Gene had two. Well . . "we" had three. Very soon after the tulips, daffodils, hyacinths, Easter eggs, narcissus and some garden planting, the cherries were ready for picking. The cherries seemed to take forever to ripen each season but in retrospect, it really happened very fast. Searching the tree each day for the first ripe cherry made it seem forever.

The cherry trees would bloom in a cloud of white blossoms and very soon after, the old apple tree would bloom. The apple blossoms were much more attractive to me. They were a rosy pink, clustered at the tip of each new growth of leaves, and more evenly spread over the tree so that you could appreciate the contrasts of color and texture. The cherry trees bloomed without greenery, and so abundantly that the tree was simply white. Like forsythia, they couldn't seem to wait for contrast.

The little green cherries appeared with the leaves and before long, we were eating semi-ripe cherries, forcing the issue and suffering the consequences.

Cousin Jessie had other needs.

Cousin Jessie lived in a two-room house in back of Grandma's house behind the grape arbor and the chicken coop. She lived there with her parents, my Uncle France, the plumber, his wife Simone, and her brothers. Aunt Simone was French and was a great storyteller. She loved exaggeration and had the ability to turn everyone's everyday life situations into a very funny account with her story telling gift. She was most always the principal character in her stories, and she really enjoyed telling them. I don't think she was ever totally accepted by Grandma as the person her baby should have married.

Cousin Jessie wouldn't go after the cherries. Putting her arms around the trunk of the tree and tilting her head vampire-like, she'd bite into the amber bulbs that mysteriously appeared only on cherry trees.

We never saw them start, we never saw them grow, they were just there. A hard shiny smooth outer skin covered a thick soft inner core of a very sticky, amber colored substance, which was probably concentrated tree sap.

We often peeled them from the tree like jewels from a crown but never thought of putting them in our mouths. I don't even know what we did with them after we pulled them from the tree except throw them away, being careful that the gooey inner core never touched flesh or clothing. They were beautiful to look at and to feel, and they were fun to peel from the tree. Only Jessie knows the taste, except maybe Carol Ann who would try anything once.

Cousin Jessie was admonished by her parents, Aunt Gene, and Grandma for biting and eating these jewels, but we would laugh and encourage her and, I suppose, admire her for her bravery. We would simply announce to our parents, "Jessie is biting the cherry trees again."

I suppose the report went to her parents via some route, but it never changed her behavior as far as I know. Even today I'm tempted to bite the cherry tree jewels, but I'm sure I never will.

For us, the cherry trees meant picking with sticky juice running to the elbow, pitting, eating, pit spitting and canning. It took a lot of work gathering the cherries and a lot of sore feet standing on the rungs of a ladder or in the fork of a tree reaching further than you knew you should for safety's sake. The cherries became cobbler and pies. I wonder if the jewels could be harvested and made into syrup for pancakes. Unlike maple syrup that has to be boiled down to a concentrate, this might be like a concentrate to which you would have to add water.

Our Pool

To cross 21st Street and play in the fields south of us was a common occurrence. The five of us would be laboriously bundled into clothing we didn't quite feel we needed, to protect us against "the elements." If we were to be really protected against the elements, it would probably have been better if we hadn't been allowed to cross south of 21st Street in the first place. South of 21st lay cornfields, cows and open, four-sided foundation ditches filled with rainwater.

Carol Ann, Tom, Jerry, Dick, and Linda Jane

Mother gave us our liberties to be and to explore in spite of parental anxieties or relief from having us underfoot. She had cleaning rituals, born and nurtured in her childhood, which she religiously adhered to.

This was probably why she allowed us to go, good for us to get the fresh air. I remember "spring cleaning" the most vividly. Part of that ritual was to wash the windows throughout the house. Now that made sense to me, for having done so, everything seemed fresh and renewed. It's a lot like washing the windows on your car. Never mind the body - just wash inside and outside the windows of your car, and it's like the whole automobile is clean. Wash your car and fail to do the windows, and it's like you haven't washed your car at all. But, another part of spring-cleaning made little sense and seemed to be without real purpose, and that was to turn the mattresses and dust the wire springs with a special brush. The long-nose cone shaped dusting brush had to be inserted into the throat of each spring and vigorously twisted to dislodge a year's accumulation of whatever. After this was completed, the springs were re-covered and the mattress, turned side for side and end for end, and replaced. I remember wondering, on going to bed after spring-cleaning, if my head was now resting above where my feet used to be. Yech! Still, it all came out fresh.

It was on one of these forays in the early spring, south of 21st Street, that we happened upon what would become many a summer's day joy, our "pool." We had spent hours playing over and around the mounds of dirt excavated from the trenches, somewhat square in shape, that would be poured with concrete to form the footings of future homes. The trenches were laden with rainwater, as they had stood at least a year without further development. A small child, such as some of us were, could have slipped into one of these trenches and, burdened with clothing meant to protect us against the elements, been slowly dragged under as the clothing soaked up the water.

It didn't happen.

Equally perilous to life and limb of heavily clothed children was a "lake" which existed near 16th and Sherman, behind an old glass works; a plant where my Daddy had briefly been employed. While he worked there, he made a marble, miniature, coffin-like box, which my Mother proudly cherished. I've never quite assimilated that period of his employment with the period of railroad work, his father's career and his employment with Chevrolet's truck and body plant on the west side of Indianapolis. Nonetheless, the lake existed. We often went there, and on one occasion discovered, half buried in mud at the shore's edge, a metal box. The box was approximately 2 feet wide, 6 feet long, and 2 feet deep. Once excavated from the sediment, it became our ship and we briefly poled ourselves about the surface of the lake.

This was salvage; our secret. We left it briefly, a week or two, continuing to use it to pole around the lake, with plans to bring the salvage home, and that we did! This magnificent find, once a ship, hauled home on the wagon, became our backyard summertime swimming pool. We were sure we were the envy of all the world's children. We had a pool!

The hose would fill the pool; it took forever! It was set out in the backyard, West of the white, wood frame garage, under the clotheslines. We couldn't use the pool on washdays. Mom hung the wash on the wire stretching from house to pole, after wiping it down with an old rag. She meticulously sorted the wash as she hung it so that the articles of clothing were hung together, in perfect order, with seams and sock heels all facing the same way. There was great pride taken in how the wash was hung for the benefit

53

Dick, Carol Ann, Linda Jane, Tom, and Jerry

of the neighbors and self. "Hang a proud wash!" I've often wondered to what extent a person would go if, after hanging their wash in a perfect symmetrical chain of clothes and wooden pins, they discovered a piece in the bottom of the basket that was missed and if now hung, would be out of sequence. Would all be rearranged so that the overlooked piece assumed its rightful position? I sometimes think that's why tall grass existed, or lawn chairs, so those pieces could be discreetly spread below the neighbor's view to dry at the sun's will. What a labor! Sheets are at their best when sun dried.

But, wash day aside, summer and no school, let's fill the pool, our prize! The tin box, dragged out into the sun, would be filled with maybe 18 inches of cold, cold water. And then came the change into our pool attire as the water warmed in the sun. I was definitely the most conspicuous. I was skinny. I was not thin, I was intolerably skinny, and I shivered in 90 degrees. The trunks I wore, string tied, were like men's boxer underwear on a thin legged stork. There was little to keep them up except hipbones and constant retying. But, preoccupation with appearance soon gave way at the encouragement of brothers and sisters and fun in our pool. Never mind that once wet, the trunks seemed to display what very little manhood there was to hide. We sometimes swam in our underwear.

Aunt Hilda, Tom, Carol Ann, Linda Jane, Dick, and Jerry

We dove like Olympians from a wooden stepladder into our pool. One after another, laughing, we displayed our original styles, playing follow the leader for what seemed like hours, swimming and splashing from ladder end and back. We marveled at the whitened and wrinkled skin of our fingertips, testimony that we had actually been swimming as long as anyone could imagine. In our minds, this placed us among the bravest, the wealthiest, having the most endurance, for we had our pool, and we knew how to use it.

Our pool box ultimately became a worm farm, or so it was meant, beside a woodpile at our self-made cottage in Owen County at Spencer, Indiana. The time the worm farm was discovered flooded with rainwater, in spite of the cover, it never smelled so bad as it did then. All the night crawlers harvested from our lawn, had drowned. We had survived the ditches, the lake and the pool. We had learned to dunk our heads beyond the crown, under water, and come up safe again. We were certainly better swimmers than worms. We certainly smelled better in life than they did in death.

The metal box was unceremoniously drained by poking holes in its sides and dumped. It could never be used again, for anything.

Horse Tea

Grandma loved to work in the yard. She hated to be inside when the weather accommodated the human body in a housedress outside. She fiddled endlessly in the yard, humming some old German tune or arguing out loud with nature and its continuous assault on an eclectic, weed less, flower filled environment. However unorthodox some of her gardening practices, things seemed to flourish under her care. She watered endlessly. She didn't deep water, but she directed the harsh spray of the hose full force on the plants, causing them to hiss and their leaves to flap as though a tropical rainstorm had suddenly struck. She often cultivated around the base of the plants with the full force of the water from the nozzle of the hose, leaving holes in the ground, splattering dirt from around the base of the plants and exposing the delicate, hair-like bleached roots. Yet, things flourished. She watered the surface intermittently throughout hot summer days. She wet the leaves in the heat of the day, but I don't recall anything in her bountiful yard that appeared scorched, brown-spotted or wilted.

Criticism or advice by me from my scant knowledge of plants, based on a book or pamphlet, was humorous to her. Though she listened, she did as she always did, but she made me feel she respected my view. Whatever I did in our yard, according to the book or pamphlet, she always exceeded.

Aunt Gene did the planting, mostly, and I learned how to plant bulbs from her. I would usually dig a nice straight furrow or follow a border to the required depth and set the bulbs in the bottom, one following the other, at a distance of six inches or so. She, on the other hand, would dig a bed with the width of a spade or more and randomly place the bulbs in the trench and then cover them up. I challenged her on this one fall when she was planting tulip bulbs.

Mother with tulip soldiers

"What are you doing Aunt Gene?" I asked.

"Planting tulips," she replied.

"Why such a ditch?"

"A ditch! What do you mean?"

"Well you don't need such a wide ditch to plant tulips," I explained.

"Well, no you don't if you want your tulips standing like soldiers in a nice straight row, single file like you do! Then they look planted, more artificial. I like things to look more natural," she answered.

After observing her tulip bed the following spring and comparing hers to what I had planted, I had to admit she had been right. I've never since planted bulbs in a nice straight line but more clustered, more eclectic.

Pamphlets I read about gardening never mentioned horse tea. When Grandma discussed the merits of horse tea for plants, she salivated as though she were talking about a delicious German dish fit for human consumption. For her, plants were living organisms that liked to be served a varied diet. After all, she wouldn't eat the same menu of prepared foods day after day, so why would plants want to, she reasoned. So, she prepared horse tea.

I recall her excitement when once we were sitting on her porch on a hot summer day and a horse-drawn wagon came up the street. It was a buckboard style wagon on automobile tires and made no noise except for the horse and driver. The black man at the reins called out, "Rags, old rags, old iron, rags, any old rags, old iron." He didn't look right or left but kept his eyes on the reins in his hands, his elbows resting on his knees in the heat of the sleepy day. His greasy, soiled hat shaded his head, and except for his hypnotic chant, he appeared to be asleep.

His passing, at first, disturbed us only slightly, as Grandma explained in answer to my question, that he collected old rags and old iron for sale as scrap. His wagon slowly passed in front of Grandma's house behind the klop, klop, klop of the horse's shod hooves on the brick.

Suddenly, Grandma came to life. Her eyes widened, she gasped a little. I looked to the street and the passing ragman's wagon and back to her and asked, "What is it, Grandma?"

I half expected to see the worst as I raised myself high enough to peer over the porch railing from the glider. She was seeing a gift.

"Horse Shit!" she quietly exclaimed.

"What?" I said.

"Horse Shit," she said. "The horse on the wagon left his mark."

So what, I thought. She was up, and Lassie, her dog, jumped down.

"Dickie, quick, go get a pail and shovel." Then she added, "Hurry, before old lady Smith sees it out there."

I felt the urgency in her voice. There was a prize to be had, but fresh horseshit?? Needless to say, I was puzzled. It smelled, even from the porch. It was golden brown, shiny and wet and had plopped to the street from beneath the horse's tail. The horse didn't miss a step in the process, and the wagon master didn't flinch, cover his nose or miss a cadent call for rags and iron.

In spite of the calm delivery of the gift, and without missing a beat, our peaceful solitude seemed turned into pandemonium. The wagon passed on.

At her command, and still puzzled, I was on my way to the garage. She called me "Dickie' whenever she wanted me to do something just like Carol Ann and Linda Jane did when they wanted a favor. I returned to the street with a coal shovel and a basket, a bushel basket. I had no idea how much there would be. She was across the street, lifting her right shoulder, then her left, in nervous anticipation, the old damp washcloth hanging around her neck. She assisted my crossing, and with shovel in hand, boldly retrieved the gift from the brick pavement, between traffic, scoop after scoop, until she was satisfied and she had all there was.

"Okay, let's go," she said.

I took one handle of the basket, and she took the other. She held onto the shovel and kept checking to be sure she missed nothing as we crossed the street. She was more concerned for what she may have missed than any on-coming traffic.

"What is this for?" I asked.

"This is plant food. This is the best food in the world. It's good for everything."

"Really!!?" I was astonished.

The bottom of the basket was covered, and I worried that I had made a poor choice of containers from my parent's garden stock - maybe it would never come clean again. I broke out in a sweat.

Knowingly she said, "You were really quick, Dickie. Don't worry about the basket. We'll hose it out."

"Oh, sure." I thought.

Grandma went right to work. She dragged out an old galvanized chicken feeder and inverted it in a slight depression she had made in the Shasta daisy and iris bed. As instructed, I pulled the hose to her from the side of the house. She dumped the horse manure into the container and then she directed the full force from the hose into the smelly pot. It hissed, boiled and foamed-a brown foam. She filled it to the top.

"What are you doing that for, Grandma?" I asked.

"This is horse tea," she answered.

"Horse tea! For horses?" I exclaimed.

She laughed a genuine raucous laugh and answered, "No, you ninny, for my plants."

She placed the base of the chicken feeder on top as a lid and patted it proudly as though she had just closed a safety deposit box on a fortune. She went on to explain.

"In a few days, after the sun has heated and fermented this concoction, I'll take dippers full off the top and put it on my plants, and I'll keep adding water until I've gotten all the good out of it that I can."

She did just that, more earnest in attending to the needs of her yard plants than to the needs of her house. When nasty weather set in, you could attack the dust in the house if you had to.

Besides horse tea, she mulched, sprayed, dusted, and pruned. She watered and weeded. Her unorthodox methods paid off because she combined her methods with a profound respect for plants and an appreciation for and an understanding of their needs, needs she met and rejoiced in supplying. It was always more important for her to feed a summer's bounty than to clean, especially on a hot summer's day in a house dress.

Home Delivery

The big old truck would lumber into the gravel driveway, rocking back and forth through the minor chuckholes, and stir up a little white dust. Twenty-first Street was a relatively quiet, two-lane, brick street and with the doors and windows of the house open in the summer you could hear the truck's engine and the gravel crunching under the tires. These sounds announced the arrival of the Crosstown Bakery truck, our Omar man! Fresh baked goods delivered to your door daily, if you wanted, or on whatever schedule you arranged with them. Ours came once every two weeks in the early morning around 7:30 A.M. The Crosstown Bakery delivered warm doughnuts, rolls, coffee cakes, bread and even pies.

As the truck slowly rolled to a stop, we were out the front door having announced his arrival to mother. The driver would slide the truck door open, step out and walk to the back of the truck where we were all waiting. This is where we wanted to be when he opened the two large doors because we didn't want to miss the wonderful odors that cascaded from the racks of trays confined in the truck. Everyone must like the smell of fresh baked dough goods in whatever form.

Excited, delighted comments about the smell aside, we turned our attention to Mother's transactions to see what was in store for this day's breakfast. We always hoped for the cake and yeast doughnuts. The first one to get into the bag at the breakfast table searched for the yeast doughnut which was the heaviest because it would have a glob or pocket of sugar glaze concentrated in the dough and it was the best. Mother would close her deal and come in to supervise further doughnut distribution.

The other home delivery system to which we subscribed, like thousands of others, was that of the milkman. The quart bottles of milk and juice, tinkling in the wire carrying case, would be deposited one by one in the insulated box sitting on the back steps. Mother would complete an order form that was slipped the night before into a clip on the inside of the lid of the piano hinged box. If she forgot, the milkman guessed and he was usually close enough. This delivery often came before the family was up and, like Crosstown Bakery, the bill was settled once every two weeks. Mother got up early to take care of that.

We never had ice blocks delivered on a regular basis in my lifetime although ice trucks or horse drawn wagons were still very much around. We did have ice delivered every now and again for special occasions for cooling watermelons or tubs of bottled beer. I remember the spray of tiny ice chips as the block was jabbed again and again with the ice pick to fracture it and break it into smaller pieces. I liked to watch it fracture deep within the crystal clear block as it took on a light blue hew and imagine I was watching a diamond cutter skillfully at work.

Once a month, the insurance man would come to the door to collect premiums. I don' know for what kind of insurance, but he came for years on a regular basis. He was a large man who always wore a white shirt and tie, his girth challenging the buttons of his shirt, especially when he sat down. Mother would sit on the other end of the couch and he would lay open his narrow but fat account book on the coffee table. She would hand him seven pennies. He would count them and record the payment on each of the required pages, which I presume represented each of the seven children. He talked a little about the weather and he seemed kind enough to me as I watched the transaction while seated on the floor.

The Fuller Brush man was another regular visitor. Mother purchased a brush of some sort or another frequently enough that he came on a regular basis. She more often bought nothing at all. He would also sit in the living room on the couch and open his case of brushes on the floor. Taking one brush after another from the case, he would explain how each could be used and Mother would patiently listen to his presentation. We sometimes thought it would never end and wondered off in boredom. The door-to-door salesmen were endless it seemed. The Jewel-Tea man came with all sorts of roasted coffee beans and ground coffee beans in bags that I did

Mother, Linda Jane, Dick, and Carol Ann

enjoy smelling. With purchases of his coffee or assorted teas, coupons were awarded and an entire set of Jewel-Tea dishes could be acquired over a period of time. The set of dishes included all of the cups, saucers, dinner plates, bowls, sugar bowel, creamer, serving bowls, meat platter and salt and peppershakers. Everyone collected them. I think Grandma and Aunt Gene next door collected more Jewel-Tea dishes than we did. They drank more coffee!

Though they were a dying breed, some doctors still delivered medical care to the home. I never knew a waiting room or it's smell until I was well into grade school after our medical home delivery died with Dr. Conger and we started going to Dr. Gick on East Michigan. I have no idea where Dr. Conger's office was located because I never went there. She always came to the home. Mother would simply call her and tell her there was a problem with one of the children and she would appear within an hour or so. She was a very kind lady, very grandmotherly. She delivered all seven of us at our homes. Bill and Ron were delivered at 4400 East 21st Street, Jerry was delivered at "Black's house" at 4415 East 21st Street, and Carol, Linda, Tom, and myself were delivered at 4350 East 21st as the home address changed.

I am amazed that all of these deliveries occurred at home because of my mother's experiences with home delivery of babies. Her older sister, Ida, married and moved to Fowler, Indiana. There she had five sons and each time, Mother would travel from Lanesville by train to Fowler to help her sister through the ordeal of childbirth and home maintenance. In the end, Ida's husband was out of work and out of money and came home to Lanesville with his pregnant wife, who was in ill health, and their sons. They moved into Mother's home place with her father and sisters. At this point in her life, Mother was recently married and was living in Indianapolis. She prevailed upon her husband, my father Art, to take her to Lanesville and then for him to leave her there so she could once again help her sister through childbirth. Ida was the oldest of the living Ringle children and "broke her father's heart when she married and moved to Fowler." Now she was home with her husband and five sons and about to deliver again. My mother and Rose Day (a "second mother" to my own) were with Ida through her delivery of twin girls, Jean and Joan. Ida had wanted a girl and now she had two but she knew they would not survive.

Bill, Ron, Jerry, Carol Ann, Linda Jane, and Dick with Dr. Conger

They were too small. Mother and Rose wrapped the infants in blankets and placed them on the open oven door of a wood-burning stove. They placed hot-water bottles around them, all in a desperate attempt to keep them warm and alive. Ida said to them, "they are not going to live, don't bother with all of that." The twins died and so did Ida. All of this makes one wonder how much Mother and Daddy must have dreaded the fate of home delivery, not being able to afford anything else.

The difference for them was Doctor Conger and their confidence in her. She came when called and, as I said, delivered seven children. Daddy and Mother gave Doctor Conger what they could and often not cash but trade of one sort or another. This Doctor came to the house regularly, opening her black case in the living room, just like Jewel-Tea and Fuller Brush, only she would extract little bottles and a syringe, a bottle of alcohol and cotton balls and Mother would line us up for inoculations. We protested and cried as we sat, one by one, on her grandmotherly lap and were swabbed and stuck.

Doctor Conger was a giving person, "a saint on earth," mother always said. She gave of herself and her personal possessions. If complimented on something she was wearing, she would immediately remove it and give it to the person who expressed their admiration. She died in an automobile accident without shoes. She had given them to one of her "clients." A saint on earth!

The best home delivery was one of love, not to say the others weren't. But, this one was more special and occurred around 4:00 or 4:30 in the afternoon each day of the week. Mother would remind us of the time if she became aware that we were letting it slip by preoccupied with play...... "Daddy's coming."

Carol Ann

"Oh! Let's go to the porch and see who gets him!"

This game is really simple. The players stood on the West end of the front porch, leaning on the sandstone cap of the brick wall or sitting in the porch swing, and we would take turns "claiming" passing cars, having determined the order of play by who got to the porch first, second, third and so on. We mostly only counted the cars traveling East on 21st Street from town, the direction of his travel home. Sometimes, if traffic was scant, we would also count the cars traveling from East to West. We used the telephone pole across the street as the marker. This method generated many an argument about which car belonged to which player. We also enjoyed making fun of the other player's "rattletrap" and bragging about our own shiny new car. But the biggest braggart of all was the one who got Daddy!

He would pull into the drive smiling and stop by the steps of the porch, a cloud of dust swirling about the car. We would run off the porch yelling "Hello Daddy," surrounding the car while announcing the winner. He would then let us ride on the running board all the way back to the garage - maybe fifty feet.

Home delivery was the greatest!

Indestructible Wagon

We had a wagon. I don't know who received it on a birthday or the occasion of Christmas or what, but we had one. It seemed to me we only ever had one, like the original was never replaced. It was

indestructible; lived forever. Except, today of course, it is history but I don't remember when it was trashed or passed on. It just faded out of the picture, replaced by a gardener's delight, the blue-green, two-wheeler.

The wagon, originally shiny red, was a "Radio Flyer;" black wheels, black wheel rims, and little metal silver hub caps with four tabs that hooked onto the rim, both hiding (and protecting) the end of the spokes and the cotter pins that held the wheels on. Of all the parts of the wagon to disappear, the little silver hubcaps were the first, all four of them, to go. The second piece to go was the handle in the tongue so that all you had were the metal tabs between which the handle was once secured. The tabs remained like the outer tines of a four-pronged garden fork missing the two middle tines. It was a lethal situation but never harmed us.

Our wagon was primarily a plaything, but we used it in our yard work as well. In the fall, it was loaded with leaves which were joyously hauled down the garden path to the "burning place" at the back of the lot, with Tommy sitting on the load, holding the leaves in the bed so not so many spilled out on the trip. Then Tommy rode back again, to the work, in the empty wagon for another load.

Bill, Cousin Bill holding Linda Jane, Carol Ann, Ron, and Jerry

During the garden season, the wagon was pulled between the rows and we heaped weeds onto the bed like hay on a wagon and hauled those to the "burning place." The weeding crews worked fast; faster than haulers could haul. We would haul until dusk, until the combination of sweat and mosquitoes drove us in, or at least to the porch for cold lemonade or ice cream from the Blue Ribbon and ice water. We basically enjoyed the work.

The wagon hauled groceries from the trunk of the car to the back door. It transported rocks from here to there for rearranged borders. It hauled dirt and large shrubs and plants that were being moved.

But, the weight, placed in the bed, far more frequently was that of us kids. We often used one of Mother's forked clothes line props to propel our playmate in the wagon by placing the forked end over the rear axle and pushing; the occupant "driving" with the lethal tongue chin or chest high. It would really fly out the gravel drive, dust billowing up, to the front of our house, then careen left in front of Grandma and Gene's house and up the hill of their drive and to the

Tom, Bobby, Dick, and Lassie

back yards again. Round and round! The stamina of the pusher would last just so long, who, with a mighty heave, would send the wagon down the hill of our drive and then out across grandma and Gene's front yard to hook up again at the back, the wagon having coasted through turns one and two. Besides it was not easy to keep the forked pole in the center of the back axle of a turning wagon.

If the wagon turned over, it was never the pusher's fault, pole or no. It was always the fault of the driver because they tried to turn too sharp. Sharp - That's a strange word, isn't it? Think about it. Sharp - Knives are sharp. Scissors are sharp, so are razors. So, how do you turn too sharp?) That's what we always yelled before the driver had a chance to blame the pusher.

"You turned too sharp!" or, "You have to keep control of the tongue!" or, "You lost control of the tongue! You have to hold tight."

Still, the driver would protest and blame the pusher, often amidst tears. "You were pushing too fast!"

A front wheel would hit a stone and jerk the tongue out of the driver's hands as the front wheels turned right or left, practically back on themselves, and the wagon would flip, pitching the driver unceremoniously out onto the gravel or whatever it was running on, the bed following in the tumbling driver's general direction. The "crashes" were frequent. They were often staged for diversion, usually at the driver's design, often to the surprise, but amusement, of the pusher.

The only hurtful episode I remember with our wagon occurred early one spring as we played across the street from our house, to the south, on Euclid Avenue. There were no houses there, but there were sidewalks. There were no sidewalks on 21st Street. Jerry, Carol Ann, Linda Jane, Little Tommy and I were all suited against the weather, caps, scarves and heavy coats; maybe it was fall. No, I'm sure it was springtime. The banks rising from the sidewalks were heavy with long green grass and the brown blades from the year before. Jerry was pushing Carol Ann, the driver, in the wagon. Faster and faster they went and the others of us running behind could hardly keep up. Jerry, bent over, was pushing with his hands on either side of the wagon bed. I remember the wagon veering left and plummeting up the grassy embankment. I remember the squeals and laughter. The wagon toppled to the right and rolled down the embankment and landed bottom side up, wheels still whirring, on top of Carol Ann who seemed to disappear completely under the overturned hollow of the metal wagon bed. As we caught up, Jerry lifted the wagon off Carol Ann and she was crying. I only remember Carol Ann crying as a child one other time, much later, when she intended to prove she could stand on a basketball as we played in our basement. She couldn't do it, and she split her chin open when she connected with the concrete in a one-point landing trying to do it. She carries the five-stitch scar to this day. Just as I don't recall the sequence of events following the bloody split chin, I don't recall much more of the hurtful wagon accident other than we loaded her in the wagon and pulled her to 21st and Euclid and called to Mother.

Jerry called "Mother, Mother," who came out the front door onto the porch.

He continued, as she attended to his pronouncement, "I think Carol Ann has a broken arm."

Only then did I realize what had happened.

Mostly, I remember the wagon as something we made into a stagecoach. Tommy and I would take a cardboard box and cut slits into the open end that would slip over the sides of the wagon tub. Fashioning a door and windows as well as an opening for the tongue to slip through, the driver was wholly contained and would drive by peering through a hole cut in the front. We made many a stagecoach out of our wagon.

"Kneel up and drive the wagon."

"Stand up and drive the wagon."

"Sit with your back to the tongue and drive it blind. I'll tell you which way to turn."

"Here, put on this blindfold and I'll tell you which way to turn."

Crash! Crash!

"Turn hard! Roll it!"

"Pretend there are Indians and you are shot."

"You're carrying gold and there are stagecoach robbers!"

Sometimes,

Tom "making repairs"

"All three of you get in and I'll push."

"Okay, but don't push too fast."

Laughter . . .

"Faster! Faster! Oh come on, faster!"

A sudden crash, bodies tumbling and the rattle and clatter of a rolling metal wagon amidst the laughter and grunts of tumbling bodies. It's a wonder our adventures weren't more frequently hurtful, and I wonder which outlasted the other, the wagon or our childhood? Indestructible? I don't think so!

Squeak, Squeak

I can't quite write out the sound the blue-green, metal glider on Grandma and Aunt Gene's front porch made as it moved back and forth. "Squeak, squeak" will have to do. Somehow it doesn't explain the sound well enough because it had more of a ring to it than I can spell. You've never heard it before, and I'll never hear it again with Grandma.

As a youngster, I visited Grandma and Aunt Gene's daily; after dinner, after homework, after chores, after dark, but each day and sometimes twice a day.

You were allowed to knock and walk in the front door, shouting "hellooo." You were usually greeted by Lassie first, and then from the kitchen or basement by Grandma or Aunt Gene. They were often still at the dinner table eating food that smelled wonderful but looked awful.

When Aunt Gene was still at work, Grandma would begin to prepare dinner, often starting at 4:00 P.M. even when she knew Aunt Gene wouldn't board the bus until 5:00 P.M. from downtown. Aunt Gene often sat down to over-cooked meals; meals that looked bad, smelled wonderful and tasted great. Grandma cooked with a lot of fat, salt and pepper, garlic and onion. Leftovers were always used, most often in barley soup. I loved her barley soup and haven't tasted any like it yet. I remember once she dropped in leftover mashed potatoes, and I was sure surprised.

Aunt Gene and Grandma

"What was that?" I asked.

"Mashed potatoes leftover from the other day," she responded.

"You put mashed potatoes in your soup?" I was amazed.

"Sure, why not. It thickens it up," she chuckled.

There was only one thing I ever ate at Grandma's that I wish I hadn't. hog's head cheese! I love cheese, all kinds of cheese, but hog's headcheese isn't made from milk. It's made from a hog's head.

You never knew what you would find boiling in the pot on Grandma's stove. One Saturday morning I popped in,. "Hellooo," I shouted. Grandma called me into the kitchen and pulled a stool over to the stove. She said "Climb up here and see what I've got in this pot." She loved to surprise the kids. It gave her a kick. I climbed up on the stool while she held my hand, careful not to touch the hot stove. She lifted the lid, and in my mind's eye, I can still see the gray hog's head bobbing vigorously around, filling the pot, steam rising, ears flopping, teeth and tongue protruding in rapidly boiling water. The frightened, bug-eyed hog's face filled the kettle and barely had room to move.

"What is that?!" I exclaimed!

"It's a hog's head!" She shouted with glee.

"What are you going to do with it?!" I asked.

"Auch du lieber!, I'm going to make hog's head cheese." She said.

"Ugh!" was all I could utter.

She laughed and muttered, "Dumbis dumbkoff! You don't know what's good."

Oh, the mess of pulling the smelly flesh from the hog's skull. Everything was used and put through the grinder once, maybe twice. Cartilage would pop and tough flesh and parts would squish and squirt as Grandma pressed the pieces into her hand-turned meat grinder she had clamped to the kitchen table. I imagine her mouth was watering the whole time (She always sprayed when she talked, but somehow it didn't matter.) The mass of ground skull flesh was mixed with herbs and spices, rolled up in a layer of hog fat and cooled. It was sliced and served on a plate or used on bread as sandwich meat. I had one bite only! Ever!

Two things I never, ever ate were bone marrow spread on bread. Grandma did. She claimed it was as good or better than butter. The other was chicken gristle, which Aunt Gene ate, cleaning the bones. But then, she only left the stem of an apple unconsumed, eating absolutely everything else!

Anyway, you never knew what was cooking, but you were always greeted by Lassie.

Grandma, Aunt Gene, and Lassie begging for the ball

"Where's your ball, Lassie, where's your ball?" I would say expectantly, to excite her. She would find a ball, usually under the dining room table, with Grandma's or Aunt Gene's direction, and I was allowed to throw the ball almost anywhere even while at times they were eating. She would tear through the house, her claws tearing at the carpet, to retrieve the ball and bring it back. You could throw the ball and then hide. Lassie would retrieve it and try to return it. If you weren't there, she would drop it and begin a frantic search to find you. Grandma would chuckle and encourage her to keep looking if you were particularly well hidden.

"Where's Dick, Lassie? Find him! Where's Dick?" She would say. Lassie would cock her head from side to side and assume an expression of bewilderment that would make Grandma laugh. Grandma loved to laugh and did so at the slightest provocation. She loved to tease and had a great sense of humor. Lassie would go to the front door and check it and Grandma would explain, "No, no, he hasn't gone home. Find him!"

The best place to hide was behind the couch. Aunt Gene, who couldn't tolerate Lassie's frustration as well as Grandma, would often tell her where you were hiding.

"He's behind the couch Lassie. Look! Look behind the couch," Aunt Gene would say and Grandma would immediately protest her giving me away.

Lassie, when directed so, would bound up on the couch and peer into the abyss behind and bark and growl. She loved the game and was free to romp anywhere in the house. The absolute best romp with her inside was to throw the ball out the enclosed back porch door so that it rolled down the steps to the back door and while Lassie chased it in the dark, (if you were lucky, the door to the basement was open and the ball would go on down giving you more time to hide) I would run through the kitchen, dining room and living room and up the wooden stairs into the dark, second story, trying to step lightly on the stairs because they creaked all over. It was gloriously exciting in the dark, bounding from bedroom to sunroom to bedroom, slamming doors as Lassie pursued from one direction and then another in her desperate growling and barking effort to corner her tormentor.

If she failed to detect that you had gone upstairs while she retrieved the ball, she would search the main floor to your delight while you waited in the darkened upstairs rooms, Grandma laughing, giving her clues until Aunt Gene would clearly state, "He has gone upstairs, Lassie, upstairs." Almost instantly her nails would click on the wooden stairs and, having caught the scent, the growling and barking would begin. It was terribly exciting and free spirited play in a world apart from the order of our house next door. Grandma and Aunt Gene seemed to love the sport of the visits and free-reign play as much as I did. It was a wonderfully happy noise. But I also felt guilty for I was sure if my Mother ever saw what I was doing at 4400, she would not have approved at all.

Grandma and I were very good friends. I behave very much like her today. Our summer visits occurred outdoors on the porch with lemonade, cookies and Lassie racing around the house. The expansive porch had a small set of side steps and a wide set of front steps directly across from their front door. It was a house Grandpa had built from plans out of Sears' catalogue. He used old railroad car timbers as floor joists and roof beams. Neighbors laughed at Grandpa Joe saying he would never be able to raise the heavy beams into place, but he did it. The foundation was made of fieldstones and cement. Grandma

Grandma and Dick

and Aunt Gene always chided us if we climbed on the fieldstone to get over the porch rail and away from Lassie. I suppose Grandpa Joe had set the example, insisting his children not climb on the foundation for fear of loosening a stone. He had collected the stones himself and some were fairly rounded and smooth. In fact, he had collected so many more than he needed that he had buried a whole pile of stones in the lot next door, just to get rid of them. He probably didn't think the smooth stones would hold too well in the foundation.

Front and back views of the house that Grandpa built

Grandma and Trixie on her front porch glider

While sitting on the cushioned metal glider, rocking to and fro in the morning sun, Grandma talked of Joe, her husband, my father's father, my Grandpa, a lot. I never knew my Grandpa Joe. I especially enjoyed early Saturday morning visits with Grandma. She sat in the glider humming as she rocked. I would join her and Lassie on the glider. Being there required little conversation or effort. It was a completely comfortable situation. Leaning on Grandma was soft and comforting. Our meager conversation between the glider's "squeak, squeak" (there's that inadequate description of the sound again), her sips of strong, black coffee from a Jewel tea cup hanging on her finger, and the humming would always lead to the same series of questions from me and answers from her. I spent countless hours listening to her going over and over the same stories and loved every warm moment.

She was the daughter of a baker whose shop was on Massachusetts Avenue.

"Pop sold doughnuts at a nickel a baker's dozen. You know what a baker's dozen is?" she would ask.

"Yeah, thirteen for the price of twelve," I answered.
"Right," she affirmed.
She lived on North Street as a little girl.

She told of her husband Joe, my Grandpa, who was sent to America by his parents at the age of fourteen to join family already here "in the land of milk and honey." He was sent on a boat to avoid conscription into the army. He spoke no English and had his name and address pinned to his coat and was sent to Indianapolis by rail. His family were butchers from the Rhine Valley in Germany. The family name used to be spelled Krëamer, but the umlauted 'e' was dropped and it became Kramer.

Grandpa Joe drank, and she would often stop the inter-urban train with a kerosene lantern and lead him home to the one-room shack that they lived in. It sat much farther back on the lot at 4400 East 21st Street. The shack stood where the garden was later after Grandpa Joe built the house.

The shack was not well sealed. Spaces between the siding boards allowed snow to blow in during the winter.

They had a milk cow and chickens. Life was tough. She described a destitute, improvised lifestyle, but she didn't let on that she saw it that way. She always talked about it as though it was just factual and fine, no worse and no better than anyone else.

She told about Jake, their dog, who was often mauled as a pup by a neighbors dog but Jake killed their dog when he grew up. She delighted in Jake's triumph. She told of my Daddy and his experience with the horse liniment and his "private parts." She told of Agnes, her daughter, drinking the homemade

67

whiskey in the middle of the night, thinking it was water, and dying as a three year old. She was a proud woman who didn't know she had lived a hard life.

She teared and choked every time she concluded this series of answers to my questions with her story of Grandpa Joe's death at the age of forty-five. How he left her with seven children and his whispered dying words, "I'm sorry Maim."

Grandma never expressed anger that he left her so young and with such a brood to provide for. I think her tears expressed her anger and sorrow for herself and what she had to face. A hug, a kiss on the cheek from me and an "I love you, Grandma," would disturb Lassie a bit and we would settle back into the silence except for the sound of the glider, "squeak, squeak."

Her old veined hands were smooth and soft, and she would let me hold and pat one and turn the thin gold wedding band during the conversation as she kept the glider in a steady motion. My legs were still too short to reach the porch floor.

You've never heard the "squeak, squeak" of the porch glider before, and you've never heard the stories as told by my Grandmother about her life. And you know, though I never thought I would hear it again, I did, just now hear the "squeak, squeak," with Grandma.

The Votive's Tongue

When I look back at some of the things we did as kids, I am amazed that we are not maimed or injured, at least physically. It is marvelous that we are alive, having survived childhood. In spite of responsible, watchful supervision, young children can place themselves in life threatening situations that could easily result in disfigurement, handicapping injuries, or even death. The invincibility and resiliency of youth is a gift but can also be a liability. The "it won't happen to me," syndrome carries us easily into precarious, self-indulgent, dangerous situations.

One of the hazards is fire and a common childhood fascination with its flirtatious dance, a threatening dance of destruction and death. Fire can be thrilling. I first learned about the excitement of fire during a puppet show in the basement of our home. Jerry, ever the entertainer, presented stories in a darkened basement with puppets. Some puppets were crudely homemade, but others had strings and all. The plays occurred in a two-room, homemade, wooden doll house. Although it seemed Jerry made up the stories as he went along, I think he thought a great deal about story lines in moments of leisure and stored them away for later use. For example, why else would he save slivers of soap bars in a jar with a little water, on the shelf with the canned goods? He added slivers of soap from the basement shower and a little more water, whenever he could. He accumulated close to a quart and a half of bluish-green slime in the jar over a period of time.

The curtain went up in the darkened basement one evening, when Jerry was in charge and both mother and daddy were gone. The stage house was illuminated with a flashlight. The puppets isolated by the light in the darkness became real, with different voices. The story line was immediately forgotten, within minutes of its presentation, as the story was greatly overshadowed by the climax. The play and dialogue progressed in a "Punch and Judy" style of slapstick violence; very funny violent falls, puppets slamming into the walls, arms and legs flopping uncontrollably about. Fire was introduced as one puppet entered holding a flaming skewer, as though its hotdog caught fire. The puppet danced about clumsily, and the contents of the playhouse stage were set afire. Suddenly a bluish green mass of slime spilled over the flaming, two-room interior, and amidst hissing and smoke, the flames were snuffed out. Was it out of control or all planned? It seems to me now that there was cause for concern. The slime ran out the front of the house stage, and the smoke rose to the ceiling. The lights in the basement came on amidst the laughter and screams. There was a mess to clean up. The slime was not much of a problem, but the smoke hung at the ceiling, filling half of the basement. That was the bigger problem for it would soon smell throughout the house. The back door was opened as well as the basement windows, and frantic fanning with newspapers ensued. I don't think Mother or Daddy smelled anything when they came home.

One rainy thunderous spring evening, our house was struck by lightening. Daddy wasn't home from work, and the darkness at around 5:00 P.M. was not right. We had been called in from play with the approaching storm because Mother was deathly afraid of lightening. When it stormed, we loved to go to the front porch and watch the display and feel the mist from the rain in our faces.

Mother, on the other hand, always lit the usual votive light by the statue of the Blessed Virgin in her bedroom. On this occasion, after lighting the blessed candle, she returned to the kitchen to continue preparing supper. Tommy and I were playing with metal toy cars, trucks and farm implements in the carpet patterns of the dining room floor. The lights flickered, and the bluish-white light of lightening flashed outside. Mother was peeling potatoes at the far end of the kitchen by the back double windows. Picking up the newspaper for the potato peels, potatoes, kettle of water and all, she moved. Just after she moved away from the windows, there was a tremendous crack and clatter. The upper cabinet doors above the counter where she had been standing flew open, and various articles of kitchen stuff exploded into the room. It was as if Paul Bunyon had hit the back of our home with his axe just above the double windows. In spite of her adrenaline-filled veins, mother remained calm and said to her saucer-eyed children, "We've been struck by lightening."

I peered into the kitchen and grayish smoke rolled out of the cabinets, some of it rolling across the ceiling, some floating toward the floor. Jerry called the fire department, and they were at our home very quickly. It was raining very hard when they arrived. The firemen were ushered through the back door, their black shiny slickers and heavy boots dripping with water. In with them bounded a huge Dalmatian, the firedog. It ran from room to room. It even went into the bedroom where the votive candle was lit, and it shook. I wondered of the fireman who followed would criticize us later for leaving an unattended candle burning in the bedroom. Jerry directed the firemen upstairs and to the front closet and the attic access panel. He had kept them from chopping a hole to discover the wicked fire by showing them the removable panel. There was no fire. Mother described a blue ball of fire that followed the scattered, now broken kitchen stuff, out of the cabinets, but there was no fire.

There was a pounding on the front door, and Carol Ann and Aunt Gene were there, soaked through as they had run from the bus stop at Twenty-first Street and Bosart, recognizing that the fire engine was at one of our homes, homes that sat side by side.

As quickly as they came, and without wielding their voracious axes, the firemen and the Dalmatian disappeared. What a mess! The Dalmatian, a big hit with us kids, had paid little attention to us and we were disappointed. We didn't even learn its name!

A silver-plated butter dish had been hit, and its little glass innards shattered. The top and bottom were both melted in only one spot each, as though a torch had been applied to them where the lightening bolt had passed straight through.

We speculated for a long time about why the bolt of lightening had struck the back of the house and didn't hit the huge cottonwood tree that stood at that very corner of the house. And, why did mother move when she did from below the cabinets as she peeled potatoes? Did Mother Mary speak to her through the votive's tongue?

....We built tee pees out of dried weeds in the fall. I wish I knew the name of these weeds. They were green, grew six feet tall or more, dried to a light gray, and were hollow inside. We gathered several of these weeds in the fall and stripped them of their branches. They were leaned against each other like poles of tee pees and dried grass was woven between them until a tee pee was formed. We didn't play in the tee pee long until we, the Indians, were raided, and our tee pee set afire with a "flaming arrow" (a wooden blue tip match struck on a rock.) The tee pee was quickly consumed in smoke and flames and all imaginary battle was suspended as we watched the structure burn in a whoosh!

Can you imagine the headlines?

TEENAGER SETS HOUSE AFIRE DURING PUPPET SHOW - Five   children die or . .

TEENAGER SAVES SIBLING IN HOUSE FIRE or . .

LIGHTENING STRIKES HOME - Three dead or . .

TEE PEE "RAID" RESULTS IN TWO DEAD or . .

FIRE RESULT OF MISCHIEVOUS MATCH PLAY! . . or

. . on and on as one thinks of what might have been and wonders if the Blessed Virgin Mary really did respond to the silent prayer of the votive's flaming tongue.

Snacks

In mid to late November, after the gardens and the fields were laid to rest for the winter, a brown pasteboard box, about one cubic foot in size, would arrive at our home. It was heavy. Mother always knew what it was but she allowed us to open it without telling us. It was full of popcorn kernels, full to the brim. They were small and cream colored, almost white. It was an early Christmas gift sent each year by Uncle John from Lanesville, Indiana. The box was shoved into the unheated kitchen pantry and left on the floor.

Bedtime snacks consisted of cookies and milk, graham crackers and milk, graham crackers with white icing and milk, ice cream and cookies and ice water, potato chips or pretzels and coke but the best of all was buttered and salted popcorn and Coke or Pepsi. Bedtime snacks followed the seasons. The cookies and milk were a result of Mother's holiday baking; hermits with black walnuts and oatmeal-raisin cookies made for Christmas holidays. Graham crackers dipped in milk, were a fill in when the cookies were not available. The graham crackers with white icing were made with the leftover icing used to frost a cake. They were special. The ice cream, potato chips and pretzels were also fill-ins.

Tommy was a specialist at eating graham crackers and milk. With his left hand he would break them and pass the half to his right hand. He would dunk the cracker into the glass of milk and while placing that half into his mouth he was passing another half to his right hand. It was a kind of conveyor system, awesome to behold, non-stop.

Popcorn did take some time to prepare so it was usually reserved for the weekends, Friday or Saturday nights, when we didn't have to get up early for school. Our home had a special four-quart kettle reserved for popcorn popping. Depending on who was fixing the popcorn, Mother or Daddy, made a distinct difference in how it was served. Mother would pop three or four kettles full and dump them one after the other into the large oval turkey-roasting pan. After popping the corn, she would then melt the butter in the popcorn kettle and pour it over the popcorn, salt it, put the lid on the roaster and shake it all up. The popcorn would be served in the roaster, placed in the middle of the kitchen table and voracious consumption would begin by those gathered around. Mother taught us to use our fingertips and to pick up a few at a time. She distributed paper napkins.

Daddy's method varied from the above. While he was popping the first kettle of corn, he melted the butter in another small pot. As soon as the first kettle was finished, he would butter and salt it in the kettle, shake it up and dump it in the middle of the kitchen table. We could start eating immediately and didn't have to wait for all of it to be popped. He would return to the stove and start another kettle. When that was finished, buttered and salted, it was dumped on top of what was left of the first kettle full. And so he would continue. I think he didn't want to wash the roaster. Daddy also demonstrated a better method of eating popcorn. Rather than using just the fingertips, he would use his entire hand. His fingers would claw into the pile of popped corn and scoop up a handful. Placing the heel of his hand up to his gaping mouth, he would shove the popcorn into his mouth and work it all in with his fingers dancing in front of his lips. We soon learned the technique. Though unacceptable in public, it was clearly a better way to eat popcorn.

As we neared the end of our fill, someone would suggest a game of 'line-up.' Ten popped kernels were placed in a row on the tabletop in front of each participant. The idea was to see who could pick up the pieces with their lips/tongue and into their mouth, one by one, faster than anyone else. Carol Ann was always the champion.

After the popcorn snack, we all participated in cleaning up the kitchen. The stove was wiped down, kettles were washed, table was cleaned and the floor was swept. To our delight, Daddy would sometimes let the dog in to sweep the floor. Faces and hands washed, we were off to bed.

Tommy required a snack of his own which I could never understand. On frequent occasions, he would be found in the dark kitchen on top of the kitchen table, eating butter. The stick butter was left in the middle of the table with the salt and peppershakers and the sugar container, all arranged neatly on a doily. The butter was left out because it was impossible to spread if it were cold. During a period after World War Two (Two meant little to me because I didn't understand World War Two as something that came after World War One nor, for that matter, did I understand "World War", a block of white substance was purchased as butter but, if you wanted it to look like butter, you had to knead in a packet of powered yellow coloring. Stick or mixed butter made little difference to Tommy. He would disappear from the family gathered in the living room around the radio, be missed by Mother and be found by her on top of the table in the kitchen eating butter.

So much for snacks!

Deannie P.

We were a motley crew, ready for anything, well equipped. My older brother, Jerry, didn't carry anything but the rest of the "terrible five" did. My sister, Carol Ann, had a six-shooter strapped on, scarf around her neck and the ever-present cowgirl hat that she occasionally let hang by the strap around her neck onto her back. She also had the rope that we would use in this particular episode, the Deannie P. affair. Linda Jane had a set of six-shooters strapped on also but she did not have her hat. My younger brother, "Little Tom," and I had cap pistols on this sunny summer's day. The five of us hung together pretty tight and had many an adventure "at the end of the lot."

Jerry, Linda Jane, Tom, Dick, and Carol Ann

"At the end of the lot," certainly did not mean that at all. We lived on a plot of land that was sixty feet wide by three hundred feet deep. What "going to the end of the lot" really meant was that we were going way beyond where the lot ended, across the inter-urban ditch, across the railroad tracks and down into the woods along Pogue's Run creek. We often went beyond that, across Pogue's Run and into the fields where a small airfield used to be. We would sometimes go as far as Massachusetts Avenue, which runs northeast out of the city and eventually turns into highway 67.

If we stayed too long on one of these adventures we would have to run most of the way home in response to Daddy's whistle. He would produce this piercing whistle by putting the index fingers of each hand into his mouth and, while pulling his cheeks apart, would blow air across his upper lip. I could never figure it out. No, that's not true..... what I never wanted to do was to put my index fingers into the cheeks of my mouth and pull them apart. My fingers always tasted salty; a taste that I have always associated with being dirty. Anyway, when we heard the whistle that meant we had to get home and if we were especially far away we had to really hurry if our lie about the imposed limits were to be believed. Usually he whistled because supper was ready, or soon to be, and Mother didn't like to hold food. She liked to have the meal all come together at the last minute and serve it hot. She always succeeded. It's a gift.

Eddie (dad's friend) and Daddy

On this ideal day in the summer, we decided to go "to the end of the lot" and pick black raspberries. This is not an easy chore because of the insects, short-lived irritations from mosquito bites and the dreaded long-lived effects from chiggers, let alone the nasty cuts from the thorns on the long canes that invariably hung out over a steep incline and held the best berries. We often held on to each other to increase the length of our reach to get at these berries.

We set out walking back through the yard, past the wooden, white frame, one car garage with its two huge wapper-jawed entry doors, past the apple tree beyond which was Grandma's chicken coop, grape arbor and the little two room house that Grandma rented to the strangest family. This was Deannie P.'s home. He lived there with his parents, Mr. and Mrs. P. though I seldom saw the Mr. and wouldn't know the Mrs. today. I don't remember that Deannie had any brothers or sisters. I don't think he did. We reached the garden and the path around it. You never walked on the garden. The garden was huge in my eyes. The rows of everything went on forever and, if you don't believe me, just try picking or weeding or hoeing one row of green beans in our garden. When you thought, "I must be half-way through by now" and dared to raise your head to look against the advice of your aching back, it was always a disappointment and you swore you wouldn't make it to the end of the row, at least not in this lifetime. Having checked the distance yet to go it was equally important to check how far you had come, which you could do without raising up, by looking back under your arm. This maneuver was important because the distance to go had to be confirmed. It was.

We walked single-file down the path, Jerry leading, then Carol Ann, Linda Jane, Dick and Little Tom, our pecking and our birth order. We left our property when we finally passed the fence post set by our Grandfather when they had a cow and really needed the fence. Down through the old inter-urban ditch that was being filled in with trash, up the other side and across the short "plateau" before the descent to the railroad bed and the tracks which went on to the right and the left forever and ever. I always wanted to cross the tracks in a hurry. I didn't like to linger there. The crushed stone in the rail-bed was more like sharp edged rocks to me and they were not the most pleasant things to walk on in thin shoes. Besides, I was sure that if one of those belching monsters came chugging around the bend and across the trestle, all five of us would not get across and, what a sad family it would be if one of us got killed, cut in half. I could just see my Daddy and Mother and brothers and sisters crying over the loss of their dear son and brother, Dick.

I don't know how long we picked black raspberries but we didn't have to go far because they were everywhere. Our plan was to take these berries home and to have them with sugar and milk. Cream would probably have tasted better but we never had cream except for that little bit at the top of the milk bottle that you had to shake back into the rest of the milk before you drank it. I tasted that stuff once and it was kind of sour and salty too; reminded me of the taste of my fingers. I'm glad we never had cream. We ate as many berries as we picked, that is Little Tom and I did, smiling quietly at each other, until we were reprimanded. Jerry was the disciplinarian of the group and he sure let you know if you crossed the line or, rather, got out of it. I'm sure, the whole time we were picking, he didn't eat more than one or two berries. He had self discipline enough to wait for the real reward back at the house and after they had been washed. Jerry had a thing for cleanliness and food, besides he knew about the tiny little green worms that thrived on the black raspberry caps. We picked until we almost filled the one-quart tin kettle that we used as a water dipper when we set the live plants in the garden.

We started back for the house. We crossed the tracks and when we reached the top of the path that leads back to the inter-urban ditch, we saw him. He was standing at the top of the path on the South side of the ditch, facing us, Deannie P.. We had often warned Deannie P. never to follow us because we didn't want him with us. We were exclusive and didn't want to be contaminated. There he stood in clothes we were certain our parents would never put us in; one foot on top of the other, moving his bent knee back and forth, tapping the tips of his fingers together, one hand against the other.

"There's Deannie," someone said.

"Wonder what he wants," said another.

"Whatcha doin'?" asked Deannie, not daring to start down the path and get caught in the bottom of the inter-urban ditch by us. As long as he was uninvited, he kept a safe distance and he always kept himself between his house and us until he was invited. There had been many a time Deannie had been chased home by us because he was uninvited. He learned to get invited first, remaining wary in the process.

"We picked some black raspberries," Jerry said.

"And we are going to have them with sugar and milk," Carol Ann tacked on.

"You don't get any because you didn't help pick them," Linda Jane added.

It didn't make any difference to us that he hadn't been invited.

We seemed to speak according to birth order, just as we walked single file.

"I'd like some............can I help now?" Deannie asked.

"Oh Deannie!" Carol Ann half shouted, sort of dismayed.

Jerry and Carol Ann began to confer and, although I hadn't helped much at all, I began to worry that a person who hadn't helped a lick was about to get a share for doing less than I had done. Jerry, Carol Ann and Linda seemed to consider the matter forever. I thought we should just tell him to get home and not to bother us when the decision was announced. Deannie was told to come on over and carry the berries home. He eagerly ran down the path, through the bottom of the ditch and up the other side to stand with us on the plateau.

"What can I do?" he asked.

Jerry answered, "You can carry the berries."

"And, if you spill any you will be sorry," finished Carol Ann in a firm voice.

74

"O.K.," Deannie said.

"Here, take them....and don't spill any," Jerry reminded.

We started down the path in the appropriate order, Deannie trailing. Jerry was leading his troops home from another successful foray into the wilds and all were returning safely to enjoy their warm home and Mother's cooking. I had not taken three steps down the path into the ditch when I saw a flood of black raspberry caps rolling past my feet, the little tin pan tumbling behind.

Deannie P. yelped. He had spilled the berries and we were between him and his home. His house must have seemed to him to be on the other side of the world at that moment, sitting there on the path as he was, having spilled the berries we had slaved to collect. Jerry, Carol Ann and Linda Jane turned around when Deannie yelled seeing what I already knew. He spilled them and everyone could see that but I said, "He spilled them."

Carol Ann was on him in a flash, darting up past us.

"Pick them up now and get every one!" she demanded.

Deannie looked up at her standing over him from his sitting position, frozen, except he seemed even closer to the ground, holding one arm over his head...for protection, I supposed. I mean, if my sister were standing over me, hissing in that tone of voice, I would be protecting myself. I had been in that position many a time.

Jerry handed him the tin pan that he had retrieved from the bottom of the ditch and Deannie sort of scooted down the path, scooping up the berries. I think we almost immediately regretted that we had given him the order to collect the berries because his hands were dirty and he obviously didn't know how delicate they were because he was kind of rolling them and smashing them against the ground as he scooped. The berries would never be the same and I don't think we cared if he got them all.

We all turned our attention to another, more important task, when Linda Jane asked the question on everyone's mind, "Well....what are we going to do to him?"

The answer came quickly from Carol Ann, "We'll tie him to the railroad track and leave him there! That will teach him to spill our black raspberries!"

I was stunned, but it was a good idea. We were all stunned. We all agreed. Deannie was the most stunned of all and began to struggle as our hands fell on him. He began to yell, "No! No!" as he writhed and struggled to break free. Carol Ann whipped off her rope and Deannie was dragged the few feet up the hill and over the plateau to the path down to the tracks. I don't see how he kept from getting hurt in the struggle. I'm sure he must have been dropped a time or two onto the sharp rocks. Deannie had little flesh for protection. We laid him on one of the rails and tied him to it, passing the rope under the rail and knotting it securely. We looked at each other, pleased with the work we had done and someone said, "Lets go!"

We left him there and retreated to the path to the inter-urban ditch where the berries had been spilled. We stopped there but we knew that Deannie P. believed that we had gone. He yelled and cried. After what seemed like a long time to me, we went back and untied him. He ran as he never had before. He disappeared over the plateau and by the time we walked up the hill from the tracks and down and up again through the inter-urban ditch, he had already made it all the way home....or he had collapsed in fright in the tall weeds somewhere and was waiting for us to walk the garden path.

I don't remember ever playing with Deannie P. again. The amazing thing to me is that he must have never told his parents of his experience at our hands for, surely, if he had, they would have walked the few hundred feet separating our homes to complain to our parents. If they did, we never heard about it. But, I believe if they had, there would have been hell to pay.

I also believe now that, even though they didn't complain to our parents then, there still may be hell to pay later. I often wonder what we would have done if, while we were sitting on that path to the interurban ditch, we had suddenly heard the whistle of the belching monster rounding the bend. Would we have succeeded in untying Deannie? Would we have had the guts to try? And, if the monster came and we didn't succeed how would we explain it? How might our lives have been changed? If his parents had called the police.......?

I want to apologize to Deannie but I have no idea where he is.

"I'm sorry Deannie." Dick has thought a thousand times.

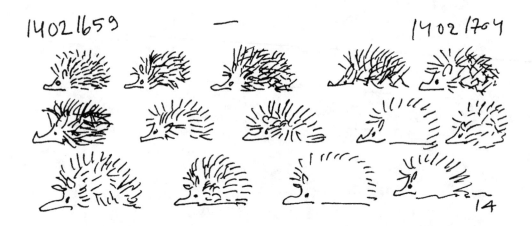

HOW TO MEASURE TIME

The day was February 14. The time was 16:59 when the operator answered my phone call, but it was just after 17:04 when I heard the voice of the man I wanted to speak with. I had to wait 5 minutes. Actually I waited 14 hedgehogs. I still remember the thorns. I drew every one of them.

The drawing above represents the relations between objective time and subjective time. The hedgehogs are actually subjective time units.

More different subjective time units are recorded and drawn on the following pages.

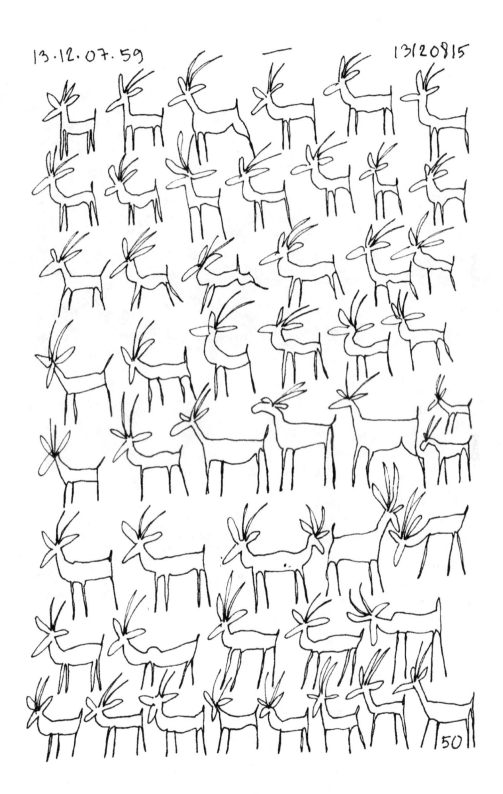

50

76+4

13120925 — 13120927

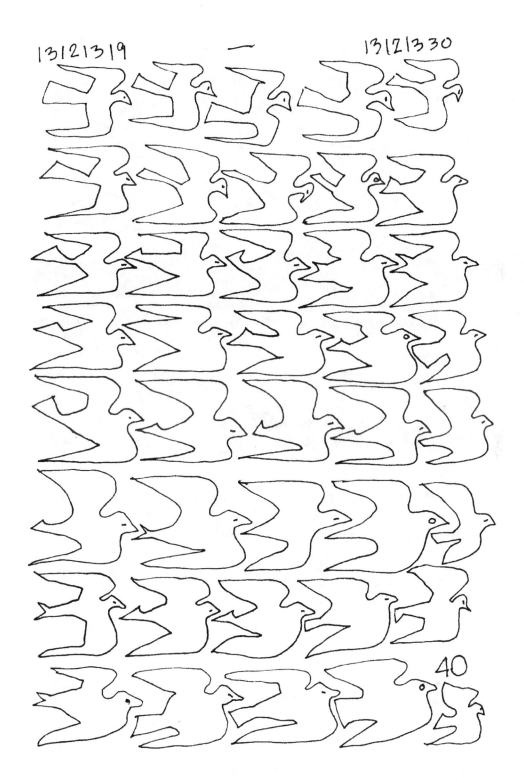

40

14120805   —   14120925

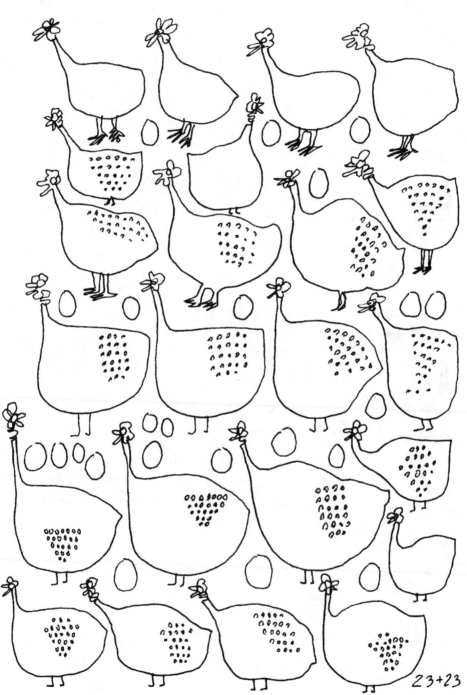

23+23

86

8

24

16121552 16121628

20

10

33

47

12

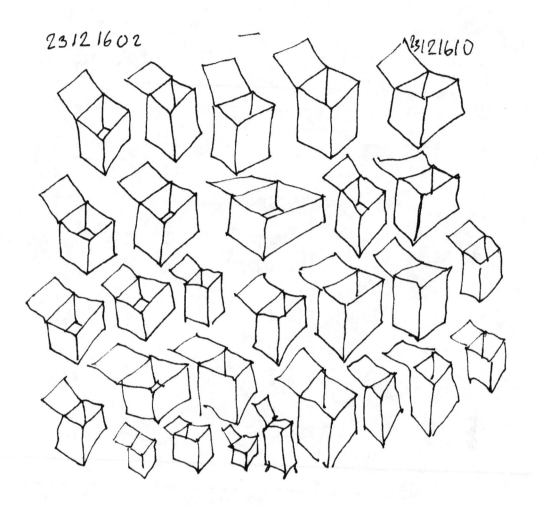

28

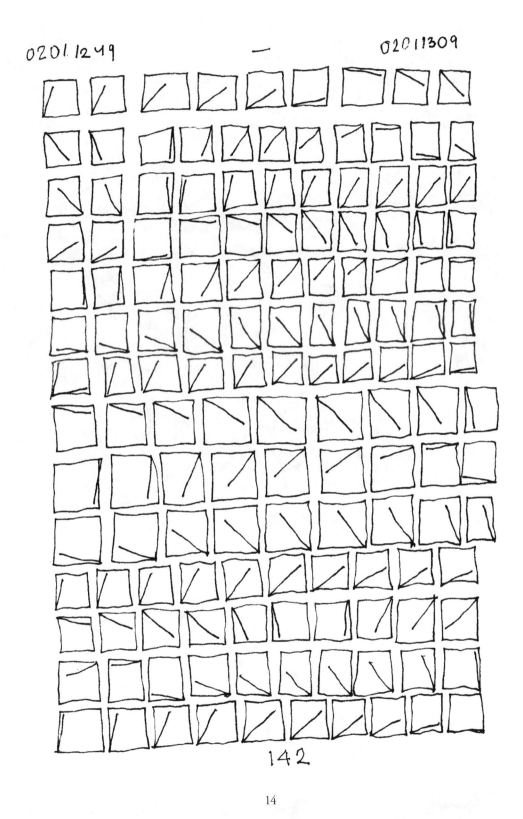

142

03011355 — 03011408

139

— 30 —

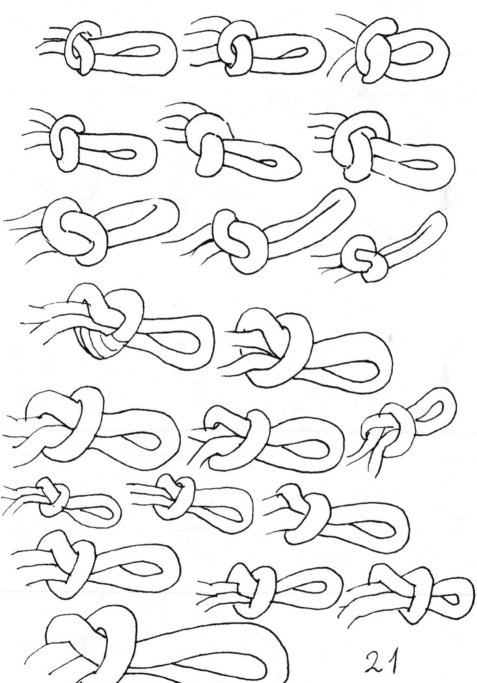

21

04011649   —   04011655

-18-

05010735 — 05010801

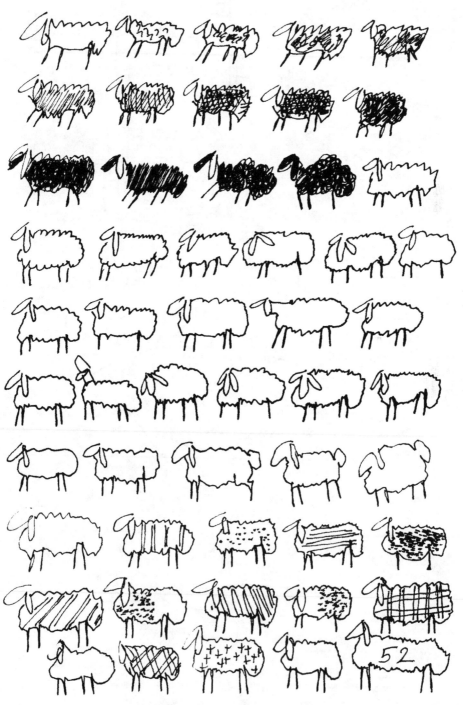

40

ה

69

65

22

10011606

10011652

61

54

ב

בבבבבבב
בבבבבבב
בבבבבבב
בבבבבבב
בבבבבבב
בבבבבבב
בבבבבבב
בבבבבבב
בבבבבבב
בבבבב

73

ו

150

83

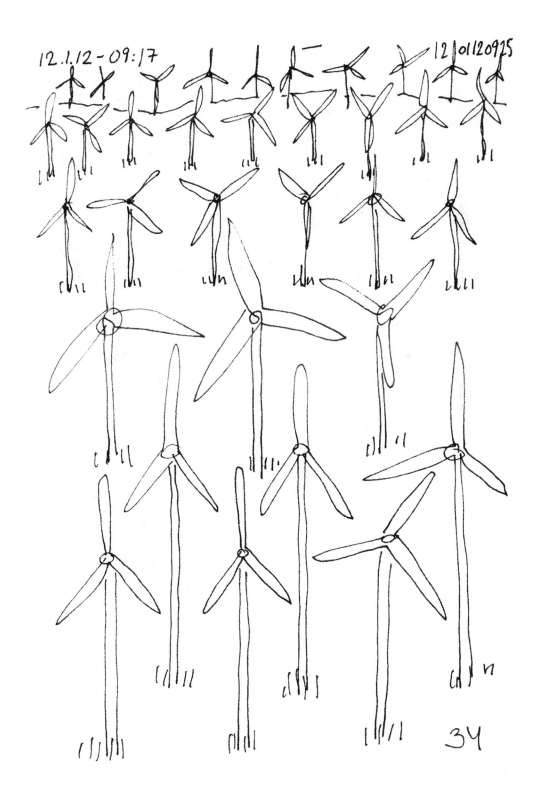

12.1.12 - 09:17

12 01120925

34

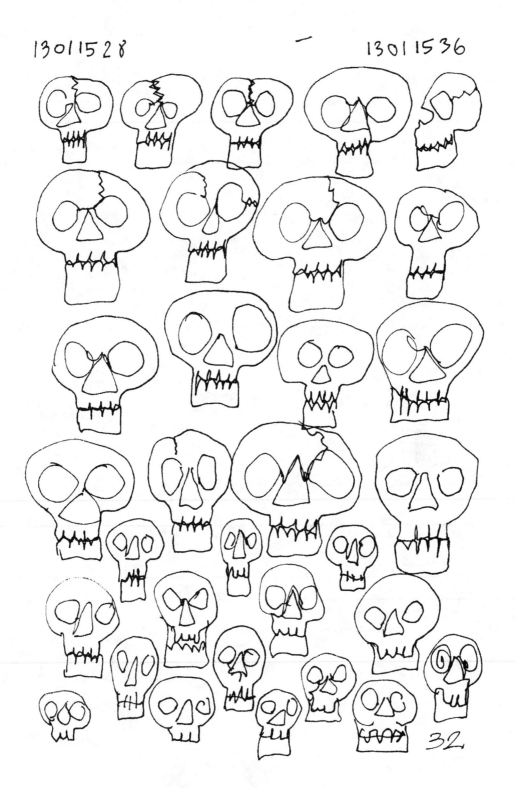

32

18

18011936 — 18011948

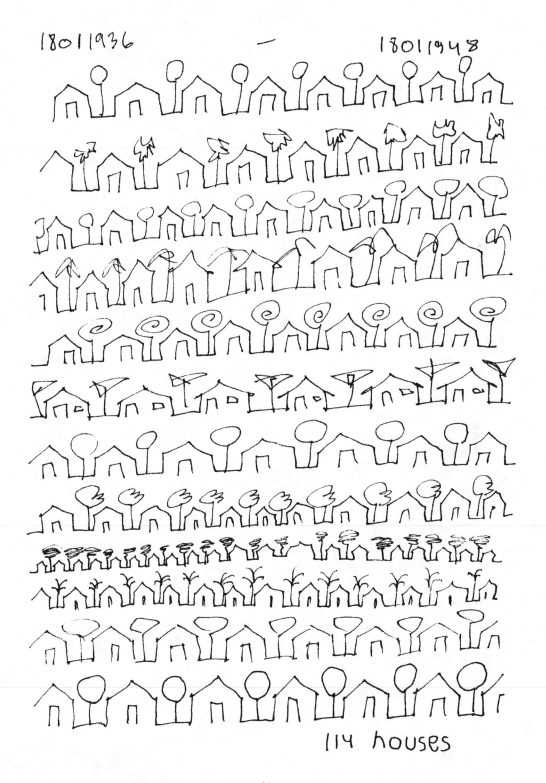

114 houses

18011956

18012012

5

20011017   —   20011044

27 minutes   90 holes

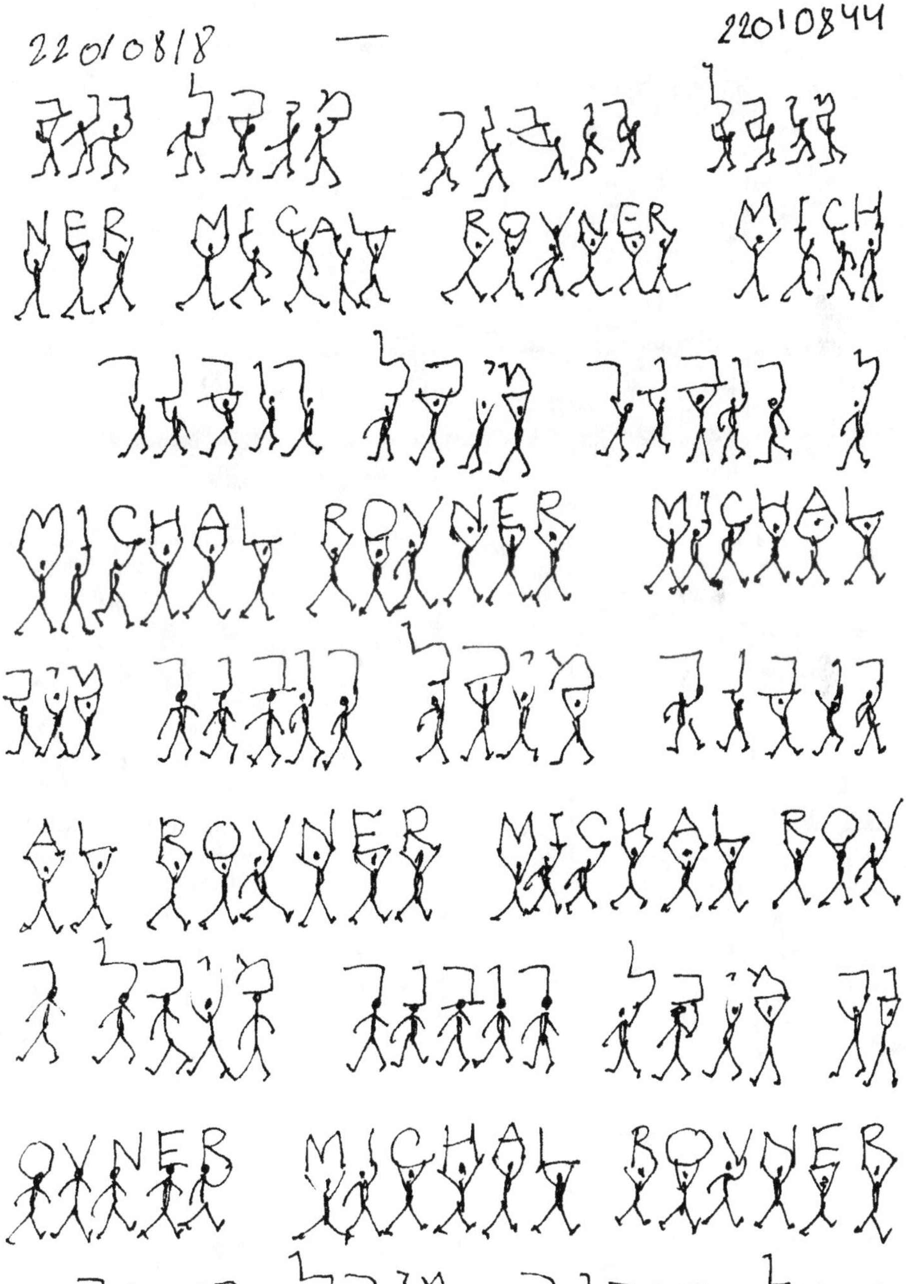

22010818 — 22010844

NER MICAL ROYNER MICH

MICHAL ROYNER MICHAL

AL ROYNER MICHAL ROY

OYNER MICHAL ROYNER

26 minutes   152 figures

34

70

24011150   — 24011210

20

36

25011025 — 25011043

213

25011052 — 25011130

28

25 011543   —   25 011555

208 × 3 = 624

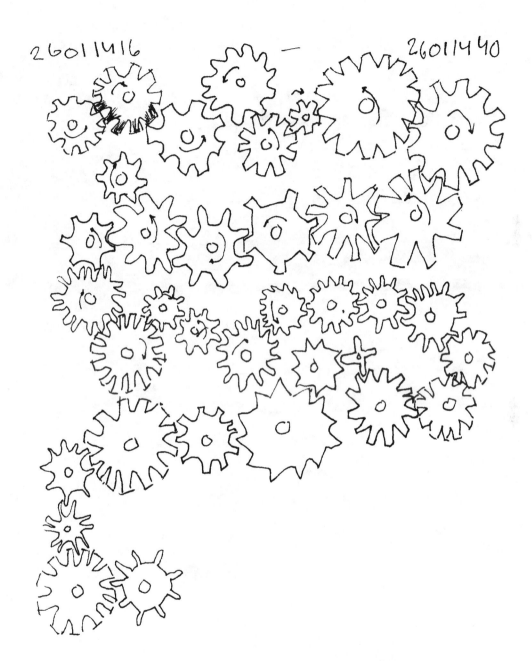

37

29011059 — 29011124

159 × 6 = 954

—

$95 \times 10 = 950$

69

31011927   31012022

55 minutes   (2+3+4....36) circles

44

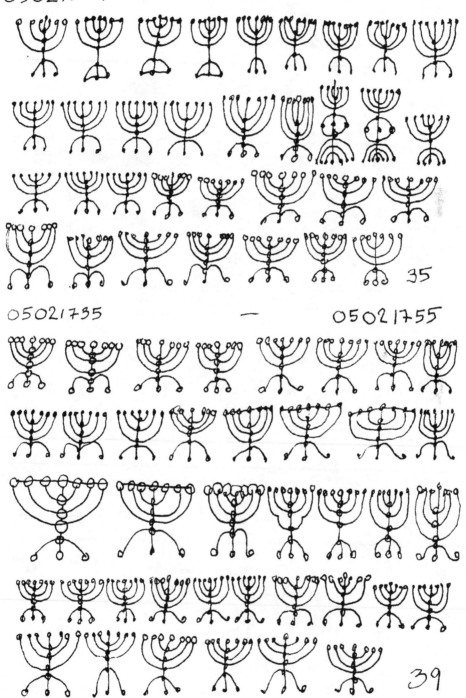

35

39

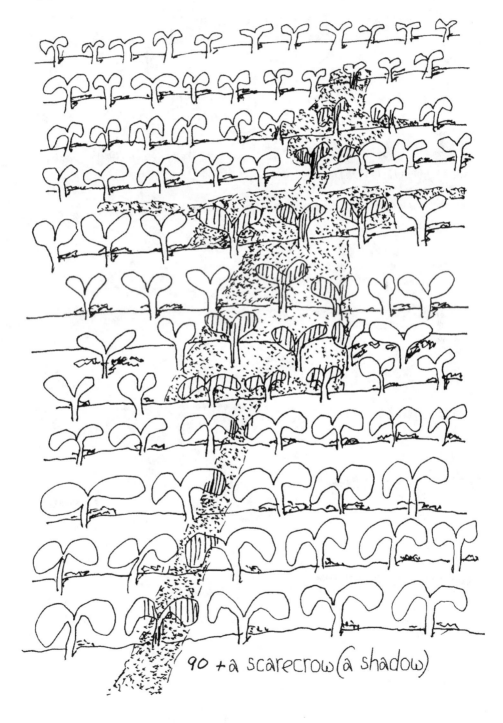

90 + a scarecrow (a shadow)

57

42

32

16021210 — 16021240

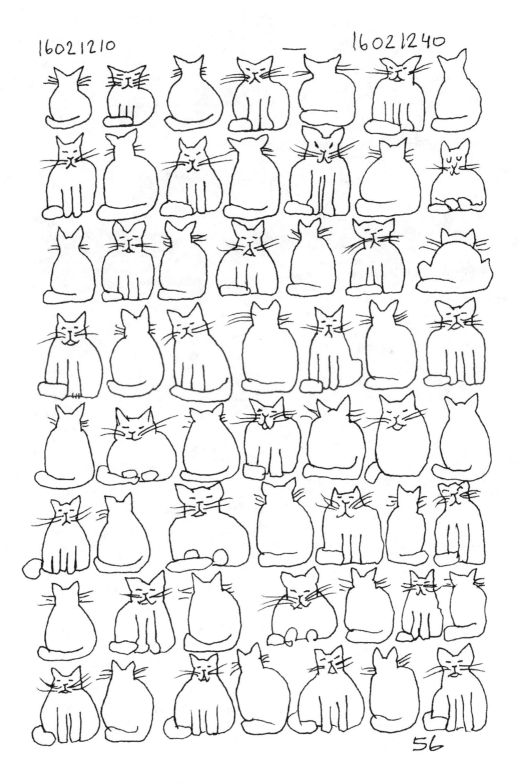

56

16021620 — 16021629

HHT HHT HHT HHT HHT HHT HHT HHT HHT HHT HHT HHT HHT
HHT HHT HHT HHT HHT HHT HHT HHT HHT HHT HHT HHT HHT
HHT HHT HHT HHT HHT HHT HHT HHT HHT HHT HHT HHT HHT
HHT HHT HHT HHT HHT HHT HHT HHT HHT HHT HHT HHT

HHT HHT HHT HHT HHT HHT HHT HHT HHT HHT HHT HHT HHT
HHT HHT HHT HHT HHT HHT HHT HHT HHT HHT HHT HHT HHT

HHT HHT HHT HHT HHT HHT HHT HHT HHT HHT HHT HHT

HHT HHT HHT HHT HHT HHT HHT HHT HHT HHT HHT

HHT HHT HHT HHT HHT HHT HHT HHT HHT HHT HHT
HHT HHT HHT HHT HHT HHT HHT HHT HHT HHT HHT

HHT HHT HHT HHT HHT HHT HHT HHT HHT HHT HHT HHT HHT
HHT HHT HHT HHT HHT HHT HHT HHT HHT HHT HHT HHT HHT

HHT HHT HHT HHT HHT HHT HHT HHT HHT HHT HHT HHT HHT
HHT HHT HHT HHT HHT HHT HHT HHT HHT HHT HHT HHT HHT

HHT HHT HHT HHT HHT HHT HHT HHT HHT HHT HHT HHT HHT
HHT HHT HHT HHT HHT HHT HHT HHT HHT HHT HHT HHT HHT
HHT HHT HHT HHT HHT HHT HHT HHT HHT HHT HHT HHT HHT
HHT HHT HHT HHT HHT HHT HHT HHT HHT HHT HHT HHT HHT
HHT HHT HHT HHT HHT HHT HHT HHT HHT HHT HHT HHT HHT
HHT HHT HHT HHT HHT HHT HHT HHT HHT HHT HHT HHT HHT

$285 \times 5 = 1425$

41

19021747   —   19021820

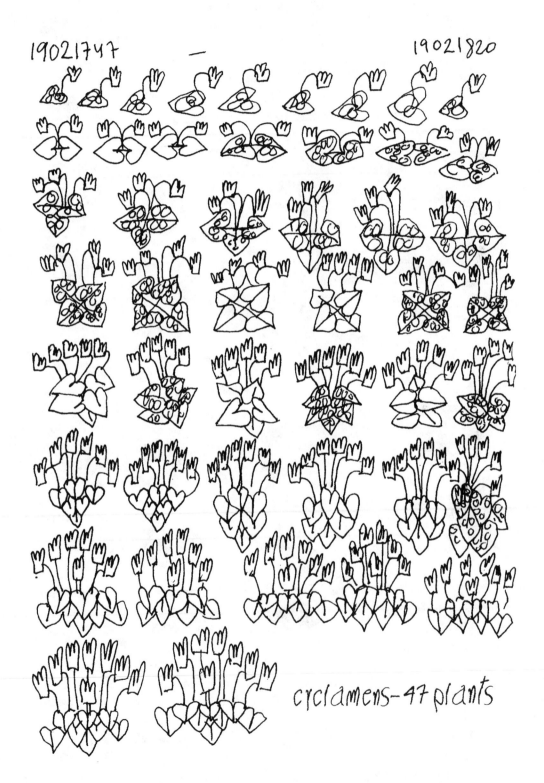

cyclamens-47 plants

195

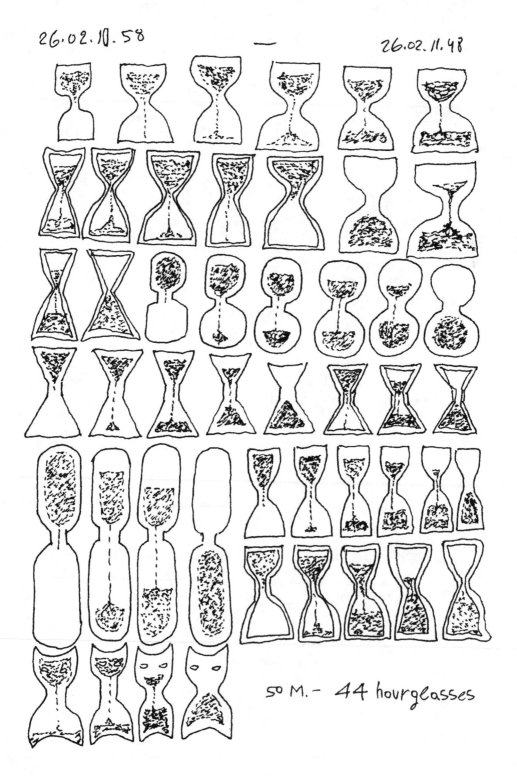

26.02.10.58   —   26.02.11.48

5° M. — 44 hourglasses

26021929 — 26021940

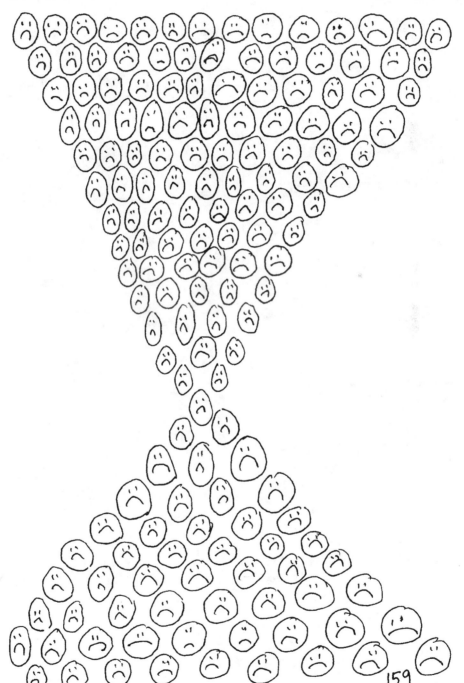

159

57

0001 0002 0003 0004 0005 0006 0007 0008 0009
0010 0011 0012 0013 0014 0015 0016 0017 0018
0019 0020 0021 0022 0023 0024 0025 0026 0027
0028 0029 0030 0031 0032 0033 0034 0035 0036
0037 0038 0039 0040 0041 0042 0043 0044 0045
0046 0047 0048 0049 0050 0051 0052 0053 0054
0055 0056 0057 0058 0059 0060 0061 0062 0063
0064 0065 0066 0067 0068 0069 0070 0071 0072
0073 0074 0075 0076 0077 0078 0079 0080 0081 0082 0083
0084 0085 0086 0087 0088 0089 0090 0091 0092 0093 0094
0095 0096 0097 0098 0099 0100 0101 0102 0103 0104 0105
0106 0107 0108 0109 0110 0111 0112 0113 0114 0115 0116
0117 0118 0119 0120 0121 0122 0123 0124 0125 0126 0127
0128 0129 0130 0131 0132 0133 0134 0135 0136 0137 0138 0139 0140
0141 0142 0143 0144 0145 0146 0147 0148 0149 0150 0151 0152 0153
0154 0155 0156 0157 0158 0159 0160 0161 0162 0163 0164 0165 0166
0167 0168 0169 0170 0171 0172 0173 0174 0175 0176 0177 0178 0179
0180 0181 0182 0183 0184 0185 0186 0187 0188 0189 0190 0191 0192
0193 0194 0195 0196 0197 0198 0199 0200 0201 0202 0203 0204 0205 0206
0207 0208 0209 0210 0211 0212 0213 0214 0215 0216 0217 0218 0219 0220 0221 0222
0223 0224 0225 0226 0227 0228 0229 0230 0231 0232 0233 0234 0235 0236 0237 0238
0239 0240 0241 0242 0243 0244 0245 0246 0247 0248 0249 0250 0251 0252 0253 0254 0255 0256
0257 0258 0259 0260 0261 0262 0263 0264 0265 0266 0267 0268 0269 0270 0271 0272 0273 0274
0275 0276 0277 0278 0279 0280 0281 0282 0283 0284 0285 0286 0287 0288 0289 0290 0291
0292 0293 0294 0295 0296 0297 0298 0299 0300 0301 0302 0303 0304 0305 0306 0307 0308 0309 0310
0311 0312 0313 0314 0315 0316 0317 0318 0319 0320 0321 0322 0323 0324 0325 0326 0327 0328 0329
0330 0331 0332 0333 0334 0335 0336 0337 0338 0339 0340 0341 0342 0343 0344 0345 0346 0347
0348 0349 0350 0351 0352 0353 0354 0355 0356 0357 0358 0359 0360 0361 0362 0363 0364
0365 0366 0367 0368 0369 0370 0371 0372 0373 0374 0375 0376 0377 0378 0379 0380
0381 0382 0383 0384 0385 0386 0387 0388 0389 0390 0391 0392 0393 0394 0395 0396 0397 0398 0399
0400 0401 0402 0403 0404 0405 0406 0407 0408 0409 0410 0411 0412 0413 0414 0415 0416
0417 0418 0419 0420 0421 0422 0423 0424 0425 0426 0427 0428 0429 0430 0431 0432 0433
0434 0435 0436 0437 0438 0439 0440 0441 0442 0443 0444 0445 0446 0447 0448
0449 0450 0451 0452 0453 0454 0455 0456 0457 0458 0459 0460 0461 0462 0463 0464
0465 0466 0467 0468 0469 0470 0471 0472 0473 0474 0475 0476 0477 0478 0479
0480 0481 0482 0483 0484 0485 0486 0487 0488 0489 0490 0491 0492 0493
0494 0495 0496 0497 0498 0499 0500 0501 0502 0503 0504 0506
0507 0508 0509 0510 0511 0512 0513 0514 0515 0516 0517 0518 0519 0520 0521
0522 0523 0524 0525 0526 0527 0528 0529 0530 0531 0532 0533 0534 0535 0536 0537
0538 0539 0540 0541 0542 0543 0544 0545 0546 0547 0548 0549 0550 0551 0552
0553 0554 0555 0556 0557 0558 0559 0560 0561 0562 0563 0564 0565
0566 0567 0568 0569 0570 0571 0572 0573 0574 0575 0576 0577 0578 0579

65

29020918

29020940

37

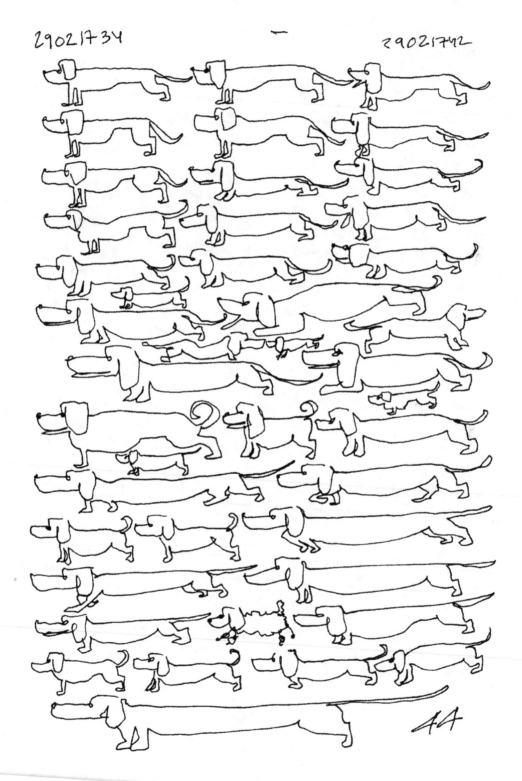

01031624   01031638

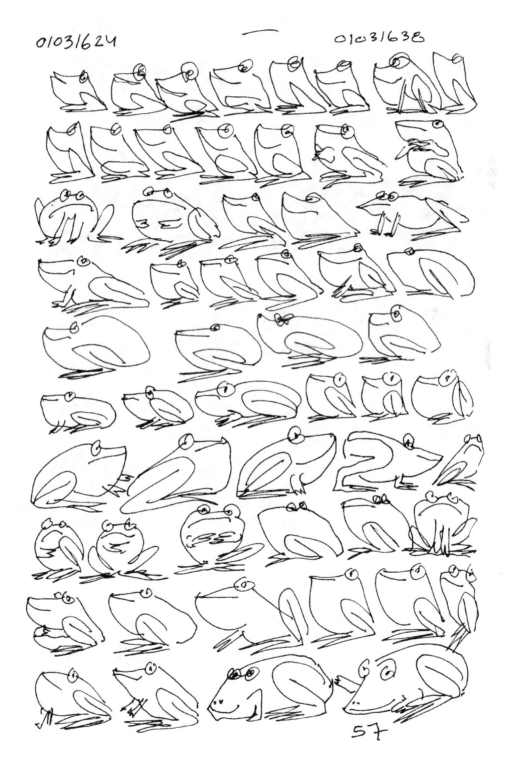

57

62

1 2 3 4 5 6 7 8 9 10 11 12 13 14 15 16 17 18 19 20 21 22 23
24 25 26 27 28 29 30 31 32 33 34 35 36 37 38 39 40 41
42 43 44 45 46 47 48 49 50 51 52 53 54 55 56 57 58 59 60
61 62 63 64 65 66 67 68 69 70 71 72 73 74 75 76 77 78 79
80 81 82 83 84 85 86 87 89 90 91 92 93 94 95 96 97 98 99
100 101 102 103 104 105 106 107 108 109 110 111 112 113 114
115 116 117 118 119 120 121 122 123 124 125 126 127 128 129 130 131 132 133
134 135 136 137 138 139 140 141 142 143 144 145 146 147 148 149 150 151
152 153 154 155 156 157 158 159 160 161 162 163 164 165 166 167 168 169
170 171 173 174 175 176 177 178 179 180 181 182 183 184 185 186 187
188 189 190 191 192 193 194 195 196 197 198 199 200 201 202 203 204 205
206 207 208 209 210 219 212 213 214 215 216 217 218 219 220 221 222 223
224 225 226 227 228 229 230 231 232 233 234 235 236 237 238 239
240 241 242 243 244 245 246 247 248 249 250 251 252 253 254
255 256 257 258 259 260 261 262 263 264 265 266 267 268 269 270
271 272 273 274 275 276 277 278 279 260 261 262 263 264 265 266 267 268
269 270 271 272 273 274 275 276 277 278 279 280 281 282 283 284 285
286 287 288 289 300 301 302 303 304 305 302 303 304 305 306 307
308 309 310 311 312 313 314 315 316 317 318 319 320 321 322 323 324 325
326 327 328 329 330 331 332 333 334 335 336 337 338 339 340 341 342
343 344 345 346 347 348 349 350 351 352 353 354 355 356 357 358 359 360 361
362 363 364 365 366 367 368 369 370 371 372 373 374 375 376 377 378 379 380
381 382 383 384 385 386 387 388 389 400 401 402 403 404 405 406 407 408 409
410 411 412 413 414 415 416 417 418 419 420 421 422 423 424 425 426 427 428
429 430 431 432 433 434 435 436 437 438 439 440 441 442 443 444 445 446
447 448 449 450 451 452 453 454 455 456 457 458 459 460 461 462 463
464 465 466 467 468 469 470 471 472 473 474 475 476 477 478 479 480
481 482 483 484 485 486 487 488 489 490 491 492 493 494 495 496 497 498 499 500
521 522 523 524 525 526 527 528 529 530 531 532 533 534 535 536 537 538 539 540
561 562 563 564 565 566 567 568 569 570 571 572 573 574 575 576 577 578 579 560
581 582 583 584 585 586 587 588 589 590 600 601 602 603 604 605 606 607 608 609 610
611 612 613 614 615 616 617 618 619 620 621 622 623 624 625 626 627 628 629 630 631
632 633 634 635 636 637 638 639 640 641 642 643 644 645 646 647 648 649 650 651
652 653 654 655 656 657 658 659 660 661 662 663 664 665 666 667 668 669 670 671 672
673 674 675 676 677 678 679 680 681 682 683 684 685 686 687 688 689 690 691 692 693
694 695 696 697 698 699 700 701 702 703 704 705 706 707 708 709 710 711 712 713 714 715 716
717 718 719 720 721 722 723 724 725 726 727 728 729 730 731 732 733 734 735 736
737 738 739 740 741 742 743 744 745 746 747 748 749 750 751 752 753 754 755
756 757 758 759 760 761 762 763 764 765 766 767 768 769 770 771 772 773 774 775
777 778 779 780 781 782 783 784 785 786 787 788 789 790 791 792 793 794 795 796
797 798 799 800 801 802 803 804 805 806 807 808 809 810 811 812 813 814 815 806 807 808
809 810 811 812 813 814 815 816 817 818 819 820 821 822 823 824 825 826 827 828 829
830 831 832 833 834 835 836 837 838 839 840 841 842 843 844 845 846 847 848 849 850
851 852 853 854 855 856 857 858 859 860 861 862 863 864 865 866 867 868 869 890
891 892 893 894 895 896 897 898 899 900 901 903 905 907 909 911 913 915 917 919 921
923 924 925 926 927 928 929 930 931 932 933 934 935 936 937 938 939 940 941 942 943 944 945
946 947 948 949 950 951 952 953 954 955 956 957 958 959 960 961 962 963 964 965 966 967 968 969
970 971 972 973 974 975 976 977 978 979 980 981 982 983 984 985 986 987 988 989 990
991 992 993 994 995 996 997 998 999 1000

63

50

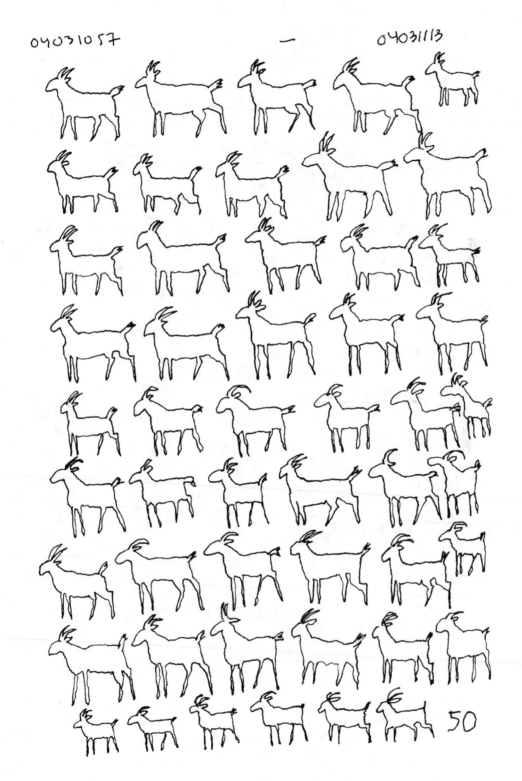

50

כמה זמן נשאר עד הפתיחה

כמה זמן נשאר עד הפתיחה

כמה זמן נשאר עד הפתיחה

כמה זמן נשאר עד הפתיחה

כמה זמן נשאר עד הפתיחה

כמה זמן נשאר עד הפתיחה

כמה זמן נשאר עד הפתיחה

כמה זמן נשאר עד הפתיחה

כמה זמן נשאר עד הפתיחה

כמה זמן נשאר עד הפתיחה

כמה זמן נשאר עד הפתיחה

כמה זמן נשאר עד הפתיחה

כמה זמן נשאר עד הפתיחה

כמה זמן נשאר עד הפתיחה

כמה זמן נשאר עד הפתיחה

34 m.

75 words, 270 letters,

How much time is left till the opening

13031923 — 13031939

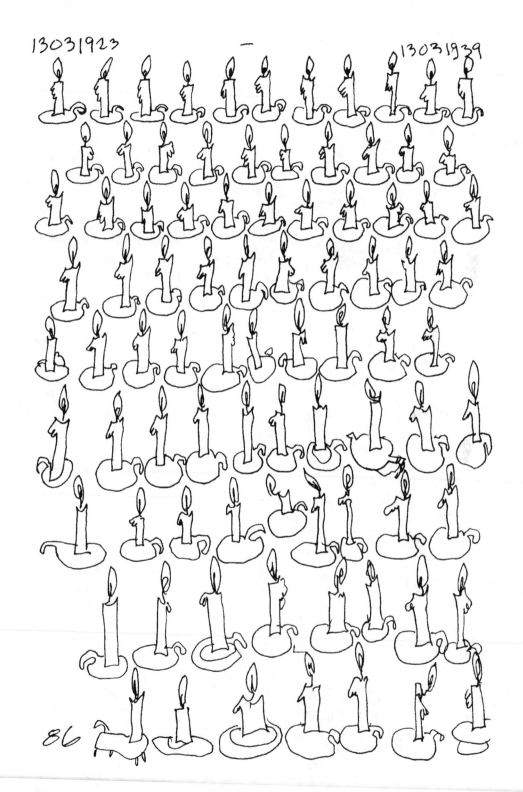

86

24

כמה זמן עבר מאז הפתיחה של דף זה

כמה זמן עבר מאז הפתיחה של דף זה (החדש)

כמה זמן עבר מאז הפתיחה של דף זה (החדש)

כמה זמן עבר מאז הפתיחה של דף זה

כמה זמן עבר מאז הפתיחה של דף זה

כמה זמן עבר מאז הפתיחה של דף זה

כמה זמן עבר מאז הפתיחה של דף זה

כמה זמן עבר מאז הפתיחה של דף זה

כמה זמן עבר מאז הפתיחה של דף זה

כמה זמן עבר מאז הפתיחה של דף זה

כמה זמן עבר מאז הפתיחה של דף זה

כמה זמן עבר מאז הפתיחה של דף זה

כמה זמן עבר מאז הפתיחה של דף זה

כמה זמן עבר מאז הפתיחה

כמה זמן עבר מאז הפתוחה

כמה זמן עבר מאז הפתיחה?

— 25 דקות —

How long has it been since the opening of this page

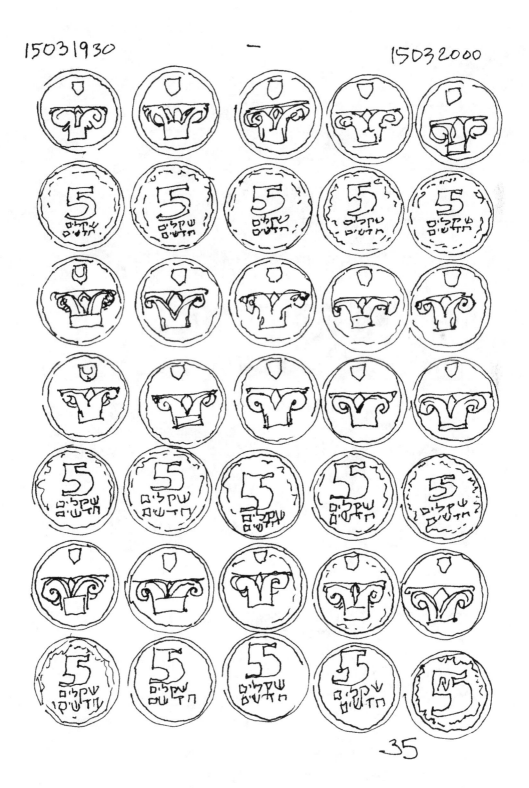

-35

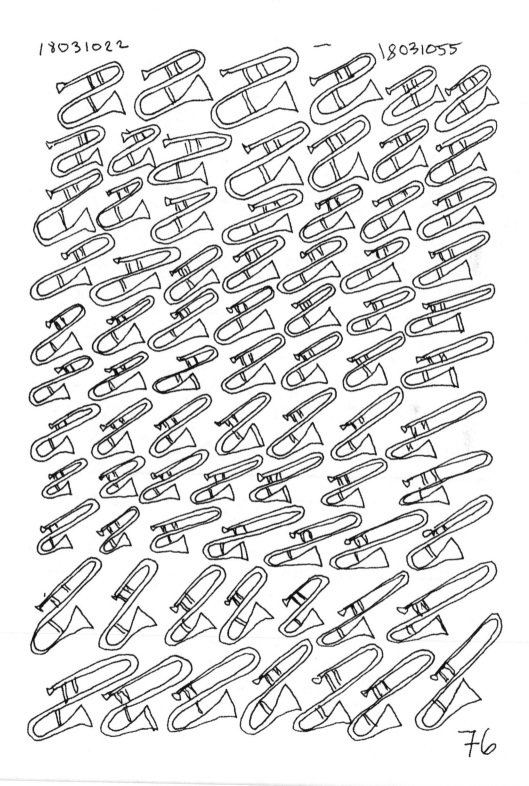

76

19031330 — 19031350

52 cypress trees   46 tombstones + 1

T0208964

"God Bless Daddy, Mother,
Bill, Ron, Jerry,
Carol Ann, Linda Jane,
Dick, and Little Tom"

"God Bless Daddy, Mother, Bill, Ron, Jerry, Carol Ann, Linda Jane, Dick, and Little Tom"

By

Richard L. Kramer

ISBN: 978-1-5882-0389-2 (sc)

Print information available on the last page.

This book is printed on acid-free paper.

1stBooks – rev. 8/15/00

Acknowledgments

It has taken three years for me to write these stories. Various family members have read them and have remembered things differently. In response to their differing memory, I have simply said, "write your own account." Because of their comments, I have remembered many other events that deserve recording and I am currently in the process of doing so.

I wish to acknowledge the suggestions and the thorough, critical reading of these stories by my sister, Carol Taylor and by two good friends, Nancy Crowder and Cathy Spencer. Acknowledgements also to my good friend Terri Ritz who typed rough drafts.

In addition, I want to acknowledge the editorial expertise of my son, Dane and his computer skills. I also would like to thank my daughter, Cass for her warm, complimentary introduction.

Dedicated to:

- **God**, who gave me life through my wonderful parents **Arthur William Kramer (Art)** and **Cecilia Frances (Ringle) Kramer (Ceal)**,

- My wife, **Margaret (Fane) Kramer (Peg)** who is incessantly supportive and tolerant,

- Our son, **Dane Edward Kramer (Dane)** who edited this book and brought it together,

- Our daughter, **Casady Lynn Kramer (Cass)** who wrote the complimentary introduction,

- My six brothers and sisters:
  William Leo Kramer (Bill) who will save me,
  Ronald Joseph Kramer (Ron) who gives me courage,
  Gerald Francis Kramer (Jerry) who fosters simplicity, health, and the pursuit of common sense,
  Carol Ann Taylor (Carol) who continually nourishes family and the love of family history,
  Linda Jane VanTreese (Linda) who is a model of commitment and strength, and
  Thomas Edward Kramer (Tom) who was a perfect childhood playmate and completes Bill's logical, definitive approach.

- **Lastly, to my** Grandma Kramer **and** Aunt Gene Kramer.

Contents

Introduction

by Casady Lynn Kramer

"I love the rain." The most common reaction I receive after making this statement is the simple question: "Why?" To me the answer is just as simple: "Dad." Everything about the rain reminds me of my childhood and the special kind of magic that it seemed to evoke in my father. I remember when the smell of rain was in the air and we were frantically gathering toys scattered in the yard from a hard day of playing. My brother and I would enjoy a nice hot dinner with Mom and Dad, but when night fell and the rain was beating on the rooftops, Dane and I would join Dad on the front porch. Dad would sit in the middle of the white wicker swing and, like bookends, we would sit on either side and snuggle up close under the blankets we had brought to the porch. We would watch the rain pouring down, feel the mist on our faces and listen to the music it beat out all around us. As Dad rocked the swing with his long, sturdy legs, each arm wrapped around one of his children, we would talk lightly of the day's events. Then, it would begin. Sometimes we had to ask but more often, as I remember, Dad would simply begin, "Once upon a time…."

It didn't take long for the magic of Dad's stories to envelop us as we lay safe at his side. He could weave a tale. Sometimes scary, sometimes weird, sometimes fantasy, but always good. His stories often had a moral. I remember one in particular of a young man who, in an effort to be included in his rich Grandmother's will, always complimented her on a hideous, life-size painting of a cowboy. The young man got into her will all right, he got the painting. As he was cursing his misfortune, the cowboy came to life and said, "Be careful what you wish for 'cause you just might get it!"

Some of Dad's stories were explanatory: "Why the weeping willow tree weeps," or "Why clouds are sometimes flat on the bottom." Whatever they were, Dad's stories were always fun. He has a wonderful imagination. Nevertheless, my favorites, (and most of the ones I remember) are the true stories he would tell about his childhood. Just picturing my father as a little kid, running around with his brothers and sisters, causing all kinds of mischief still puts a smile on my face. As far as I am concerned, no one can tell a story like my Dad. I hope you will agree.

Section 1

Personal Development

Unhappy, and Didn't Know Why

When I was very young, two or three at the most, I was sent to Lanesville, Indiana for a period of time one summer. I was very unhappy being sent away from home and I do not remember anyone explaining to me why I had to go. Aunt Till arrived and before I knew it, we were on the train to New Albany and from there we went to Lanesville. The only thing I remember about the train trip was passing through the deep gorges and tunnels of the knobs, Floyd Knobs. I must have slept most of the way. The northern portion of Indiana is flat but in the south, where Lanesville is located, there are hills and the knobs.

I spent an eternity in Lanesville that summer. I didn't know what to do with myself. There was nothing to do, no one else to play with, and I missed my older sisters and brothers. I also missed, most of all, my Mother. I slept in the childhood home of my Mother, Aunt Till and Aunt Olive's home. There was also a man there called Uncle John. He passed the hours of the day sitting on the roofed porch between the house and the smokehouse. For some reason, he had a collection of comic books. He would doze, snoring on occasion, while I thumbed through the books. I couldn't read the stories, but I looked at the pictures while sitting on the cool floor of the porch.

Cousin John and Dick
(smokehouse in background)

Various people came to visit to try to cheer me up but I persisted in my foul mood for as long as I was there. On one `big occasion,' I was sent across the creek to spend the night at Uncle George and Aunt Hilda's home. Wading in the creek was fun, but beyond that there was little difference for me. Their home sat above the creek on the side of a hill. They were tenants in half of the house that belonged to an old lady that they insisted I address as "Aunt Lou." She was a large lady who was always sitting in a chair. On the following morning, after breakfast, I decided it might be entertaining to lie on my side and roll down the hill toward the creek. Aunt Hilda would not have this, but I insisted on doing it anyway. After several admonitions to stop from Aunt Hilda, I stuck my tongue out at her thinking she did not have the authority to tell me to do anything; she was not Mother. When I stuck my tongue out at her, she slapped me across the face and told me never to do that again. I never stuck my tongue out at her again and I stopped rolling down the hill. However, I did stick my tongue out for pictures, never cooperating with the adults taking the picture. I don't know why I couldn't have been happier with the situation. After all, people were going out of their way to entertain me.

I was taken by hand into town, two blocks away, for ice cream. Aunt Till always had a supply of the soft mint candies I really liked in her two-door cupboard that sat in the kitchen. If she ran out, we would make a special trip to the grocery store to buy more of them. The store always had wieners made of pork, which I really liked with mustard after they were boiled. My aunts were nice to me when they put me to bed. I should have felt like royalty and made the most of it, but something just did not fit.

Uncle John Ringle and Dick
(St. Mary's steeple in background)

It seemed to me I was there too long and I was beginning to think that I was not wanted at home any more. I was really down on the whole situation. I couldn't stand to listen to Uncle John snoring by the cistern on the porch, I was tired of exploring the smokehouse and the root cellar, tired of playing in the creek, tired of walking up the hill to the church and the graveyard, and bored with the comic books and the walks into town. Then it happened. The telephone rang. The telephone hung on the wall in the kitchen. Everyone in Lanesville had the same ring, a double "ring, ring." Aunt Till answered the phone and almost before I was told that I had a new baby brother in Indianapolis, the whole of Lanesville knew that my Mother, Cecilia, had given birth. The local operator, who connected the calls, always listened in and proceeded to

spread the word to the entire town. Word spread like a grass fire with a healthy wind to its back. As for me, I was amazed that there was another person in the family. I hadn't noticed any difference in my Mother's shape. If I did, I had no idea what was happening. She must have been pregnant right before my eyes, but I still had no idea why I was sent away. I endured the separation from family in Indianapolis for about two months with an alien family in Lanesville; a family that treated me well, loved me, but who I didn't understand or want to be with.

Just as suddenly as my bag was packed and I was taken from Indianapolis to Lanesville, my bag was packed and I was taken from Lanesville back to Indianapolis. The return home was gratifying, and I was glad to be there. The smell of the home was the same as I remembered, and the feel of the bed was the same. My older sisters were the same as ever, but they made over a new arrival, my little brother, Tommy. I still don't know why I had to be sent away.

Lent

You might get the idea by the title that this is a short story about a person who has loaned something to someone else. It's not. It is about a period in the yearly calendar of the Catholic Church. The four weeks of Lent arrive in the early spring (sometimes very late winter and into early spring because of the calendar which dictates these events). It is a period that is akin to 'forever' when you are a child who has given up candy for the duration of lent. Family custom followed church custom and you were expected to "give something up for lent" as a penance in atonement for your sins. Lent ended on the Easter Sunday following Good Friday. I cannot, for the life of me, understand why the Friday on which we remember the crucifixion and death of Jesus is referred to as "Good." "Bad" seemed more appropriate, or maybe "Sad."

The children always gave up candy. At least I know that Tommy and I did. We stuck to it too. Mother helped. However, giving up the consumption of candy didn't stop us from collecting all that we could during the four weeks of lent.

At play, in the back yard, we would hear the back door of our neighbors' house open and we would instinctively stand up so that we could see over the hedge. We were hoping it was Mrs. Fultz so that we could say, "Hello Mrs. Fultz," in as nice a tone as we could muster.

Tommy at the hedge

If it were she, she would wave and say hello and then tell us to, "Wait there a minute." She would go back into the house and Tommy and I would look at each other knowingly. She would soon come out again and cross her drive to the hedgerow. Handing a couple of candy bars, usually Hershey bars, across the hedge, she would say something like, "Here, take these. You boys are so nice." Tommy and I would thank her in a voice that conveyed surprise, like we really didn't expect to be given candy bars.

"Why thank you Mrs. Fultz! Thank you very much!"

The transaction complete, we were tempted to sneak behind our garage and eat them on the spot. During lent, Mother kept a watchful eye. She would soon appear at the back door, call and wave hello to Mrs. Fultz who was making her way toward the back of their property to do who knows what, and then she would say to us, "OK, Dick and Tom, bring those in here." She would call out a "Thank you." to Mrs. Fultz as we approached the back door with the candy bars in hand.

"Well, you know this is Lent and we need to put those in the tin until Lent is over." Mother would then go to the kitchen pantry and retrieve a large, round cookie tin and pry it open. She would extend it to us for the deposit. By the end of Lent the tin was nearly filled with confiscated candy.

We knew Lent was nearing an end when we boiled and colored several dozen eggs. On the first nice day, we gathered weathered grass and fashioned nests all about the yard in plain view but also under bushes and in stands of tulips. Mother would then want a tour of the yard to see the nests we had made. On Easter morning, after mass and while we were changing clothes, Mother or Daddy would go out into the yard and run from nest to nest and put in the very eggs we had colored. While we were still in the process of changing, Daddy would come to the base of the stairs and call to us that he had seen the Easter Bunny and that we had better hurry. Of course, we never got down in time to see the bunny because "he had just left." "Oh, there he goes," Daddy would say while looking out a window that was too high for us to see out of, usually the kitchen window toward the back of the lot. We scrambled with our baskets out the back door and collected the eggs from the nests. They didn't let us miss any either, suggesting we look here or there. We were none the wiser simply thinking we were collecting eggs left by the bunny and that we would add to the ones we had colored.

The same stuff went on with the idea of Santa Claus only that went on for a much longer period of time, prompting us to be better than "good."

Oh, if we could have seen out the window.

The One and Only First Grade Event

St. Francis de Sales Grade School was a large one. The old, two-story brick building with four rooms downstairs and four rooms upstairs couldn't accommodate the eight grades neatly quartered in one building as it once did.

The first grade was taught by a slight nun, Sister Ernesta, in a large room located directly behind the priests' house and off the hallway that led from their home to the sacristy of the church. The second grade was taught across the playground in the convent, the sisters' home. The church, the school and the convent all had Avondale Street addresses and faced west. My Father and all his brothers and sisters had attended grade school at St. Francis, a German-speaking parish, except maybe for Dolores, my Daddy's youngest sister, one of Grandma Mary and Grandpa Joseph's daughters.

Tom, Sister Ernesta, and Dick

I never knew Grandpa Joseph. After he died, Grandma sent Dolores to live with some relatives in Texas, because she had too many mouths to feed on a railroad man's pension or whatever income she had, if not from her other children, sent to work before their time.

Anyway, they had all attended St. Francis de Sales Grade School. The summer I turned six, I knew I would be starting school in the fall. Going never bothered me much, because it seemed like our family school. We had history there. Besides, my Father and all my Kramer aunts and uncles, I was preceded by three older brothers and two older sisters. I don't know if they all attended the first grade in the room off the sacristy of the church, but that's where I went.

Sister Ernesta had taught my oldest brother, Bill, and all the rest, and now here I was. I felt connected.

Besides, for years, and before I attended grade school, we had cut up sheets of letters and numbers and placed a set of each in little cloth pouches for Sister Ernesta's new first graders. So, I already knew the nuns.

The nuns had a convivial relationship with the Kramer household. They would often walk the tracks from Sherman Drive and pick blackberries or black raspberries with Mother, always in their habits, only with their sleeves rolled up. Some of them had hair on their arms. Once, they were back picking berries, and a rain shower suddenly came up. The starched parts collapsed, and the bibs rolled up. Mother and the two nuns raced to the house and could hardly stop laughing. One would pull the bib down and let it go. It would roll right back up like a window shade and set them all laughing again amidst speculation about what their Mother Superior would think.

Sisters of St. Francis
(Sister Ernesta in center)

We seemed to be a class of about fifty, but Sister Ernesta, who towered over us at all of five feet, wore the black robes of power and mystery, her face surrounded with the same stiff, cardboard-like white frame of starched cloth and long, squared stiff bib of the Sisters of Saint Francis.

She was quietly talking and we were quietly listening to her instructions. We were all in our seats and there was a moment when Sister Ernesta stopped talking and the room was filled with silence.

Then everyone heard it, even those who were furthest away, the splattering of water on the wooden floor.

One of the students, one of my classmates, too afraid to ask to leave the room, had "lost her water." We knew she had peed. She was quickly approached by Sister Ernesta and escorted from the room. There was a whisper but nothing more from the class. That's all I remember of my first grade experience at St. Francis de Sales, and that was the first day of my formal education.

Prayers

Teeth were brushed and the face was washed with a cloth and then came time to get out of your clothes and into pajamas. Before getting into bed we were asked to kneel beside it and say our night prayers. Mother was the culprit. She insisted that we say our night prayers and many prayers for that matter, before and after meals, during storms, for the conversion of Russia, morning prayers, the Angelus and the rosary.

Night prayers included the Our Father, the Hail Mary, the Glory Be, and the blessing for the family. The blessing was said in two or three seconds. "God bless Daddy, Mother, Bill, Ron, Jerry, Carol Ann, Linda Jane, Dick and Little Tom." That accomplished, we were able to get under the covers, adjusting the pant legs of our pajamas so that they were not twisted and we were off to sleep.

Another prayer we were encouraged to say after we were tucked in was, "And now I lay me down to sleep, I pray the Lord my soul to keep. If I should die before I wake, I pray the Lord my soul to take." I sort of cringed at the line, "If I should die before I wake," and often lay awake wondering what it would be like if I really should die before I awoke. I came to the realization that if the event of death should occur before I awoke then I wouldn't know it would I? Pondering the mystery of death, I was asleep before I knew it and was awake when I did know it.

Well, morning prayers were very similar to night prayers. The Our Father, the Hail Mary, and the Glory Be. I included a prayer of my own which echoes the "Now I lay me down." It goes, "Good morning Lord, I'm awake, and my soul You did not take. Thank You for a good night's sleep. Throughout this day my soul please keep!"

Morning prayers were muttered while showering, brushing your teeth or dressing so that when you got to the breakfast table you could answer in the affirmative to Mother's query, "Did you say your morning prayers?"

Under the threat of nuclear destruction and the news of the Children of Fatima and their "sealed messages" which only the Pope in Rome was allowed to read, we were encouraged through the Catholic Church to pray the rosary for the conversion of Russia and because the family that prays together, stays together. Each evening, after the supper dishes were finished and the kitchen floor was swept clear of debris, Mother would invite us to her bedroom to light a candle in front of a statue of the Blessed Virgin and to pray the rosary. Daddy most often ignored the invitation, continuing to read the evening paper or to watch the television. We would often set the bedroom door to near closure to shut out the sound of the television. The monotonous rhythm of the rosary would begin; the Apostles Creed, a Glory Be, three Hail Mary's and another Glory Be. Then the meat of the thing ensued; five decades, each introduced by one of five glorious mysteries, one of five sorrowful mysteries, or one of five joyful mysteries. The set of mysteries used

Daddy ignoring the rosary

depended on the week or the season or calendar of the church, if not all three. Someone kept track of all this and published a guide of which Mother had a copy for our use. She would often ask one of the older children to lead the rosary and provide them with the guide. Five decades, each introduced by the Our Father followed by ten Hail Mary's and a Glory Be to the Father.

During these evening interruptions for prayer, I always thanked God for the bed around which we were kneeling for it was possible to lift yourself off your knees for relief by pressing your elbows into the mattress.

"Holy Mary, Mother of God, pray for us sinners now and at the hour of our death. Amen!"

"Holy Mary, Mother of God, pray for us sinners now and at the hour of our death. Amen!"

"Holy Mary, Mother of God..." Ten times five equals fifty. There were fifty-three Hail Mary's, six Our Father's, six Glory Be to The Father's, one Apostles Creed and, as though that wasn't enough, there was a prayer to be said at the close of the rosary that started with "Remember O most Gracious Virgin Mary that never was it known, that anyone who fled to thy protection, implored thy help, or sought thy intercession, was left unaided. Inspired by this confidence I fly unto thee........ etc., etc."

When the rosary was finished and the candle blown out, we would lift ourselves off aching knees and emerge from the bedroom into brighter light.

On many occasions, when traveling home from the cottage, someone would suggest that we say the rosary sometime after passing the Ten O'clock line. It was usually Mother or Jerry. Well, who could refuse? On these occasions, Daddy was a captive participant. In the darkness of the car, we would fumble among the contents of our pockets for the rosary we always carried and we would begin the countdown. For entertainment, I would often ignore the counting of the beads and see if I could simply predict when the last Hail Mary of a decade would be said.

There was also a period of time when we would be called to say the Angelus. I have no recollection of how this prayer begins. While working in the garden on Saturday's, we could hear the bells of St. Francis de Sales Church tolling the noon call to prayer. Mother would have us gather and say the Angelus. This was a European custom and the Catholic Church here was making an attempt at domesticating it. It failed.

Prayer was a part of my life, prayer is a part of my life and I suppose, prayer will be a part of my life until my death. While prayer was a part of my life as a child as much because it was expected and accomplished by rote as it was demanded, prayer is now a part of my life because I do believe in a Supreme Being and do desire to give praise and thanks for a multitude of gifts, not the least of which is the family into which I was born and the parents who nurtured me.

Aunt Lottie

Charlotte was my grandmother's sister. That made her my great-aunt, but I always knew her as Aunt Lottie. When Charlotte was a little girl of eight or nine years of age, she had an accident while roller-skating near the family home on Massachusetts Avenue. My Grandmother always related that Charlotte was skating and fell backwards onto a broken gate and one of the rusty nails pierced the back of her skull and she later developed meningitis. The illness left her deaf and deranged. Her parents (my great-grandparents) cared for her until their deaths. Then her care fell to the siblings. Since Grandma was the only one of her siblings in Indianapolis, the burden of care fell to her. From the age of twenty-one or so, Charlotte spent her time living with Grandma and living at Central State Hospital on West Washington Street in Indianapolis. She spent more time at Central State, Seven Steeples, than she did at Grandma's home next door to us on East 21st Street.

Aunt Lottie was all of five feet and ten inches tall. She weighed no more than 110 pounds, very thin. She dressed in long sleeved black dresses that reached her ankles, dresses that her mother might have worn in the late eighteen hundreds. She was accomplished at crocheting. She never sat to crochet but carried her current piece with her and performed her miracles with thread and needle while she walked about. Charlotte also prayed incessantly from a little black book that she always carried with her in one of the pockets of her long skirt.

When Aunt Lottie was with Grandma, it was for brief periods of time, maybe three months, and then she would be returned to Central State. My Grandmother's patience with her would be exhausted. Grandmother was determined to cure her with her own methods through reasoning and arguing. When Aunt Lottie was with Grandma, she would often come next door to our home and help my Mother with housework. Mostly she would do the ironing. She wouldn't speak but she was exceedingly gentle with everything and with anyone she encountered, silently appearing and silently leaving. She often presented my Mother with a piece of her handiwork from her crochet needle. Her eyes were downcast and we paid little attention to her comings and goings. She was just there from time to time. I think she enjoyed helping Mother with the chores of our home because Mother placed no demands on her whatsoever. The work she did was always just fine and appreciated.

On the other hand, this was Grandma's younger sister and she was determined to have Aunt Lottie behave as normal as possible.

I only heard Aunt Lottie's voice on a couple of occasions. On one of those occasions Charlotte was simply screaming. While playing in the back yard on a hot summer's day, I heard this shrill screaming coming from the other side of Grandma's house. I ran over to their drive and saw Aunt Lottie sticking out the window in the stairwell, her arms flailing in the air. Grandma was inside, behind her, holding the sash against her back and pushing down. Grandma was saying something but I couldn't understand what was going on. By the time I got into the house through the back door, the incident had ended and Aunt Lottie had disappeared into her upstairs bedroom. Grandma was muttering something about her sister and how she intended to make her behave. I thought it best to leave. Mother advised me to forget it after I told her what I had seen.

It was an odd sensation. I mean, here was this loving Grandmother with whom I spent countless hours, behaving in, what appeared to be, a cruel manner toward another human being. It just didn't fit.

There were other occasions when Grandma's treatment of her sister seemed amusing and somewhat appropriate and more acceptable. Aunt Lottie, praying if not crocheting, often stood in front of the huge bush in front of Grandma's house. Between prayers, she would admonish the travelers on 21st Street for going too fast. She pressed back into the branches of the bush that towered above the first floor of the house as though she were the Madonna at Fatima, praying and intermittently yelling at the motorists. "Slow down! Don't go so fast." Grandma would put up with this until she had enough. Aunt Lottie's admonitions would draw me toward the front of Grandma's house from play in our back yard. I would encounter Grandma unwinding the hose from the side of her house. She would signal to me to be quiet but there seemed to be little need for Charlotte was deaf. The signal to be silent indicated to me that

maybe Grandma knew that Aunt Lottie wasn't as deaf as she behaved. I never learned the truth of that matter.

Grandma would pull the hose up the side steps of her porch and out to the front rail behind the towering bush. Having already turned on the spigot, she would turn the nozzle open and spray toward Aunt Lottie through the bush. Aunt Lottie would run toward the street and continue her prayers. Grandma would come off the porch, trailing the hose, and run toward her out the drive. Aunt Lottie would retreat to the other side of the street while grandma struggled with the nozzle of the hose to get the best force available. She would hold the nozzle as high as she could, sending an arch of water across 21st street in an attempt to get her sister to stop her behavior. Aunt Lottie simply stepped backwards out of reach of the water. I have to admit that it was fun to participate in this activity and I had to laugh. Grandma was trying to tame the beast in Aunt Lottie the only way she knew. She thought that if she got her wet enough, she would cease her public and embarrassing display and come into the house to change clothes.

Who knows what went on in the mind of my great Aunt Lottie? There were times when she was obviously lucid but most of the time she was a mystery. Hearing her yell at the motorists on 21st Street was only the second time I ever heard her voice and it was clear.

While Aunt Lottie was confined at Central State, Grandma and Aunt Gene would visit her at least once a month. For them, it was an entire day of the weekend for they had to take the bus. These visits occurred on Saturdays and I was allowed to go with them from time to time. We would arrive at Central State Hospital and walk to the main building. Eventually, Aunt Lottie would appear, escorted by an aide. We usually sat in a swing, a two-seater, with the seats facing each other. To make it move you had to pump the deck with your feet. There were long periods of silence. Aunt Lottie would just sit and stare and listen while Grandma and Aunt Gene talked to one another and to her. Mostly, it was as if she were not there at all. They would give her a jar of peanut butter and she seemed appreciative but there was little other interaction. I remember most the long trip back on the bus to the East side and home and what a long exhausting day it had been.

I don't remember when Aunt Lottie died or why she died but she passed from my childhood. Trying to remember without the help of Grandma or Aunt Gene is impossible. The best I can think of is that it is like walking into an unknown and realizing that you have stepped into a cobweb. The webbing is all over your face and your immediate reaction is to step back and brush it off as quickly as possible, hoping that the spider is not somewhere in your hair or on your clothes.

She was there in my life, she was strange and different, she was quiet and gentle, she wove intricate patterns and she was patient, waiting and praying.

The Lump

Before the bathroom was installed at our house, it was not a simple matter to take a bath. Preparations were made beyond what I realized were required for as I was at play, unaware. Sunday was the day to go to Mass at St. Francis de Sales Church near Brightwood and, in preparation, Saturday night was bath night. Mother would heat water in buckets and kettles on the stove. The blue flames aglow under the containers seemed warm in the darkened kitchen in spite of their color. While the water was heating, the round galvanized tub, placed on the kitchen floor, was surrounded on three sides with kitchen table chairs draped with towels. Surrounded so, there was some privacy and the draped chairs created a windbreak and held in some of the precious heat.

Mother decided who was bathed and when. I suppose, from week to week, she tried to change the order in which she called us so that occasionally we would be bathed in unused water. No one wanted to be called. The older ones were allowed complete privacy. They would go into the darkened kitchen, close the door and after a time, emerge robed with their hair in a towel. My brother, Tommy, and I were still being bathed.

I don't have any recollection of Mother or Daddy bathing or how they did it. I didn't wonder about it then but I wonder about it now.

With clean underwear and pajamas at the ready, Tommy or I would be called to the bath. Daddy would urge us on our way by just being there. We didn't dare to be called the second time. When called, our response was immediate for he took note of that with a glance. Entering the kitchen, we were told, "Close the door and get your clothes off." Sitting on the cold linoleum floor, the untied shoes were pulled off, then the socks. That was a mistake. Taking off the shoes was smart because you couldn't get the pants off over them, but we should have left the socks on until the long legged pants were removed. I still sometimes forget that today. I suppose we removed the socks because it was easier to do it while still sitting on the floor. Standing then to remove the pants over hot, sweaty feet almost killed us on occasion and made a lot of noise as we fell. While holding onto the doorknob, the back of a chair of the kitchen table, we struggled to remove the pants. The sweaty feet stuck to the linoleum and stuck to the inside of the pant leg. I did not like to walk to the tub across the linoleum floor with sweaty feet. I wonder why we weren't advised to take off our socks at tub side. We were allowed to wait to remove our underwear at tub side just before we stepped in. Then Mother would pull the T-shirt off over our head as we raised our arms at her command. Naked we sat in the tepid, sometimes used, scummy water. Mother was always aware of water temperature, checking it from time to time with her elbow. If it seemed to cool to her she would add hot water from the large, spouted, hot water kettle that kept heating on the stove. She would carefully direct the flow so as not to scald us. The added warmth would induce a shiver and we would fight the urge to pee. You never wanted to admit to Mother that you made pee in the water but if it happened you were obliged to tell her. If you did pee in the water it probably guaranteed that the next to bathe would have fresh water.

It was my call. "Dick, time for your bath."

After I was sitting in the tub, Mother started at the top. Using a soaped washrag, she washed my face with that awful ivory soap, rinsed it, and re-soaped the rag. She said little, only speaking to instruct me to cooperate so I wouldn't get soap in my eyes. The chest was scrubbed, the arms raised and the pits swabbed. Each of the arms, top and bottom, front and back, were washed. The hands, between each finger, were washed and then the back. The washing of the back was the best; it was soothing. To feel the water lifted in a cupped hand and poured at the nape of the neck felt good. Soaped and rinsed, the back was finished and all was well.

Mother's hands were soft but Aunt Gene's hands were the softest of all. She had the softest hands of any I can remember. She occasionally wiped our faces and necks at her kitchen sink in the summertime. Her hands were soft.

Then came the dreaded, "Okay, stand up. Let's wash your behind and the rest of you." Soaped rag in hand, Mother went to work. I turned to face front and supported myself, right hand on her left shoulder,

left hand on the back of a towel draped chair, and, in the dim light, she quietly exclaimed, "What is that lump?"

"Where?" I asked.

"Here," she said as she pointed without touching.

I looked down and saw the lump. On the left side and above the convenience, there was a protruding lump.

"When did that happen?" I was asked.

"I don't know," I said.

"Art! . . . . Art! Come in here!" Mother shouted. Her call created a commotion of sorts and the news spread quickly, "Dickie has a hernia!"

"Oh my God, I have a hernia! What's that?" I thought.

A doctor's appointment was made, first with Doctor Gick and then with some other doctor downtown in the Hume Manser Building. All the doctors in the world were housed in the Hume Manser Building. It was confirmed. I had a hernia. However, it was determined that it was too soon to operate and that we should try to treat the hernia with a truss. This truss was a painful device I was supposed to wear daily. Upon hugging me good-bye on a school day, Mother would often deftly check to see if the truss was in place before I left.

"Do you have a handkerchief?" she would ask while patting my backside checking to see if she could feel the hard, plastic band of the truss around my waist. The truss had an oval, half-egg protrusion that was to be placed directly over the lump to push the hernia back into my body. The lump never disappeared, but then the truss was seldom in place in spite of its grip on an active child. It probably more often pressed the lump out rather than in by sliding above or below the assigned spot.

I wish I had one of the trusses today that I was supposed to have used in the hope of support or in the hope of correcting this deformity, so I could burn it! Whatever happened to those instruments? I don't know. I can see the first one today as clearly as I saw it then.

In the mornings I put on the truss as part of preparation for school. After being hugged I would announce that I had forgotten something. Rushing upstairs, I hurriedly removed the device and hid it for the day under the stack of my underwear in the bottom drawer. Was Mother ever the wiser?

Bathing was hard work in the dimly lit kitchen. Only one bath was really scary, the bath the night the lump was found.

Games

Around dusk, someone would suggest, "let's play hide and seek." The grimy sweaty kids would be gathered and all would join in. "So, who is 'it?' " Usually, a smaller one was selected and they had to hide their eyes at the designated home base and count very slowly to ten. While 'it' counted, we scrambled to be the best concealed but nearest home base so as to get home free. This was truly agonizing, trying to decide where to hide and not to have decided as you heard "six, seven, eight ...." Almost frantic to find a place, as you watched others conceal themselves, you would fling yourself into half lit places, like under bushes you wouldn't crawl into in full daylight because of the bugs. Somehow the dusk hid things as though they weren't there and you were at liberty to lie on the ground under a bush without fear. The greater fear was being seen by 'it' and hearing your name called out, having no chance to beat 'it' to home base. If you didn't beat 'it' to home base then you became 'it' and had to do the seeking. I think the rules changed from time to time. Sometimes you were just out - sometimes you became 'it'.

It was that way with most of the games we played like "king of the mountain," "redrover, redrover, send so and so over," or "mother may I," with it's baby steps, giant steps, scissor steps and free steps, which were always in dispute as to their execution. There was also "freeze," "rock school" on the front steps of the house, "drop the handkerchief," which always seemed silly to me, "crack the whip," "follow the leader," and some game we played as a variation on "redrover" by throwing a ball over the old frame garage to a team on the other side, a game I never understood.

The most favorite game of all for me was "tin can alley." Though it was often very confusing, it was a variation on "hide and seek." This game was also played at dusk and required 'it' not only to find those hiding, but also to protect home base (a tin can) from being kicked. Any tin can would do. It would be placed somewhere in the open yard or driveway, and 'it' would place a foot on the can and count to a specified number slowly while hiding the eyes. Every one who was 'it' peeked to see where hiders were going. As in "hide and seek," depending on the rules set down at the start, you, the seeker, might find someone and beat them back to the can and place your foot on the can before them, and then they had to help you capture others. Of course, there were variations here also. Even if your foot were on the can, it had to have enough pressure on it to prevent your opponent from kicking the can out from under your foot. If those sought beat the seeker to the can and kicked the can away 'it' had to retrieve the can, replace it in its assigned spot, and start again. Another of anyone hiding could also burst from concealment and try to beat 'it' to the can and kick it if 'it' strayed too far a field while searching for those hiding. Also, while 'it' was racing for the can, having found a hider, another hider could race to the can, kick the can and save the found hider from 'it.'

Why don't you read that last paragraph again?

Tin can alley was rough. Shins were kicked around the can, people were shoved into bushes followed by threats of "I'm gonna tell." In spite of the roughness of this game, I don't recall any serious injuries, only bruises and hurt feelings.

My younger brother, Tommy, and I had a game of our own. Armed with one of Grandma's old iron cow stakes, used in the garden as row markers, we pretended we were exceedingly strong and would take turns swinging the iron rod through the rusted upright wires of the fence along the garden path. The fence separated our garden area from the neighbors. This was a forbidden activity, but it was exceedingly entertaining. We didn't do a lot of fence cutting at one time but only a few uprights on each occasion, just enough to satisfy our need to feel we were powerful conquerors. Tommy had taken his turn, and I took the rod, gripping it like a baseball bat, Tommy at my left and behind me. I swung at the fence and five or six wire strands gave way like butter. I swung much harder than necessary and the momentum carried the rod right past my left shoulder and struck Tommy in the forehead just above his left eye. I can still feel the rebound in the iron rod and hear the dull thud.

He immediately began to run for the house, clutching his left eye. He started to cry and I ran after him.

"No, Tommy, no! Don't go in," I said as I pulled him behind a bush by the neighbor's garage.

"It hurts," he said.

"Let me see," I said.

Seeing it convinced me that it hurt, but I was panicking. They would find out we were doing wrong, and we would be punished.

"It will be all right. Just wait," I said. But it got worse. The swelling increased and bulged beneath his eyebrow. It was getting dark in color.

"Oh, Tommy," I exclaimed. "We'll tell them it was a baseball bat, that I accidentally hit you with a baseball bat while practicing my swing."

Tommy marched to the back door, climbed the steps and went in. I can't for the life of me remember the outcome.

No one was ever injured so seriously at "tin can alley" when they, by rights, should have been.

School Is Out / Boredom Sets In

The last day of school for the summer was always cause for celebration. Everyone was always promoted to the next grade and big plans were made in our minds for all the time off during the summer. Within a week, boredom set in and we were at the tails of Mother's dress asking her what there was to do. She would suggest we play with the dominoes or the checkerboard but none of her suggestions piqued our interest. Tinker toys was a favorite pastime but there never seemed to be enough parts to make the elaborate designs we had in mind, let alone those on the paper that came inside the Quaker Oats style box. Often, the parts didn't fit together tightly enough and the contraption would collapse before it was finished.

She might suggest we play with the clay and make something with it. Clay came at Christmas and was usually saved until summer. The box had six sticks of clay, each wrapped with a thin sheet of clear paper. There were sticks of red, green, yellow, blue, gray and brown. It was always a thrill to open the clay sticks and to promise yourself that, "no matter what I make, I will separate the colors when I finish." All of the clay eventually ended up brown. Even though we would play with the clay in the basement where it was cooler, the pieces would stick together and would finally be folded into one. Instead of making the layout of a country cottage with a garden with corn stalks and tomato plants, we found ourselves making a fort from the old West or a log cabin in Kentucky. It was easier to work with brown. Sometimes it would be so hot, even in the basement, that we would cool the clay in the refrigerator so we could continue to form it into logs.

Mother's suggestions were endless. "Make a telephone out of tin cans and a string," she suggested. Though we tried, it didn't really work. Then she came up with the best idea of all, recalling her own childhood. "Make some mud pies and bake them in the sun," she said.

"How do we do that?" we asked.

Her instructions were simple and short. "Get a bucket from the basement and put some water in it. Then, take it outside and find some dirt from the garden. Mix some of the water with the dirt in another container. Here use this." She handed us an old kettle and a spoon. "Then mix it up and pat the pies out in your hands and lay them on something to dry in the sun."

We went right to work. We learned a lot about adding water to dirt so that it wasn't too runny or too thick to handle. Most of the first mud pies crumbled as we tried to remove them from the board on which they were drying. We learned that a painted board was better for drying than an unpainted one but that a piece of metal was the best. Mother may have loaned us a cookie sheet on which to dry the pies. We also found that the deeper we dug into the ground for the dirt, the better the pies held together. We turned out stacks of pies in the following days, intent on finding the right mix and the right drying surface and the right drying time. We had found clay in our own back yard and using the sun to do the finish work was a lot easier than waiting on the refrigerator to cool the Christmas clay.

All of the pies wound up back on the garden plot but the making and the baking and finding the right mix occupied a lot of our time. We never again asked what there was to do that summer because we always knew we could make and perfect mud pies. We added pieces of shredded grass clippings to the mixture of mud and water to hold them together as they dried, but breaking one in half was not at all appetizing. Mother, in her wisdom, knew how to get us off the tails of her dress. We went from pies to cookies that we decorated with dandelion and violet blossoms found in the yard, sticking them into the 'cookie' before they began to dry. The cookies were sold for a penny apiece to Grandma and Aunt Gene, to Mother and Daddy and to other members of the family. They would pretend to eat them by breaking off pieces and throwing them into the yard exclaiming how good they were to our delight. We all had a good laugh over the mud pies and cookies.

We also entertained ourselves by making braids of long stemmed clover blossoms and wearing them as crowns. Carol Ann and Linda Jane were best at braiding.

Making hollyhock ladies was fun but you had to work fast because the open blossom would begin to wilt fairly soon after it was picked. We always started with preparing the head before we picked the dress. Have you ever made these?

We collected cottonwood grapes and kept them in a container until they dried and burst open, creating a mound of white fluff. The bunches of seedpods were especially plentiful after a summer storm. The fluff would be released into the air as we lifted it in our hands to the wind much as the blossom of the dandelion. Snapdragon blooms were plucked and were entertaining for a brief period of time as we squeezed the sides to open the "mouth." We made "ink" from all sorts of wild plant fruit that was collected, crushed, and mixed with water. Catalpa fingertips were fun but also short lived. It was difficult to cover all ten fingers without help. Though we looked incessantly, I never found the four-leaf clover that I must have overlooked.

Mud pies were the best.

At The End of His Rope

I knew he wouldn't do what I was afraid of, but I was certain he might. I wished I was the younger and could stand and watch, like Tommy. The water was colder than usual, and I was scared to death to let go and do what he was telling me to do. I never saw him swim, yet he was determined that we should know how to swim and he intended for us to learn that very day in ten minutes or less.

Mother was really concerned about one of us drowning at Graybrook Lake, and I suspect she shared her concern frequently with Daddy. Her worry probably influenced her disposition and caused her to be tense the whole time we were at the cottage. We didn't worry much about drowning when we went out in the boat and rocked it from side to side or moved from stem to stern, stepping over the oars and oarsman; or when we beat the water with oars trying to splash each other. All of this activity occurred around the bend in the lake, out of Mother's sight. We didn't worry about falling in off the end of the dock while fishing or chasing each other. We didn't fear drowning until Daddy became as determined to teach us to swim as he was determined to allay Mother's fear.

Mother dipping lake water off of the first dock

As I said, I never saw Daddy swim so it's safe to assume he didn't know how. I don't suppose he ever knew how because swimming is like a lot of other things, once you learn, you never forget. That surprises me a little, what with his ease at being on or around the water, deep water, and his childhood on 21st Street near Pogue's Run and the swimming holes. Of course, it's possible the swimming holes were not over his head, and he simply stood up to get out after jumping in.

Tom, Dick, Carol Ann, And Linda Jane

Also, I suspected he didn't really know how to swim because of his chosen method of instruction. He didn't get into the water with us, but used a more direct approach. He tied a large towing hemp rope around our skinny waists and instructed us to climb down the ladder and let go. Yep, that was it, tied the rope around our waist, had us climb down into the water and told us to let go.

When you think about it, you can imagine it working, and you get this image of a concerned man who is calmly explaining to his two little shivering boys that he is sure he knows what he is doing. He believes this will work and he wants to teach them how to swim because he doesn't want them to drown. He is encouraging; he is talking reassuringly in a confident voice. Well, that approach certainly would have been a positive addition to being treated like a tea bag and being cursed at for not producing.

I must say that he did take the time to wrap the end of the harsh hemp rope in a white rag, which he taped with black electrical tape. This cushioned it against the skin. That did demonstrate some concern for us on his part, but that was about it. I know today that he was confident then, and he would not let us drown.

The lesson went something like this.

"Daddy, I don't want to do this," as he tied the rope around my waist.

No response.

"Is that too tight?" Daddy asked.

"No, I don't think so." I responded.

"Okay, now I'm going to hold you up with this rope so you won't go under, and you are going to learn to swim," he encouraged.

I had to pee and said nothing.

"Climb down the ladder," Daddy instructed.

"But what if . . . ," I stammered.

He cut me off saying, "I've got the rope. Climb down the ladder."

"The water's cold," I complained.

"God damn it, climb down the ladder," he exclaimed.

"Oooooooo, it's cold!" I complained further.

"Get in the water . . . . Do it faster and it won't be so cold," he shouted.

"It's cold," I said for the very last time.

As I slowly lowered myself, the cold line of water marched up the ankles, around the calves, rising as I slowly lowered myself, kind of almost tickling as it rose to the trunks and the crotch. The water changed temperature and became even colder than it was, becoming the coldest ever on the back. So there I was, the water ringing my neck.

"Now, let go and swim," Daddy demanded

"Nooooooooo . . . .!" I answered.

"'God damn it, let go of the dock and swim!" he insisted.

The underside of the dock was absolutely full of spider webs and spiders. They were long legged, skinny bodied, water spiders. The light brown, crunchy shells of the Katy-did bugs were hanging all over, like the ornaments on the bottom side of a Christmas tree. The undersides of the boards on the deck were spotted with a kind of white mold. The pilings, which had been driven into the muddy lake bottom through holes cut in the ice, were still covered with their bark. Oh, what a vivid scene . . . then the toe of a shoe was pushing at my shoulder and a voice booming.

"Let go of the God damn dock, go on, I got you, get out there, you won't drown."

The whole lake knew of my plight and the folks across the lake must have been watching. I imagine they stopped whatever they were doing, wherever they were doing it, to watch Art Kramer teach his boys to swim and to listen to his method.

None of his yelling and pulling or his nudging with his foot, being watched, or the sight of the underside of the dock motivated me to take the plunge and let go, as much as the realization that my feet were so deep in the dark green water, that they were colder than the top of me, and I couldn't see them. I was sure something was rising to have a sample.

In that instant, I tried to swim.

I don't know how many attempts it took or how many times he let us sink before he pulled us up, but both Tommy and I learned to swim. Our Daddy taught us off the end of our dock on the end of a rope. City pool swimming at Longacre hadn't prepared us as much for the deep water as we thought it had. We were blue lipped, red waisted but proud.

Mysterious Frank

Spring arrived and new life presented itself in the form of tulips, hyacinths, budding trees and hedgerows. People came outdoors and cleaned up their yards. We had cleaned them up in the fall but there was always the winter refuse to clean out of the hedgerow. Our hedge row was a long one running from the front yard all the way back to the neighbors' garage on the West side of our home. Sometimes the hedgerow would get too tall and in the early spring we would cut it completely back and the new growth would break out at the base of the plants. When we cut the hedgerow back there was a lot to burn, so much so that it could not be burned all at once. Clearing the hedgerow fully exposed our neighbors to the West, the Fultz's. The adults could see them and talk to them above the hedge when it was tall and children would be picked up and held or stood on a tree stump that was in the row so that Mrs. Fultz could see us. Mrs. Fultz lived in a very small two-bedroom house that sat well back on the lot so that her front door was about twenty feet behind the back door of our house. The original developers had intended to build a larger home in front of this 'temporary' one which would stand in line with the other homes on 21st Street. This was never accomplished. Also in the home were Rose, Art and Frank Fultz, the children of Mrs. Fultz. As long as I can remember, Mrs. Fultz was old. Even Rose seemed old and I never thought of her as a daughter but used to think that she was a sister of Mrs. Fultz. Art worked every day at the gas company. Rose took care of the home and her mother but Frank was a mystery.

Even during the winter months you would see Mrs. Fultz occasionally and Rose and Art regularly, coming and going. Art always had a cigar in his mouth and both he and Rose were very friendly people. So was their mother for that matter. Frank would never be seen.

In the spring, with the hedgerow cleared, a full view of the neighbors home was provided. Frank would come out of the front door of the house and begin to perform some of his own spring-cleaning. He never looked at us and never spoke to us. He was a thin, tall man, almost too thin for his height. He would close the storm door very quietly as if he were sneaking out of the house. There was no porch on the house, just two concrete steps down to the yard. He would stand for a while facing the steps and then remove a handkerchief from his right back pocket. He would unfold it and hold it by one of the corners and begin to clean the top step by snapping it at the step. He would do this for a long time. We would continue to play but we were intent on staying where we could watch his activity. After ten minutes of cleaning the step with the snap, snap, snap of his handkerchief, he would refold it, place it in his pocket, and sit on the step. He wouldn't sit there very long before he would get up and walk to the middle of their front yard. We had to reposition our play further into our back yard so that the corner of our house did not block our view of what was going on. Mother would sometimes quietly admonish us for she knew we were intent on watching. On some occasions she would simply call us in. If she did call us in, we would go to the upstairs bedroom and watch Frank from the West windows. We could see what he was doing because the huge Red-haw tree had not yet put on its leaves.

Frank would stand in the middle of their large front yard facing 21st Street. Suddenly, he would raise both arms above his head while pivoting sideways and execute a cartwheel. His cartwheels were not show material but I couldn't execute one half as well. In the process of turning the cartwheel, his comb from his shirt pocket and coins from his pants pockets would tumble out to the ground. He would then spend the next several minutes snapping his handkerchief at the grass in a meticulous process of locating each coin. This could go on longer than we could stand to watch. The strange thing is, once he was satisfied he had found all of the coins, which he placed back in his pockets as he found them one by one and, after he combed his hair and placed the comb in his shirt pocket, he would resume his stance, throw up his arms, pivot and do another cartwheel. The search for comb and coins would begin again with the snapping of the handkerchief.

There were also times when Frank, after his brief respite on the cleaned front step, would walk to a spot in the yard and begin snapping at it with his handkerchief. He would do this until the tip of the handkerchief had cleared all of the grass in that particular spot down to the dirt. I often wondered if he felt he was missing a coin and was determined to find it in that particular spot. I never saw him retrieve anything.

Mother must have done something right because we never made fun of Frank nor chided him. He never looked at us nor spoke to us though he must have known we were watching. Of course, we didn't speak to him either. Still, I was tempted to step over the hedgerow and walk to the step and just sit down beside him on the cleaned step. I thought about it but I never did follow through, probably out of fear of what I imagined might happen.

Parents' Night Out

Sometimes the only way to get the hard or semi-hard deposits out of your nose is to stick the index finger, or whichever finger you are accustomed to using, up your nose and scrape its insides with your fingernail. Opening the nasal passages was important and blowing your nose into a handkerchief didn't always work.

Clean handkerchiefs were always available in the top bureau drawer in Mother and Daddy's bedroom. That was the only source of supply. Ironed and neatly folded, the stack was always there. We never ran out. On occasion, when picking my nose, I would suddenly cause it to bleed!

I learned to put my head back, press on the bleeding side of the nose, breath through the other and place a damp, cold cloth at the back of my neck.

My nose seemed to bleed easily. Sometimes spontaneously and with out picking, a sneeze or a cough would start it. It bled if I was struck in the middle of the back with an open hand. What malady was this? Did others have nosebleeds so easily? I don't remember my last nosebleed as an adult, but I remember the gaiety with which my brothers and sisters sometimes caused my nose to bleed.

Every now and then it happened that Mother and Daddy would both be gone from our house, leaving Jerry and Carol Ann "in charge." Usually, it was on a Wednesday night when Daddy went bowling and Mother had a P.T.O. meeting or ladies club or whatever at St. Francis de Sales School and Church.

Daddy left shortly after dinner, and as she left, Mother would leave instructions to behave. We behaved all right! As we chose to behave, but not, I'm sure, as she would have had us behave. We played hide and seek. The clothes hamper in the bathroom was a favorite of the smaller ones. Closets, among smelly shoes and behind the hanging clothes, behind the couch, behind the floor length drapes, not daring to breath much, under the kitchen table among the chair legs, behind doors and under beds with carpeted floors were our hiding places. We didn't hide much under beds with linoleum floors because of all the dust balls; those light gray transparent puffs of dust always seemed to be there like clouds that settled on the floor. No one ever hid in the dark recesses of the basement! We had our rules.

Tiring of hide and seek, we would sometimes raid the kitchen cabinets for kettles, lids, and table knives and work up a marching band. It sometimes worked, but mostly we would make such a din that Art, our neighbor next door, must have easily heard us and wondered what was going on. As I look at that now, Jerry must have been quite proud at how he kept us entertained. We never washed the kettles, lids or knives that served as band instruments, but we did put them away, with sweaty hands, lest their use be discovered.

Another fantastic bit of adventure that Jerry showed us, I remember, was to turn on all the lights in the house and walk slowly, peering into a mirror held at our waist. The ceilings, identified as we went from room to room, gave you a slight dizzying feeling of imbalance and an exciting, different view of things. On occasion, we would do the same thing, entertaining ourselves, with all the house lights out and using a flashlight.

On one of these evenings, after Tom had gone to bed, my sisters convinced me, against my better judgment, to let them dress me up like a girl. Using their articles of clothing and their makeup, they had me dress in a skirt, blouse and scarf. The makeup was added after I was outfitted. Adding insult to injury, they took a picture.

Dick after "makeover"

I guess there was a limit to ideas. Without Mother or Daddy in the house, no one was interested in sedate games like tic-tac-toe or connect the dots. Besides, it took far too long to set up a game like connect the dots.

We were chasing each other through the house, and I think Jerry said with a devious giggle, "Let's make Dick's nose bleed." That was scary, to be singled out like that. Besides, there were many times, especially at school, when I didn't think it would stop bleeding after it started. Mother was called to St. Francis de Sales Grade School many a time to get it stopped or to bring a clean shirt or handkerchief. Mother wasn't at home now.

23

I ran but got caught on the stairway to the basement. Turning the corner, through the kitchen doorway, my right hand hit the light switch, and the light came on as I bounded down the stairs. Jerry's hand caught me flat in the middle of my upper back. I stopped on about the third step. Sure enough, the warm, slick, salty stuff ran out of my nose and over my lip.

"Ah! His nose is bleeding," Jerry said. They assisted me to the bathroom warning me not to tell Mother.

We were in bed before Mother came home. She always got home before Daddy. I wonder today if she knows how we behaved on parents' night out.

The Cure

A letter from my Mother to her sisters in Lanesville, Indiana:
(Note that parenthetical phrases are my comments.)

Dear Till, Olive and Hilda,

Hope you all are well. This has really been a busy spring. It seems like one of the kids are sick all of the time. (She really means that one kid is sick and then another, not that the same kid is sick and then the same kid is sick again.) I have been able to get some of the spring-cleaning finished between the illnesses. The bedrooms have been done but none of the closets have been cleaned. There are still all of the clothes to go through. Linda is tired of Carol Ann's hand-me-downs and I really ought to try to find a way to get Linda some of her own things. (Meaning new ones, but she didn't know how she could manage it financially.) I have been able to get the windows on the downstairs washed but there are still the upstairs ones to do. The windowsills all need to be painted but Art says it is dumb to do it every year. He'll do it though. (If he didn't he wouldn't hear the end of it.)

Linda was sick first and missed a few days of school. Then Carol Ann got it and she gave it back to Linda. I think it is because they are in such a small room that they give it to each other. They finally got over the sore throat and then little Tommy got it. They have a fever and a sore throat and that lasts about three days but they are so tired that I keep them home a few days more just to be sure they are over whatever it is. It's probably some sort of flu. If they complain and stay home or say they are sick, then I make them stay in for the day. I think sometimes they use the fact to get more sympathy so I don't allow them to go out to play in the afternoon or the evening when they say they are feeling better. (If you claim to be sick in the morning then there is no reason for you to go out in the evening for any reason. If you are sick, you need your rest.)

After Tommy was about over it, Dick got sick with a sore throat. He stayed home from school and I made sure he got plenty of liquids like the hot lemonade. Mom Kramer brought over some chicken soup. She is a dear person and always tries to help but she comes over and through the back door at the worst time yelling my name so loud that she scares me to death. I do love her for the way she tries to help me. And, I don't mean that she doesn't help me, she does.

Well, I will keep you posted but Dick is calling and I want to get this in the mail before the mailman comes so goodbye for now,

Love, Ceal   XX OO

Aunt Hilda's response to my Mother:
(Again, parenthetical phrases are mine)

Dear Ceal.

We are all fine. I do so wish we were closer so that we could help you with your children. It must be difficult with so many sick at once and then to have the same one get sick again. We have had the flu here as well. Alberta has been under the weather (here she means ill as we are all under the weather all of the time if you think about it) for more than a month. Till and George, and I have not had any of this flu and I sure hope we don't get it. I'm always afraid that George will bring it home from school and give it to the rest of us because he is in daily contact with so many children and many of them have been sick with the symptoms you describe.

Olive has not been feeling well. She comes home from the shirt factory and lies down on the couch and is just too tired to do anything. Till and I want her to go to the doctor but she says she doesn't have the time. (Or the money.)

This is a short letter just to let you know that we did receive your letter and to let you know that you and your family are always in our prayers. It's short also because I'm making all of the gowns for the Schellambager wedding and I still don't have all of the material. Some of them expect miracles.

Love, Hilda

P.S. Picnic plans are being made and we think we will make over $10,000.00 this year.

P.S. Oneda just stopped by and said to tell you all hello. She, Johnny, and family are fine.

Oh yes, my throat hurts and I wouldn't kid about that. Yeah, I stayed home from school today because my throat hurt so bad I didn't want to swallow my own spit. I broke out in a sweat thinking that I was going to have the same thing that Ron had had last year when he was sick for most of the spring and summer, scarlet fever! I knew "scarlet" meant red but he didn't look red from what I remember of that bittersweet spring and summer.

I remember that one morning Ronnie was ill and the routine of the household was sort of put on suspension. Daddy was home and he and Mother were waiting on the doctor to arrive. She diagnosed his ailment as a serious kind of flu called scarlet fever and she took the time to give elaborate instructions to my parents about how to contain the disease so as not to spread it to the rest of the family. After the doctor left, one of the first things Daddy did was to drive two nails into the walls or the woodwork at the top of the stairs and to hang a heavy bedspread over the doorway to sort of contain the air that Ronnie was breathing.

Then I remember some similar pounding on the front porch. When we were outside playing later that day, we saw the board that had been nailed to the front of our house. It had been nailed right through the asbestos redbrick like siding and it read, "Quarantine, Scarlet Fever, Do Not Enter." In a way this seemed like we were very special and it set us apart from the rest. We were able to continue our regular routines as a family but with the restriction that only a few members of the family could go upstairs to tend to Ronnie. I'm sure there were all kinds of precautions laid down for those who went upstairs during that long, long period of time like how to handle the wash, changing the bed, getting rid of the waste, and the washing of the hands before and after contact with anything that was connected to that area of the house. We went to bed in makeshift beds on the floor of the living room, the living room couch and the dining room daybed through all of this.

Ronnie was isolated from the rest of the family, save the caretakers, for an eternity. Daddy spent a lot of time upstairs with him. During that time, they built model airplanes out of balsa wood, glue, and very thin paper. The planes were shellacked when completed and stored in the attic. They were rediscovered several years later when Daddy turned the attic spaces into closets. It was the first time we saw them. The day Ronnie was declared 'safe' we were escorted upstairs to see him and to wish him well. Then, one day, he was allowed to come downstairs and there was a celebration that he had survived. Only then did I realize the seriousness of the situation and learned that he could have died. Died!

So, here I am with a sore throat wondering if I am the next to have the dreaded scarlet fever. Somewhere along the way, through all of these childhood illnesses my parents contended with, my Father decided that he could do as well as any M.D. at treating early symptoms. My Mother agreed and acted as the attendant nurse. I hated to have to admit that I had a sore throat because I knew that when Daddy got home from work at Chevrolet he would suggest that they had to "paint the throat." I hoped that maybe he would decide, as he looked into my throat, that my tonsils had to be removed. One summer, Carol Ann, Linda, and Ron had their tonsils removed, one after the other and they got to eat all of the ice and ice cream that they wanted. Unfortunately, that was not the case with me. I had a raw, red throat that simply needed painting. They always had a supply of Methiolate and long sticks with cotton on the end. Oh, I hated to hear the words, "let's paint his throat."

Where one nail would do, Daddy drove two. So it seemed the same with the painting of the throat. Where one coat was enough, he would apply two or three. The gagging was awful as he probed with the cotton tipped stick.

"Open up," he would command. "Put your head back and stick your tongue out."

Following this initial effort, if the illness persisted into the following day, the treatment would intensify. The throat would be painted and then they would debate the merits of the highly dreaded enema. They pretended not to make the decision in front of the patient but the discussion occurred within earshot and the sweating persisted.

"Where is the damn thing?" Daddy would ask as he looked for the device.

Mother would answer, "It's right in here Art, just a minute, I have to be sure it is clean. I'll scald it first."

The water could be heard to run in the kitchen and then in the bathroom and then they would appear, the two together. Mother would hold the orange, swollen, bladder-like reservoir high and the Vaseline coated tip of the four inch black nozzle would be inserted gently into the rectum. The nozzle was connected to the bladder by a long rubber tube. Once inserted, the black nozzle released the tepid water when the clip was released. The higher the bladder was held, the greater the flow.

At this point, instructions were given and encouragement to "hold it, don't let go." You felt as if you couldn't take another drop and they would say "this is almost enough." I felt as if we were well beyond enough and that I would make a mess. I always thought I would lose control when the probe was removed, that the stream would follow. I was then helped to the bathroom and was thankfully left alone to purge myself of the fluid. It was embarrassing because everyone in the house at the time knew what was going on, that the dreaded enema was being administered. Sympathy was in the air and you could see it in the eyes of the siblings who were hanging around in the dining room to catch a glimpse of you as you hurried from the bedroom to the bathroom.

My motto became, "don't report a sore throat until you can't eat." But as I reflect on the treatment of early symptoms that my parents conducted, I realize there may have been two things going on. One is that their early interventions really worked and prevented more serious illnesses. The other is that the threat of their early interventions was, in and of itself, a cure.

Tommy Was Good

I vaguely recall the work of busting up the basement floor. I didn't bust it up but Daddy and the older ones did. They carried it all out the back door and I helped by hauling it away in the wagon. I think the basement floor was lowered about 14 inches after we were hooked up to the sewers of the city. It was a mess. It must have been. It was more of an adventure for me; not real work, and yet another affirmation that no job was too big to tackle. If you wanted it done, you could do it yourself. It was from exposure to situations like these that taught me I could do anything. Never mind you've never done it before, just think about it, plan it (but don't plan too long), and just do it. Half the effort was in just getting started and when the job was done, you wondered why you were ever worried about whether you could do it in the first place and why it took so long to get started.

These projects also taught me no matter how much you plan, you can't anticipate everything you might run into and there would be delays and endless trips to the hardware store, Interstate Hardware.

I'll never forget the trips to Interstate Hardware on Sherman Drive. It was the same way we went to go to church. Turn right out of the driveway, go to Sherman Drive and turn right to Interstate, just before Massachusetts Avenue. Daddy would charge into the hardware store. The hardware was a lot like our mess in the basement. Everything was in disarray and the shelves, laden with dust, overwhelmed the inner space of the store. They practically met you at the door.

"Denny!" Daddy would shout as he entered the store. Denny was the proprietor, always standing behind the U-shaped counter amid his catalogues, an unlit cigar butt in his mouth, secure between his teeth. With his glasses on his forehead and the phone secure against his ear, propped by his shoulder, he would grunt some acknowledgement that we had arrived.

In spite of the fact he was obviously talking on the phone, Daddy would ask for whatever it was he needed in some foreign language.

Daddy and Denny had what seemed to me to be a rude relationship. I was usually embarrassed when I went with Daddy to Interstate, but I also found their bantering amusing. They would curse at each other while laughing, though they appeared angry. I don't know of any other situation in which Daddy used foul language except in anger. I was also attracted to the liberties we were given in the hardware store.

"God damn it, Art, I'm busy on the phone," Denny would growl.

"Well, just tell me where it is, and I'll find the Goddamn thing myself like I always do," Daddy would respond.

'Aisle three, near the paint," Denny directed, "bottom bin."

With that, we entered the maze of shelving and dusty bins. Daddy went on his search and I wandered freely, peering into the shelves and bins, wiping my hands on my pants after fondling oily pieces of pipe called elbows, nipples, female and male adapters, all of which were intriguing. My first suspicions about the anatomy of the human body were confirmed at Interstate Hardware.

Denny often did not have in stock what was needed, and the two would argue and improvise or argue and criticize.

"You never have what I need. I don't know why I bother to come here," Daddy would say laughing.

"Well, Goddamn, Art, I can't stock every Goddamn thing you need!" Denny retorted.

I wondered why. The place seemed full to me, dark, dirty and full of everything. I was amazed at the number of times Denny gave accurate directions to the bin or shelf, and Daddy came away with what was needed. When he did, Daddy complained about the price no matter who was around or behind the counter.

"Well, Goddamn it, Art, I have to make a living! Hell, you would complain about the sunset if you weren't ready for it!" Denny would say.

We always left on a friendly note, Daddy exclaiming that he would see him later. It never quite fit, but I think they really liked each other.

When the basement project was finished, we had an island that supported the hot water heater, furnace, and gun rack. The old monstrous coal furnace had been converted to a forced air oil furnace. It forced hot air up through its tentacles providing small patches of warmth in a cold house above. These

29

registers were briefly occupied, while getting ready for school on cold winter mornings, letting warm air course up the pant legs or skirt. The favorite register, and most convenient to the breakfast table, was in the dining room.

The furnace occupied most of the island in the basement. The island created an oval, and the entire floor, tiled in brittle black squares, sloped to the drain outside the shower, next to the basement toilet. This oval and the slope of the floor created a whole new playground. Because of the basement project, we played in the basement as never before. The favorite sport was to sit on a metal roller skate with metal roller skates on your feet and propel yourself around the island again and again, pushing against the floor with your hands. The down side was past the hissing oil burner, while the up side began at the base of the stairway, under the clotheslines toward the south end.

The champion oval racer was Tommy. No one could beat his time, clocked with Daddy's stop watch, or more often, counted with "one, one thousand, two, one thousand, three, one thousand, four..." No one could beat his time. The metal wheels against the tiled concrete can still be recalled today. He was the youngest, and he was the best.

Years later, Tommy had a blue scooter, gas powered. I don't know who paid for all the gas he burned in that scooter, but he was the best in time on that as well. This oval was around the garden, and just as he spent hours sitting on a skate, he spent hours on that damn blue scooter, whizzing around the garden plot.

The garden plot was turned over each spring for years by an old man and a team of horses. I don't know where they appeared from, but it was always an exciting event for me to see that blade cut smoothly through the earth, laying it open for further preparation and planting. Our garden always generated some sense of pride and covered the back of the lots of our home and that of Grandma's and Aunt Gene's.

Planting was a joyous time, and the garden looked good. So why was Tommy allowed to create this unsightly path around it? It pissed me off. It made it hard to mow. I really think it pissed me off because he was so damn good on skates on our oval basement track, and he was so damn good on his scooter around the garden as well. I told myself he had more time to practice.

A Walk With Purpose

After the evening meal, Grandma would sometimes bolt from her back door and head back the driveway in her thin-soled, soiled shoes. She seemed intent on reaching some pre-determined point. She lifted her shoulders, right then left with her left-right stride, swiftly covering the distance from the back door to the grape arbor, past the huge maple tree.

The maple tree stood as testimony to her ability to grow things. It had happened one summer, after the construction of a two-car brick garage, that we wanted more trees on our property than we had at the time. So we harvested small, sapling maple trees from somewhere on North Sherman Drive or along White River. After we had planted the "best" of the lot, we had laughingly offered the "runt of the litter" to Grandma.

Complete optimism is a fault of mine inherited from my Grandma. She took the runt and stuck it into a hastily dug and ill-prepared hole in a bed of lily of the valley amidst currant bushes. The tree exploded into life, nourished by Grandma and surpassed all others planted in the front yards and back yards alike. She eventually moved the currant bushes, due to excessive shade, but the lily of the valley and spearmint flourished. She reminded us frequently how we had laughed when she planted her tree.

As she swiftly walked back the driveway, shoulders in opposing cadence with her stride, she would occasionally brush the back of her left hand against the back of her dress and across her buttocks. I would watch this swift march from our back porch and call, "Hi, Grandma."

She would continue swiftly, raise her right hand in a kind of regal, impersonal salute and continue her march.

I wasn't aware then of what was going on, although I do recall the putt, putt puttering as she walked swiftly back her driveway.

Now that I'm middle aged, I know that she wasn't so much in a hurry to go anywhere in particular, as she was in a hurry to escape the confines of her house, to relieve herself of gas and to brush herself clear of any odors, leaving them hurriedly behind.

Man's Best Friend

Big old dog! I can't tell you how big he was, because I was so small when we had Captain. His dog pen lay beyond the garage just before the garden plot. The cherry trees offered their shade in the morning and some other big old tree offered the same in the evening. A doghouse stood in the middle of the high fenced pen. Captain was some sort of retriever, I think. He got out of his pen only when Daddy let him out. We weren't allowed to let him out. When Captain's gate was opened he would tear around the home place and romp with Daddy, who complained he never really had time to train him as a good hunting dog. I don't know how often Captain got to show his stuff at the hunt, but he sure knew how to entertain his master and us kids. Daddy would fill a bucket with water. After showing a golf ball to Captain, Daddy would drop it in the bucket and it would sink to the bottom. Without hesitation, Captain would plunge his head into the pail and come up snorting with the ball in his mouth. I used to wonder what possessed him to do that. Did he open his eyes? How did he keep from drowning if he opened his mouth to get the ball?

Captain

Captain left one night. Sometime during the following day, when Mother discovered the pen was empty, she called Daddy at work. She seldom called him there. You were to call only in emergencies. This probably wasn't a real emergency, but I thought she did the right thing. After dinner that same evening, and in a drizzle, we got into the car and drove around the east side of town. It seemed to be as long a trip as from Indianapolis to Lanesville, Mother's birthplace. It finally got dark and was cold and damp. It was only 7:00 P.M., but it seemed like midnight to me. Daddy and Mother decided to give up looking for Captain. Daddy pulled into the service drive of the huge water tower at 10th and Arlington Streets to turn around to go home when two bright green eyes were reflected in the headlights. It was Captain! We took him home; he was thin and shivering. He died on the back porch the next day, releasing his runny brown bowels as he lay on his side, his back to the wall, head at the top of the basement stairs. His death prompted another call to Daddy at work.

We were sheltered from the labor of Captain's disposal. Someone came to pick him up. We didn't bury him like we did the pet parakeet, whose neck was broken in the pantry door. The parakeet belonged to my oldest brother Bill, who was away at GMI (General Motors Institute) in Flint, Michigan. With the bird on his shoulder, Tommy stepped into the dark kitchen pantry and closed the door to see what the bird would do. But, as he stepped in beside the trash can and pulled the door shut quickly, the bird scrambled through the air for the light and his neck was caught between the door and jamb. He plopped to the floor, jerked twice and was dead. Tommy felt really bad.

Anyway, after Captain, Spike appeared. Spike was a hound dog; a handsome, short, muscular, boxy-headed dog with long ears. He was a hunting dog, supposed to be good for tracking rabbit. I wasn't old enough to go hunting, but Daddy took the older ones. Daddy would go with Bill and Ron and sometimes with other folks. He always complained about Spike. Spike was considered a mean dog. Once, Grandma went with me to feed Spike in Captain's old pen, and he came at her. He didn't bite her, but she meant it when she called him a "sowmench." I think that's German for "son of a bitch."

Spike was chained to the doghouse, and he would frequently hang himself by jumping over the fence from the top of his house. The chain wasn't long enough for his feet to reach the ground on the other side and, because the doghouse weighed more than he did, he would hang himself. Spike tried different sides of the pen, but since the doghouse was in the center of the pen, it made no difference. So, no matter how smart he was to try different sides, it always came out the same. Dumb! Whoever saw Spike hanging would throw him back over, and he

Carol Ann, Linda Jane,
Dick, and Spike

would breath again. Usually, Mother was the one who saw him out the back kitchen window. She would tear outside and just throw him back over.

Tom, Dick, and Spike

Spike also bit Tommy's ear. Tommy liked to fold Spike's long ears between his thumb and the index finger and rub the pinched ear back and forth on itself. It felt as smooth as silk. On one of these occasions Spike nipped Tommy's ear.

Shortly after, on a hunting trip, Daddy came home without Spike or rabbits. He always said, "The dog ran a rabbit and never came back." Daddy claimed he called and looked for him for a long time. I think he shot Spike.

The following summer, Daddy came home from work and called me outside. As I stood nearby, he opened the back door of the car, picked up a rope and coaxed another hound dog out of the back seat floor. I was delighted, but I never forgot about Spike and my suspicion. Daddy told me how he bought the year old dog from some man at work who always kept the dog chained to a fence. The man described the area on the west side of Indianapolis as smoky. "That's it! We'll call him Smokey," I said.

Then, "Oh, can I name him?" I asked.

"Sure, he's yours," Daddy answered.

Smokey had quite a life at our house. He was well cared for. The routine was the same as for Spike; feed the dog and burn the trash. Table scraps were added to his can of food in moderation because after a dinner with five to seven kids at the table, there weren't many scraps left. The plates were scraped with a spoon into one as they were removed from the table and dog food added. I always enjoyed feeding the dog and burning the trash. You could dally and get out of the kitchen chores, a little while anyway.

The bag of trash was dumped into the fireplace and the dog fed and petted a little. Then the trash would be arranged a little until the various boxes and containers became a city. The match would be lit and strategically placed to represent a fire in an apartment, a fire in a factory, or a fire in an office building. The flame would slowly consume the city while sirens roared in the imagination and people screamed and raced to the outskirts (ants and spiders). The firemen never saved the city. It always burnt so fast, too fast, and the drama was over. Sometimes the brown grocery bag was placed in the chimney of the fireplace, open end down, and as the city was consumed, the bag would ignite, burn in a flash, and large chunks of ember lit shards of black paper were fired out of the flue by the heat of the updraft. The drama ended abruptly, often enough with, "Richard Louis, bring that plate in here now! We want to finish dishes!" It was frequently at the very height of the drama, but that was easily abandoned with the threat of reprisal in Carol Ann or Linda's voice calling from the back door.

Smokey was often unchained and allowed to run rabbits at the end of the lot. He ran rabbits well and frequently returned with blood all over his mouth, triumphant in the chase. I don't know if he just killed the rabbits he caught or actually ate his fill. I suspect he did both. Most probably, he only unearthed a litter and killed or ate the little helpless ones. I liked him anyway. He was my link to that wild side. I was secretly proud when he came back bloody and imagined he could provide for us both if need be.

Dick, Tom, and Smokey

Daddy took Smokey hunting only a few times, because, like Spike, he never performed like a hunting hound dog. Spike was his own dog and did as he pleased on a hunt, but from what I heard, Smokey was no good because he cowered in fear when the shotgun sounded. He soon began to cower on the ground in anticipation of the blast when anyone took aim. That was okay with me also. It didn't diminish his stature in my book. After all, I didn't like shotguns either. I understood.

When we went with Smokey to the end of the lot and Pogue's Run, he was glad we were with him, tail wagging, panting, nose to the ground. But, his nostrils soon tempted him away, and he was off on the chase. We almost always returned to the house without him, long bored with skipping stones or

launching a bottle into the creek and bombarding it with stones, while scrambling along the bank, until we hit and sank it.

During the summer, Smokey would pass the heat of the day dozing. I could lie in the grass in the sun and pat the ground next to me, calling him over, and he would stretch out on his side with his back next to me. He would doze while being petted or he was content to lay undisturbed.

He spent each winter outdoors until the temperature dropped and the wind howled and Mother felt that no amount of doghouse winterizing had been adequate. She would come to the foot of the stairs in the middle of the night, flip on the light and call quietly, "Dick, come and let the dog into the basement."

Smokey and Dick

Without hesitation, and thankful that she was so sympathetic; I would pull on my play clothes and bring him into the basement. A rug was spread on the concrete island next to the furnace and Smokey was content. He was tethered there so as to limit probable deposits in the laundry room area. Knowing he was warm and sound asleep made the return to my bed, after a "Thanks Mother," all the warmer.

During spring renovations to the yard, Smokey's doghouse was moved every few years because he destroyed the grass around his house to the extent that his chain allowed. He eventually wound up in front of the two-car brick garage daddy built out of the nine loads of brick he got at a dollar a load from the destruction of the old St. Francis de Sales School House. The school building was the traditional four rooms up, four rooms down, two story structure where my father, his sister, Aunt Gene, and other brothers and sisters had all gone to grade school as had all of us, except Tommy.

At sixteen, a sophomore in high school, I went to work at J.C. Penney's on the circle and worked every evening after school until 5:00 P.M. The bus to downtown was in front of Scecina and, books in hand; I caught it religiously each afternoon. I would arrive at 3:30 and go to work, picking up lay-aways throughout the three floors of the store, between "running packages" that customers finally paid off, some, 50 cents at a time. All new lay-aways would be shelved, hung or stored in Z - corner. The cards appropriately marked would be turned in to the office. The bell announcing the store's closure would sound, "bong, bong, bong, bong," and it was time to take the employee's cart of packages to the doors of the main floor. All the packages were sealed with a tag to be matched on exit by the employee. After delivering the cart of packages to the assigned department head on duty, I would return to the lay-away area on the second floor to relieve Mr. Williams, the store comptroller, my boss, at accepting the money bags. Exchanging each employees tag for their numbered moneybag, they were stored in stacks of tens in the money cart. The count of bags was reconciled and a tag yet on the board signaled a bag still out. When finally all were in, the heavy, money laden cart was shoved out of lay-away past the machines that clattered earlier, registering payments and the racks and racks of files holding cards with outstanding balances. The cart was left standing outside lay-away while I ran through the kitchen and into the employee's locker room to cut the lights on that part of the second floor. The cart was then pushed to the office area on the other side of the second floor, routing it past the elevators, and into the safe. The safe was secured, lights doused, and all left the store. I would hurry to Meridian Street to catch the East 21st Street bus in front of the Board of Trade Building. The ride home was quick enough and I looked forward to crossing 21st Street after the bus passed, and being greeted by the rattle of Smokey's chain as he came out of his doghouse to meet me on the gravel drive. I always went straight to him before I went in to the dinner that Mother kept warming on the stove.

One Saturday evening, I was walking up the gravel drive and reached the top of the little rise and realized I didn't hear Smokey's chain. I looked to the garage and the doghouse was gone.

"Oh, they've moved his doghouse again. I wonder where to?" I thought.

I went to the spot. It was raked clean and grass seed was already sprinkled about. I went around the West side of the garage and looked all about.

"Mother!" I called as I went bounding in the back door. Mother was re-warming dinner.

"Hi, Mother. Where's Smokey?" I asked.

She fumbled with the contents of the skillet and without looking at me she said, "You better ask your sister."

"Carol Ann?" I asked.

"Yes," she said

"Where is she?" I asked.

"In her bedroom," she answered.

"Carol Ann!" I called, and as she came out of her room I added, "Where's Smokey?"

She said, without hesitation, "I had him put to sleep."

"You what!! Why?!" I was dumbfounded.

"I took him to the pound and had him put to sleep. He was dribbling all over the place," she explained.

Smokey had lost bladder control and did drip. I suppose others said things in her defense or just said things. I don't know, I didn't hear them. I know Smokey had grown old, I just hadn't known when.

I did ask someone about his doghouse. It might have been Carol Ann, but I don't remember the exact answer she gave me. It was given to someone and I remember thinking how incredible this was that "they" were so thorough. Here I was at work at Penny's all day. I had gone out the front door to catch the bus that Saturday morning before anyone else was up, and while I was at work, Carol Ann and her accomplices had taken my dog to the pound, gotten rid of his house and cleaned up the site. At what point in the day did my wonderful friend die without being told good-bye?

I have forgiven Carol Ann and "them" inside, whoever they were, but I've never told them so. I think, though, until I tell them, I will not really have forgiven them. I don't think they even know they need my forgiveness. If they don't know it, then do they need it?

They were probably right in what they did in that Smokey needed merciful treatment, and it's with that reasoning I've forgiven. I haven't forgiven their failure to involve me in the decision or the lack of opportunity to face the truth and say good-bye to my friend.

Section 2

Family Ties

C.C.C.

There were a couple of rabbit hutches attached to the back of the wood frame garage. They were homemade and covered with chicken wire, top, sides, and bottom. The rabbits, stepping around on the chicken wire, must have hurt their feet; at least it seemed that way to me. They were large rabbits and were seldom taken out to play. My oldest brother, Bill, raised rabbits to eat, not as pets. "Hasenpfeffer," Grandma said. Bill did have a hard time killing them. He would take one from the cages by the ears and carry it into the garage and close the door. He would sit in the garage and pet the rabbit for a long time before he could finally hit it in the back of the head with a club. Sometimes hitting it once wasn't enough. That must have been tough because you can imagine how you could become attached. Mother would pass sentence, so to speak, by asking him to kill a couple of rabbits for dinner- hasenpfeffer. He would decide which ones and then often could hardly eat. On occasion, the female rabbit would kill her newborn before Bill got them separated. I believe she couldn't imagine living in such a small space with eight other rabbits and self-preservation kicked in. We were never allowed to open the cages and play with them but we did feed them clover through the chicken wire and we did stick our fingers through the wire to touch their sides and feel the soft, cool fur. There was a pet store smell about the rabbit hutches, probably the food pellets.

Carol Ann, Bill, Jerry, and Linda Jane with rabbits

It wasn't at the same time, but my second oldest brother, Ron, decided to raise chickens. Grandma had chickens for the eggs but Ron raised chickens for the chicken meat. He purchased a factory made chicken coop from friends of the family. It looked like a piece of cake and ice cream roll because of the shape. It had a little door on one end and two, four-pane windows on either side. The rounded roof was removable. It was hinged so that it could be lifted and raised while sliding it to one side. That way a person could stand up and clean the coop. I don't know if raising rabbits or chickens had anything to do with the war or the depression that followed, but I've wondered what would motivate parents to allow their oldest boys to engage in these activities.

Carol Ann, Dick, Mother, Linda Jane, and Jerry with rabbits

Ron received his live, golden little chicks in brown pasteboard boxes. The chicks would be released into the coop and a light bulb would often have to be left on all night for the warmth. The following day he would remove the dead chicks. Through the night, as they clamored for the warmth of the light bulb, some of those in the middle, nearest the bulb, would be crushed by the weight of the others. I'm not sure how successful Ron was at raising chickens but, ultimately, like the rabbit venture, the chicken raising came to an end. However, the big difference between the rabbits and the chickens was the coop. The hutches, one sunny afternoon, were unceremoniously dismantled. They were torn from the back of the frame garage and trashed but the coop underwent a transformation. Like Cinderella's pumpkin became her coach, the coop became our clubhouse. We worked several days cleaning it up. There was the sweeping, hosing, scrubbing, and splashing of bleach water that Mother had us do to make it safe and clean. It had to dry out forever before we were able to give it a fresh coat of white paint and finally seat ourselves inside of it, snug on throw rugs and old comforters. It was then that deliberations began on the name of the club.

Our club was finally named the "C.C.C." The three letters were painted above the little door in an arch and it stood for the "Catholic Children's' Club." The club was launched with five charter members and ended with the same membership. We had a president (Jerry), a vice president (Carol Ann) and a secretary (Linda Jane) although we did not keep minutes. We didn't recruit new members because we

39

didn't want other members. It was our club. Besides, the coop wasn't big enough for a larger membership body. Five was just right!

We had no by-laws, but what we did have was a self-imposed system of merits and demerits. There were no written guidelines for how you could earn merits or have them taken away. We sort of made that up as we went along. For example, complimenting another person, not just club members, by saying "that's a nice shirt," or "that's a good color for you," or "I like the way your hair looks," or "you look good today," and so on, you could earn one merit. Doing something nice for another person like taking out the trash when it was their job but they forgot or by making their bed or picking up their laundry and taking it to the hamper, earned a couple of merits. Cursing, teasing or making fun of another person meant demerits!

Holy card of St. Ann

The number of merits earned or lost was somewhat arbitrarily applied. It depended on the value of the nicety extended to another person or the severity of the infraction. As an example of an infraction consider this. Suppose you threw a green apple at another person. Questions to be considered would be, "Was it tossed to tease or thrown with force? Did it miss, tossed or thrown or did it strike? If it struck, was it tossed or thrown? Did it hurt or not? If it hurt, how much? And, did the perpetrator laugh or apologize immediately?" You get the point. It was very complicated. Imagine the number of demerits you could receive if you threw the green apple with malice, intending to strike the person and do harm and you did, it hurt a lot, leaving a red mark or bruise and then you laughed at the "cry baby!" Ha! Name calling besides! It could add up. At weekly club meetings, all of these things were hashed out. Under scrutiny, however, lies were told and denials prevailed as well as false claims of good deeds.

Of course, someone had to keep the book in which were added merits earned and demerits deducted. These records were tallied weekly at our regular C.C.C. meeting. Changes were made at the meeting as the individuals recalled events not recorded. At the end of the tally some one of the membership was recognized for having earned the greatest number of merits for that week. After a few weeks, it became clear that the person who kept the book was always the winner, Carol Ann, the vice president. I've often wondered if she added merits to her column. I mean, she kept book on everybody and the book was with her all the time. Having the book, she could see, in an on-going way, where she stood. She might have emerged from her room with the knowledge of where she stood, said three nice things and go right back to her room to post the profits.

In recognition of being the week's first place earner of the most merits, a little something or another, like a holy card, was presented. The system went by the wayside soon enough because at least four members lost interest due to the lack of positive reinforcement (no prizes).

The chicken coop was eventually moved to the cottage at Graybrook Lake and used as a storage shed until it also went by the wayside due to a lack of paint. It fell to flames consuming termites and all - set afire where it stood. I thought we should have set it afire at home after the first meeting of the C.C.C.

Addendum to C.C.C.

Here is a copy of the original record of merits and demerits for the members of the Catholic Children's' Club. Carol Ann was the "grand prize" winner, her name boldly outlined in addition to her hand-scrawled announcement at the bottom of the first page of the record.

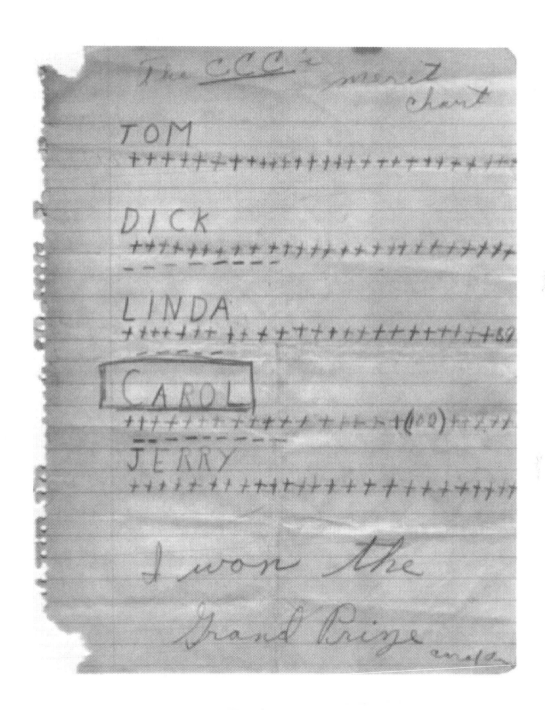

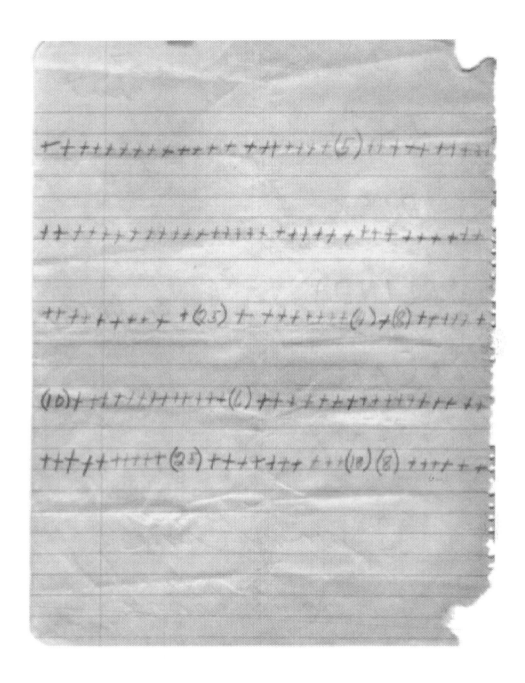

+++++++++/++++++H++   82

8+5   64

                                    261
+++++++56++++++++++++++12+2

            267
++ 77-16++/+8

                    136
+++++++++++++5+5++++++7+

Tommy earned 82 merits over the four or five week period that the club existed and received no demerits - the numbers check out!

Linda Jane earned 266 merits less the 5 demerits for a total of 261 - the numbers check out!

Carol Ann earned 276 merits less the 9 demerits for a total of 267 - the numbers check out!

Jerry earned 136 merits and received no demerits - the numbers check out!

However, I only earned 69 merits over the four or five-week period the C.C.C. was active, less my eight demerits for a total of 61, yet the record shows 64.

I cannot figure out what might have generated the parenthetical figures in Tommy's, Linda Jane's, Carol Ann's, and Jerry's recorded line of merits. Some of them are extraordinarily large, i.e. "102" and "77" in Carol Ann's line; "89," "25" and "56" in Linda Jane's line; and "25" and "18" in Jerry's line of merits. These three all have other figures in their lines. Tommy has one "5" and I only have extra numbers of "8" and "5" tacked on the end. Even if my figure were accurately tallied, I still clearly came in last.

The order of first to last at the finish was Carol Ann, Linda Jane, Jerry, Tommy, and Dick. I have some questions!

Connections

In Indianapolis, as was true of everywhere else in the country, when telephones were introduced to the home, "party lines" were available. They were less expensive by the month than a private line. A party line meant that your telephone was on the same service as that of another home telephone line. The telephone company instructed the homeowner what to listen for in order to know that a call was meant for them. Our particular ring was two short rings and a long one while the other household on the same line was one short ring and one long. I never understood how the caller got the correct household when both had the same numbers until I grasped the concept of the operator. On a party line, you knew when the others were receiving a call because of the ring but you never knew when they were making a call and were using the line. Often times, if we wanted to make a call and picked up the receiver, there was conversation on the line meaning the other household on the party line was using the system. With a brief "Oh, sorry," the receiver would be hung up and the wait to use the phone would begin. The only way to find out if your line was free to place a call was to pick up the receiver and hope for a dial tone. Otherwise, the brief apology was in order. Party line members often got angry with their other party line members, though they never knew who they were or where they lived, for taking so much time on the phone. On the other hand, there was a great deal of cooperation because if you needed the line in an emergency, they would hang up and open the line for your use.

We did not have a party line as long as Aunt Gene and Grandma. We, soon, were the proud owners of the private line. There were nine people in our home, including five teenagers. The line was private until Mother called Lanesville, Indiana, her birthplace. About twice a year Mother would place a call to her home place in Lanesville to talk to her sisters, my Aunts, Bertilla and Olive. When she decided to place the call, she informed those in the house what she was about to do and called us to her skirt to stand by. We would fumble about on the linoleum of the kitchen floor and wait, bored.

Her conversation went something like this:

(Mother) "Oh darn, I got a busy signal." We began to scatter and Mother would say, "No, no. Come back here. I must have dialed wrong. I'll try again." She dialed again as we regrouped at her feet.

(Mother) "Hello, Virginia?,... Yes, this is Ceal in Indianapolis. Connect me with 1524,.....thank you....Yes,...no, everyone is fine....OK, yes, yes, I will....Thanks!" We waited while the telephone at 1524 rang.

(Mother) "Hello, Till, this is Ceal.....no, everyone is fine...no, everything is OK." They always assumed the worst, otherwise, why would anyone be making a long-distance call when sending a letter was so much less expensive? Mother continued, "I just wanted to call to let you know we are well and to see if everything and everyone was OK there.....Yes, we are doing fine......No, Art is in the other room.....What?.....Oh, hello Hilda, how is George.....Good!....Till!, I think Hilda is on the line....Yes, Virginia must have connected her...Yes....Well, whenever I call the word goes out.....Yes, it does. It's good to hear your voices! You sound so clear. I wish we were as close as.....What!?....Oh, hello, Cornelia!....Cornelia is on the line. Cornelia, how are you?.....Yes, we are all fine. I just decided to call home to say hello. How is Uncle Dominic?.....Oh, I see....OK. No, thanks, we are all fine....No they are all here, everyone is well, thank goodness! OK, Good-bye Cornelia. Yes, good-bye,....I love you too.....Till? Hilda?, are you still there?.....Oh, thank goodness! I didn't, know if you got cut off or not. Oh, Olive.....Till must have put you on while Cornelia was on the line.....Oh, you heard all of that?......No, they are all here and I want them to say hello......Yes.....Yes.....Everyone is fine.....What?....Oh, hello Germaine, and who else is on the line, is that you Oneda?....Yes, we are all OK. I hope everything is OK with you also?.....Good......Oh?.....Good......Oh, that's wonderful!....Good, I'm glad for you. Say hello to all your families for me....Yes, thank you.....thank you...yes, I love you too. I'll write soon.....Yes, I'll tell him.....OK, thanks and good-bye.....Yes, thanks.....Olive and Hilda, I want the kids to say hello.....No, it will just take a minute.....Its not costing too much. Here, wait, this is Tommy."

"Tommy, say hello to Aunt Hilda," Mother instructed as she handed the receiver to Tommy.

"Hello, Aunt Hilda....Yes, I'm fine......Oh? Hello Aunt Till." Tommy says.

"Speak louder," instructed Mother for she realized Aunt Till was again on the line and Aunt Till was very hard of hearing.

So Tommy would shout, "Hello Aunt Till."

The passing of the receiver went on like this on both ends for about five minutes, Virginia, the operator in Lanesville continuing to take it upon herself to plug other people into the conversation she just knew Mother would "want to say hello to."

After we finished our turn on the telephone, we were free to go and Mother was left to say her goodbyes. I could hear her from the dining room saying how much she missed them, how much she wished they lived closer, that she would write soon and that they should tell anyone who had not been on the phone with them that she sends her greetings and those of "Art as well." Art, Daddy, never got on the phone but continued to read the daily newspaper in the living room.

"Thank you.....thank you...yes, I love you too. I'll write soon.....Yes, I'll tell him...." Mother concluded.

These infrequent calls were important but draining on Mother. You could see both the joy and the sadness in her face as she finally hung up the receiver, sometimes a tear or two, while smiling, would spill from her eyes before she could catch them with the apron she took from her waist.

Sunday Relaxation

In my childhood, Sundays were a day of rest and relaxation. Sundays began with 9:00 a.m. Mass at St. Francis de Sales unless we were going to Lanesville then we went to the 6:00 A.M. Mass. After Mass and breakfast we would celebrate birthdays, have company or visit other families. We stayed in our good clothes longer on Sunday than on any other day and lined up in various groupings for pictures by the spiraea bushes in front of our home - Mother wielding the telescopic Kodak.

(Left to Right in back) Bill, Mother, Daddy, Ron
(Left to Right in front) Jerry, Linda Jane, Tom, Carol Ann, Dick

In the summer, our Sunday relaxation took several forms that often only involved our family. I remember the gatherings and visits and celebrations and pictures and so on, when the good clothes and shoes stayed on, but the fondest and warmest memories are of the Sundays spent with just the immediate family. A Sunday drive in the car was such an event. We would head east on 21st Street. The first site just up the street to be pointed out was Black's house, Mother and Daddy's first house, Harry's Grocery Store, Naval Avionics and then country.

Harry's Store was really small and sat at the corner of Drexel and 21st Street, about four blocks from our home. It seems to me we went to Harry Grassoff's Grocery at least once each day, sometimes twice, either because we forgot something or Mother forgot something. I can still see the store's interior clearly. The bell on the door tinkled when you went in. The floor was wooden and worn. It creaked in places. Harry cut the meat, weighed it and wrapped it in brown paper. He secured it with paper tape and marked the price on the paper with a grease pencil that he always tucked behind his ear, all in one motion. He stocked the shelves and helped us find the items we couldn't find. He reached those we couldn't reach, and he checked us out. If there were more than one customer, he was everywhere doing everything, but he always had time.

He also "carried" people. The money Mother sent went on the account; what we purchased went there also. Harry was a very nice man of some unknown nationality. He didn't seem American to me but more middle-eastern and mysterious. He was a small man. Some years later, he hired a neighbor, Josephine, as his check out clerk.

When the store "Walt's" opened at 21st and Linwood, only one block from home, we stopped going to Grassoff's Grocery with our wagon. That's too bad because Walt's didn't carry anyone for anything. Walt's was more like the Standard Store in Brightwood where we did our weekly, heavy shopping on Friday or Saturday evenings. When Walt's opened, Harry's soon closed. Even round shouldered Josephine left Harry's and took a checkout job at Walt's. At Walt's and Standard, you paid as you "goed."

We still had to go to the drugstore for Alophon pills for Daddy. The drugstore was just across the street from Harry's, and when I went there I always wondered about Harry and how he was doing.

I stared in awe at Naval Avionics as we passed and was sorry we lived so close. As I recall, they made bombing sights during the Second World War. I figured this place was marked for an atom bomb when we were attacked and we wouldn't stand a chance at home. Even in school at St. Francis, I thought it was ridiculous that we practiced the "duck and cover" method of survival practice when Naval Avionics was so close. Remember the drill? "When you see the flash, duck and cover." Duck and cover meant we were to crouch under our desk in a little ball and cover our heads and face with our hands and arms. If we were forewarned enough, we could go from the classrooms into the hallway and duck and cover there. What a joke! But it gave us the hope that we could survive the atom bomb, and hope was important. Anyway, on to the country to enjoy this day.

There were berries to look for, the old persimmon tree, paw paws and walnuts. We would visit Geist Reservoir. Parking the car, we walked to the dam and visited the spillway. What a sight: the blue-green, deep water behind the huge curved concrete top of the dam and the green, mossy, slimy face of the spillway with a steady curtain of water pouring over! I marveled at how "they" got the thing so level at such a span so that the water flowed over so evenly. This, to me, was the beginning of Fall Creek.

Dick and Jerry at Geist

I was amazed that we always found our way home from Geist. I never believed I could ever find my way to Geist and back. I know I couldn't then, and I'm not so sure today. Fall Creek Parkway, the bridge to cross and the embankment, was much like the cliff at our Pouge's Run, where people fired at targets into the dirt. I wonder how much lead from rifles and shotguns has been pumped into that hillside.

After several stops to do or see this or that, all familiar sights, and when we were on our way home, the notorious five in the back seat would put heads together and raise an agreed upon shout for watermelon or ice cream.

"Okay let's go, one, two, three ...." Jerry would conduct and the chorus was raised.

"We want ice cream, we want ice cream, we want ice cream. I scream, you scream, we all scream for ice cream," and so on.

We would laugh and roll about in the back seat, exaggerating our inability to stay upright at corners and continuing our chant, sometimes mistakenly chanting for watermelon too late in the summer season. If that were pointed out by Mother, we would readily switch to ice cream, knowing the power we wielded and that the Blue Ribbon on 10th Street always had ice cream no matter what the season.

Whatever the chant, Mother and Daddy would talk quietly to one another above the din and frolic in the back seat. While we chanted, we carefully watched this consultation, poking and congratulating each other, for, we always got our wish, seasonal or otherwise.

I suspect, when we went on these trips, Mother and Daddy had financially planned to be able to meet our "demands" else we didn't go for such drives, but we knew no better. We knew from the start, when a Sunday drive was suggested, that we would endure the scenes and raise a chant on the return trip. I don't know who knew we were near the home place to suggest we begin the chant to divert the driver, Daddy. I suspect it was Jerry and Carol Ann. It was a game.

And so we would wind up stopping at a roadside market for watermelon or at the Blue Ribbon Ice Cream Parlor for ice cream.

If we got a watermelon, we took it home, arriving about dusk, and invited Grandma and Aunt Gene to join us. Newspapers were spread on the back steps of our home and the watermelon was cut and passed out piece by piece. Seeds were spit in all directions but usually "accidentally" at each other, and friendly

fights ensued with rind and watermelon juice and mosquitoes. Not to worry, as amid the laughter and chase, we could be hosed down along with the steps.

I remember once when fastidious Linda was particularly annoyed with Little Tom and warned him only once that if he did whatever it was he was doing "one more time," he would be sorry. He did. With the scooped out butt end of the watermelon in her right hand, she chased him down, and very quickly, I might add. She caught him with her left hand, and there, for all to see, whipped him to the ground. As he sat up, she plopped the watermelon bowl on top of his burr cut head and ground it back and forth as though she were grinding the juice from half an orange. Juice ran down all around and Grandma whooped and laughed, Daddy too, while Mother called out "Linda Jane!" as though she would stop. When Linda Jane decided to, she stopped and walked back and plopped the rind into the bucket and smacked her hands as if brushing them off, congratulating herself for having accomplished a difficult task so handily and easily.

If we got ice cream from Blue Ribbon, we took it home, and, after inviting Grandma and Aunt Gene to join us, it was taken into the kitchen and served in bowls. Mother and Daddy decided what to buy. Daddy's favorite was black walnut but that was more expensive. Vanilla was the standby. Neopolitan was often the choice for it was a layered combination of vanilla, strawberry and chocolate. They usually purchased two one quart blocks or one half gallon in the blue and white thick paper wrapping.

In our kitchen, the block laid open, would be sliced into squares with the same butcher knife used to dissect a watermelon. Ice cream was always served with ice water.

I remember the "pop" of the watermelon and the familiar rip of the paper wrapping under the knife. What wonderfully caring, responsive parents, the best in the world!

Other Sunday relaxation affairs were Fall Creek fishing trips. Preparations for these trips began Saturday evening as the sun went down. Daddy would begin to "water the lawn," or so it appeared to me. When I was sure the grass had enough, he would still sit on the steps at the back door and spray the yard, brown beer bottle in hand - Schlitz.

When enough water had been sprayed over the back yard, he would come in the house and wait awhile. Then he would get a flashlight and invite his children to the harvest. We were instructed to be quiet and to step lightly. We were going to harvest night crawlers.

I had seen robins do it after a rain. They were real good at it. We had turned over boards and stones and had discovered huge pink-banded worms that we picked up on sticks, hoes, or shovels and carried them to Grandma's chickens. The chickens were delighted and competed for the fat, cool, damp worms. We enjoyed watching them compete as we dangled the long, slimy things from the transporter. I was amazed at how long they could get before they snapped and curled about the hen's beak. The hens also seemed amazed that a squirming worm suddenly surrounded their beaks, but putting their beaks to the ground, they clawed the worm off and devoured them cleanly.

So we were going to catch night crawlers! I learned that the water filled their burrows and they came up for air to keep from drowning. Stepping lightly into the cool, glistening grass, the flashlight casting its beam, Daddy would suddenly thrust his hand into the grass and triumphantly say "Ah ha!" Pulling easily, the worm would slip from the hole in the ground and he would place it into a one pound coffee can that he had saved for the harvest.

If you approached heavily on foot, the vibration would drive the worm underground as if it were a stretched rubber band suddenly released. I came upon two huge worms at the same time. They were lying next to each other. I was going to get two at once! Training the light on them in my left hand, I slowly moved my right hand above them, secretly hoping a vibration of some sort would cause me to miss. I thrust my hand on the pair and lost them both in opposite directions but was left with the milky white, sticky residue all over my palm and fingers. I learned later they were "mating." This was enough for me. I couldn't wash my hands at the back porch sink fast enough.

Sunday morning, after church, we went fishing on Fall Creek with the harvested worms. Daddy, and whomever, would fish while Mother scoured the banks for berries. The younger children would be allowed to stay in the car and listen, much to our frightened delight, to such programs on the car radio as "The Creaking Door" and "The Shadow Knows."

"Who knows what evil lurks in the hearts of men? The Shadow Knows," a deep voice would say. The screams, shouts and hugs of delight at the mere introductions of those programs are vivid. Forget the stories, the intros were enough!

On occasion, with Daddy still fishing and baiting his hook with Saturday evening's night crawlers, Mother would drive home from the Fall Creek site and make fudge and popcorn for snacks and then return.

These were the relaxing but emotionally exhausting Sundays I remember most. Chanting for watermelon or ice cream or screaming at the intro of "The Creaking Door," all in a car that transported us as a family into our imaginations and the power we thought we held over our parents.

Jessie is Biting the Cherry Tree

We had cherry trees. There were three. Actually, we had only one and Grandma and Aunt Gene had two. Well . . "we" had three. Very soon after the tulips, daffodils, hyacinths, Easter eggs, narcissus and some garden planting, the cherries were ready for picking. The cherries seemed to take forever to ripen each season but in retrospect, it really happened very fast. Searching the tree each day for the first ripe cherry made it seem forever.

The cherry trees would bloom in a cloud of white blossoms and very soon after, the old apple tree would bloom. The apple blossoms were much more attractive to me. They were a rosy pink, clustered at the tip of each new growth of leaves, and more evenly spread over the tree so that you could appreciate the contrasts of color and texture. The cherry trees bloomed without greenery, and so abundantly that the tree was simply white. Like forsythia, they couldn't seem to wait for contrast.

The little green cherries appeared with the leaves and before long, we were eating semi-ripe cherries, forcing the issue and suffering the consequences.

Cousin Jessie had other needs.

Cousin Jessie lived in a two-room house in back of Grandma's house behind the grape arbor and the chicken coop. She lived there with her parents, my Uncle France, the plumber, his wife Simone, and her brothers. Aunt Simone was French and was a great storyteller. She loved exaggeration and had the ability to turn everyone's everyday life situations into a very funny account with her story telling gift. She was most always the principal character in her stories, and she really enjoyed telling them. I don't think she was ever totally accepted by Grandma as the person her baby should have married.

Cousin Jessie wouldn't go after the cherries. Putting her arms around the trunk of the tree and tilting her head vampire-like, she'd bite into the amber bulbs that mysteriously appeared only on cherry trees.

We never saw them start, we never saw them grow, they were just there. A hard shiny smooth outer skin covered a thick soft inner core of a very sticky, amber colored substance, which was probably concentrated tree sap.

We often peeled them from the tree like jewels from a crown but never thought of putting them in our mouths. I don't even know what we did with them after we pulled them from the tree except throw them away, being careful that the gooey inner core never touched flesh or clothing. They were beautiful to look at and to feel, and they were fun to peel from the tree. Only Jessie knows the taste, except maybe Carol Ann who would try anything once.

Cousin Jessie was admonished by her parents, Aunt Gene, and Grandma for biting and eating these jewels, but we would laugh and encourage her and, I suppose, admire her for her bravery. We would simply announce to our parents, "Jessie is biting the cherry trees again."

I suppose the report went to her parents via some route, but it never changed her behavior as far as I know. Even today I'm tempted to bite the cherry tree jewels, but I'm sure I never will.

For us, the cherry trees meant picking with sticky juice running to the elbow, pitting, eating, pit spitting and canning. It took a lot of work gathering the cherries and a lot of sore feet standing on the rungs of a ladder or in the fork of a tree reaching further than you knew you should for safety's sake. The cherries became cobbler and pies. I wonder if the jewels could be harvested and made into syrup for pancakes. Unlike maple syrup that has to be boiled down to a concentrate, this might be like a concentrate to which you would have to add water.

Our Pool

To cross 21st Street and play in the fields south of us was a common occurrence. The five of us would be laboriously bundled into clothing we didn't quite feel we needed, to protect us against "the elements." If we were to be really protected against the elements, it would probably have been better if we hadn't been allowed to cross south of 21st Street in the first place. South of 21st lay cornfields, cows and open, four-sided foundation ditches filled with rainwater.

Carol Ann, Tom, Jerry, Dick, and Linda Jane

Mother gave us our liberties to be and to explore in spite of parental anxieties or relief from having us underfoot. She had cleaning rituals, born and nurtured in her childhood, which she religiously adhered to.

This was probably why she allowed us to go, good for us to get the fresh air. I remember "spring cleaning" the most vividly. Part of that ritual was to wash the windows throughout the house. Now that made sense to me, for having done so, everything seemed fresh and renewed. It's a lot like washing the windows on your car. Never mind the body - just wash inside and outside the windows of your car, and it's like the whole automobile is clean. Wash your car and fail to do the windows, and it's like you haven't washed your car at all. But, another part of spring-cleaning made little sense and seemed to be without real purpose, and that was to turn the mattresses and dust the wire springs with a special brush. The long-nose cone shaped dusting brush had to be inserted into the throat of each spring and vigorously twisted to dislodge a year's accumulation of whatever. After this was completed, the springs were re-covered and the mattress, turned side for side and end for end, and replaced. I remember wondering, on going to bed after spring-cleaning, if my head was now resting above where my feet used to be. Yech! Still, it all came out fresh.

It was on one of these forays in the early spring, south of 21st Street, that we happened upon what would become many a summer's day joy, our "pool." We had spent hours playing over and around the mounds of dirt excavated from the trenches, somewhat square in shape, that would be poured with concrete to form the footings of future homes. The trenches were laden with rainwater, as they had stood at least a year without further development. A small child, such as some of us were, could have slipped into one of these trenches and, burdened with clothing meant to protect us against the elements, been slowly dragged under as the clothing soaked up the water.

It didn't happen.

Equally perilous to life and limb of heavily clothed children was a "lake" which existed near 16th and Sherman, behind an old glass works; a plant where my Daddy had briefly been employed. While he worked there, he made a marble, miniature, coffin-like box, which my Mother proudly cherished. I've never quite assimilated that period of his employment with the period of railroad work, his father's career and his employment with Chevrolet's truck and body plant on the west side of Indianapolis. Nonetheless, the lake existed. We often went there, and on one occasion discovered, half buried in mud at the shore's edge, a metal box. The box was approximately 2 feet wide, 6 feet long, and 2 feet deep. Once excavated from the sediment, it became our ship and we briefly poled ourselves about the surface of the lake.

This was salvage; our secret. We left it briefly, a week or two, continuing to use it to pole around the lake, with plans to bring the salvage home, and that we did! This magnificent find, once a ship, hauled home on the wagon, became our backyard summertime swimming pool. We were sure we were the envy of all the world's children. We had a pool!

The hose would fill the pool; it took forever! It was set out in the backyard, West of the white, wood frame garage, under the clotheslines. We couldn't use the pool on washdays. Mom hung the wash on the wire stretching from house to pole, after wiping it down with an old rag. She meticulously sorted the wash as she hung it so that the articles of clothing were hung together, in perfect order, with seams and sock heels all facing the same way. There was great pride taken in how the wash was hung for the benefit

Dick, Carol Ann, Linda
Jane, Tom, and Jerry

of the neighbors and self. "Hang a proud wash!" I've often wondered to what extent a person would go if, after hanging their wash in a perfect symmetrical chain of clothes and wooden pins, they discovered a piece in the bottom of the basket that was missed and if now hung, would be out of sequence. Would all be rearranged so that the overlooked piece assumed its rightful position? I sometimes think that's why tall grass existed, or lawn chairs, so those pieces could be discreetly spread below the neighbor's view to dry at the sun's will. What a labor! Sheets are at their best when sun dried.

But, wash day aside, summer and no school, let's fill the pool, our prize! The tin box, dragged out into the sun, would be filled with maybe 18 inches of cold, cold water. And then came the change into our pool attire as the water warmed in the sun. I was definitely the most conspicuous. I was skinny. I was not thin, I was intolerably skinny, and I shivered in 90 degrees. The trunks I wore, string tied, were like men's boxer underwear on a thin legged stork. There was little to keep them up except hipbones and constant retying. But, preoccupation with appearance soon gave way at the encouragement of brothers and sisters and fun in our pool. Never mind that once wet, the trunks seemed to display what very little manhood there was to hide. We sometimes swam in our underwear.

Aunt Hilda, Tom, Carol Ann,
Linda Jane, Dick, and Jerry

We dove like Olympians from a wooden stepladder into our pool. One after another, laughing, we displayed our original styles, playing follow the leader for what seemed like hours, swimming and splashing from ladder end and back. We marveled at the whitened and wrinkled skin of our fingertips, testimony that we had actually been swimming as long as anyone could imagine. In our minds, this placed us among the bravest, the wealthiest, having the most endurance, for we had our pool, and we knew how to use it.

Our pool box ultimately became a worm farm, or so it was meant, beside a woodpile at our self-made cottage in Owen County at Spencer, Indiana. The time the worm farm was discovered flooded with rainwater, in spite of the cover, it never smelled so bad as it did then. All the night crawlers harvested from our lawn, had drowned. We had survived the ditches, the lake and the pool. We had learned to dunk our heads beyond the crown, under water, and come up safe again. We were certainly better swimmers than worms. We certainly smelled better in life than they did in death.

The metal box was unceremoniously drained by poking holes in its sides and dumped. It could never be used again, for anything.

Horse Tea

Grandma loved to work in the yard. She hated to be inside when the weather accommodated the human body in a housedress outside. She fiddled endlessly in the yard, humming some old German tune or arguing out loud with nature and its continuous assault on an eclectic, weed less, flower filled environment. However unorthodox some of her gardening practices, things seemed to flourish under her care. She watered endlessly. She didn't deep water, but she directed the harsh spray of the hose full force on the plants, causing them to hiss and their leaves to flap as though a tropical rainstorm had suddenly struck. She often cultivated around the base of the plants with the full force of the water from the nozzle of the hose, leaving holes in the ground, splattering dirt from around the base of the plants and exposing the delicate, hair-like bleached roots. Yet, things flourished. She watered the surface intermittently throughout hot summer days. She wet the leaves in the heat of the day, but I don't recall anything in her bountiful yard that appeared scorched, brown-spotted or wilted.

Criticism or advice by me from my scant knowledge of plants, based on a book or pamphlet, was humorous to her. Though she listened, she did as she always did, but she made me feel she respected my view. Whatever I did in our yard, according to the book or pamphlet, she always exceeded.

Aunt Gene did the planting, mostly, and I learned how to plant bulbs from her. I would usually dig a nice straight furrow or follow a border to the required depth and set the bulbs in the bottom, one following the other, at a distance of six inches or so. She, on the other hand, would dig a bed with the width of a spade or more and randomly place the bulbs in the trench and then cover them up. I challenged her on this one fall when she was planting tulip bulbs.

Mother with tulip soldiers

"What are you doing Aunt Gene?" I asked.

"Planting tulips," she replied.

"Why such a ditch?"

"A ditch! What do you mean?"

"Well you don't need such a wide ditch to plant tulips," I explained.

"Well, no you don't if you want your tulips standing like soldiers in a nice straight row, single file like you do! Then they look planted, more artificial. I like things to look more natural," she answered.

After observing her tulip bed the following spring and comparing hers to what I had planted, I had to admit she had been right. I've never since planted bulbs in a nice straight line but more clustered, more eclectic.

Pamphlets I read about gardening never mentioned horse tea. When Grandma discussed the merits of horse tea for plants, she salivated as though she were talking about a delicious German dish fit for human consumption. For her, plants were living organisms that liked to be served a varied diet. After all, she wouldn't eat the same menu of prepared foods day after day, so why would plants want to, she reasoned. So, she prepared horse tea.

I recall her excitement when once we were sitting on her porch on a hot summer day and a horse-drawn wagon came up the street. It was a buckboard style wagon on automobile tires and made no noise except for the horse and driver. The black man at the reins called out, "Rags, old rags, old iron, rags, any old rags, old iron." He didn't look right or left but kept his eyes on the reins in his hands, his elbows resting on his knees in the heat of the sleepy day. His greasy, soiled hat shaded his head, and except for his hypnotic chant, he appeared to be asleep.

His passing, at first, disturbed us only slightly, as Grandma explained in answer to my question, that he collected old rags and old iron for sale as scrap. His wagon slowly passed in front of Grandma's house behind the klop, klop, klop of the horse's shod hooves on the brick.

Suddenly, Grandma came to life. Her eyes widened, she gasped a little. I looked to the street and the passing ragman's wagon and back to her and asked, "What is it, Grandma?"

I half expected to see the worst as I raised myself high enough to peer over the porch railing from the glider. She was seeing a gift.

"Horse Shit!" she quietly exclaimed.

"What?" I said.

"Horse Shit," she said. "The horse on the wagon left his mark."

So what, I thought. She was up, and Lassie, her dog, jumped down.

"Dickie, quick, go get a pail and shovel." Then she added, "Hurry, before old lady Smith sees it out there."

I felt the urgency in her voice. There was a prize to be had, but fresh horseshit?? Needless to say, I was puzzled. It smelled, even from the porch. It was golden brown, shiny and wet and had plopped to the street from beneath the horse's tail. The horse didn't miss a step in the process, and the wagon master didn't flinch, cover his nose or miss a cadent call for rags and iron.

In spite of the calm delivery of the gift, and without missing a beat, our peaceful solitude seemed turned into pandemonium. The wagon passed on.

At her command, and still puzzled, I was on my way to the garage. She called me "Dickie' whenever she wanted me to do something just like Carol Ann and Linda Jane did when they wanted a favor. I returned to the street with a coal shovel and a basket, a bushel basket. I had no idea how much there would be. She was across the street, lifting her right shoulder, then her left, in nervous anticipation, the old damp washcloth hanging around her neck. She assisted my crossing, and with shovel in hand, boldly retrieved the gift from the brick pavement, between traffic, scoop after scoop, until she was satisfied and she had all there was.

"Okay, let's go," she said.

I took one handle of the basket, and she took the other. She held onto the shovel and kept checking to be sure she missed nothing as we crossed the street. She was more concerned for what she may have missed than any on-coming traffic.

"What is this for?" I asked.

"This is plant food. This is the best food in the world. It's good for everything."

"Really!!?" I was astonished.

The bottom of the basket was covered, and I worried that I had made a poor choice of containers from my parent's garden stock - maybe it would never come clean again. I broke out in a sweat.

Knowingly she said, "You were really quick, Dickie. Don't worry about the basket. We'll hose it out."

"Oh, sure." I thought.

Grandma went right to work. She dragged out an old galvanized chicken feeder and inverted it in a slight depression she had made in the Shasta daisy and iris bed. As instructed, I pulled the hose to her from the side of the house. She dumped the horse manure into the container and then she directed the full force from the hose into the smelly pot. It hissed, boiled and foamed-a brown foam. She filled it to the top.

"What are you doing that for, Grandma?" I asked.

"This is horse tea," she answered.

"Horse tea! For horses?" I exclaimed.

She laughed a genuine raucous laugh and answered, "No, you ninny, for my plants."

She placed the base of the chicken feeder on top as a lid and patted it proudly as though she had just closed a safety deposit box on a fortune. She went on to explain.

"In a few days, after the sun has heated and fermented this concoction, I'll take dippers full off the top and put it on my plants, and I'll keep adding water until I've gotten all the good out of it that I can."

She did just that, more earnest in attending to the needs of her yard plants than to the needs of her house. When nasty weather set in, you could attack the dust in the house if you had to.

Besides horse tea, she mulched, sprayed, dusted, and pruned. She watered and weeded. Her unorthodox methods paid off because she combined her methods with a profound respect for plants and an appreciation for and an understanding of their needs, needs she met and rejoiced in supplying. It was

always more important for her to feed a summer's bounty than to clean, especially on a hot summer's day in a house dress.

Home Delivery

The big old truck would lumber into the gravel driveway, rocking back and forth through the minor chuckholes, and stir up a little white dust. Twenty-first Street was a relatively quiet, two-lane, brick street and with the doors and windows of the house open in the summer you could hear the truck's engine and the gravel crunching under the tires. These sounds announced the arrival of the Crosstown Bakery truck, our Omar man! Fresh baked goods delivered to your door daily, if you wanted, or on whatever schedule you arranged with them. Ours came once every two weeks in the early morning around 7:30 A.M. The Crosstown Bakery delivered warm doughnuts, rolls, coffee cakes, bread and even pies.

As the truck slowly rolled to a stop, we were out the front door having announced his arrival to mother. The driver would slide the truck door open, step out and walk to the back of the truck where we were all waiting. This is where we wanted to be when he opened the two large doors because we didn't want to miss the wonderful odors that cascaded from the racks of trays confined in the truck. Everyone must like the smell of fresh baked dough goods in whatever form.

Excited, delighted comments about the smell aside, we turned our attention to Mother's transactions to see what was in store for this day's breakfast. We always hoped for the cake and yeast doughnuts. The first one to get into the bag at the breakfast table searched for the yeast doughnut which was the heaviest because it would have a glob or pocket of sugar glaze concentrated in the dough and it was the best. Mother would close her deal and come in to supervise further doughnut distribution.

The other home delivery system to which we subscribed, like thousands of others, was that of the milkman. The quart bottles of milk and juice, tinkling in the wire carrying case, would be deposited one by one in the insulated box sitting on the back steps. Mother would complete an order form that was slipped the night before into a clip on the inside of the lid of the piano hinged box. If she forgot, the milkman guessed and he was usually close enough. This delivery often came before the family was up and, like Crosstown Bakery, the bill was settled once every two weeks. Mother got up early to take care of that.

We never had ice blocks delivered on a regular basis in my lifetime although ice trucks or horse drawn wagons were still very much around. We did have ice delivered every now and again for special occasions for cooling watermelons or tubs of bottled beer. I remember the spray of tiny ice chips as the block was jabbed again and again with the ice pick to fracture it and break it into smaller pieces. I liked to watch it fracture deep within the crystal clear block as it took on a light blue hew and imagine I was watching a diamond cutter skillfully at work.

Once a month, the insurance man would come to the door to collect premiums. I don' know for what kind of insurance, but he came for years on a regular basis. He was a large man who always wore a white shirt and tie, his girth challenging the buttons of his shirt, especially when he sat down. Mother would sit on the other end of the couch and he would lay open his narrow but fat account book on the coffee table. She would hand him seven pennies. He would count them and record the payment on each of the required pages, which I presume represented each of the seven children. He talked a little about the weather and he seemed kind enough to me as I watched the transaction while seated on the floor.

The Fuller Brush man was another regular visitor. Mother purchased a brush of some sort or another frequently enough that he came on a regular basis. She more often bought nothing at all. He would also sit in the living room on the couch and open his case of brushes on the floor. Taking one brush after another from the case, he would explain how each could be used and Mother would patiently listen to his presentation. We sometimes thought it would never end and wondered off in boredom. The door-to-door salesmen were endless it seemed. The Jewel-Tea man came with all sorts of roasted coffee beans and ground coffee beans in bags that I did

Mother, Linda Jane, Dick, and Carol Ann

59

enjoy smelling. With purchases of his coffee or assorted teas, coupons were awarded and an entire set of Jewel-Tea dishes could be acquired over a period of time. The set of dishes included all of the cups, saucers, dinner plates, bowls, sugar bowel, creamer, serving bowls, meat platter and salt and peppershakers. Everyone collected them. I think Grandma and Aunt Gene next door collected more Jewel-Tea dishes than we did. They drank more coffee!

Though they were a dying breed, some doctors still delivered medical care to the home. I never knew a waiting room or it's smell until I was well into grade school after our medical home delivery died with Dr. Conger and we started going to Dr. Gick on East Michigan. I have no idea where Dr. Conger's office was located because I never went there. She always came to the home. Mother would simply call her and tell her there was a problem with one of the children and she would appear within an hour or so. She was a very kind lady, very grandmotherly. She delivered all seven of us at our homes. Bill and Ron were delivered at 4400 East 21st Street, Jerry was delivered at "Black's house" at 4415 East 21st Street, and Carol, Linda, Tom, and myself were delivered at 4350 East 21st as the home address changed.

I am amazed that all of these deliveries occurred at home because of my mother's experiences with home delivery of babies. Her older sister, Ida, married and moved to Fowler, Indiana. There she had five sons and each time, Mother would travel from Lanesville by train to Fowler to help her sister through the ordeal of childbirth and home maintenance. In the end, Ida's husband was out of work and out of money and came home to Lanesville with his pregnant wife, who was in ill health, and their sons. They moved into Mother's home place with her father and sisters. At this point in her life, Mother was recently married and was living in Indianapolis. She prevailed upon her husband, my father Art, to take her to Lanesville and then for him to leave her there so she could once again help her sister through childbirth. Ida was the oldest of the living Ringle children and "broke her father's heart when she married and moved to Fowler." Now she was home with her husband and five sons and about to deliver again. My mother and Rose Day (a "second mother" to my own) were with Ida through her delivery of twin girls, Jean and Joan. Ida had wanted a girl and now she had two but she knew they would not survive.

Bill, Ron, Jerry, Carol Ann, Linda Jane, and Dick with Dr. Conger

They were too small. Mother and Rose wrapped the infants in blankets and placed them on the open oven door of a wood-burning stove. They placed hot-water bottles around them, all in a desperate attempt to keep them warm and alive. Ida said to them, "they are not going to live, don't bother with all of that." The twins died and so did Ida. All of this makes one wonder how much Mother and Daddy must have dreaded the fate of home delivery, not being able to afford anything else.

The difference for them was Doctor Conger and their confidence in her. She came when called and, as I said, delivered seven children. Daddy and Mother gave Doctor Conger what they could and often not cash but trade of one sort or another. This Doctor came to the house regularly, opening her black case in the living room, just like Jewel-Tea and Fuller Brush, only she would extract little bottles and a syringe, a bottle of alcohol and cotton balls and Mother would line us up for inoculations. We protested and cried as we sat, one by one, on her grandmotherly lap and were swabbed and stuck.

Doctor Conger was a giving person, "a saint on earth," mother always said. She gave of herself and her personal possessions. If complimented on something she was wearing, she would immediately remove it and give it to the person who expressed their admiration. She died in an automobile accident without shoes. She had given them to one of her "clients." A saint on earth!

Carol Ann

The best home delivery was one of love, not to say the others weren't. But, this one was more special and occurred around 4:00 or 4:30 in the afternoon each day of the week. Mother would remind us of the time if she became aware that we were letting it slip by preoccupied with play...... "Daddy's coming."

60

"Oh! Let's go to the porch and see who gets him!"

This game is really simple. The players stood on the West end of the front porch, leaning on the sandstone cap of the brick wall or sitting in the porch swing, and we would take turns "claiming" passing cars, having determined the order of play by who got to the porch first, second, third and so on. We mostly only counted the cars traveling East on 21st Street from town, the direction of his travel home. Sometimes, if traffic was scant, we would also count the cars traveling from East to West. We used the telephone pole across the street as the marker. This method generated many an argument about which car belonged to which player. We also enjoyed making fun of the other player's "rattletrap" and bragging about our own shiny new car. But the biggest braggart of all was the one who got Daddy!

He would pull into the drive smiling and stop by the steps of the porch, a cloud of dust swirling about the car. We would run off the porch yelling "Hello Daddy," surrounding the car while announcing the winner. He would then let us ride on the running board all the way back to the garage - maybe fifty feet.

Home delivery was the greatest!

Indestructible Wagon

We had a wagon. I don't know who received it on a birthday or the occasion of Christmas or what, but we had one. It seemed to me we only ever had one, like the original was never replaced. It was

indestructible; lived forever. Except, today of course, it is history but I don't remember when it was trashed or passed on. It just faded out of the picture, replaced by a gardener's delight, the blue-green, two-wheeler.

The wagon, originally shiny red, was a "Radio Flyer;" black wheels, black wheel rims, and little metal silver hub caps with four tabs that hooked onto the rim, both hiding (and protecting) the end of the spokes and the cotter pins that held the wheels on. Of all the parts of the wagon to disappear, the little silver hubcaps were the first, all four of them, to go. The second piece to go was the handle in the tongue so that all you had were the metal tabs between which the handle was once secured. The tabs remained like the outer tines of a four-pronged garden fork missing the two middle tines. It was a lethal situation but never harmed us.

Our wagon was primarily a plaything, but we used it in our yard work as well. In the fall, it was loaded with leaves which were joyously hauled down the garden path to the "burning place" at the back of the lot, with Tommy

Bill, Cousin Bill holding Linda Jane, Carol Ann, Ron, and Jerry

sitting on the load, holding the leaves in the bed so not so many spilled out on the trip. Then Tommy rode back again, to the work, in the empty wagon for another load.

During the garden season, the wagon was pulled between the rows and we heaped weeds onto the bed like hay on a wagon and hauled those to the "burning place." The weeding crews worked fast; faster than haulers could haul. We would haul until dusk, until the combination of sweat and mosquitoes drove us in, or at least to the porch for cold lemonade or ice cream from the Blue Ribbon and ice water. We basically enjoyed the work.

The wagon hauled groceries from the trunk of the car to the back door. It transported rocks from here to there for rearranged borders. It hauled dirt and large shrubs and plants that were being moved.

But, the weight, placed in the bed, far more frequently was that of us kids. We often used one of Mother's forked clothes line props to propel our playmate in the wagon by placing the forked end over the rear axle and pushing; the occupant "driving" with the lethal tongue chin or chest high. It would really fly out the gravel drive, dust billowing up, to the front of our house, then careen left in front of Grandma and Gene's house and up the hill of their drive and to the

Tom, Bobby, Dick, and Lassie

back yards again. Round and round! The stamina of the pusher would last just so long, who, with a mighty heave, would send the wagon down the hill of our drive and then out across grandma and Gene's front yard to hook up again at the back, the wagon having coasted through turns one and two. Besides it was not easy to keep the forked pole in the center of the back axle of a turning wagon.

If the wagon turned over, it was never the pusher's fault, pole or no. It was always the fault of the driver because they tried to turn too sharp. Sharp - That's a strange word, isn't it? Think about it. Sharp - Knives are sharp. Scissors are sharp, so are razors. So, how do you turn too sharp?) That's what we always yelled before the driver had a chance to blame the pusher.

"You turned too sharp!" or, "You have to keep control of the tongue!" or, "You lost control of the tongue! You have to hold tight."

Still, the driver would protest and blame the pusher, often amidst tears. "You were pushing too fast!"

A front wheel would hit a stone and jerk the tongue out of the driver's hands as the front wheels turned right or left, practically back on themselves, and the wagon would flip, pitching the driver unceremoniously out onto the gravel or whatever it was running on, the bed following in the tumbling

driver's general direction. The "crashes" were frequent. They were often staged for diversion, usually at the driver's design, often to the surprise, but amusement, of the pusher.

The only hurtful episode I remember with our wagon occurred early one spring as we played across the street from our house, to the south, on Euclid Avenue. There were no houses there, but there were sidewalks. There were no sidewalks on 21st Street. Jerry, Carol Ann, Linda Jane, Little Tommy and I were all suited against the weather, caps, scarves and heavy coats; maybe it was fall. No, I'm sure it was springtime. The banks rising from the sidewalks were heavy with long green grass and the brown blades from the year before. Jerry was pushing Carol Ann, the driver, in the wagon. Faster and faster they went and the others of us running behind could hardly keep up. Jerry, bent over, was pushing with his hands on either side of the wagon bed. I remember the wagon veering left and plummeting up the grassy embankment. I remember the squeals and laughter. The wagon toppled to the right and rolled down the embankment and landed bottom side up, wheels still whirring, on top of Carol Ann who seemed to disappear completely under the overturned hollow of the metal wagon bed. As we caught up, Jerry lifted the wagon off Carol Ann and she was crying. I only remember Carol Ann crying as a child one other time, much later, when she intended to prove she could stand on a basketball as we played in our basement. She couldn't do it, and she split her chin open when she connected with the concrete in a one-point landing trying to do it. She carries the five-stitch scar to this day. Just as I don't recall the sequence of events following the bloody split chin, I don't recall much more of the hurtful wagon accident other than we loaded her in the wagon and pulled her to 21st and Euclid and called to Mother.

Jerry called "Mother, Mother," who came out the front door onto the porch.

He continued, as she attended to his pronouncement, "I think Carol Ann has a broken arm."

Only then did I realize what had happened.

Mostly, I remember the wagon as something we made into a stagecoach. Tommy and I would take a cardboard box and cut slits into the open end that would slip over the sides of the wagon tub. Fashioning a door and windows as well as an opening for the tongue to slip through, the driver was wholly contained and would drive by peering through a hole cut in the front. We made many a stagecoach out of our wagon.

"Kneel up and drive the wagon."

"Stand up and drive the wagon."

"Sit with your back to the tongue and drive it blind. I'll tell you which way to turn."

"Here, put on this blindfold and I'll tell you which way to turn."

Crash! Crash!

"Turn hard! Roll it!"

"Pretend there are Indians and you are shot."

"You're carrying gold and there are stagecoach robbers!"

Sometimes,

"All three of you get in and I'll push."

"Okay, but don't push too fast."

Laughter . . .

"Faster! Faster! Oh come on, faster!"

Tom "making repairs"

A sudden crash, bodies tumbling and the rattle and clatter of a rolling metal wagon amidst the laughter and grunts of tumbling bodies. It's a wonder our adventures weren't more frequently hurtful, and I wonder which outlasted the other, the wagon or our childhood? Indestructible? I don't think so!

Squeak, Squeak

I can't quite write out the sound the blue-green, metal glider on Grandma and Aunt Gene's front porch made as it moved back and forth. "Squeak, squeak" will have to do. Somehow it doesn't explain the sound well enough because it had more of a ring to it than I can spell. You've never heard it before, and I'll never hear it again with Grandma.

As a youngster, I visited Grandma and Aunt Gene's daily; after dinner, after homework, after chores, after dark, but each day and sometimes twice a day.

You were allowed to knock and walk in the front door, shouting "hellooo." You were usually greeted by Lassie first, and then from the kitchen or basement by Grandma or Aunt Gene. They were often still at the dinner table eating food that smelled wonderful but looked awful.

When Aunt Gene was still at work, Grandma would begin to prepare dinner, often starting at 4:00 P.M. even when she knew Aunt Gene wouldn't board the bus until 5:00 P.M. from downtown. Aunt Gene often sat down to over-cooked meals; meals that looked bad, smelled wonderful and tasted great. Grandma cooked with a lot of fat, salt and pepper, garlic and onion. Leftovers were always used, most often in barley soup. I loved her barley soup and haven't tasted any like it yet. I remember once she dropped in leftover mashed potatoes, and I was sure surprised.

Aunt Gene and Grandma

"What was that?" I asked.

"Mashed potatoes leftover from the other day," she responded.

"You put mashed potatoes in your soup?" I was amazed.

"Sure, why not. It thickens it up," she chuckled.

There was only one thing I ever ate at Grandma's that I wish I hadn't. hog's head cheese! I love cheese, all kinds of cheese, but hog's headcheese isn't made from milk. It's made from a hog's head.

You never knew what you would find boiling in the pot on Grandma's stove. One Saturday morning I popped in,. "Hellooo," I shouted. Grandma called me into the kitchen and pulled a stool over to the stove. She said "Climb up here and see what I've got in this pot." She loved to surprise the kids. It gave her a kick. I climbed up on the stool while she held my hand, careful not to touch the hot stove. She lifted the lid, and in my mind's eye, I can still see the gray hog's head bobbing vigorously around, filling the pot, steam rising, ears flopping, teeth and tongue protruding in rapidly boiling water. The frightened, bug-eyed hog's face filled the kettle and barely had room to move.

"What is that?!" I exclaimed!

"It's a hog's head!" She shouted with glee.

"What are you going to do with it?!" I asked.

"Auch du lieber!, I'm going to make hog's head cheese." She said.

"Ugh!" was all I could utter.

She laughed and muttered, "Dumbis dumbkoff! You don't know what's good."

Oh, the mess of pulling the smelly flesh from the hog's skull. Everything was used and put through the grinder once, maybe twice. Cartilage would pop and tough flesh and parts would squish and squirt as Grandma pressed the pieces into her hand-turned meat grinder she had clamped to the kitchen table. I imagine her mouth was watering the whole time (She always sprayed when she talked, but somehow it didn't matter.) The mass of ground skull flesh was mixed with herbs and spices, rolled up in a layer of hog fat and cooled. It was sliced and served on a plate or used on bread as sandwich meat. I had one bite only! Ever!

Two things I never, ever ate were bone marrow spread on bread. Grandma did. She claimed it was as good or better than butter. The other was chicken gristle, which Aunt Gene ate, cleaning the bones. But then, she only left the stem of an apple unconsumed, eating absolutely everything else!

Anyway, you never knew what was cooking, but you were always greeted by Lassie.

Grandma, Aunt Gene, and Lassie begging for the ball

"Where's your ball, Lassie, where's your ball?" I would say expectantly, to excite her. She would find a ball, usually under the dining room table, with Grandma's or Aunt Gene's direction, and I was allowed to throw the ball almost anywhere even while at times they were eating. She would tear through the house, her claws tearing at the carpet, to retrieve the ball and bring it back. You could throw the ball and then hide. Lassie would retrieve it and try to return it. If you weren't there, she would drop it and begin a frantic search to find you. Grandma would chuckle and encourage her to keep looking if you were particularly well hidden.

"Where's Dick, Lassie? Find him! Where's Dick?" She would say. Lassie would cock her head from side to side and assume an expression of bewilderment that would make Grandma laugh. Grandma loved to laugh and did so at the slightest provocation. She loved to tease and had a great sense of humor. Lassie would go to the front door and check it and Grandma would explain, "No, no, he hasn't gone home. Find him!"

The best place to hide was behind the couch. Aunt Gene, who couldn't tolerate Lassie's frustration as well as Grandma, would often tell her where you were hiding.

"He's behind the couch Lassie. Look! Look behind the couch," Aunt Gene would say and Grandma would immediately protest her giving me away.

Lassie, when directed so, would bound up on the couch and peer into the abyss behind and bark and growl. She loved the game and was free to romp anywhere in the house. The absolute best romp with her inside was to throw the ball out the enclosed back porch door so that it rolled down the steps to the back door and while Lassie chased it in the dark, (if you were lucky, the door to the basement was open and the ball would go on down giving you more time to hide) I would run through the kitchen, dining room and living room and up the wooden stairs into the dark, second story, trying to step lightly on the stairs because they creaked all over. It was gloriously exciting in the dark, bounding from bedroom to sunroom to bedroom, slamming doors as Lassie pursued from one direction and then another in her desperate growling and barking effort to corner her tormentor.

If she failed to detect that you had gone upstairs while she retrieved the ball, she would search the main floor to your delight while you waited in the darkened upstairs rooms, Grandma laughing, giving her clues until Aunt Gene would clearly state, "He has gone upstairs, Lassie, upstairs." Almost instantly her nails would click on the wooden stairs and, having caught the scent, the growling and barking would begin. It was terribly exciting and free spirited play in a world apart from the order of our house next door. Grandma and Aunt Gene seemed to love the sport of the visits and free-reign play as much as I did. It was a wonderfully happy noise. But I also felt guilty for I was sure if my Mother ever saw what I was doing at 4400, she would not have approved at all.

Grandma and Dick

Grandma and I were very good friends. I behave very much like her today. Our summer visits occurred outdoors on the porch with lemonade, cookies and Lassie racing around the house. The expansive porch had a small set of side steps and a wide set of front steps directly across from their front door. It was a house Grandpa had built from plans out of Sears' catalogue. He used old railroad car timbers as floor joists and roof beams. Neighbors laughed at Grandpa Joe saying he would never be able to raise the heavy beams into place, but he did it. The foundation was made of fieldstones and cement. Grandma and Aunt Gene always chided us if we climbed on the fieldstone to get over the porch rail and away from Lassie. I suppose Grandpa Joe had set the example, insisting his children not climb on the foundation for fear of loosening a stone. He had collected the stones himself and some were fairly rounded and smooth. In fact, he had collected so many more than he needed that he had buried a whole pile of stones in the lot

next door, just to get rid of them. He probably didn't think the smooth stones would hold too well in the foundation.

Front and back views of the house that Grandpa built

Grandma and Trixie on her front porch glider

While sitting on the cushioned metal glider, rocking to and fro in the morning sun, Grandma talked of Joe, her husband, my father's father, my Grandpa, a lot. I never knew my Grandpa Joe. I especially enjoyed early Saturday morning visits with Grandma. She sat in the glider humming as she rocked. I would join her and Lassie on the glider. Being there required little conversation or effort. It was a completely comfortable situation. Leaning on Grandma was soft and comforting. Our meager conversation between the glider's "squeak, squeak" (there's that inadequate description of the sound again), her sips of strong, black coffee from a Jewel tea cup hanging on her finger, and the humming would always lead to the same series of questions from me and answers from her. I spent countless hours listening to her going over and over the same stories and loved every warm moment.

She was the daughter of a baker whose shop was on Massachusetts Avenue.

"Pop sold doughnuts at a nickel a baker's dozen. You know what a baker's dozen is?" she would ask.

"Yeah, thirteen for the price of twelve," I answered.
"Right," she affirmed.
She lived on North Street as a little girl.

She told of her husband Joe, my Grandpa, who was sent to America by his parents at the age of fourteen to join family already here "in the land of milk and honey." He was sent on a boat to avoid conscription into the army. He spoke no English and had his name and address pinned to his coat and was sent to Indianapolis by rail. His family were butchers from the Rhine Valley in Germany. The family name used to be spelled Krëamer, but the umlauted 'e' was dropped and it became Kramer.

Grandpa Joe drank, and she would often stop the inter-urban train with a kerosene lantern and lead him home to the one-room shack that they lived in. It sat much farther back on the lot at 4400 East 21st Street. The shack stood where the garden was later after Grandpa Joe built the house.

The shack was not well sealed. Spaces between the siding boards allowed snow to blow in during the winter.

They had a milk cow and chickens. Life was tough. She described a destitute, improvised lifestyle, but she didn't let on that she saw it that way. She always talked about it as though it was just factual and fine, no worse and no better than anyone else.

She told about Jake, their dog, who was often mauled as a pup by a neighbors dog but Jake killed their dog when he grew up. She delighted in Jake's triumph. She told of my Daddy and his experience with the horse liniment and his "private parts." She told of Agnes, her daughter, drinking the homemade

whiskey in the middle of the night, thinking it was water, and dying as a three year old. She was a proud woman who didn't know she had lived a hard life.

She teared and choked every time she concluded this series of answers to my questions with her story of Grandpa Joe's death at the age of forty-five. How he left her with seven children and his whispered dying words, "I'm sorry Maim."

Grandma never expressed anger that he left her so young and with such a brood to provide for. I think her tears expressed her anger and sorrow for herself and what she had to face. A hug, a kiss on the cheek from me and an "I love you, Grandma," would disturb Lassie a bit and we would settle back into the silence except for the sound of the glider, "squeak, squeak."

Her old veined hands were smooth and soft, and she would let me hold and pat one and turn the thin gold wedding band during the conversation as she kept the glider in a steady motion. My legs were still too short to reach the porch floor.

You've never heard the "squeak, squeak" of the porch glider before, and you've never heard the stories as told by my Grandmother about her life. And you know, though I never thought I would hear it again, I did, just now hear the "squeak, squeak," with Grandma.

The Votive's Tongue

When I look back at some of the things we did as kids, I am amazed that we are not maimed or injured, at least physically. It is marvelous that we are alive, having survived childhood. In spite of responsible, watchful supervision, young children can place themselves in life threatening situations that could easily result in disfigurement, handicapping injuries, or even death. The invincibility and resiliency of youth is a gift but can also be a liability. The "it won't happen to me," syndrome carries us easily into precarious, self-indulgent, dangerous situations.

One of the hazards is fire and a common childhood fascination with its flirtatious dance, a threatening dance of destruction and death. Fire can be thrilling. I first learned about the excitement of fire during a puppet show in the basement of our home. Jerry, ever the entertainer, presented stories in a darkened basement with puppets. Some puppets were crudely homemade, but others had strings and all. The plays occurred in a two-room, homemade, wooden doll house. Although it seemed Jerry made up the stories as he went along, I think he thought a great deal about story lines in moments of leisure and stored them away for later use. For example, why else would he save slivers of soap bars in a jar with a little water, on the shelf with the canned goods? He added slivers of soap from the basement shower and a little more water, whenever he could. He accumulated close to a quart and a half of bluish-green slime in the jar over a period of time.

The curtain went up in the darkened basement one evening, when Jerry was in charge and both mother and daddy were gone. The stage house was illuminated with a flashlight. The puppets isolated by the light in the darkness became real, with different voices. The story line was immediately forgotten, within minutes of its presentation, as the story was greatly overshadowed by the climax. The play and dialogue progressed in a "Punch and Judy" style of slapstick violence; very funny violent falls, puppets slamming into the walls, arms and legs flopping uncontrollably about. Fire was introduced as one puppet entered holding a flaming skewer, as though its hotdog caught fire. The puppet danced about clumsily, and the contents of the playhouse stage were set afire. Suddenly a bluish green mass of slime spilled over the flaming, two-room interior, and amidst hissing and smoke, the flames were snuffed out. Was it out of control or all planned? It seems to me now that there was cause for concern. The slime ran out the front of the house stage, and the smoke rose to the ceiling. The lights in the basement came on amidst the laughter and screams. There was a mess to clean up. The slime was not much of a problem, but the smoke hung at the ceiling, filling half of the basement. That was the bigger problem for it would soon smell throughout the house. The back door was opened as well as the basement windows, and frantic fanning with newspapers ensued. I don't think Mother or Daddy smelled anything when they came home.

One rainy thunderous spring evening, our house was struck by lightening. Daddy wasn't home from work, and the darkness at around 5:00 P.M. was not right. We had been called in from play with the approaching storm because Mother was deathly afraid of lightening. When it stormed, we loved to go to the front porch and watch the display and feel the mist from the rain in our faces.

Mother, on the other hand, always lit the usual votive light by the statue of the Blessed Virgin in her bedroom. On this occasion, after lighting the blessed candle, she returned to the kitchen to continue preparing supper. Tommy and I were playing with metal toy cars, trucks and farm implements in the carpet patterns of the dining room floor. The lights flickered, and the bluish-white light of lightening flashed outside. Mother was peeling potatoes at the far end of the kitchen by the back double windows. Picking up the newspaper for the potato peels, potatoes, kettle of water and all, she moved. Just after she moved away from the windows, there was a tremendous crack and clatter. The upper cabinet doors above the counter where she had been standing flew open, and various articles of kitchen stuff exploded into the room. It was as if Paul Bunyon had hit the back of our home with his axe just above the double windows. In spite of her adrenaline-filled veins, mother remained calm and said to her saucer-eyed children, "We've been struck by lightening."

I peered into the kitchen and grayish smoke rolled out of the cabinets, some of it rolling across the ceiling, some floating toward the floor. Jerry called the fire department, and they were at our home very quickly. It was raining very hard when they arrived. The firemen were ushered through the back door,

their black shiny slickers and heavy boots dripping with water. In with them bounded a huge Dalmatian, the firedog. It ran from room to room. It even went into the bedroom where the votive candle was lit, and it shook. I wondered of the fireman who followed would criticize us later for leaving an unattended candle burning in the bedroom. Jerry directed the firemen upstairs and to the front closet and the attic access panel. He had kept them from chopping a hole to discover the wicked fire by showing them the removable panel. There was no fire. Mother described a blue ball of fire that followed the scattered, now broken kitchen stuff, out of the cabinets, but there was no fire.

There was a pounding on the front door, and Carol Ann and Aunt Gene were there, soaked through as they had run from the bus stop at Twenty-first Street and Bosart, recognizing that the fire engine was at one of our homes, homes that sat side by side.

As quickly as they came, and without wielding their voracious axes, the firemen and the Dalmatian disappeared. What a mess! The Dalmatian, a big hit with us kids, had paid little attention to us and we were disappointed. We didn't even learn its name!

A silver-plated butter dish had been hit, and its little glass innards shattered. The top and bottom were both melted in only one spot each, as though a torch had been applied to them where the lightening bolt had passed straight through.

We speculated for a long time about why the bolt of lightening had struck the back of the house and didn't hit the huge cottonwood tree that stood at that very corner of the house. And, why did mother move when she did from below the cabinets as she peeled potatoes? Did Mother Mary speak to her through the votive's tongue?

....We built tee pees out of dried weeds in the fall. I wish I knew the name of these weeds. They were green, grew six feet tall or more, dried to a light gray, and were hollow inside. We gathered several of these weeds in the fall and stripped them of their branches. They were leaned against each other like poles of tee pees and dried grass was woven between them until a tee pee was formed. We didn't play in the tee pee long until we, the Indians, were raided, and our tee pee set afire with a "flaming arrow" (a wooden blue tip match struck on a rock.) The tee pee was quickly consumed in smoke and flames and all imaginary battle was suspended as we watched the structure burn in a whoosh!

Can you imagine the headlines?

TEENAGER SETS HOUSE AFIRE DURING PUPPET SHOW - Five   children die or . .

TEENAGER SAVES SIBLING IN HOUSE FIRE or . .

LIGHTENING STRIKES HOME - Three dead or . .

TEE PEE "RAID" RESULTS IN TWO DEAD or . .

FIRE RESULT OF MISCHIEVOUS MATCH PLAY! . . or

. . on and on as one thinks of what might have been and wonders if the Blessed Virgin Mary really did respond to the silent prayer of the votive's flaming tongue.

Snacks

In mid to late November, after the gardens and the fields were laid to rest for the winter, a brown pasteboard box, about one cubic foot in size, would arrive at our home. It was heavy. Mother always knew what it was but she allowed us to open it without telling us. It was full of popcorn kernels, full to the brim. They were small and cream colored, almost white. It was an early Christmas gift sent each year by Uncle John from Lanesville, Indiana. The box was shoved into the unheated kitchen pantry and left on the floor.

Bedtime snacks consisted of cookies and milk, graham crackers and milk, graham crackers with white icing and milk, ice cream and cookies and ice water, potato chips or pretzels and coke but the best of all was buttered and salted popcorn and Coke or Pepsi. Bedtime snacks followed the seasons. The cookies and milk were a result of Mother's holiday baking; hermits with black walnuts and oatmeal-raisin cookies made for Christmas holidays. Graham crackers dipped in milk, were a fill in when the cookies were not available. The graham crackers with white icing were made with the leftover icing used to frost a cake. They were special. The ice cream, potato chips and pretzels were also fill-ins.

Tommy was a specialist at eating graham crackers and milk. With his left hand he would break them and pass the half to his right hand. He would dunk the cracker into the glass of milk and while placing that half into his mouth he was passing another half to his right hand. It was a kind of conveyor system, awesome to behold, non-stop.

Popcorn did take some time to prepare so it was usually reserved for the weekends, Friday or Saturday nights, when we didn't have to get up early for school. Our home had a special four-quart kettle reserved for popcorn popping. Depending on who was fixing the popcorn, Mother or Daddy, made a distinct difference in how it was served. Mother would pop three or four kettles full and dump them one after the other into the large oval turkey-roasting pan. After popping the corn, she would then melt the butter in the popcorn kettle and pour it over the popcorn, salt it, put the lid on the roaster and shake it all up. The popcorn would be served in the roaster, placed in the middle of the kitchen table and voracious consumption would begin by those gathered around. Mother taught us to use our fingertips and to pick up a few at a time. She distributed paper napkins.

Daddy's method varied from the above. While he was popping the first kettle of corn, he melted the butter in another small pot. As soon as the first kettle was finished, he would butter and salt it in the kettle, shake it up and dump it in the middle of the kitchen table. We could start eating immediately and didn't have to wait for all of it to be popped. He would return to the stove and start another kettle. When that was finished, buttered and salted, it was dumped on top of what was left of the first kettle full. And so he would continue. I think he didn't want to wash the roaster. Daddy also demonstrated a better method of eating popcorn. Rather than using just the fingertips, he would use his entire hand. His fingers would claw into the pile of popped corn and scoop up a handful. Placing the heel of his hand up to his gaping mouth, he would shove the popcorn into his mouth and work it all in with his fingers dancing in front of his lips. We soon learned the technique. Though unacceptable in public, it was clearly a better way to eat popcorn.

As we neared the end of our fill, someone would suggest a game of 'line-up.' Ten popped kernels were placed in a row on the tabletop in front of each participant. The idea was to see who could pick up the pieces with their lips/tongue and into their mouth, one by one, faster than anyone else. Carol Ann was always the champion.

After the popcorn snack, we all participated in cleaning up the kitchen. The stove was wiped down, kettles were washed, table was cleaned and the floor was swept. To our delight, Daddy would sometimes let the dog in to sweep the floor. Faces and hands washed, we were off to bed.

Tommy required a snack of his own which I could never understand. On frequent occasions, he would be found in the dark kitchen on top of the kitchen table, eating butter. The stick butter was left in the middle of the table with the salt and peppershakers and the sugar container, all arranged neatly on a doily. The butter was left out because it was impossible to spread if it were cold. During a period after World War Two (Two meant little to me because I didn't understand World War Two as something that

came after World War One nor, for that matter, did I understand "World War", a block of white substance was purchased as butter but, if you wanted it to look like butter, you had to knead in a packet of powered yellow coloring. Stick or mixed butter made little difference to Tommy. He would disappear from the family gathered in the living room around the radio, be missed by Mother and be found by her on top of the table in the kitchen eating butter.

So much for snacks!

Deannie P.

We were a motley crew, ready for anything, well equipped. My older brother, Jerry, didn't carry anything but the rest of the "terrible five" did. My sister, Carol Ann, had a six-shooter strapped on, scarf around her neck and the ever-present cowgirl hat that she occasionally let hang by the strap around her neck onto her back. She also had the rope that we would use in this particular episode, the Deannie P. affair. Linda Jane had a set of six-shooters strapped on also but she did not have her hat. My younger brother, "Little Tom," and I had cap pistols on this sunny summer's day. The five of us hung together pretty tight and had many an adventure "at the end of the lot."

Jerry, Linda Jane, Tom, Dick, and Carol Ann

"At the end of the lot," certainly did not mean that at all. We lived on a plot of land that was sixty feet wide by three hundred feet deep. What "going to the end of the lot" really meant was that we were going way beyond where the lot ended, across the inter-urban ditch, across the railroad tracks and down into the woods along Pogue's Run creek. We often went beyond that, across Pogue's Run and into the fields where a small airfield used to be. We would sometimes go as far as Massachusetts Avenue, which runs northeast out of the city and eventually turns into highway 67.

If we stayed too long on one of these adventures we would have to run most of the way home in response to Daddy's whistle. He would produce this piercing whistle by putting the index fingers of each

Eddie (dad's friend) and Daddy

hand into his mouth and, while pulling his cheeks apart, would blow air across his upper lip. I could never figure it out. No, that's not true..... what I never wanted to do was to put my index fingers into the cheeks of my mouth and pull them apart. My fingers always tasted salty; a taste that I have always associated with being dirty. Anyway, when we heard the whistle that meant we had to get home and if we were especially far away we had to really hurry if our lie about the imposed limits were to be believed. Usually he whistled because supper was ready, or soon to be, and Mother didn't like to hold food. She liked to have the meal all come together at the last minute and serve it hot. She always succeeded. It's a gift.

On this ideal day in the summer, we decided to go "to the end of the lot" and pick black raspberries. This is not an easy chore because of the insects, short-lived irritations from mosquito bites and the dreaded long-lived effects from chiggers, let alone the nasty cuts from the thorns on the long canes that invariably hung out over a steep incline and held the best berries. We often held on to each other to increase the length of our reach to get at these berries.

We set out walking back through the yard, past the wooden, white frame, one car garage with its two huge wapper-jawed entry doors, past the apple tree beyond which was Grandma's chicken coop, grape arbor and the little two room house that Grandma rented to the strangest family. This was Deannie P.'s home. He lived there with his parents, Mr. and Mrs. P. though I seldom saw the Mr. and wouldn't know the Mrs. today. I don't remember that Deannie had any brothers or sisters. I don't think he did. We reached the garden and the path around it. You never walked on the garden. The garden was huge in my eyes. The rows of everything went on forever and, if you don't believe me, just try picking or weeding or hoeing one row of green beans in our garden. When you thought, "I must be half-way through by now" and dared to raise your head to look against the advice of your aching back, it was always a disappointment and you swore you wouldn't make it to the end of the row, at least not in this lifetime. Having checked the distance yet to go it was equally important to check how far you had come, which you could do without raising up, by looking back under your arm. This maneuver was important because the distance to go had to be confirmed. It was.

We walked single-file down the path, Jerry leading, then Carol Ann, Linda Jane, Dick and Little Tom, our pecking and our birth order. We left our property when we finally passed the fence post set by our Grandfather when they had a cow and really needed the fence. Down through the old inter-urban ditch that was being filled in with trash, up the other side and across the short "plateau" before the descent to the railroad bed and the tracks which went on to the right and the left forever and ever. I always wanted to cross the tracks in a hurry. I didn't like to linger there. The crushed stone in the rail-bed was more like sharp edged rocks to me and they were not the most pleasant things to walk on in thin shoes. Besides, I was sure that if one of those belching monsters came chugging around the bend and across the trestle, all five of us would not get across and, what a sad family it would be if one of us got killed, cut in half. I could just see my Daddy and Mother and brothers and sisters crying over the loss of their dear son and brother, Dick.

I don't know how long we picked black raspberries but we didn't have to go far because they were everywhere. Our plan was to take these berries home and to have them with sugar and milk. Cream would probably have tasted better but we never had cream except for that little bit at the top of the milk bottle that you had to shake back into the rest of the milk before you drank it. I tasted that stuff once and it was kind of sour and salty too; reminded me of the taste of my fingers. I'm glad we never had cream. We ate as many berries as we picked, that is Little Tom and I did, smiling quietly at each other, until we were reprimanded. Jerry was the disciplinarian of the group and he sure let you know if you crossed the line or, rather, got out of it. I'm sure, the whole time we were picking, he didn't eat more than one or two berries. He had self discipline enough to wait for the real reward back at the house and after they had been washed. Jerry had a thing for cleanliness and food, besides he knew about the tiny little green worms that thrived on the black raspberry caps. We picked until we almost filled the one-quart tin kettle that we used as a water dipper when we set the live plants in the garden.

We started back for the house. We crossed the tracks and when we reached the top of the path that leads back to the inter-urban ditch, we saw him. He was standing at the top of the path on the South side of the ditch, facing us, Deannie P.. We had often warned Deannie P. never to follow us because we didn't want him with us. We were exclusive and didn't want to be contaminated. There he stood in clothes we were certain our parents would never put us in; one foot on top of the other, moving his bent knee back and forth, tapping the tips of his fingers together, one hand against the other.

"There's Deannie," someone said.

"Wonder what he wants," said another.

"Whatcha doin'?" asked Deannie, not daring to start down the path and get caught in the bottom of the inter-urban ditch by us. As long as he was uninvited, he kept a safe distance and he always kept himself between his house and us until he was invited. There had been many a time Deannie had been chased home by us because he was uninvited. He learned to get invited first, remaining wary in the process.

"We picked some black raspberries," Jerry said.

"And we are going to have them with sugar and milk," Carol Ann tacked on.

"You don't get any because you didn't help pick them," Linda Jane added.

It didn't make any difference to us that he hadn't been invited.

We seemed to speak according to birth order, just as we walked single file.

"I'd like some............can I help now?" Deannie asked.

"Oh Deannie!" Carol Ann half shouted, sort of dismayed.

Jerry and Carol Ann began to confer and, although I hadn't helped much at all, I began to worry that a person who hadn't helped a lick was about to get a share for doing less than I had done. Jerry, Carol Ann and Linda seemed to consider the matter forever. I thought we should just tell him to get home and not to bother us when the decision was announced. Deannie was told to come on over and carry the berries home. He eagerly ran down the path, through the bottom of the ditch and up the other side to stand with us on the plateau.

"What can I do?" he asked.

Jerry answered, "You can carry the berries."

"And, if you spill any you will be sorry," finished Carol Ann in a firm voice.

74

"O.K.," Deannie said.

"Here, take them....and don't spill any," Jerry reminded.

We started down the path in the appropriate order, Deannie trailing. Jerry was leading his troops home from another successful foray into the wilds and all were returning safely to enjoy their warm home and Mother's cooking. I had not taken three steps down the path into the ditch when I saw a flood of black raspberry caps rolling past my feet, the little tin pan tumbling behind.

Deannie P. yelped. He had spilled the berries and we were between him and his home. His house must have seemed to him to be on the other side of the world at that moment, sitting there on the path as he was, having spilled the berries we had slaved to collect. Jerry, Carol Ann and Linda Jane turned around when Deannie yelled seeing what I already knew. He spilled them and everyone could see that but I said, "He spilled them."

Carol Ann was on him in a flash, darting up past us.

"Pick them up now and get every one!" she demanded.

Deannie looked up at her standing over him from his sitting position, frozen, except he seemed even closer to the ground, holding one arm over his head...for protection, I supposed. I mean, if my sister were standing over me, hissing in that tone of voice, I would be protecting myself. I had been in that position many a time.

Jerry handed him the tin pan that he had retrieved from the bottom of the ditch and Deannie sort of scooted down the path, scooping up the berries. I think we almost immediately regretted that we had given him the order to collect the berries because his hands were dirty and he obviously didn't know how delicate they were because he was kind of rolling them and smashing them against the ground as he scooped. The berries would never be the same and I don't think we cared if he got them all.

We all turned our attention to another, more important task, when Linda Jane asked the question on everyone's mind, "Well....what are we going to do to him?"

The answer came quickly from Carol Ann, "We'll tie him to the railroad track and leave him there! That will teach him to spill our black raspberries!"

I was stunned, but it was a good idea. We were all stunned. We all agreed. Deannie was the most stunned of all and began to struggle as our hands fell on him. He began to yell, "No! No!" as he writhed and struggled to break free. Carol Ann whipped off her rope and Deannie was dragged the few feet up the hill and over the plateau to the path down to the tracks. I don't see how he kept from getting hurt in the struggle. I'm sure he must have been dropped a time or two onto the sharp rocks. Deannie had little flesh for protection. We laid him on one of the rails and tied him to it, passing the rope under the rail and knotting it securely. We looked at each other, pleased with the work we had done and someone said, "Lets go!"

We left him there and retreated to the path to the inter-urban ditch where the berries had been spilled. We stopped there but we knew that Deannie P. believed that we had gone. He yelled and cried. After what seemed like a long time to me, we went back and untied him. He ran as he never had before. He disappeared over the plateau and by the time we walked up the hill from the tracks and down and up again through the inter-urban ditch, he had already made it all the way home....or he had collapsed in fright in the tall weeds somewhere and was waiting for us to walk the garden path.

I don't remember ever playing with Deannie P. again. The amazing thing to me is that he must have never told his parents of his experience at our hands for, surely, if he had, they would have walked the few hundred feet separating our homes to complain to our parents. If they did, we never heard about it. But, I believe if they had, there would have been hell to pay.

I also believe now that, even though they didn't complain to our parents then, there still may be hell to pay later. I often wonder what we would have done if, while we were sitting on that path to the interurban ditch, we had suddenly heard the whistle of the belching monster rounding the bend. Would we have succeeded in untying Deannie? Would we have had the guts to try? And, if the monster came and we didn't succeed how would we explain it? How might our lives have been changed? If his parents had called the police.......?

I want to apologize to Deannie but I have no idea where he is.

"I'm sorry Deannie," Dick has thought a thousand times.

74 WAYS TO MEASURE TIME

iUniverse books may be ordered through booksellers or by contacting:

iUniverse
1663 Liberty Drive
Bloomington, IN 47403
www.iuniverse.com
1-800-Authors (1-800-288-4677)

ISBN: 978-1-4917-7733-6 (sc)
ISBN: 978-1-4917-7734-3 (e)

Library of Congress Control Number: 2015915558

Print information available on the last page.

iUniverse rev. date: 11/11/2015

74
WAYS
TO
MEASURE TIME

E H U D   S C H O R I

74
WAYS
TO
MEASURE TIME

CHAPTER ONE

Sunday 16th June 1963

It was late when Betty and Jill left Peter's flat. Betty had been wanting to leave for over an hour, the thought of school looming as dark as the hazy fog which had been cloaking London all that week. But Peter had ignored her and kept putting on records which they'd had to listen to. It was clear that Peter fancied Jill, and not Betty. She wasn't surprised by that. It wasn't that Jill was so much prettier than her, just that Jill was the more adventurous of the two. Jill was the rebel, the one who talked back to the nuns and had the red welts on her hands to show it. Jill was the one who sneaked a bottle of whisky into the dorm one night, Jill who smoked Russian cigarettes and kissed boys outside the cinema. Jill did other things too.

Around ten-thirty, Jill had given Betty a clear-off look

and Betty went and sat in the tiny bathroom while Jill and Peter made noises. Betty, familiar with this situation, blocked her ears. Jill could be so noisy. She wished she were back in her little bed at the top of the convent school in Highgate Village. She wasn't jealous of Jill, she was concerned about her. Betty had always been the sort to look after other people, and Jill certainly needed looking after. They'd run into each other on their first day at school, and each recognized something they needed from the other. Jill needed a sensible friend, Betty needed someone to outrage her.

Twenty minutes later Jill popped her tousled head around the door.

'C'mon, you,' she said. 'He's asleep.'

Jill took a packet of Pall Mall cigarettes and a half-full bottle of wine and they headed out into the thick fog. The legendary pea-soupers were a thing of the past since the Clean Air Act in the Fifties, but grimy London was still capable of coughing up a lungful of fog from time to time, particularly around Highgate, where the grand houses largely ignored the restrictions on open fires. Tonight the fog looked thick enough to trap in a teacup and the gaslights offered only the vaguest guide to the way home.

The girls crossed Highgate Road and turned up Swain's

Lane, up the long hill, the East Cemetery railings to their right. On the other side of the street, almost invisible, stretched a terraced row of Georgian houses, keeping watch over their dead neighbours across the way. Jill slowed as they climbed the long hill, tired now, and puffing grumpily like a toddler. A couple of dim street lights, high above the pavement, offered a little light, but shadows lurked everywhere. Within the cemetery itself the only thing obscured by the fog was an inky blackness. Jill peered into the darkness, gripping the railing as she swigged from the bottle. Betty stopped to watch her, tired and barely able to raise a tut.

'Come on,' Betty said. 'We have exams in three weeks.'

'Three weeks,' Jill replied, 'not tonight.' She belched – a low rumble that Betty thought loud enough to raise the residents on both sides of the road.

Footsteps.

'Shh,' Betty said, and pulled her friend along.

A tall man, black in the gloom, slowed to peer at the girls as they slunk past, even Jill shamed into hiding the bottle. He made as if to speak but Betty hurried them along.

'He had a good old look,' Jill snorted.

'He was probably worried about you.'

'Me? Why would he be worried?' Jill asked, mystified.

'Because you're staggering about and it's late, come on,' Betty repeated.

'I'm not ready to go back,' Jill said, pulling away from Betty. 'Where can we go?'

Betty stared at her friend, exasperated. 'We have to go back to school, now!'

'You go back,' Jill said, not even looking at her. Instead she was gazing through the railings into the cemetery.

'What are you looking at?' Betty asked.

Jill turned to her, a wicked look on her face. 'Come on, Bets, let's climb over.'

'In there?' Betty replied, incredulous. 'Are you mad?'

'A little,' Jill said. She put the bottle down on a low wall before the railings and clambered up, showing her knickers. 'Give us a leg up,' she said.

'No,' Betty said. 'No way.'

'Fine, I'll do it myself,' Jill said. And with the uncanny ability of the drunk rebel, she pulled herself up and picked her way carefully over the blunt spikes at the top. She grunted as she dropped down into the grass on the other side. Already half concealed by darkness and fog, Jill's grinning face appeared at the railings, a thin white hand slid through and grabbed hold of the bottle, then she retreated and disappeared.

Betty sighed. She didn't want to go over the railings,

but she knew that over the railings was where she would be going. That was her role.

She took much longer over the ascent, being sober and careful. Even so, she managed to graze a knee and tear her tights, her only good pair. 'Damn you, Jill!' she hissed quietly, not wanting to wake the dead. 'Where are you?'

But there was no answer. Betty walked slowly in through the graves, visible as great white blobs. The clouded gaslights on the street outside did not penetrate more than a few feet in, but once her eyes had adjusted somewhat, she could pick out pale smears of broken gravestones and the black grass between them. At least Jill hadn't climbed into the West Cemetery, with its dank forest of oaks and cracked stone.

'Jill! It's getting cold. Come on.'

Betty shivered and stepped slowly through the grass. If she squinted she could just make out hulking stone tombs on either side. Terraces of the dead. Creepers clutched at the graves as if trying to stop them moving.

'Jill?' She stopped and listened but there was no response. Betty carried on along a leaf-strewn half-path, with each step her constant low-level worry gradually increasing even as the air grew colder. Rounding a corner in the lane of tombs she froze and clapped a hand across her mouth to hold in the scream.

A dull yellow glow, seemingly without source, lit a terrifying tableau. Jill knelt on a low slab between the terraces, open-mouthed tombs gaping dumbly at her and at the dark, cowled figure which towered above her, face obscured. As the terrified Betty watched, the figure signalled to Jill to stand, which she did slowly, still clutching the bottle of wine. Jill stared up into the dark maw of the creature's hood, apparently transfixed. She tilted her head slightly, exposing her pale throat. Warm breath misted the narrow gap between her and the tall figure.

Suddenly the temperature dropped even further as the figure shifted and bent towards the girl. Betty began to shiver uncontrollably, partly through the intense cold but also through the flooding fear. Perhaps sensing her presence, the figure stopped and slowly turned its head towards her.

'No . . . no . . .' Betty heard herself whisper as she finally saw into the hood. Two piercing eyes of bright yellow glared back at her. They stayed, staring at one another for what seemed like minutes.

Betty willed herself to turn and run but could no more have done so than could the occupants of the surrounding tombs.

6

Then the figure plunged its head and tore Jill's throat out.

The bottle dropped to the slab and smashed, dark wine staining the stone.

Released, Betty shrank back and ducked around the corner. Legs like rubber, she slumped down against a cold, cold tomb and sobbed in fear. The noise was hideous, a crunching, slavering frenzy that echoed around the tombs. Underneath, almost lost, was a soft gurgling from Jill as her lifeblood was drained.

Betty blocked her ears again.

Kathy woke with a start and twisted to grab the notepad by her bed, knocking over the half-full water glass on the night stand. Ignoring the spill, she scribbled furiously on the pad for a half-minute before coming to a frowning stop. Again the dream, so vivid in the last few moments before she woke, had drained out of her memory and seeped away like the water now soaking its way into the rug. Only one thing remained: the image of a tall man in a dark suit with wide lapels stepping towards her, leering horribly and carrying a cane. She struggled to escape but found herself bound as the man's twisted features came ever closer. But just under the surface, she was aware there was so much more to this dream.

7

She looked at the scribbling. Half of it was illegible, the rest may have been words but made little sense. London Church. Swaingate. Bishop. Amber. She stared so hard her eyes lost focus, there was nothing to grip on to here. She'd hoped a couple of phrases, locked into the paper, might provide a key to a fuller memory of the dream. *Another dumb idea of yours, Kathy.*

She got up and stumbled through into her bathroom. A slim, pale brunette stared back at her from the mirror, long hair tangled from a restless sleep. She stuck out her tongue. Grey and lumpy. She'd read a magazine article the other day which told you what sort of person you were according to your tongue type. Grey and lumpy hadn't featured. *Stop reading stupid magazines, Kathy.*

Downstairs her mom had made toast and coffee. They grunted at each other, neither were morning people. Kathy's father was different. Before he had gone into hospital he'd wake early every morning, make porridge and fruit shakes and talk non-stop as Kathy and her mom shuffled around, ignoring him. He had never got the hint. But neither had he ever seemed annoyed that he was talking to himself. They'd loved him for it. And now he was in hospital and with the prognosis changing for the worse every other day, they missed his irritating chatter more than anything.

Kathy forgot her earlier resolution and began leafing through one of her mom's magazines. Clothes she had neither the courage to wear, nor the money to buy. Perfumes that made her allergies flare, celebrities she found vacuous. She flicked the pages quickly, yawning, her cereal forgotten.

'Bad night again?' her mom, Susan, asked, sitting down opposite with a black coffee. Kathy nodded.

'The dream? The same one?'

Kathy nodded again.

'You could talk to Doctor Gelion about it.'

Kathy sighed. 'I don't know, Mom, I've been thinking about this and I'm not sure I should carry on with the sessions.'

'Really?' her mom said. 'Are you sure that's a good idea?'

Kathy looked down at her magazine, to escape her mom's searching gaze. A full-page picture of a red London bus looked back at her. *Come to London*, the caption read. Kathy studied the picture more closely, something catching her eye. A young girl, maybe six or seven, sat on the top deck of the bus, staring towards the camera, towards Kathy. She looked familiar, like . . .

'Kathy?' Susan said.

'Sorry,' she replied, looking up. 'Look, I haven't had a panic attack for months now.'

'No, but these dreams . . . And I can tell you're not happy.'

'Neither of us are happy, Mom. How can we be, with Dad in hospital?'

'It's more than that. It's that college. Are you being bullied?'

'No,' Kathy said. It was sort of the truth. Being ignored by the entire student body wasn't *technically* bullying.

'Go and see him today,' her mom said. 'If you don't feel he has anything useful to say about the dreams, then sure, stop. But give it one more try, okay?'

Kathy nodded.

'Oh, and a package came for you today, I left it by the door.'

Ten minutes later Kathy slammed the door behind her and scanned up the street for signs of the bus she needed. Then suddenly remembering, she rummaged through her handbag and pulled out her keys. Opening the door again she reached through and grabbed the parcel. The bus was coming – she slammed the door a second time and ran to the stop.

The bus was around half full; she found a double seat and slid in next to the window as the driver hit the gas and they pulled away from the stop. Kathy yawned again as she inspected the parcel. It was maybe A4-sized and felt like a book or a picture frame. Wrapped in brown paper and stamped with half a dozen portraits of the Queen of England. It was postmarked Highgate, UK.

London again, Kathy thought. She began to unwrap the package but stopped as she became conscious of someone sitting behind her and to her left. Turning her head slightly, she saw a long-haired man, craggy-faced, maybe in his mid-fifties, maybe older. He was watching her intently. Kathy sighed to herself. How had she become such a weirdo-magnet? She stuffed the unopened parcel into her bag and stared out the window, trying to shrink into herself.

Lockers slammed up and down the hall, each firing a tiny bolt of panic through Kathy's jangled nerves. She left her bag, containing the unopened parcel, in the locker, taking just a notepad and her foxed copy of *Vanity Fair*, the book they were studying in Eng Lit class. She closed her locker quietly and slipped off down the corridor, keeping to one side as the louder, more popular students thronged past, laughing and chatting.

'Hey, Kath,' someone said.

'Hi Scarlet,' Kathy said, spinning to see one of the few girls who knew her name, even if she did get it a little wrong.

'How you doing?' Scarlet asked. A few weeks earlier, Scarlet had been one of the unfortunate girls who'd found Kathy curled up in the girls' bathroom, heaving with fearful sobs after a panic attack. As a way to begin a friendship, it wasn't exactly ideal, but Kathy appreciated the kindness.

'I'm good,' Kathy said, smiling shyly. 'I feel a lot stronger lately.'

'Good to hear,' Scarlet said. 'You going to Marshall's party on Saturday?'

Kathy forced herself to look up into Scarlet's eyes, the way Dr Gelion had told her to do in a role play. 'They're people just like you,' the doctor had said. 'There's nothing to be frightened of.'

'I haven't been invited,' Kathy said.

Scarlet snorted. 'You don't need an invite to Marshall's party, everyone's going.'

Kathy's skin crawled at the thought of a heaving room of unknown people who'd just brush past her. She'd stand by the wall for a couple of hours, nursing one drink, chat awkwardly with the three people who knew her name and then slip away, unnoticed.

But she knew she should try, and she was glad to be asked. Dr Gelion would tell her she must go, so would her mother. She nodded.

'Great,' Scarlet said. 'I'll text you, okay?'

Kathy watched her go, almost smiling, then leaped a mile as a locker slammed behind her.

'And how's college?' Doctor Gelion asked gently, the way he did everything. He opened doors gently, he typed on his laptop gently, he picked up his pen gently, he put it down again just as gently. Kathy yearned for him, just once, to lose it and slam a filing cabinet door shut and scream 'Fucking prick!'

'College sucks,' Kathy replied. There was no point coming to a shrink and downplaying things. You had to give him something to work with. 'Everyone ignores me. I get Cs for all my grades, however hard I try. As an experiment I stopped studying one term, guess what I got?'

'C?'

'Bingo.'

'Have you made any new friends?'

Kathy hesitated for a moment. 'I've been invited to a party.'

'That's excellent news,' Dr Gelion replied. 'Are you going?'

'Yes,' Kathy said. 'I don't have to stay long, right?'

'That's up to you. But it's terrific that you decided to

13

attend. What do I always say to you?'

Kathy rolled her eyes, then grinned. 'One step at a time.'

'That's right, one step at a time. Now what about your sleeping?'

'Still bad,' she said, suddenly cold in the air-conditioning. 'I have terrible dreams, but I can never remember them, except for one part . . . I've been trying to write it all down as soon as I wake up, but the memories of the dream just sort of disappear as I pick up the pen.'

'You say there's one part you remember?'

Kathy told him about the man with the cane and being bound.

'Feeling trapped in your dream is a common motif and you shouldn't take it literally,' Dr Gelion said.

'What about suits with wide lapels and Gothic dandies carrying canes? Are they common motifs?'

Dr Gelion laughed gently. 'Not so much.'

'Dr Gelion?'

'Yes, Kathy?'

'Can you hypnotize me? So I can remember the dream?'

Dr Gelion was silent for a while. Kathy expected him to tell her, gently, that he didn't believe in hypnotherapy.

'Okay,' he said. 'We can give it a try.'

Usually Kathy sat in a high-backed leather chair facing

14

Gelion, but he asked her to lie down for the hypnosis.

'Do you swing a watch?' Kathy asked, laughing nervously.

'No watch necessary,' Gelion replied, his voice descending to an even greater level of gentleness, like down pillows wrapped in cotton wool. He sat at the foot of the couch. 'Close your eyes.'

Kathy did as he asked.

'I want you to relax, Kathy,' Gelion cooed. 'Just for a while, forget everything and listen to my voice. I'm going to count backwards from five, then you'll be in a state of extreme relaxation. Five, four, three, two and one. Kathy, how do you feel?'

Kathy took a while to answer. 'Fine. I feel fine,' she said.

'Tell me about the man with the cane,' Gelion said.

Kathy was in a burlesque nightclub. She could feel the pounding of music but could hear nothing. She was surrounded by dancers, skins shining in the thudding lights. They heaved and thrashed in time with the beat. The club looked to have a Gothic theme, vampires and Goths, virgins and grotesques. A young man of exquisite beauty passed her, brushing against her shoulder, staring deep inside her as though looking for her soul. Kathy looked down and realized she was wearing a simple black dress, tight so that the tops of her breasts threatened to escape. She felt excited and aroused, a fluttering, warming sensation deep within.

On the stage, a beautiful young woman danced, alone, performing a show. She seemed familiar. Kathy moved towards her but was distracted by someone tugging her dress. Turning, Kathy saw a young girl, perhaps seven.

'Who are you?' Kathy asked.

'I'm Amber,' the girl replied, smiling.

Then Kathy was in a different room, strapped to a wall, and the man with the cane was there; she noticed his shoes for the first time, pointed and shiny. Under the black jacket he wore a cream shirt, with ruffles and long cuffs. He twirled the cane and grinned at her madly.

'She needs you, Kathy,' he hissed. 'Amber needs you.'

'Wake up, Kathy.'

And then Kathy sat up, her heart pounding.

Gelion looked at her, concerned. 'You were becoming agitated,' he said. 'So I brought you out.'

Kathy nodded, trying to remember, wishing he'd stop talking. Something fluttered briefly within her and then was gone.

'Do you remember?' he asked.

She shook her head. 'Just the same as before, the man with the cane.'

'Who's Amber?'

Kathy looked up at him, surprised. 'I had – have – a sister called Amber. I haven't seen her since we were tiny.'

'You mentioned her a couple of times,' Gelion said. He tapped his notebook gently and looked down at his own scrawled shorthand. 'Like you thought she was in trouble?'

Kathy frowned, the memories still not there.

'Where is she now?' Gelion asked.

Kathy shrugged. 'I don't know, it's complicated. In London maybe?'

Gelion stood and walked to the window, staring out over the swarming city.

'I think maybe you need to find her,' he said.

Kathy stepped out of the office. Yellow cabs rolled by and the familiar smell of Manhattan swamped her senses. She set off towards the subway but on a whim decided to take the bus instead. She felt good and wanted to hold on to the feeling – staying overground would help, she liked resting her head against the window of the bus and watching the suburbs crawl by.

As she spun on her heels, she saw a familiar man

walking towards her. *Is that the creepy bus guy?* Kathy couldn't help but stare as he passed, his long greasy hair flopping in time with his jerky gait.

Is he following me? Kathy wondered with a shudder.

She quickened her step and hurried down to the bus stop, turning to look, but the man was nowhere to be seen. If it had been him and he had been following, he'd now disappeared.

Kathy found herself scanning the street as the bus crawled up Second Avenue, heading towards the bridge. *Great*, she told herself. *Now you've got something else to get worked up about.*

Remembering the bus journey earlier, she looked around. There was no one close by. She pulled out the parcel and ripped open the thick brown paper.

Inside lay a leather-bound book, a little bigger than A4, with ridges on the spine. At first she thought it was fake leather. A fancy 'olde-fashioned' notebook like they sold in Bloomingdales to wannabe writers who had more money than words. But the smell alone told her this book was genuinely old, and well-used. The leather was red, cracked, and the spine creaked with age as she opened the cover. The recto page was filled with words in a language she didn't even recognize. The letters didn't look like anything she'd seen before. More like squiggles. Was this shorthand? On the verso, on what was really the lining of the book, was a scrawled message.

Dear Kathy,

Bring this to Oliver Samson – British Museum. Trust him but no one else.

Stay safe.

With all my love

Amber

Kathy looked up and out the window as the black pylons of Brooklyn Bridge flickered past, clouding her view of the dull grey Hudson.

CHAPTER TWO

Kathy popped a Puralex as she waited for the laptop to fire up. Just the act of taking the little pill helped to calm her. How annoying that she should have had such a great session with Dr Gelion only for her mood to be brought down by that creepy guy. It didn't matter how many times she told herself it was coincidence, the little voices, inaudible but there nonetheless, kept telling her he was after her. But that was what the pills were for: they helped with the panic attacks, helped her ride over the rough times.

She'd gone through the book cover to cover and, apart from the inscription, hadn't understood a word. There were inexplicable diagrams, symbols and old woodcuts of weird creatures, devils and demons, winged men.

Dr Gelion had suggested she follow up on the notes she'd made after her dream.

'How would I do that?' she'd asked. 'I don't know what Swaingate is, or the London Church.'

'Well, gee,' Dr Gelion had replied, smiling gently at her. 'I'm no expert, but don't you teenagers usually go straight to the internet when you don't know stuff?'

'Oh,' Kathy had said, grinning, 'I should Google it?'

'You should indeed – Google it.'

Kathy typed *Swaingate* into the box and hit enter. She could feel the calming influence of the drug trickle through her consciousness, giving everything a soft edge. She got a few hits: some engineering company; a sci-fi author named Colin Swaingate; a Swaingate, Missouri. But nothing jumped at her.

She tried the London Church – again nothing concrete: a hundred churches in London; a couple of restaurants; a bar in Dakota.

Clearing the box, she typed in *Swaingate + the London Church* and after a moment's pause typed in *+ Amber*. She pressed enter and her stomach lurched at the page that came up, Puralex or not. Suddenly she remembered.

It was the burlesque club she'd been in under hypnosis. The homepage was a web of pictures: jostling, twisted bodies locked in metamorphic poses, the same horror shows she'd seen before. Mostly dressed as vampires but there were other undead creatures in there, as well as a fair sprinkling of virgins and victims. Kathy had had a Goth friend at high school who sometimes would drag her along to raves and parties, before the panic attacks had turned murderous. It had always seemed dumb and hokey to Kathy, just a stupid kids' fancy dress party. But as Kathy clicked through the website, exploring the torture chamber, the crypt, the chill-out slab room, she could see this place was a whole new level. Something inside her stirred a little.

The costumes were amazing. The web page played a grungy, deep-throated track which felt familiar to her. Some of the more hard-core members had their own biogs. Here was Karla, vampish and sexy. Next Vlad, snarling theatrically at the camera. Maybe it was the obvious sense of belonging they all had that attracted Kathy. It was that being part of something she missed in her own life. The vampire costumes were silly but it was just for fun, right? Like *Rocky Horror*. She found herself leaning forward, trying to get a better view of the stage in the background. There were dancers there, some in cages, some swinging from high rope. One girl in particular caught her eye. Dark-haired and dressed in pure white, she clung to the bars of her cage, butt out, back arched. Yearning for rescue, or for something else? But it was her face which captured Kathy's attention. She looked like a more beautiful version of Kathy. Was this Amber?

Kathy clicked through the biogs, looking for Amber, but instead found herself looking at someone called Antwain, and for the second time she jerked in surprise. It was the boy from her dream, the beautiful boy. And boy was he beautiful. Dark skin, toned without being over-muscled. She watched a short video of him dancing bare-chested with a scantily-dressed vixen and felt herself grow warm as he writhed on-screen. She squeezed her thighs together and shivered.

My God, she thought, *is that Puralex I took?* Embarrassed at herself she returned to the home page and scanned the options at the top. Clicking on *contact us*, a mailbox popped up with contact@thechurch.vampirecorps.com. She rattled off a quick email.

> *Hi,*
>
> *I'm hoping to get in contact with an old friend, who is a member. Her name is Amber Bilic, though she may have changed her surname. If you know her, could you ask her if she'd like to get in touch with me?*
>
> *Kathy Moore*

She sent the email, returned to the search page and scrolled down. Swaingate, it turned out, was a place in London, a tiny triangle on a road called Swain's Lane, which ran past Highgate Cemetery. It just happened to be where the Church nightclub was located, close to the gates to the cemetery itself. That explained the Gothic theme, she thought.

Suddenly feeling hot, Kathy escaped and went downstairs to the cooler kitchen where her mom was rattling cups. Kathy listened for a while, interpreting the cup-rattling code to see how well her father had been today. Low-frequency, gentle clunks meant her mom was sad and distracted. A brighter prognosis meant cheery clattering, while an argument with the doctors sometimes led to the dustpan being needed.

Things seemed okay today. 'How was Dad?' Kathy tried.

Susan turned, smiling. 'We went for a spin around the gardens today. He even read for a while in the sun.'

'That's great news,' Kathy said. Being slightly removed from it, Kathy saw things a little different to her; there were good days and bad, and her mom's mood followed these tightly. Kathy stood back and could only see a gradual decline. The cancer was winning.

Susan turned back to the sink.

'Mom?'

'Sweetie?'

'I was thinking today about my family – in England.'

She didn't want to say her 'real' family.

Without turning Susan said, 'Okay.'

'And I thought, well . . . I really don't know too much about them.'

Now Susan did turn. She walked to the table and dried her hands, eyeing Kathy curiously.

'I'm happy to answer any questions you have, Kathy. We've never tried to keep anything from you.'

'Oh I know, Mom, I know that,' she said. 'It sounds odd now that I come to think about it. But it's me. I don't really understand why, but I've never really wanted to find out more. I just ... I just accept that they're there and I'm here and that's how it is.'

'I'll put the kettle on,' Susan said.

A few minutes later, they settled in their usual seats at the table and grinned at each other nervously.

'Okay, so you probably know most of this story,' Susan said, 'but let me just go over it again. Your parents and your sister, Amber, were born in Romania. There was a revolution there twenty years ago and they fled to England. The family settled in London and stayed with your Aunt Elizabeth, your mother's half-sister. Now unfortunately, as with this type of civil unrest, it followed them to London. We don't know exactly how it happened, but your father was killed. Your mother was pregnant with you at the time. She and Amber had to escape again; she came to New York, where you were born.'

Susan stopped and grinned at Kathy at this point. She paused, as if waiting for Kathy to say something. Kathy just smiled nervously and sipped her coffee, waiting for Susan to continue.

'Unfortunately,' Susan said, 'your mother was found by the Immigration Department, working in a hotel, and was sent back to England, along with Amber. Because you were born here, they gave her the option of letting you stay, and we were lucky enough to find you at the orphanage and brought you home to live with us.'

Kathy wondered if she'd be choking up now without the soothing effect of the drug. But she felt strangely disconnected as she listened to the tragic story of her own family. It was as if a shroud cloaked her early history, like it wasn't a real part of her. She struggled to cut through the cloth as her mom continued.

'It was a desperately difficult decision your mother had to make,' Susan said, watching Kathy closely. 'You mustn't blame her.'

I don't, Kathy thought. *I don't blame her at all. I'm glad she left me here*. She knew this wasn't how she was supposed to feel. This wasn't how it happened in the

26

soaps on TV. She was supposed to get all angry and tearful and demand to find her mother, now!

'Things were very uncertain and there was still trouble for your family in London. It wasn't the place for a baby,' Susan continued.

'And then she too was killed,' Kathy said, staring down into her coffee. Even her own mother's death hardly stirred an emotion. What was wrong with her? It couldn't just be the Puralex. 'Was she killed because of this . . . revolution?'

Susan shook her head. 'No, she died in Highgate—'

Kathy looked up sharply. 'Highgate?'

Susan paused before responding. 'Yes, that's where your Aunt Elizabeth lives. She has a big old house overlooking the cemetery.'

Now she felt something, as though part of her had been awoken by the mention of this Highgate Cemetery.

'Do you still keep in touch with my Aunt Elizabeth?'

'We used to, but not so much these days. We still send Christmas cards and the odd note on how you're doing at school.'

'And what happened to Amber?'

'The family thought it was too dangerous to let her stay in London. She went to a foster home. But Elizabeth is in contact with her now though and, the last I heard, Amber's just fine.'

27

Kathy tried to picture her sister as a tiny, frightened child being led away from a grand London town house by strangers, but even such a tragic tale as that couldn't hold her interest. Her mind's eye was drawn across the dream road to a Grimm's fairytale cemetery scene. She shook her head, her mind frazzled.

'So how did my mother die?' she asked.

Susan sighed and cupped her hands around her empty coffee mug. 'She was murdered.'

'Yes, but how? Was she shot, strangled – how?'

'Do you really want to know all this? Do you really think it will help?'

'Yes, yes I do,' Kathy said. She was looking for something that would penetrate this balloon that surrounded her, stopping her from feeling. She wanted pain and sadness, she wanted a dark, sickening anger.

'Her body was found, drained of blood, in a crypt, in Highgate Cemetery,' Susan said, mechanically, the way a cop in a TV show might. 'Her killer was never found.'

And all Kathy could think about was Swain's Lane, Highgate Cemetery, and the man with the cane.

'Hello?'

'H-hello? Is that Elizabeth Fallon?'

'Yes it is, who's calling?'

28

'It's Kathy – Kathy Moore. Sorry, I mean Kathy Bilic, your n—'

'Kathy? My God, you're calling from America?'

'Yes. Hello.'

'It's so nice to hear from you. How *are* you?'

'I'm good thanks. How are you?'

'I'm getting old, Kathy, never ask an older lady how she is. Otherwise you'll be old yourself by the time she's finished listing her ailments.'

Kathy laughed. There was a silence.

'So,' Elizabeth asked, 'was there something in particular you wanted? It's just nice to talk of course, but . . .'

'Oh yeah. Look I was kind of hoping that maybe I could, y'know, get in contact with Amber?'

There was another silence, longer this time.

'Hello?' Kathy said.

'Oh sorry, darling, yes. About Amber. The thing is . . . she's disappeared. I don't know where she is.'

Kathy's stomach flipped and she leaned against the wall for support. The black-suited man. Was he real? Was Amber kidnapped? Held in some awful dungeon?

'When did she disappear?' Kathy asked.

'Two weeks ago,' Elizabeth replied, her voice wavering as some solar flare hit the satellite a hundred miles over the Atlantic. Two weeks ago was when Kathy had

29

started having the dream, the dream of her sister held by inhuman forces.

'We didn't worry at first,' Elizabeth said. 'She's been working as a journalist and she often goes off for a few days on a story. But this time, she didn't reappear. Then a nice man called Oscar contacted me to see if I'd heard from her, as she often stays here with me, you see. We called around but no one had seen her or heard from her. We have reported it to the police and she's been officially listed as missing.'

Kathy felt sick. She slumped down on to the floor, curling up, the phone still clasped to her ear. Finally something had started to penetrate her comfort zone, her balloon of emotional resistance was slowly deflating. *You wanted to feel something, Kathy*, she told herself. *You wanted the pain. Now you've got it.*

'Can I come?' Kathy asked in a tiny voice.

'Sorry? What was that?'

'Can I come?' Kathy repeated. 'Can I visit you? In London?'

Now there was the longest pause of all. Kathy wondered if the connection had been broken, then she realized her aunt was crying.

'Please?' Kathy said.

'I'd love to meet you,' Elizabeth said, her voice

just holding. 'Susan's letters – I know you're a fine young woman.'

Kathy waited for the *but*.

'I'm just not sure it's safe here,' Elizabeth said.

'But the revolution isn't still going on, is it?' Kathy asked. 'Who'd even know who I was?'

'Oh Kathy,' Elizabeth said. 'There's so much you don't know.'

'I want to come,' Kathy said. She had intended to tell her aunt about the red leather book, but thinking about it now, and remembering the inscription inside the cover telling her to trust no one but Oliver, she held back. 'I'm coming, and I'd like to stay with you, but I can get a hotel . . .'

She couldn't have got a hotel. The cost of the flights would wipe out most of her savings from her Saturday job. She'd have precious little spending money while there.

'Of course you can stay with me,' Aunt Elizabeth said, suddenly firmer and perhaps sounding a little offended. 'I won't have you staying in some ghastly London flea-pit.'

'Great,' Kathy said. 'I'll send you the flight details. Do you have email?'

Elizabeth laughed. 'Of course. I may be old, but I'm still with it.'

They exchanged email addresses and Kathy hung up with a grin on her face. She was going to London.

Now she just had to break the news to Susan.

CHAPTER THREE

7th October 1971

Brian Travis locked the Cortina and pulled at the handle to check it was secure. Ever since his old Capri had been stolen from outside his flat in Archway, he'd been extra careful. Couldn't even leave your flat unlocked to pop down the shops these days, they'd have the lot inside ten minutes, all them immigrants. Sometimes felt like Bridgetown round here these days. Brian looked up and down the lane. He always parked here, between the high brick walls at the north end of the cemetery. Swaingate was just down the road; the Flask pub opposite, where he'd sometimes stop for a pint of mild and a bowl of water for Gooner. Brian shivered in the cool evening. A fog had rolled in in the last half-hour or so. *Just a quick walk today and maybe we'll see about that pint*, he told himself.

Gooner whined and thumped his tail impatiently.

'Come on then, lad,' Brian said. They walked down to the gate and plunged into the West Cemetery, trotting up the steps into the woods. Gooner disappeared almost instantly amongst the jumble of graves and trees. Brian trudged along the gravel path, heading towards the Circle of Lebanon, a couple of hundred yards up the hill, into the cemetery.

The fog crept up behind him and wrapped its ghostly tentacles around his stocky frame. Not a superstitious type, Brian appreciated days like this. They kept the tourists away. He felt the cemetery was his alone to enjoy – well, him and Gooner. Lately there'd been more of those idiotic news items on the telly about the vampire and, as usual, the place had been overrun with loonies carrying stakes and crucifixes, leaping out from behind gravestones and frightening Gooner.

'Gooner!' he called, then gave his special whistle. The dog answered with a bark from somewhere deep within a thicket. Once the labrador had come back to him carrying a rabbit corpse, stinking and maggoty. It wasn't just dead humans here. There was plenty of wildlife in the cemetery, going about their business killing and eating one another. That's how it all started – with dead foxes drained of blood.

34

He read some of the inscriptions as he passed the graves. Here was Harold Coutts-Burnett, who'd owned half of London once. Then Mary Jennings, famous for being the first person to be buried in this cemetery, at a young twenty-three years old. Most of the graves in this part of the cemetery were overgrown with weeds and creepers. Over the decades the shifting soil had jammed the already-crowded stones closer together, forcing them into odd angles. A Celtic cross leaned drunkenly over the path, looking like it might fall at any moment.

As he peered across the graves, into the fog-obscured distance, Brian thought he saw someone. A tall man in a dark coat. He stopped for a second, hoping for a clearer view, but the man had disappeared. Maybe it had just been his imagination. Probably a tree, half seen. He carried on and, after a couple of minutes, he reached the Circle of Lebanon, a great cedar acting as its centrepiece. Without the fog, the church of St Michael of Highgate would have been visible further up the hill, at the edge of the cemetery, its great stained-glass windows watching over the dead below.

'Once around and then to the Flask,' he told himself, shivering again. As he trotted down the steps and entered the circle, the temperature dropped further. *The weatherman hadn't predicted either fog, or such a drop in the mercury*, he thought, sniffing. *That BBC never got it right.*

'Gooner!' he called again. This time though, there was no answer. He carried on, the temperature growing ever colder. The fog closed in around him. Trapped between the rows of tombs, solemn in their regard, the gloom seemed to fold in on itself, swamping him. He began to hurry a little, wanting his dog and his ale. The only sound was the crunching of his feet on the sharp gravel beneath. There was no birdsong, not even the hum of traffic from the Highgate Road. It was as if he, Brian Travis, was the only living creature on the planet. The Planet of the Dead. He shook his head and tried to force a laugh out at the idea. It died in his throat. Then, sensing something in his peripheral vision, he spun around to look. But it was just a pattern of moss on a tomb door. For a moment he'd thought it was the dark figure of a man.

Brian whistled for his dog, listened, then whistled again. Still no answer. A tiny icicle of fear began to grow along his spine, drip-dripping down. 'Gooner!' he yelled. He stopped for a minute to listen.

Nothing.

Brian ran, chest heaving, belly wobbling. 'Gooner!' he called, panting. Just how big was this damn circle anyway? Where was the exit? The tombs carried on seamlessly ahead of him, curving away to a vanishing point to his left. Surely he'd done a full circuit? He carried on running and puffing, his body complaining about the unaccustomed exercise.

And then he saw it, the exit. A sense of relief swept over him and he staggered out into the gloom, panting, sweat pouring from his face, despite the now-intense cold.

Then something dark came at him with incredible speed from behind a tomb. Brian screamed as he saw glowing eyes.

The dog thumped into him, knocking him over and licking his face in raptures. Evidently Gooner had been as worried as he had.

'Christ on a bike, Gooner!' Brian said. 'You scared the crap out of me.' But he hugged the dog tightly, greedily soaking up the animal's warm vitality.

'Come on,' he said, getting to his feet with difficulty. 'Let's get to the Flask, I need a drink.'

Shadows assailed them as they hurried back to Swaingate. The swirling fog formed itself into dark-coated figures which dissipated as soon as they were formed. Gooner stayed close to Brian's heel as they went, as aware as he was that there was something not quite right about the cemetery tonight.

Brian's heart lurched as he saw a glow ahead of them

on the path, down the slope. He stopped and Gooner crouched down, whimpering slightly.

'Who's there?' Brian called out. 'I can see you. I have a dog.'

But the glow remained, wavering slightly. Brian took a step forward. Was this the tall man he thought he'd seen earlier?

But no, with a huge sense of relief, Brian realized it was the glow of the lamplight outside the gates, part hidden by the trees. *There's no more welcoming sight on the Earth*, he thought, then headed off towards the pub.

Brian had two pints, as it happened, and shared a packet of pork scratchings with Gooner. He felt silly about his fears and didn't mention to Harry, the landlord, what he'd experienced. He felt better after the drinks though and bade everyone a cheery goodnight.

As they left the pub Brian turned up his collar.

'Time to go home,' he said to Gooner, who seemed to agree as he ran towards the car. But a few yards from the Cortina, the dog stopped short.

'What is it?' Brian asked. Fur bristling, a dull moaning growl in his throat, Gooner stood, staring at the car.

Brian peered ahead. There was something . . . no, some*one* in the driver's seat. He stepped forward slowly, shivering, his gut churning with icy fear. A dark figure sat behind the wheel. As Brian approached, the light from the street lamp opposite gradually came into play to reveal the face.

It was a corpse, that of a woman, in an advanced stage of decomposition. Her straggly blonde hair only partially masked her worm-eaten visage. The hands, cracked and withered, were resting loosely on the steering wheel. She wore a white dress, stained yellow. Brian felt bile rise in his throat but couldn't tear his eyes away. Gooner grumbled in the fog behind, as if asking who would do such a thing?

Later, back in the Flask and after the police arrived, a constable came and asked him for the car keys. Brian had been given some pills to make him stop shuddering and swaying.

Brian stared up at the young policeman, confused. 'Why do you want the keys?' he asked.

The policeman shuffled nervously. 'The doors are locked, sir. We don't want to break in if we don't have to.'

'How can the doors be locked?' Brian asked, clutching his pint like a lifeline. 'How could that ... thing have been put there if the doors are locked?'

But the policeman simply stared back at him, unable to answer.

* * *

'You have to go now?' Susan said. 'Right now?'

'It's important to me,' Kathy said, staring at her feet. She felt awful about it, especially as she'd decided not to tell Susan about Amber's disappearance. She didn't want her mom worrying about her.

'But what about your father?'

Kathy glanced up at her mother. Was this an acknowledgement of what they both knew? That he was nearing the end?

'I'll only be gone a few weeks,' Kathy said. 'Just until college starts again.' There, she thought, gauntlet laid down. 'Are you telling me he hasn't got weeks?'

Susan turned away and started clattering cups violently in the sink. Kathy slipped out of the room and went to check flight prices.

Whilst checking American Airways' website, a mail notification popped up. Kathy clicked on it without thinking.

Kathy,

Any friend of Amber's is a friend of ours. Why not drop into the Church some time and we'll see if we can't put you in touch with her?

Remember, dress to impress.

40

Power,

Antwain

Kathy read the email again, icy fingers brushing against her exposed skin. Part of her was excited by the thought of meeting Antwain, especially as he seemed to know where Amber was. But why be so mysterious about it? Why not just say, 'Sure I know Amber, I'll pass your details on to her'? Were they that keen for new customers they had to play dumb games?

Feeling a little naughty, Kathy fired off an immediate response.

If I drop by, should I ask for you? I'm new to London and don't know anyone there.

A few minutes later, while Kathy pretended to continue with her travel plans, a reply came back.

Sure, Kathy. I'd love to show you around. Ask for me when you get here, Antwain.

Kathy had to forcibly restrain herself from responding straight away. She went and made herself a coffee, waited half an hour, counting the time before sending back a brief email. A girl needs to play it cool, she knew that much.

Look forward to it,

    K

Then she closed down mail to rid herself of the distraction and got back to the flight search.

Kathy found that she could just about afford the flights if she left at three a.m. from Newark, which was one hell of a trek from Flushing but worth it for the saving. She booked a flight for Sunday morning with a return three weeks later. London was six hours ahead and the flight took the same amount of time. Kathy got in a fluster trying to work it out and ended up thinking she might arrive at the same time she left, until Susan explained it all to her. Kathy was one of those bright girls who can be inexplicably dumb with some things.

Susan was in an *okay* mood. She seemed to have accepted Kathy needed to do this thing. It wasn't as though her daughter had ever asked for much.

'In a way it might be best if you're not here over the next few weeks anyway,' her mom said as Kathy packed. Kathy sensed Susan was trying to convince herself, rather than Kathy. 'The doctors say he's making progress.'

'I'll come with you to see Dad tomorrow. Anyway I'll be back in three weeks, I promise,' Kathy said.

Susan nodded and tried to smile, her heart clearly not in it.

Kathy had decided to try and get some sleep on Saturday evening, not sure if she'd be able to sleep on the plane. Buzzing with nervous energy, she took a couple of Puralex, even though it had been less than twenty-four hours since the last two. They weren't sleeping pills, but they did calm her down and help her to empty her head of the mad spinning thoughts and anxieties which usually filled it. As she lay down though, her phone buzzed. It was a text from Scarlet, reminding her about the party.

Kathy shook her head. She couldn't go. Not now. She turned off the phone and lay back down. But it was too early. Despite the pills, she just lay there thinking about Amber and Antwain, and Dr Gelion's voice floated through her mind congratulating her on being invited to a party. *One step at a time, Kathy. One step at a time.* She imagined what it might be like to dress in vampire costume and dance like the undead at the Church.

After an hour of lying there, eyes wide shut, Kathy sat bolt upright.

'Screw it,' she said. 'I'm going to the party.'

* * *

'Good to see you,' Scarlet shouted in her ear, over the booming music. 'You don't come out too often.'

Kathy smiled. 'I don't get invited too often,' she replied, then immediately regretted it, feeling like she was whining.

'Don't wait for invites,' Scarlet said. 'Just put yourself out there, girl.'

Kathy nodded and sipped her drink, something with vodka in it. She wasn't supposed to be drinking on top of the drugs, but she figured a little sip wasn't going to hurt.

'You wanna dance?' Scarlet asked.

Kathy glanced over at the dance area; jostling, jumping happy bodies gleamed in the strobe lighting Marshall had put up. A DJ swayed slowly as he mixed one record into the next seamlessly, one fingertip on his laptop, another against his massive headphones.

'Maybe in a while,' Kathy shouted, suddenly feeling a little panicky. Marshall was there dancing with Megan Lars, a perky blonde who, rumour had it, gave great blow jobs.

'Well I love this song, so I'm gonna, okay?' Scarlet said, her hot breath against Kathy's ear. Then she was gone, leaving Kathy alone and defenceless. She shuffled closer to the wall and took a deep breath. She recognized most of the people at the party, but didn't know any of them well enough that she could just go and start talking. She was aware that that was what normal people did do. Just walk up and start talking. That was the point of a party, but the thought of doing it made Kathy's skin crawl. It just wasn't going to happen. This was what it was always like for her.

She saw Marshall and Megan dirty dancing for a while and suddenly drained her vodka. Scarlet waved at her and motioned her over. Kathy hesitated a second, then thought *Oh what the hell*.

She walked over on to the makeshift dance floor, watched Scarlet's shapes. Time slowed as Kathy closed her eyes and imagined she could feel the vodka creep through her system. Suddenly she was back in the Church. Antwain danced on the stage as he performed a sword show with a near-naked Amber. The crowd danced, some drank wine as they watched them and Kathy felt the thumping drive of the music through her feet, up into her core, driving into her like sex. She found herself nodding along, then swaying, and before she knew it she was dancing along with the others, following the moves, in tune with the pack.

Someone jostled her and her eyes snapped open. She was back at the party; standing in the middle of the dance floor. Megan nudged Marshall and pointed at her, smirking. Kathy straightened her back and began to dance. Maybe it was the dream, maybe the Puralex and vodka, maybe the thought that in a few hours she'd be on a plane over the Atlantic, but something clicked in Kathy and she found expression and release through dancing. Like she was inhabiting someone else's body, or someone else was in hers. A familiar fluttering sensation unfolded in her belly. Where had she felt that before?

Scarlet pouted at her and Kathy swung closer, provocative. She spun, her back to her partner, and wasn't surprised to find Scarlet's hands on her body, sliding down her flat stomach. Kathy pulled away and seized Scarlet's hand, then pulled her in close and slid down against her torso. Everything worked smoothly, each girl seemed to be able to mind-read the other, and a circle gathered around, watching the display.

Scarlet's eyes were half closed as she ran her hands down Kathy's chest. The music reached a crescendo. Kathy gasped as something awoke inside her and she slipped in closer to her partner. The boys in the circle leered and catcalled. Scarlet's head went back, exposing her neck. Kathy danced on, transfixed by the marble-smooth skin.

But then Scarlet had pulled back and Kathy realized the song had ended and the DJ had mixed in some chill-out track.

'Who's Oliver?' Scarlet asked, smiling and puzzled.

'What? Oliver?' Kathy said, her head still swimming.

'You said, "Stay away from Oliver" just now.'

'Did I?'

'Are you okay?' Scarlet asked, resting her cool palm against Kathy's cheek. Kathy closed her eyes, hoping Scarlet was going to kiss her. Then she opened them, realizing what an idiot she must look. *What's wrong with me? I'm not even into girls.*

Scarlet winked at her and walked off to get a drink. The circle broke up. Kathy stood, shaking for a moment, then looked up to find Marshall's eyes on her, for an instant, before he was dragged off by Megan. What a weird night. And what was the whole Oliver thing about? If Amber was somehow trying to communicate with her, she was being a little too cryptic.

'I guess weirdness runs in the family,' she muttered to herself. She shivered slightly, a little scared by herself, then turned to go.

'Which gate?' Susan asked for the third time.

Kathy sighed and kept walking, Susan bumbling along behind her, knocking into people. She'd wanted to come alone, having had a cool fantasy about riding the early-hours subway, with just her carry-on bag. She'd thrown in

47

a few pairs of pants, shorts and a couple of tops, her money, Amber's red leather book, her Puralex and of course her inhaler. What else did a girl need? Susan had firmly rejected the subway idea when she'd heard what time the flight left and had insisted on driving her to the airport, then staying with her while she checked in.

'It's Gate Twenty-four, but Mom I keep telling you, you can't come through. We have to say goodbye here.'

'But your flight doesn't leave for two hours,' Susan protested.

'I have security, and passport control, and I want to buy a magazine.'

'I think I saw a news-stand just over there,' Susan said. 'I'll buy you a magazine . . .'

'Mom,' Kathy said, stopping to address her foster-mother, 'it's going to be okay.'

Susan burst into tears and Kathy hugged her. This is why she'd wanted to come alone.

'Let's say goodbye here,' she said. 'I love you, Mom.'

'I love you too, honey.'

'I'll be back sooner then you know,' Kathy said, a little break now creeping into her own voice. She ended the hug and Susan stood for a second, as if she were going to say something else. Then she waved and hurried off into the crowd.

The airport was busy even at this time, though not nearly so crazy as the last time Kathy had been here – on her way to Bermuda for a family holiday a few years back. Kathy sighed and hoisted her little bag. Susan had given her a little money in case she needed more clothes, but she didn't want to use that. Her parents were not wealthy. Besides, the weather was supposed to be okay in London this time of year.

Kathy excused herself past a sprawling family and their luggage, then looked up and saw the long-haired man. Walking towards her. Her breath caught in her throat as he looked over at her, for an instant their eyes met, then he looked away and changed direction, hurrying off. Kathy rushed after him, determined to find out why he was following her.

'Hey you!' she shouted, wondering if this was such a good idea – but he couldn't attack her in Newark Airport, could he? Plenty of cops here. The man scuttled down a set of stairs and Kathy ran after him.

'Hey!' she yelled, again. People had stopped to look by now and Kathy thought maybe she shouldn't yell again – she didn't want to get herself arrested. The man pushed past some people on the stairs and ducked off to the left at the bottom of the steps. Kathy got stuck behind a large lady who was having trouble with her suitcase. By the time she got to the bottom the man was gone – a sliding door out to a car park, his escape route. Kathy wandered out, but suddenly felt insecure.

'Who are you?' she muttered. 'What do you want?'

CHAPTER FOUR

27th March 1983 – Highgate Cemetery

Viduc scanned the nameplates on the tombs as he passed. Jacob trudged along behind him, huffing. As usual he'd protested about having to carry the equipment.

'You – assistant,' Viduc had reminded him back at the house. 'Me – Hunter.'

Jacob had rolled his eyes. 'Yeah, about that, we do a lot of hunting but never seem to do any finding.'

'No bad thing,' Viduc said, grinning. 'I not sure you really ready to find vampire. Shit you pants.'

Jacob scowled and held up a stake. 'I'm ready. You find me one and I'll do what I need to.'

Now, in the cemetery in the small hours, Viduc wondered if Jacob's nerve was still there. He had grave doubts about the boy, but assistants were hard to find.

The group was dwindling. Just two full-blood Hunters remained of a sect that had once numbered a hundred thousand. Beggars can't be choosers, and these days the young seemed more interested in dressing up as vampires than trying to destroy them. Like Viduc, this boy had no Hunter blood in him, but he wanted to kill vampires, which made him okay in Viduc's book.

'Like a game of chess,' Viduc said. 'The vampire knows we look for him. We make this cemetery into a prison but he needs to feed. He comes out rare, only when he is too weak and nearly dead. Maybe once every ten years?'

Jacob grunted by way of response. Viduc stopped to inspect a tomb, then shook his head and moved on.

'All the time we are doing the research. Looking for who he is, where he comes from. He tries to throw us off the scent. Hides in different tombs. Does mad things to confuse.'

A small cloud hushed the gibbous moon and Viduc stopped, waiting for the light to return. Jacob started to say something but Viduc held up a hand to silence him. The cloud passed and silver light revealed the nameplate over the tomb Viduc stood before.

Gantry.

'This the one,' he said softly. 'I know what he is. And I know where he is.'

Jacob sighed and dropped the gear with a clank.

Viduc was on him in a flash, gripping the boy's denim jacket and pinning him against a neighbouring tomb door, a look of fury twisting his Slavic features. He struggled for a minute to get control of his temper, then took a deep breath.

'Quiet – or we get killed here tonight,' he hissed, finally. Viduc released the boy and turned to pick up his tools.

'Okay, okay,' Jacob whispered, shocked by the intensity of the man's anger. He dusted himself off and glared at the old man's back.

Viduc took a crowbar from the old leather toolbag Jacob had been carrying. He jammed it into the crack between the tomb and its door. Glancing over at Jacob for support, Viduc grunted and pushed. Nothing. Viduc rested and signalled Jacob over with a flick of his head. The two men took hold of the crowbar and pushed as one. An owl hooted in the trees somewhere to their left and the wind tickled along the crescent. Still they heaved, silently, sweat trickling down their necks and on to their backs.

Then, with a crack to wake the dead, the door snapped open. The men waited, listening. The owl had stopped hooting – perhaps it too was listening. Finally satisfied,

Viduc took hold of the heavy stone door and dragged it open, crushing the springtime weeds which had grown up against it.

A stench of damp stone and decay assailed them: Jacob coughed into his sleeve. Viduc handed him a torch and took the same for himself. The torches were powerful, ex-army, and the batteries were fresh, but even so they seemed to illuminate little within the tomb, as though the darkness within had its own corporeal form and was intent on swamping the beams, dampening their vitality. The men descended the steps into the gloom, breath misting before them in the cold air.

The tomb was huge – one large, high central chamber, with doors in every wall, leading to further rooms, all lined with coffins. Engraved marble slabs lined the floors and decorated the walls. *In memoriam. RIP. With God. Requiescent in Pace.* All the crypts along this row were the same: family crypts, dug deep over the years as new generations of the great North London families left instructions that they be interred with their ancestors. New rooms were dug, extensions were planned, a local architecture practice specialized in maximizing space underground – real estate for the dead. This was a prestigious address.

Viduc turned slowly within the main chamber

looking for the right door, then walked through into the next chamber. Jacob tripped along after him, no longer looking so cocky, staying close to his master. Viduc located the sarcophagus easily enough. The inscription on the top read:

William Edward Gantry 1819–1901

'This is him?' Jacob whispered, as the older man ran a finger along the case, almost lovingly. 'William Gantry?'

Viduc nodded. Then shook his head. 'His name not Gantry. But he in this tomb. It take me thirty years, but I find the bastard.'

'And are you sure it's him? I mean, are you sure Gantry, or the man in his tomb, is the one you're looking for?'

Viduc looked up at the young man and held out an arm, drawing his attention to the other sarcophagi in the room. 'See the dust?'

Jacob looked around and nodded. 'Sure.' The other boxes were grimy with the accumulated filth of a hundred years.

Viduc ran a finger along the top of William Gantry's casket and held it up. 'Not so much dust on this one.'

Jacob looked down. Viduc was right. Gantry's box was comparatively clean.

'No one been buried here for seventy-six years,' Viduc

said. 'This box opened much more recently. Maybe ten years?'

Jacob shrugged. 'Maybe someone came in to clean this one,' he suggested.

'You losing your nerve?' Viduc asked, eyeing him closely.

Jacob shook his head.

'Come on,' Viduc said, 'help open this.'

Jacob hesitated. 'Will he be . . . you know – alive?'

'I think not,' Viduc said. 'He hasn't fed for years. He is being careful. So he is weak. He will wake only slowly, we have enough time.'

As the slab fell clear Jacob gasped at what he saw. The body within lay at rest, with not a trace of decomposition. The man, supposedly dead for over eighty years, looked as if he were just taking a quick nap.

'Believe Viduc now?' the old man asked wryly.

Jacob looked up at the old man, suddenly aware that this wasn't a dumb game any more. They held each other's gaze for a moment. Then Jacob grinned, involuntarily, the tension getting too much. He began to speak.

'I suppose—'

But he was cut short when a hand shot out of the box and seized him by the throat. Jacob gurgled a muffled scream. Viduc looked down in alarm to see the vampire's yellow eyes were wide open, his face twisted into a snarl. Viduc hefted the stake. The vampire hissed to see it and began to lift itself out of the box. It moved slowly though, weak, and hampered by the grip on Jacob's throat that it showed no signs of releasing. The boy's eyes bulged as he fought for breath. But Viduc was quick and sure. With a practised twist, he rammed the sharp wooden stake deep into the vampire's chest.

The vampire screamed and thrashed inside the box. Viduc held his weight down on the stake, forcing the vampire back down. It took minutes to die, its yellow eyes flashing, its foul-breathed, open mouth screaming into Viduc's ear as the three held themselves in the awkward tableau, intimate, sharing this moment. The vampire turned its attention to Jacob in the last few seconds as though searching for help. Its hand still clutched Jacob's throat, though the grip was growing weaker. Jacob looked down, his sight dimming as if an echo of the fading light in the vampire's eyes. At that moment, as they each teetered on the very precipice of the abyss, something passed between them, the vampire and Jacob. Then the grip was relaxed and Jacob slumped to the floor.

Once he was sure the vampire was dead, Viduc came to check on his assistant. He helped Jacob up into a sitting position and grinned at the young man.

'First time not so bad, eh?'

Jacob nodded, stroking his reddened throat tenderly.

'Next time, I let you have the stake, yes?'

Viduc stood and began collecting his things. Jacob watched his master crouching down, tucking tools into the leather bag.

The young man's eyes flashed vampire-yellow.

CHAPTER FIVE

Kathy bent her head back as far as it would go, her pale throat exposed to the cool morning air. Aunt Elizabeth's house towered above her. A terraced town house opposite the cemetery itself, it seemed to rise up and up as if stretching high to get the best view over the graveyard. Kathy counted five storeys, including the basement – or cellar, as they'd say here.

'Sorry about the weather,' Elizabeth said, joining her after paying the taxi driver. Kathy had been pleased to find her aunt waiting for her at the airport, holding a little sign with her name on it. They'd hugged tightly, an instant bond forming. 'So like your sister,' Elizabeth had said. 'So like your mother.'

The taxi journey had taken forty-five minutes, the old-fashioned black cab zipping through the back streets; lines of terraced houses on either side guarded by lines of parked cars. Amber's red leather book lay at the bottom of Kathy's bag. She'd intended to call the mysterious Oliver the minute she'd touched down at Heathrow Airport, but she felt unaccountably nervous at the prospect. Though Amber's note had told her to trust no one else, something had happened at the party, when Kathy had felt Amber was inside her, trying to express something, to warn her. She shook her head; Oliver could wait another day or two – at least she'd give the jet lag time to relent.

Kathy had recognized the cemetery from her search on Google images and had peered intently through the taxi window as they'd headed up Swain's Lane.

'Mom said you had a grand old house,' Kathy said, 'but I had no idea.'

Elizabeth shrugged. 'It was my father's money, and my husband made some wise investments with it before he died. Too big for me now, really, but I can't bear to leave. So many loving memories.'

Kathy looked up at her aunt. Elizabeth looked to be in her early sixties, a decade or so older than Kathy's mother would have been. She was an attractive older woman, even if her waist was thickening and her skin a little tight now against the strong cheekbones that seemed to run in their family. *If I look like her in forty years*, Kathy thought, *I won't complain*.

'Come on, then,' Elizabeth said, lifting Kathy's little bag. 'Let's get you and your insufficient luggage inside.'

As she passed the threshold, something made Kathy look up again. A curious stone carving sat atop the lintel, twisted and complex in its shape. Kathy paused to look, aware of something unusual about it. She didn't recognize the pattern, it was more that seeing it had somehow changed the atmosphere. Like it was projecting some kind of power, like the feeling you get when you enter a church. She shook her head and followed her aunt into the house.

If the house had looked large from the outside it seemed absolutely vast inside. Elizabeth gave her a brief tour and then left Kathy to explore while she went downstairs to make tea. The ceilings were so high they could have accommodated another floor. There were three sitting rooms and two sets of staircases. Upstairs were countless bedrooms, most of which looked as if they hadn't been used for years. Corridors headed off at strange angles, leading to hidden rooms and secret doors. The entire basement had been converted to an open-plan area with a kitchen-diner and lounge. Steps led up to an ancient walled garden, dense with birdsong and dripping with flowers. Kathy fell in love with the house immediately. It felt like a sanctuary. How relieved her parents must have been, all those years ago, to escape a revolution and find refuge here, in this beautiful place.

Kathy's room was at the top of the house.

'I thought you'd accept the extra effort getting up here for the sake of the view,' Elizabeth said, showing an understanding of her young niece. 'You have a rest; have a sleep if you like. Get yourself together then come down for a bite to eat.'

Though the freshly-laundered sheets called softly, Kathy went first to the window, to see that which had been calling her. She sat on the window-seat for a good quarter hour, staring out of the window, hands to the pane, looking out over the hundreds of graves, statuary and monuments visible from here, lit by the moon. She could see paths and lanes, there a circle of mournful tombs. Much of the cemetery was obscured by greenery. This was the West Cemetery, the older part, her research had told her that. It was very old, to judge by the ancient ash and oak trees driving their way up to the heavens. With a shudder she thought of the trees' roots and what they entwined and held below.

Kathy's attention was suddenly captured by a movement off to the left, to a section of the cemetery visible between the trees – a cut of moonlight acting like a light on a stage. Her eyes flicked across and she saw a little girl stepping lightly between the gravestones, well away from the path. Had she become separated from a late-tour group? Not at this time. As she watched, the girl suddenly stopped and looked up, directly towards Kathy, whose heart skipped a beat. The girl looked familiar – was it . . . ?

But then the girl stepped quickly to her left and disappeared behind the branches of an ash tree. Kathy waited for a moment but she didn't reappear.

She was torn away eventually by the calling of the bed. She undressed and climbed in between the cool linen, her jet-lagged limbs soaking up the cotton luxury. As she drifted off, the memory of the girl's haunting face stared back at her from the brooding cemetery.

When Kathy woke the little girl was sitting on the end of her bed, watching her with large eyes, a look of disappointment on her face. Kathy studied her closely – *was* this the same girl she'd seen in the cemetery? Surely not. She could clearly see the family resemblance in this girl's features. She couldn't possibly remember her sister, of course. Kathy hadn't even been two when her mother went back to England, taking Amber with her. But there was no doubt in her mind – the girl, it was Amber.

'You haven't been to see Oliver yet,' her sister said,

accusingly. She had a sweet English accent and a sad face.

'I will,' Kathy replied.

'When?'

'Soon, I'll call him soon.'

'Good,' Amber said.

Kathy opened her eyes and sat up quickly. There was no Amber, of course. As always it was just a dream. A vivid dream. Kathy checked the clock – she'd been asleep for a couple of hours. She washed her face, getting ready for breakfast downstairs, Before she left the room, she turned and inspected it one more time. The four-poster bed. The wall-hangings. The flock velvet wallpaper. Her meagre belongings jumbled at the foot of the bed. Something caught her eye – above the door again another strange symbol like the one above the front door of the house. This one was made of a black stone – it was embedded into the door frame. She shut her eyes – she could feel a presence, but a good one, and she grinned in delight. She felt safe here, like she somehow belonged. Like she was *home*.

Over a continental breakfast held in the kitchen-come-diner, Kathy asked her aunt about the cemetery.

'Is it open to the public?' Kathy asked. 'I see they run tours. I wanted to go for a wander.'

'The West Cemetery you can only visit as part of a tour group,' Elizabeth replied, sipping a coffee from white bone-china. 'Part of the East Cemetery is open to the public at weekends. One used to be able to visit either at any time, but there was some trouble and they restrict entry there now.'

'What sort of trouble?'

Aunt Elizabeth eyed her cautiously. 'Tomb-robbers, Satanists – poor misguided souls, really.'

'I read about them on the internet. I also read there were some murders,' Kathy said, toying with her food. 'And you know, strange sightings and things.'

'It was mostly all made up, but it created quite a media frenzy. You don't want to believe everything you read on the internet.' Elizabeth shrugged and poured herself some more coffee. 'So thanks to a few crazy people, I'm afraid you can't just wander about in the west section – that's the area you can see from your window.'

'Oh,' Kathy said, disappointed. She heard a bird singing cheerily through the open French doors. The weather had brightened while she'd been asleep. 'Last night I saw a little girl walking in there alone . . .'

Elizabeth looked up at her sharply. 'A little girl?'

Kathy nodded. 'She disappeared behind a tomb. I wondered what she was doing there alone and at night.'

'She must have been with someone,' Elizabeth said, sipping her coffee.

Kathy shook her head. 'No, she was alone, I am sure. Might she have been the daughter of a gravedigger, or something like that?'

Elizabeth nodded quickly. 'Yes, that's probably who she was.' Then she laughed sharply.

'What is it?' Kathy asked, smiling.

'You're just like your sister you know, always asking questions, always looking for more.'

Kathy watched her aunt closely. The older woman looked down at her plate, the atmosphere suddenly awkward.

'I don't suppose you've heard from Amber?' Kathy asked cautiously. Elizabeth shook her head. Kathy regretted asking. Now was not the right time to pepper her aunt with questions about her lost sister. Kathy began eating, just to fill the time that stretched across the table between them.

'Go and see the East Cemetery,' Elizabeth said after a minute or two. 'That's nice too. Is that what you want to do today? Visit the cemetery?'

'I thought maybe I shouldn't go too far afield on my first day,' Kathy said.

'Of course. We could pop in to a pub if you like? Have a lovely English ale?'

'Sure, I saw a bar called the Church as we drove here. Is that nice?'

Elizabeth shook her head. 'You don't want to go there. There are much better pubs around here. No shortage of good pubs in Highgate.' She laughed again, a little forced. Kathy got the sense her aunt was nervous about something. It was strange, meeting a relative for the first time – was that the reason? Kathy felt a hundred questions crowding her mind, but held her tongue, sensing it wasn't the right time to push it. Dr Gelion would have approved – *One step at a time, Kathy.*

Later, though the clouds had rolled over again, they walked up Swain's Lane, the West Cemetery to their left. Kathy trailed her fingers along the wrought-iron bars, looking through into the gloomy bone yard. A stone angel, one hand missing, sat atop a plinth looking up to heaven, as though hoping for rescue. These ancient graves were untended, the families of the deceased also long gone. Creepers and vines had invaded many of the graves; a bushy plant sat proudly atop one slab, as though the plant had decided the monument was there for its own advantage.

As Kathy walked, she saw paths leading off up the hill into the dense trees. This had been a garden once – a flower-filled, meticulously designed garden cemetery, built at a time when Americans were unceremoniously planting each other in the dusty plots of frontier towns.

'Fascinating, isn't it?' Elizabeth said. 'Some people ask me if it's not altogether too creepy, living where I do. I think it's peaceful. There are few places in London so quiet and so green.' Kathy nodded, understanding perfectly.

Elizabeth took them to a cosy little pub called the Flask where Kathy, at a beer-stained table, politely sipped a half-pint of dark bitter ale. Her aunt drank a whole pint very quickly and Kathy's eyes widened in alarm. They chatted about Kathy's step-mom and -dad for a while. Kathy's eyes wandered around the place as they talked. Pictures of old kings and queens lined the walls, along with black-and-white photographs of the cemetery and the pub in the past. There were a dozen or so people in, and Kathy found herself staring at a girl with a blonde pony-tail who sat two tables away, drinking with a friend. The blonde girl was talking loudly about the legend of the Highgate Vampire.

'Another one, dear?' Elizabeth asked, pointing at Kathy's mostly-full glass.

Kathy looked back, startled. 'No, no thanks,' she said.

'Some crisps?'

Realizing that Elizabeth was going back to the bar regardless, Kathy nodded and her aunt got up. Just at that moment, the blonde girl's friend also rose, to visit the bathroom. After a moment's consideration, Kathy stood and walked quickly over to the girl, who was busy scribbling something in a notebook.

'Excuse me,' Kathy asked. The girl looked up. She was pretty, with clear English skin. She seemed no older than Kathy.

'Sorry to bother you, but I overheard you talking about the Highgate Vampire?'

The girl nodded, a little warily, Kathy thought. Maybe she was bothered like this a lot.

'I'm Kathy, I'm staying just across the road from the cemetery.'

'Okay?' the girl replied in a rich London accent. 'Do you want to join a tour? We go every day.'

'You're a tour guide – makes sense. Yes – well, no . . .' Kathy began. 'I'd like to just go in and have a look around the cemetery, would that be possible?'

'Not in the West Cemetery. Even I don't have a key to the West Cemetery – sorry.'

'No, no. I mean the East Cemetery – that's fine. I'd really like to just wander on my own, get the feel of the place.'

The girl shook her head, frowning. 'Sorry. It's a working cemetery, you see. We can't have members of the public wandering around, falling into open graves, that sort of thing. There is a smaller section of it you can walk around on your own, but only at weekends I'm afraid.'

Kathy nodded and was about to leave, when something stopped her. Something, or someone, spoke to her. *Try again.*

She sat opposite the girl. 'Look, I understand all that,' she said, 'and I'm sure you get loads of people wanting you to make an exception. But I really feel I need to go there. To see the old part. My mother's buried there, you see,' she lied.

The girl's face softened a little.

'I only need an hour or so,' Kathy went on quickly, pressing home the advantage.

The girl grinned. 'You're lucky I like Americans,' she said, and scribbled on a piece of paper.

'Six-thirty tomorrow morning, be at Swaingate. Call me and I'll let you in. You can look around for a while before the first tour starts, but you have to be out by eight, and if you get caught by one of the diggers, you never saw me.'

Kathy took the note with a grin and looked down at it. *Becky 07582 453189.*

'Thanks,' she said. She stood just as Becky's friend returned. Kathy made her way back to the table where her aunt regarded her curiously.

'Do you know that girl?'

'I do now,' Kathy said, flushed with excitement. She'd never have had the courage to approach someone like that back home. Was this Amber again, somehow inhabiting her, strengthening her? She took a deep pull of her beer. 'Maybe I will have another of these,' she said, and laughed.

Kathy looked up into Antwain's dark eyes; he was standing close and for a moment she felt claustrophobic, like she needed to escape and run out into the dark night. But she didn't. She held his gaze steadily and felt a flush deep down inside her, warmth spreading outwards from her loins and tingling her skin. It was the same sensation she'd had at the party. The fluttering warmth she was beginning to associate with Amber's presence within her.

Antwain leaned in closer still and his lips parted slightly. Kathy closed her eyes and felt his mouth on hers, hard and just slightly rough. He kissed her hungrily and she kissed back, knowing this was wrong, knowing that Antwain was dark, dangerous. But the wrongness merely fuelled the fire inside her and when Antwain's hand cupped her breast she let it stay. And she wondered if it wasn't really her doing this. Was this Amber – the part of Amber that seemed to have become part of her in recent weeks?

She drifted down, spiralling into ecstasy. She was dimly aware that Antwain had picked her up and lain her on the bed, then he was on top of her and somehow they were both naked and she could feel him hard against her thigh. He positioned himself, questioning with a gentle motion and she nodded urgently, yes. He lifted his head and she saw his face.

Antwain's eyes shone bright yellow. He smiled and revealed a set of elongated canines, cruel tips jagged and white. Antwain snarled and his head ducked forward towards her throat.

Kathy sat up in bed, chest heaving, alone in a darkened room. She sat there, on fire, yearning, gulping air, her head spinning.

'God damn you, Amber,' she muttered. She picked up the red book from the bedside. 'Can't you just stay out of my dreams for one night?'

Kathy lay back down. The dreams were more intense here in England and she remembered them better. Part of her wanted more. When Amber – visited her, she felt more alive than she could remember. Is this what it was like for normal people? She wondered. Everything intense and sharp? How can a dream be more real than reality itself?

Kathy was up at five-thirty and drank three tiny cups of coffee as she stared at the clock hands, willing them to move faster. At twenty-past six she left the quiet house and walked up the lane to Swaingate. Peering through the barred gate the cemetery seemed deserted. Kathy dialled Becky's number and listened to the ring tone.

'Hello?'

'Becky? It's Kathy, we met at the pub last night.'

'Oh yeah, my new American friend. I wasn't sure if you'd come.'

'Are you kidding? I've hardly slept I'm so excited.'

'You are? Okay. Are you at the gate?'

'Yeah.'

'Wait there, I'll be there in a tick.'

Kathy leaned against the high brick wall. At this time of the morning the sun had not yet risen, just a light twilight glow. She could hear morning birdsong from somewhere within the cemetery and the background hum of the city. Then, floating towards her she heard the singing of a child.

'Solomon Grundy. Born on a Monday. Grew up on Tuesday. Married on Wednesday . . .'

The singing was coming from the cemetery. Wondering if this was the girl she'd seen, Kathy moved back to the gate and popped her head around to see.

A figure stood at the gate. Kathy leaped backwards in alarm and ended up on her backside on the pavement.

'Are you okay?' Becky asked, puzzled at Kathy's reaction.

Heart pounding, Kathy stared back, then burst out laughing.

'Sorry, I thought you . . . I'm just a little overexcited, I guess.'

Becky opened the gate, shaking her head. 'You Yanks are all crazy.'

Beyond the gate lay a wide, gravel driveway, leading off down a gentle slope. Smaller paths led off from either side, into the trees.

'Do you know where your mother's grave is?' Becky asked once she'd locked the gate behind them.

'What? Oh, yes, I think so, over there,' Kathy said, waving vaguely down the slope to the right.

Becky looked doubtful for a moment, but then said, 'Okay, you've got an hour and fifteen minutes. I'll meet you back here quarter to eight, okay? Then I've got to be back for the first tour.'

Kathy nodded and the girls parted. Kathy watched her new friend walk up the gravel path towards a small cemetery building. Then she spun on her heel and trotted briskly away down the road, all the time wanting to plunge deep inside the graveyard.

Now she was actually here, inside the cemetery, alone, Kathy had a brief panic about what she was to do next. The drive within her to come here had been intense, but what she was supposed to do now was anyone's guess. She wandered without purpose for a while, following paths randomly, going deeper and deeper into the sea of graves. The sounds of London receded, even the birds had gone respectfully silent.

As she walked in the shade of the trees, she thought of the reports she had read – dead foxes, charred bodies all drained of blood. She shivered slightly. The morning cold was biting; she was wearing just a light, if oversized, black cardigan donated to her by her aunt. The temperature seemed to be dropping. She chose a path at random and headed off into a wooded area. She settled into a comfortable walking pace and drank in the peaceful yet cold beauty of it all.

A panicked bird exploded out of the undergrowth before her, causing her to start. She laughed at herself. So jumpy! Then she carried on.

After a few minutes, Kathy stopped and buttoned up her cardigan. Looking around, she seemed to be in an even older part of the cemetery. The tombs here were cracked and dark, fifty thousand nights of cold and fog having left their impression. She entered a narrow, sunken lane between two rows of slab-topped tombs and crept along, entranced by the eldritch beauty, awed by the age. Her breath misted before her as she approached a crossroad.

And then it happened. She'd been half expecting it. Nothing about this was random, there was a reason she was here, she felt that deeply. Turning left, Kathy pulled up hurriedly. A tall figure wearing a black cloak walked on the path some fifty yards away from her. An almost physical fear enveloped her, something tangible, seeming to emanate from the apparition. She began shivering, a brief shudder that quickened in intensity until she was shaking uncontrollably. And yet something drew her onwards at the same time. She felt an urge to race after the figure and confront it.

Kathy's stomach churned as she watched the figure seemingly float away. It must have been seven feet tall – that was impossible. The figure turned a corner and was then gone. Kathy willed her stiff legs to move and she walked quickly after it. Peering around the corner she saw the path ahead was empty. Where had it gone? She carried on further, breathing shallowly, creeping along the path. Mausoleums lined the way, heavy slabs blocking their entrances. Who was it? She searched for an answer. Lichen and black grime obscured the nameplates. Kathy reached the end of the row and was surprised to find she'd reached a dead end. She turned around, but there was nothing behind. Had the dark figure climbed over one of the tombs? She suddenly realized it was no longer cold and, though she was fully weirded out by the disappearing figure, the sickening fear in her gut had gone. It was replaced with . . . excitement.

She checked her watch and was astonished to discover it was time to go, the sun now creeping over the trees. How could she have lost an hour like that? She hurried back to the gate, getting herself lost a couple of times – she made it, just a couple of minutes late. Becky was there, checking her watch impatiently. She smiled when she saw Kathy.

'Did you find . . . ?' she began, but then stopped as she caught a good look at Kathy's face. 'Are you okay? Your face is so pale.'

Kathy hesitated a moment, but then described what she'd seen. Becky listened carefully, then inspected Kathy's face intently.

'What?' Kathy asked. 'What's wrong?'

'You're telling the truth, aren't you?' Becky said.

'Of course, why would I make up something like that?'

Becky laughed. 'You'd be surprised – we get a lot of weirdos and freaks around here, claiming they've seen all sorts of things.'

'But you believe me, right?'

Becky nodded. 'What you saw – it's been seen before. Not by me,' she added, hastily.

'What is it?'

Becky looked around. A man approached, also dressed in the green of the cemetery staff.

'I can't talk now, let's meet at the Flask this evening, okay? Six-thirty?' Becky unlocked the gate and ushered Kathy through, looking behind her at the approaching man. 'We can talk about it there.'

'Yes, okay,' Kathy said impatiently as she passed through the gate. 'But just tell me – what is it, this thing I saw, what's it called?' But she already knew the answer.

Becky slammed the heavy iron gate and grinned through the bars. 'It's called the Highgate Vampire, of course.'

And then she was gone.

CHAPTER SIX

Kathy decided she mustn't put things off any longer. The thought of phoning Oliver, perhaps meeting him, made her very nervous – the old fears resurfacing. She sat on her bed, window open and the sounds of London floating in. Kathy took a deep breath, trying to channel the spirit of Amber that seemed to fill her with such confidence. Then she dialled the number she'd got from an old, smelly, phone book.

It rang, and rang. Kathy imagined an old-fashioned pulse-dial phone in a dusty room at the museum.

She was about to give up when someone answered. 'British Museum, how can I help?'

'Um, could I speak to Oliver Samson please?'

'Department?'

'Sorry, what?'

'Do you know what department he's in?'

'Erm, vampires?' Kathy said, screwing up her face as she realized how ridiculous that sounded.

'Putting you through.'

Kathy blinked. *They actually have a vampire department?*

But this time the phone went unanswered; after a few rings it clicked over to voicemail. A man's recorded voice spoke. 'Hello, this is Oliver Samson, Occult. I'm not in my office just now but if you'd like to leave your name and a number I'll call you back as soon as I can.'

After the tone, Kathy spoke. 'Hello, this is Kathy Moore . . . sorry, Kathy Bilic. Amber Bilic's sister. She sent me a book and gave me your details . . .' Kathy couldn't think what to say next. She'd planned what she wanted to say and practised in front of the mirror before she'd called, but now everything had flown out of her head. She gave her number and hung up. Well what are you meant to say to the head of the vampire department?

She shrugged, feeling better about having got the phone call out the way. She contemplated contacting Antwain too, while she was on a roll. Her face flushed, but she decided against it. Her aunt was desperate to show her the sights of London. Antwain would have to wait.

'One step at a time,' she muttered to herself, and went downstairs.

* * *

83 A.D.

Marius lifted his end of the stretcher, careful not to get the poles caught up in the leather scabbard dangling from his belt. Lachrimus was at the front, the great scars he'd picked up in Germany standing proud on his muscled forearms. The men were on burial detail. Some kind of plague had hit the garrison in recent days and Marius had watched as many of his flint-hard cohorts had crumpled and expired like frost-hit tulips. These were men hard enough to walk all day on bloodied feet, then fight German mercenaries without complaint. These were men who'd stand on frozen ground for eight hours on guard duty, soiled with their own excrement, wet with their own urine, oblivious to any discomfort. But this plague was something else, an enemy within.

Being assigned to burial duty brought dread. Indeed it was often used as punishment. Not in this case though. With so many legionaries down everyone healthy had to take a turn. They had to trudge down to the graveyard, carrying the body of a comrade complete with arms and armour, perform the death rituals and come back for the next one. Thankfully they didn't have to dig the graves too. Local Britons were enslaved to do that; twisted, filthy creatures the locals were, but they could dig. That was all they seemed to do sometimes, grubbing about in the heavy soil, pulling up heavy vegetables, black with stinking British soil.

A soldier's life was hard, but the alternative was far worse – a life of slavery, or back-breaking labour in a prison camp. Those were the other options for a man of Marius's station, orphaned at birth, living hand to mouth, stealing and fighting in Rome's crowded streets. He'd joined up as soon as he was able, and was grateful for it. The one thing he could do without was the almost permanent constipation he'd had to deal with for the last few years. Whatever he ate or drank, whatever sort of exercise he did, he couldn't get things moving. The cramps were crippling sometimes. But everyone had a chronic problem – a rash, a cracked rib, the clap. Everyone had something to complain about.

The men moved off, silently, and made their way out of the camp, the sentry nodding in recognition as they passed. Fog sidled through the gate alongside them. It was early and the Decurion had told them they must dispose of the night's dead before roll-call. Down the rough track away from the gates they trudged, visibility poor, the thin poles cutting into their hands. The body of Lucullus bounced slightly as they walked, heavy in full armour, to be buried with his weapons beside him, ready to carry on fighting enemies in the next life. Marius prayed to Mars he himself would not be struck down. Only another five years in this accursed country and he'd be able to return to his native Umbria, with his pension and a land grant. He'd marry a virgin or a young widow, he cared little for looks, as long as she could cook and bear children.

Onwards through the freezing fog the men trudged.

Suddenly Lachrimus stopped dead, looking out into the dank blackness. Marius scanned the surrounding area, twenty-five years' experience in the legion telling him when to keep quiet and listen. If Lachrimus had stopped, he'd done so because there was something to stop for.

Gradually, slowly, the men lowered the stretcher and, as quietly as they could, each unsheathed his short-sword. Marius could hear nothing. Perhaps the faint hush of the wind, but nothing else. Even the filthy, inedible British birds had decided to keep quiet for once. Lachrimus signalled Marius to wait and took a few steps off into the darkness. Marius stayed with his dead comrade, waiting. Then a low whistle summoned him and he crept silently through the fog to join his fellow.

Lachrimus was crouched over the body of a dead sheep, head up, scanning the gentle hillside. Marius saw the beast had been killed recently; blood streamed from its torn throat. Dogs, most likely. But then he started as the beast opened its eyes and kicked a couple of times, its soul not quite having left its body. This is what Lachrimus must have heard. But what had killed it?

'We'll take the carcass back after burying Lucullus,' Lachrimus said, not looking at him. Then he plunged his sword up inside the throat and into the animal's brain, stilling it instantly. Lachrimus pulled the sword out and wiped the gore from the flat blade, thoughtfully.

'Wolves,' he said, finally. Then with an economical flick of the head, he indicated they should get back to their task.

Ten minutes later they arrived at the graveyard and carried on through the gate to a row of freshly dug graves. Marius shivered. The temperature had plunged still lower, as it did often just before dawn. The fog curled around them, almost tangible, plucking at their body heat. A faint brightening of the sky afforded them a small amount of light. They could see a few feet away now, to the wooden headstones that littered the ancient burial ground. It had been here long before the Romans arrived, though the soldiers had opened up a separate section for themselves, refusing to be buried alongside the savage natives. On a clear day Londinium could be seen from the graveyard, off down the hill, thick smoke tendrils reaching to the skies. The curling Thames burnished silver in the weak British sunshine.

Lachrimus tipped Lucullus's body into the grave with a clatter of armour and weapons. Marius clucked in disapproval. 'He's landed on his front,' he said. 'That's no way for a Roman soldier to lie.'

'You straighten him if you want,' Lachrimus said, shrugging. He sat on a mound of earth and pulled out a pouch of bitter leaves to chew on, showing no sign of feeling the cold even as Marius's teeth started to chatter. Being able to handle extremes of temperature was something the Roman soldier prided himself on, hot or cold. Marius had heard a tale of one soldier in Northern Germany who'd walked for so long in frozen temperatures, carrying a load of heavy logs, that his arms had snapped off.

Marius sighed and dropped down into the grave, being careful not to land on Lucullus. It wasn't right, being buried upside down. One needed to be on one's back, looking up towards heaven. It wasn't too much to ask, was it, after seventeen years' service for Rome, that your comrades buried you the right way up? Marius rolled the body over and straightened the limbs carefully. He positioned the sword and spear on either side and stood to admire his work. The cold was intense now, even in the shelter of the grave.

Marius heard Lachrimus cough.

'Hold the torch over,' Marius called.

But in answer Lachrimus just coughed again, a strange, choking sound. Marius felt a stab of fear – was Lachrimus too succumbing to the plague? Hoisting himself up, he peered over the edge of the grave and hung there, astonished at what he saw.

A huge man, wrapped in a monk's cowl or some such garment, towered over Lachrimus, still sitting on the mound of earth. Lachrimus's short spear was rammed through his own throat, back to front. Blood cascaded down the shaft and poured from the tip as the soldier's black eyes bulged in horror at the sight of Death riding towards him.

The monster lifted the thrashing Lachrimus as if he were a straw doll and held him high. The red fountain sprayed its ichor into the hooded cowl, as if the creature were bathing in it.

Marius had seen enough. He dragged himself out of the grave and unslung his own spear. A Roman legionary was not easily frightened, yet even the veteran Marius, who'd marched and slaughtered his way across Europe, found his fingers grow white with pure terror as he gripped the cypress-wood shaft of the pilum.

Marius knew what he must do – a fast run, a hard thrust, retreat and unsheathe the short sword, as he'd been trained to do, as he'd done a thousand times before. Lachrimus had stopped thrashing now but continued moving his limbs weakly as the blood flow weakened.

Marius readied himself for the charge, but the creature, without turning, held out a hand and uttered a phrase in an unknown language.

'*Missum, juhaya.*' The voice was gravelly, echoing as if in a stone tomb. Marius found himself frozen to the spot. He could not move his feet. His hands gripped the spear uselessly as the creature finished its meal. Then Lachrimus's body was hurled into the grave without ceremony. The tall figure turned to the still-frozen Marius and towered above him. Marius looked up into the dark cowl, seeing the creature's face for the first time. Flashing yellow eyes glared back at him, the hint of a strong nose and cheeks, the mouth and chin obscured by shadow.

The figure reached out a hand and, for the first time in over a week, Marius's bowels opened. For a moment he felt a sense of relief, almost gratitude. And then the figure reached into his gaping mouth, gripped his upper jaw and tore the top of his head off.

* * *

Kathy and Elizabeth had just about reached the top of the London Eye when Elizabeth began talking, unprompted, about Amber.

'She used to stay with me from time to time, you see. When she was researching a story in London.'

'Where did . . . where *does*, she live normally?' Kathy asked.

'In Yorkshire, where her foster-family took her to live after your mother's death. It was thought by the adoption agency that she should be housed well away from London.'

'Did you ever see her?'

'Yes, once a year. She always wanted to come back to Highgate with me. There's something about this place that seems to draw our family. When she grew up she'd visit regularly and earlier this year she came to stay for longer, six weeks or so. It was lovely to have her here.'

Kathy smiled and waited for her aunt to go on. They were looking north, across the sun-washed city. Kathy had been surprised to find out how flat London was – apart from one outcropping of skyscrapers to the east, most of the buildings were just a few storeys. How could you fit six million people into a city with just a handful of skyscrapers?

'The police don't seem to care,' Elizabeth was saying. 'As soon as I told them she was an investigative journalist, they lost interest. "She'll be undercover," one of them said. "She won't thank you if you stick up missing person posters."'

Kathy shrugged. 'Well maybe they're right. You said yourself that she'd sometimes disappear.'

Elizabeth stared out to the north-west and pointed. 'There's Highgate – you can just about make out the cemetery.'

Kathy peered, wondering if she needed glasses. Glasses and an inhaler, all this season's essential accessories for the nerd-about-town.

'She would have told me,' Elizabeth said. 'She wouldn't just walk out of the house without saying something. She left all her clothes, notebooks, even her contact lenses.'

'Laptop?' Kathy asked.

'No, she took that, she always took that – and her phone.'

Kathy wondered if she should mention the book to her aunt. Amber had sent it, presumably because she knew she was in trouble and might not be coming back. If Elizabeth took the book to the police, might they take the disappearance more seriously?

But why hadn't Amber told her aunt if she was in fear of something? Why not just leave the book with Elizabeth? *Trust him but no one else*, the inscription had read. Kathy kept quiet. She liked her aunt, but she wasn't quite ready to trust her.

After the trip they walked across Waterloo Bridge, Kathy captivated by the views up and down the river.

'Personally,' Elizabeth said, 'I think the city looks better from eye-level. That's how it was intended to be seen.'

Kathy had to agree. If New York gave you a hundred opportunities to look down over the scurrying city you'd escaped, London gave you the chance to look up with aspiration at what could be achieved. Grand old buildings, displaying wealth and style, faced the river. Crafty architecture, capturing ancient glories, peeped out from behind the scramble of modern office buildings and phone shops.

They ate in a quiet café down a shambling alleyway in Covent Garden. Kathy gently brought the subject back to Amber.

'Do you have any idea where she might have gone?' she asked. 'Was she working with anyone?' Kathy was surprised when her aunt shook her head, no. So Elizabeth didn't know about Oliver. Or was pretending she didn't. More reason to feel glad she hadn't shown her the book.

'Did she go out much?'

'She did sometimes go up to the Church,' Elizabeth said, grimacing.

'You didn't approve?'

Elizabeth shook her head. 'Full of odd-bods and weirdos. It used to be a lovely church, a real one, St Michael's. But it shut in the Eighties and was deconsecrated.'

'Why?'

Elizabeth grimaced again before answering. 'There was a murder there. A priest was killed, horribly, in the crypt. They said it was a tramp, or a junkie.' She took a bite out of her sandwich and raised her eyebrows at Kathy.

'But why would they deconsecrate a church because of a murder?' Kathy asked.

Elizabeth shook her head, still chewing.

'I don't know,' she said, finally. 'It lay unused for about ten years, then some developer bought it and turned it into a tacky nightclub. They put on rock bands and live shows in the crypt now.'

'Under a church?' Kathy asked, thinking of the pictures she'd seen of the Church on the internet. The cavernous rooms, the fantastic fabrics, giant crystal chandeliers and the many bars.

'It's a labyrinth under there, you know?' Elizabeth said. 'Even under my house, there are tunnels, crypts, underground caverns. Perfect place for them I suppose, it's all Goths and odd-bods. They're attracted by the area. What better place for vampire-seekers than catacombs under Highgate Cemetery? Ancient they are, the Romans built some of them.'

'Wow,' Kathy said.

'The Highgate Society screamed blue murder when the new owners got planning permission to open a nightclub,' Elizabeth said, spearing a cornichon on her salad plate. 'Sometimes you can hear the music floating up from the cellar – everything's connected, you see, through drains.'

'Everything's connected,' Kathy repeated, slowly looking out through the open door to the sunlit street outside. A long-haired man stood on the other side of the road, looking towards her. Then a van flashed past and he was gone.

Kathy wasn't even surprised.

CHAPTER SEVEN

Kathy had intended to go for a walk around the cemetery perimeter in the afternoon but they were back so late she decided against it. Elizabeth had hailed a taxi after lunch and taken Kathy to the Tower of London. They'd spent two hours wandering through the towers, marvelling at the architecture made sublime by age, at the elegant brutality of the weapons. Beautiful and spectacular though it was, she'd been unable to stop thinking about the cemetery, the book, the long-haired man and of course Amber. There was so much she needed to do, her head spun with it all. She wondered if this was how it felt to be Amber, to have a head full of questions, suspicions, to be driven by the need to know more.

Back in her bedroom, Kathy opened her laptop and logged in via her aunt's broadband. As she waited for the browser to open, she noticed a tiny flashing light on her phone, a voicemail. Why had she not heard the phone ring before? Then she remembered she'd been asked to turn her phone to silent in the theatre at the Tower. She'd forgotten to turn it back on. She hit the keypad and waited for the message.

'Er, hello, Kathy? This is Oliver Samson. Thanks so much for your message. I was very . . . interested to hear from you. I didn't know Amber had a sister. I'd very much like to meet with you if you have time. I'm in meetings all day tomorrow and during the day on Wednesday, but if you'd like to come to the museum around six p.m. we can chat then. Just ask at the main desk and they'll direct you to my office. If that's a problem give me a call back, otherwise I'll expect to see you then. Oh, and if you still have the book, please do bring it along. Um, thanks, Kathy, thanks.'

Kathy took a deep breath to calm the excitement in her stomach; she was getting closer. Oliver's voice sounded clear; quite old, but strong, deep. She imagined Oliver as a tall, dark, handsome professor-type, an Indiana Jones crossed with a Hugh Grant. *This is not a date, Kathy*, she reminded herself. *You're trying to find your sister.*

Turning back to her laptop, she hit the history button to find the Church website. She was looking for opening hours. Midnight till dawn, of course. Well maybe she should pay a visit sometime, but not tonight; she was

94

tired even thinking about meeting Becky at the Flask in an hour, let alone go on afterwards. Not tonight.

Elizabeth looked a little relieved when Kathy said she was going out.

'I'm flagging a little, I must admit,' she said from the comfort of an armchair in the front sitting room. 'Might have an early night.'

'Thanks for today,' Kathy said, smiling.

'No, thank you,' Elizabeth replied. 'It's good to have you here.'

'It's good to be here,' Kathy said.

She left the house and trotted down the steps to the street. The sun was still strong and warm and tiny specks of pollen glittered as they swam through the thick evening air. The cemetery opposite called her, but Kathy ignored it. She looked right, down the hill, towards the Church. *Another time, no not tonight*, she thought, and turned left towards the Flask.

Becky was a few minutes late, and Kathy wandered about the pub, clutching a half-pint self-consciously. To give herself something to do, she examined the collection of black-and-white photographs which adorned the walls. Here was a shot from the Thirties, looking up Swain's Lane – grainy and faded, not much seemed to have changed, though there were fewer cars back then. A picture of a scraggy-haired man holding a skull.

Further along was a picture taken within the cemetery itself, the Circle of Lebanon visible in the middle-ground. Figures dotted around suggested the cemetery had been open to the public at that time. In the foreground, a little girl stood, looking towards the camera. Something about her drew Kathy's attention. She was too far from the camera to have been the subject, but close enough that her features were distinguishable. Kathy peered closely in the dim light of the old pub.

It was the little girl she'd seen in the west graveyard from her bedroom window. She was sure of it. Even the same dress, with the blue ribbon sash. Hoping to get a clue as to her identity, Kathy looked to the inscription. It read: *Highgate Cemetery – 1973*.

Kathy stepped back, her heart thudding, telling herself not to be silly. It can't have been the same girl.

'Spooky, huh?' a voice spoke into her left ear.

Kathy leaped in fright, spilling her drink on the thick carpet. A couple of old men at a nearby table burst into laughter and Kathy stared at the newly arrived Becky, her heart now thumping harder than ever.

'Sorry,' Becky said, hand over her mouth in mortification.

Kathy looked back for a minute, then grinned. '*I'm sorry, I'm a bag of nerves.*'

'Let me get you another drink,' Becky said.

A few minutes later, at a quiet table, the girls sat opposite one another, grinning. Kathy had felt an instant connection with Becky and she had the unfamiliar sensation that the feeling might be reciprocated. Had she found a friend?

'So,' Becky said, taking out a notebook, 'tell me again about what you saw. If you want to, that is.'

'Sure,' Kathy replied, glancing down at the notebook. 'What's that for?'

Becky tilted her head to one side. 'This is my vampire-sighting diary. I record it in here whenever people see, or feel, something odd in the cemetery.' As she spoke, she flicked back through the pages, thick with black ink.

'There seem to be a lot,' Kathy said.

'Not all of them are genuine,' Becky said, opening the book at a random page. 'Like this one. Amanda Barnett in August 2003 says she saw the ghost of Henry VIII charging along the Highgate Road at midnight.'

'How do you know she didn't?'

Becky smiled, 'She said Henry was riding a dragon. The thing is, most of the sightings that I think are genuine follow certain patterns. The vampire does things in a certain way and at certain times.'

'For instance?'

'Well, the sightings seem to increase every ten years. Like he can go that long without a feed, but then must emerge to drink blood.'

Kathy blinked. 'How long have you been doing this?'

'Only a few years, since I started working here. Before that my father kept the records.'

'He's a guide as well?' Kathy asked.

'He was,' Becky said, her eyes dropping to the book she held in her hands. 'He's dead now.'

'I'm sorry,' Kathy said. She had this silly urge to tell Becky that she too, had no father, as if that would ingratiate her with her new friend. Dr Gelion would have considered it a sign of Kathy's improving social skills that she managed to keep her mouth shut.

'So anyway,' Becky said, 'tell me your story.'

Kathy took a deep breath and felt herself slide back to the cemetery. She recounted the events as she remembered them. The increasing cold, the sense of being lost, then the sight of the tall figure and its disappearance.

'You know there isn't an area like the one you describe in that part of the cemetery,' Becky said, scribbling furiously.

'Why would I make it up?' Kathy replied, slightly miffed.

'Oh, I'm not saying you did,' Becky replied hurriedly. 'My father interviewed someone years ago who described the same thing. Like he's been transported into a completely different part of the cemetery, where the lanes and the tombs get all mixed up and moved. They also pretty much all say it was really cold when they saw the vampire.'

'What else?' Kathy asked, fascinated.

'A lot of people just feel the cold but don't see anything,' Becky said. 'Look, there've been reports of a vampire, or something, here since Roman times. We're on a ley line here, you see. Two in fact.'

'A ley line?'

'Druids and witches and occultists believe that there are lines of natural energy running under the earth. Two of these lines are said to run right through the cemetery. One goes through this pub, the second runs through St Michael's – you know it's now a nightclub. They meet somewhere in the cemetery.'

'Do you believe in all that?' Kathy asked. 'Do you believe there's a real vampire here? Or is this just ghostly material to add to your spooky tours?'

Becky shrugged. 'Sure, I use this stuff in my tours.

Why not? People love it, and the tips are better when you scare people. But I do genuinely believe there's something. I don't know what it is, but I'm trying to find out. If you listen to the so-called experts, one says it's a ghost or spectre, the other claims to have actually killed it – the vampire.'

Kathy nodded keenly, worried she might have offended her new friend by suggesting her research might be for mercenary motives.

As Becky wrote some more in her book, Kathy sipped her drink, thinking about the Romans. What was it her aunt had said? That some of the tombs under the Church had been built by the Romans.

'Everything's connected,' she muttered.

'What's that?' Becky asked, looking up.

'Nothing,' Kathy said.

'So was there anything else?' Becky asked.

Kathy thought. 'Well, unless you count the little girl.'

Becky narrowed her eyes, watching Kathy intently.

'From my window in my aunt's house, across the street, I saw a little girl wandering around on her own.'

'What was she wearing?'

'A white dress, with a ribbon sash – blue I think. Old-fashioned.'

'Millicent,' Becky said, grinning.

'Millicent?' Kathy replied doubtfully. 'That's her name?'

'That's just what Dad called her. She's been seen many times. Sometimes people just hear her singing, usually when the activity is at its height. Dad said she was like a siren, a warning that death was on its way.'

'I thought I saw her in a picture on the wall over there,' Kathy said, pointing. Becky didn't even look.

'Yes, that's her,' Becky said, leaning forward and dropping her voice. 'The day after that photo was taken, a body was found.'

'In the cemetery?'

'Yes, a woman. Her body was drained of blood.'

'What other things does he do, this vampire?'

'Well. A convent girl was found, drained of blood, in 1963. A priest was killed, in St Michael's in 1993. They blamed it on a tramp, but many people believe it was the vampire. Animals were found around that time too, their throats torn out, drained of blood.'

'Since 1993?'

Becky shook her head and took a drink before continuing. 'In the early Seventies vampire-hunters claim to have staked the Highgate Vampire.'

'And since then . . . ?'

'Since the Seventies there have been no bodies found *officially*, though plenty of people have been reported missing around here, and we do find the odd dead animal still.'

'But I saw *something*,' Kathy said, leaning forward.

'Oh there've been plenty of sightings,' Becky agreed. 'Just no bloodthirsty deaths.'

Kathy thought this over for a while. 'It's as though the vampire is being more careful,' she said. Becky nodded. 'Like he's learning about the modern world.'

Kathy frowned. 'So who did the vampire-hunters stake, if not the vampire?'

Becky shook her head. 'I don't know. I wondered if maybe they somehow destroyed the vampire's body, but his spirit still floats around the cemetery. That would also fit with what others say. Maybe they are right – the vampire is both physical and ethereal.'

'Like a vampire ghost?' Kathy asked.

Becky laughed at the idea. 'I guess so. But I don't know.'

Kathy wondered if this was what Amber had been investigating. What had happened to the Highgate Vampire? Maybe Oliver would yield some answers.

'Another drink?' Kathy asked. Becky looked at her watch, then yelped in alarm.

'No, sorry I have to go. Meeting my boyfriend ten minutes ago.'

Kathy felt a momentary pang of being left out again. But she shook her head. She couldn't expect Becky to be her best friend suddenly.

'Okay,' she said as Becky stood. 'Look, thanks very much, it's been really interesting.'

'I've enjoyed it too,' Becky replied, smiling at her. 'Are you in town for a while? Maybe we could meet up again.'

'I'd like that,' Kathy said, trying not to let her smile swallow the world. 'Hey, have you been to the Church? You know, the nightclub?'

Becky pursed her lips. 'No. I hear it's a bit weird, all burlesque, Gothic and that.'

'I thought it sounded interesting, and I wanted to see the tunnels and crypts underneath,' Kathy said

Becky nodded. 'We can go there if you like. What about Friday?'

'Sounds good.'

'Okay if I bring Jack?' Becky asked.

Kathy hesitated, but then wondered if it might not be a good idea to have a boy along. She nodded. 'Sure.'

Kathy realized they'd been in the pub longer than she'd thought. Though night had not yet fallen, the sun had dropped down below the horizon and a dull grey haze dimmed what light remained. Kathy walked slowly up the lane, trailing her hands along the black iron cemetery bars. She peered in at the mass of greenery, witch hazel branches swaying in the evening breeze, lush grass grasping at the mottled stone of the nearby tombs.

Detecting a movement to her left, back the way she'd come, she turned her head and saw the long-haired man. He stood on the pavement, watching her, unable or unwilling to hide. Kathy's heart lurched again. She was tired of this. Who was he? Part of her wanted to go and confront him right now. But the vampire-hunter stories Becky had told her in the pub had sapped her confidence – more freaks. Suddenly she wanted a Puralex, she wanted to go home. She walked off up the street, briskly. After ten yards she spun to look. The man was following her, not getting any closer, but definitely following her.

Kathy wanted now to run, she wanted to sprint across the road and up to her aunt's house. But she feared that running would trigger something, make him chase after her. Also, though he may well have already known where she lived, that wasn't certain. She didn't want to lead him to her home. She thought quickly and had an idea. Gripping the railings she hoisted herself up. She found a foothold on a blunted fleur-de-lis and sprang lightly up on to the upper bar. Nervously stepping between the spikes at the top, she looked down the street to see the man was trotting toward her, a look of alarm on his craggy face. Closer than ever, she could see his hair was greasy and lank; he looked unwashed, like a tramp.

Kathy dropped lightly down inside the cemetery and stood up, coming face to face with the man on the other side of the bars.

'Stop . . .' he began, but Kathy was already away, threading her way through the close-spaced graves, putting distance and masonry between her and her pursuer. She ran for a few minutes then ducked behind a large, age-blackened tomb, breathing heavily. She fumbled for her inhaler, feeling the tightness in her chest, often a precursor to an asthma attack. The man's voice – had she detected a slight accent when he'd spoken? She took a deep breath and held it, listening. Nothing.

Kathy waited a few minutes longer, then decided she'd better move. The light was fading fast and she didn't want to get lost. Keeping low, she picked her way between the graves, moving up the slope, parallel with the road. She caught occasional glimpses of the tree-swamped railings to orientate herself.

Then voices. Kathy ducked down behind a stone angel. It was too late for a tour group. Was it grave-diggers?

'This is pointless,' a girl's voice said. 'We don't even

know what we're looking for.'

'We'll know it when we find it,' a male voice answered. 'We'll feel it. His presence.'

'What and then Bishop will favour you?'

'Of course he will, he wants this more than anything.'

The voices were growing closer. Kathy shivered in the cooling evening air, breathing gently, through her mouth.

'Bishop takes and takes, he does not give—'

'Shut up!' Then Kathy heard a snarl, savage, like a dying dog. Unable to control herself, she yelped in fright and instantly there was a thump as something landed beside her. A thin hand grasped the collar of her thin jacket and lifted her up as though she were hollow. It was the man who held her, or more correctly a boy. He could not have been older than sixteen. Pale-faced and haunted, he looked like a junkie, but his immense strength suggested another explanation for his appearance.

Behind him stood a girl, perhaps a couple of years older than the boy. Dark-haired and horribly thin, she stared back at Kathy as a starving dog might look at a fat cat. Kathy struggled, punching the boy's chest. He dropped her on to her feet and seized her arms, clasping her hands together behind her back with a steely and painful grip.

Kathy wished now that the sun had not disappeared so quickly, she wished she had stayed on the other side of the railings.

'Well looky here,' the boy said. 'Should we?'

The girl continued staring at Kathy. Eventually she responded with a shrug. 'Sure.'

'Wait,' Kathy said, but the boy ignored her. He twisted her head around roughly, exposing her throat. Suddenly the scent of the wild garlic and the cut grass sharpened. Her body, sensing the approach of death, super-charged her senses in the desperate hope an escape might be found.

OhmyGodohmyGodohmyGod.

Through the corner of her eye Kathy saw the boy's mouth open, revealing a set of curved, white teeth with massively elongated canines. His breath was potent, without being entirely repulsive, like the stink of one's own body. His head snapped towards her and Kathy felt a sudden, sweet agony as the teeth broke her flesh. Time stood still, then there was another thump and she had a faceful of grass. Both vampires snarled and Kathy looked up, dazed, in time to see the long-haired man in the grey coat – he was thrusting something into the girl's chest. The boy had been knocked off his balance by the newcomer and howled as he saw his girlfriend stagger back, clutching the stake protruding from her chest, blood cascading with each heartbeat.

The boy leaped on the old man who was ready and crouched, rolling and throwing his assailant forward on to the flat surface of a grave. The old man's arms whirled and rammed another stake into the boy's chest. The man backed off, watching the thrashing death-throes of the two vampires carefully, keeping himself between them and Kathy, who sat, back against stone, clutching her neck where the vampire's bite burned like phosphorus.

It took a few minutes for them to die, yellow eyes flashing in the gloom, snarls and yelps gradually growing weaker. Eventually the movement stopped. The old man held up a hand, signalling Kathy to stay where she was. And soon after, the bodies crumbled to dust. Kathy stared in amazement. A light breeze was enough to blow the fine powder from the stones, until there was no trace at all that the vampires had ever existed, apart from the crumpled clothing they'd been wearing. The old man walked forward and reclaimed his stakes. Then he turned to Kathy and inspected her throat.

'You are injured,' he said. 'Bitten by vampire. This not good.'

'Who are you?' Kathy asked. The shock was starting to affect her now and she began shivering.

'My name is Harry Viduc. I am a friend. Now come,' he said, lifting her to her feet and slipping a wiry arm around her. 'We must get you back to your aunt's house.'

Kathy was too shocked to resist.

CHAPTER EIGHT

Elizabeth dabbed gently at the wound, peering intently in the bright light of an angle-poise lamp. Kathy lay on a sofa, a towel under her head and shoulders. The old man sat in an armchair opposite, looking out of the window into the dark night.

'It's not too bad,' Elizabeth said. 'The skin's broken and there's blood loss, but the major artery wasn't damaged.'

'She need *morcana*,' the man said gruffly.

'Yes.'

'What's that?' Kathy asked, alarmed.

'A salve,' Elizabeth said. 'It guards against vampire infection.'

'Infection?'

'Yes, vampirism can be passed through the transfer of blood. Enzymes within the blood recreate in the new host. But it can be combated.'

'I thought vampires were supposed to be . . .' Kathy said, 'you know, supernatural?'

'Oh they are,' Elizabeth replied. 'They most certainly are. But there's still a physical process.' She took a dark glass bottle and poured a small amount of the liquid within on to a pristine white surgical pad. Kathy flinched as the cold liquid stung her burning throat, but then there was a blessed cooling as whatever the stuff was began to work.

'How do you know this?' Kathy asked, as her aunt bit off some surgical tape to hold the pad in place. 'What do you know about vampires?'

Elizabeth laughed, then cut herself off. 'My dear, what don't I know about vampires? I've been studying them for fifty years, and my father before me. Vampires in general, and the Highgate Vampire in particular.'

Kathy stared at her in surprise.

'My friend Harry here has been hunting the vampire even longer than I, haven't you, Harry?'

The old man grunted and nodded in his armchair.

'I've been seeing him for a few days now,' Kathy said, nodding towards Harry. 'He's been following me, even in New York.'

'Hmm,' Elizabeth said. 'Perhaps Harry needs to work on his espionage skills. Harry was watching you with one notion only, to protect you. Since Amber disappeared, we felt your life was in danger.'

'From who?'

Elizabeth frowned. 'Well *that* we're not too sure about. We know little about the threat, but we do know why they might want to find you.'

'Tell me what you do know,' Kathy said, the nagging pain of the bite feeding her impatience.

'The vampires you saw tonight were acolytes,' Viduc said. 'They belong to Bishop's Nest.'

'What's Bishop's Nest?' Kathy asked. 'None of this makes sense.'

'Bishop is a vampire,' her aunt said. 'He's been alive for nearly two hundred years. A very powerful vampire.'

'And he's the Highgate Vampire?'

Viduc snorted. 'He wish.'

Elizabeth shook her head. 'No. The Highgate Vampire, we think, is older – much older. We think Bishop wants to find him and, well . . . re-install him in his rightful place.'

'Which is?'

'As King of the Vampires.'

Viduc spoke up again from his armchair. 'Or maybe something else.'

Elizabeth pursed her lips thoughtfully. 'Harry thinks

Bishop may wish to steal the older vampire's power.'

'They can do that?'

'We think so, but we don't know. There's so much information we don't have now. Amber was collecting vampire lore, but now she's gone . . .'

Kathy thought immediately of the book, tucked away in her bag upstairs. Did Elizabeth know about that? She shivered.

'Don't worry,' Elizabeth said, noticing. 'You're safe here, there are glyphs over the doors, powerful magic. No vampire can come in here.'

'Is that the weird carving I saw when I first arrived?' Kathy asked. Elizabeth nodded. 'And why would they want me, anyway?' Kathy continued.

'Because of who you are, Kathy,' Elizabeth said.

'Who am I?' Kathy asked, breathlessly.

'You're one of us, Kathy,' Elizabeth replied. 'You're a Hunter.'

12th April 1993

Draco went alone. It wasn't that he didn't trust the others, though the fewer involved the better, as far as he was concerned. The real reason he went alone was that he knew he wouldn't be coming back and he didn't want anyone else's death on his conscience.

He'd finally cracked the code the night before, as the toddler clucked and tugged at his leg. His wife slept quietly upstairs, already pregnant again. There could be no other torture as horrific as the thought he would have to leave his family. But he knew that if he did not do this thing then they would never be safe. He was doing it for them, and Magda would understand. As would the children, in time.

He hadn't written the tomb's location in the book but left the book for Magda. It contained plenty of other vital information besides the coded location of the tomb. No one would follow him. They wouldn't figure out the secret. Harry's veins ran rich with Hunter blood, but his head was filled with straw. Harry Viduc was convinced he knew the truth about the three prisons and there was no reason for anyone else to argue with him. Draco understood the truth though, it all came down to the interpretation of the prophecy they'd found in the vampire's book of lore.

The Third Prison Shall Claim Him for Ever.
The Lines of Power shall reveal the Tomb.
The Tavern, the Church and the Daughter of Queens
Have Rings to hold him.

He'd torn out the page in his own notebook which held the clues to the crypt's location, the measurements he'd made. He didn't want anyone coming after him.

He reached Swaingate and ran his hand over the iron glyph which formed part of the pattern of the ironwork. Only a handful of people understood what this pattern was. Thankfully Elizabeth was a member of the Highgate Cemetery Society and had made arrangements to affix this symbol here, and all around the perimeter of both cemeteries. Draco opened the gate now with the heavy key he'd stolen years before. Checking up and down the street to make sure the coast was clear, he entered the cemetery and closed the gate behind him with a clank weighted by finality.

He slipped off the path and wended his way through the scattered gravestones, sure of his route. He knew this part of the cemetery so well. When he'd finally learned of the location of the tomb, he'd smiled with grim satisfaction, visualizing its door, having passed it a hundred times on his solitary stalkings. When he'd discovered what was at the bottom of its steps, everything had clicked into place and a plan had started to form in his mind. It was a plan he'd resisted for months. He'd wanted so much to believe there was another way.

He reached the row after a few minutes and stood

before the tomb for as long again, staring at the inscription. *Havering*. A respectable family, fabulously wealthy in their time but perfectly respectable money. Northern mills, not slave plantations. They didn't deserve to have their crypt invaded, their resting place corrupted by this horror, this cuckoo. But this long-dead family were about to host one more unexpected visitor. Draco closed his eyes and took a long, last deep breath of the spring air. Then he hefted his crowbar and stepped towards the tomb door.

No, Draco was not coming back. And no one would ever find his resting place.

CHAPTER NINE

Kathy had been infuriated when her aunt refused to answer any more questions about vampires and had instead insisted she go to bed. Kathy felt sleep must be as far as the moon, her head buzzing with the mass of new and extraordinary information it had had to cope with. But despite that, or maybe because of the sheer weight of it, she actually fell asleep almost straight away. Her last drowsy thoughts were not of the vampire attack, or the thrashing deaths Viduc inflicted upon them, but of a little girl skipping along a gravel path, humming a tune so familiar, yet just beyond the limits of her memory.

The man with the cane came to her again that night, his hair wild and flowing. They were in a dark cavern, or room; a faint light flickered in the centre, leaving the outer edges in dark mystery. Hints of movement, shadows of shapes lurked in the dark, just beyond the limits of understanding. She was bound again, dressed in a flimsy gown. Her breasts felt sensitive and her loins intense with heat as the man approached. He pulled at the handle of the cane, unsheathing a concealed sword, thin and long. He held the wicked blade to her throat, where the boy-vampire had bitten her.

'So close,' he said. 'You were so close, Kathy.' He smiled and his thin face, all cheeks and teeth, split with the twisted smile.

'Close to what?' she asked. Part of her wanted him to touch her.

'Close to the truth,' he replied. 'Close to me. Close to all you've ever dreamed of.'

'I don't want that,' she said.

'Your protestation lacks passion,' he said. 'You want the same thing as your sister, as your mother, as your poor father.'

'You know nothing about them,' she spat.

He laughed, walking away into the darkness. 'Come to me, Kathy,' he said, as he walked. 'You will find everything you've been searching for.' He turned around. 'Even the things you know are impossible.'

Then he was gone and Kathy was awake and sweating. She sat in bed for a few minutes, face in hands, listening to the hollow call of an owl in the trees across the road.

After a while, her heart slowed. Feeling thirsty, she reached for a glass of water on the night stand.

Finishing the drink, she realized she needed the bathroom. On returning, she walked to the window and lifted the curtain. The cemetery was swamped with black velvet. Just a few hours ago she'd been attacked by two undead creatures somewhere in that darkness, and yet she felt no panic, no aversion, no need to run home to New York. The cemetery still drew her. Something was calling, something in the darkness. And whatever it was she did not fear it.

Now what would Dr Gelion say about that?

Elizabeth was gone when Kathy awoke. There was a note on the table.

> *Harry V and I needed to see someone, rather urgent I'm afraid. Sorry to leave you alone so soon after your experience. You're safe in the house and there's plenty of food. Get some rest. We'll be back around eight p.m. and you can ask me as many questions as you like.*
>
> *Love*
>
> *E*

Kathy sniffed. She had no intention of staying in the house, with or without glyphs, and she didn't need Harry for protection. Nonetheless, she took a Puralex before texting Oliver to confirm their appointment.

She spent the morning doing some homework, first researching more about the legend of the Highgate Vampire. She called up the many arguments and interviews, but found it hard to tell fact from fiction. She moved on, now researching the Roman buildings in the area of the tunnels, and yet more accounts of other ghostly sightings. Finally she took another look at the Church website. She fired off another email to Antwain.

Hey, I am in London now. Would love to stop by the Church, heard great things. Maybe see you there Friday?

Kathy made herself a sandwich for lunch and ate it in the sitting room, looking out of the window up the street towards the gates to the West Cemetery. A line of people stood waiting for one of the guided tours. *Why not?* Kathy thought to herself. She hurriedly washed the plate and, grabbing a key from a hook near the door, she left the house and ran up the street to join the end of the line, just as the gate opened and the tourists started to shuffle through.

Reaching the gate, Kathy was slightly disappointed to find Becky wasn't running this tour, but then she realized it might have seemed a bit weird if she had, like Kathy was stalking her or something. Their guide was an elderly lady, carrying an incongruous walkie-talkie and wearing an enormous hat that threatened to slip down over her eyes at any moment. Kathy paid her money and went through. Beyond the Gothic stone gatehouse lay a paved colonnade, overlooked by a brooding ash tree. This area, big enough to accommodate the horse-drawn funeral carriages favoured by wealthy Victorians, separated the entrance from the cemetery itself, or the lands of the living and the dead, as the guide told them. There were fourteen on the tour and Kathy heard a couple of American accents. She decided to keep shtum if possible. She didn't want Brittany from Omaha ruining the tour by attaching herself to Kathy.

The West Cemetery was the older part of the cemetery of Highgate, itself one of seven such 'Garden Cemeteries' built during the Industrial Revolution to cope with the soaring population and the plummeting life-expectancy wrought by the upheaval it caused. The group moved uphill, through dense woods. Hundreds, probably thousands of graves lay scattered, apparently randomly, among the ancient tree roots. Kathy peered into the gloom of the woods to her left. A huge old oak had sprung up amidst a group of lichen-struck gravestones and seemed intent on tossing them aside in slow-motion. She was

121

surprised most not by the dead but by the amount of life in the cemetery. Small animals rustled through the abundant vegetation. She smelled wild garlic and the heady scent of honeysuckle half obscuring a weeping angel. Her cotton sweater was soon covered with aphids clinging grimly on. Butterflies looped and waggled crazily overhead. The birdsong was deafening.

'In 1839,' the guide was saying up ahead, 'the Bishop of London sanctified Highgate Cemetery as an emergency measure after the population of London doubled within ten years. There had been massive overcrowding in the cemeteries too, with bodies being dug up after a few months so the graves could be used again.'

Kathy found it difficult to concentrate on what the tour guide was telling them. She fell behind the group, less interested in which famous old politician was buried where than standing, drinking it all in, enjoying the sensory overload.

But when she heard Brittany asking about the vampire, she trotted ahead to hear the answer.

The guide seemed quite annoyed the question had even been asked. 'It's a load of rubbish and brings us nothing but trouble and expense,' she said frostily as Brittany squirmed under the glare of this formidable old English lady. 'I have never seen or heard anything remotely supernatural, not in all my days.'

Kathy tried not to frown. She wondered if the matter was ever discussed over sherries at the Highgate Cemetery Association Christmas Party. If so, this lady and Becky were likely to have had some big rows.

'I have, however, seen the results of such nonsense: supernaturalists, vampire-hunters, Satanists, witches – both black and white – and your average, everyday drunken yobs charging around trying to find ghosties and ghouls. Lately we've even had young hoodies trying to prise the Highgate Society plates off the railings, though why they'd want those, heaven alone knows.'

The tourists glanced at each other, raising eyebrows as the guide warmed to her theme. 'Jeez lady,' Kathy heard someone mutter behind her. 'Don't have a stroke.'

'We've had people breaking into crypts, even stabbing corpses with wooden stakes, we have seen it all. In the Seventies there was a media frenzy. One night a televized vampire hunt was held – against our wishes, I'll have you all know – and you won't be surprised to find out, they never found a vampire,' she said. 'But since then we've had trespassers hold seances on tombstones, splash graffiti on mausoleums, even animal sacrifices.' The old lady leaned forward and pointed a bony finger at Brittany. 'I tell you this, dear, I'd prefer a real vampire to

123

that lot any day.' Then she winked.

The group laughed as one, the tension relieved. Kathy thought things over; if the old lady was telling the truth, then it seemed the Highgate Vampire was to be found in the West Cemetery.

As they set off again Kathy turned to look behind, just as something black flashed across the path behind them. A cat? She shivered slightly and ran off to catch up with the group again.

After the tour, Kathy popped back to her aunt's house. She had some time to kill before she needed to head to the museum to meet with Oliver. Checking her emails, her heart leaped to see she had a reply from Antwain.

Great to hear you're in London, M'Lady. Would love to show you around. Text me when you're in the queue and I'll come out to get you. Send me a snap of yourself so I'll recognize you.

Ax

The cynical part of Kathy told her that Antwain wanted a picture of her so he could decide whether she was worth pulling out of the queue. She decided not to reply just yet, there were a couple of other things she wanted to do while she had the house to herself. First she went into the entrance hall and picked up the big old telephone receiver.

'Mom? It's Kathy.'

'Hey sweetie, how is it there? I was hoping you'd call today.'

'It's not too early is it?' Kathy asked, suddenly remembering the time difference but not sure exactly what time it might be there.

'Don't worry.' Susan laughed. 'I've been up a while.'

'Sorry, Mom, I should have phoned yesterday. Still settling in, you know?'

'How's London?'

'Way cool. Everything's just so old, I mean, this cemetery. I can't get over how beautiful it is here.'

'You're not spending your whole time wandering around old cemeteries I hope?' Susan said, her voice thin on the line.

'No way, we went on the London Eye and we visited the Tower of London and Covent Garden.'

'And your aunt – how is she?'

Kathy could have kicked herself – why hadn't she asked after Dad? Now it seemed she hadn't been thinking about him, which wasn't true.

'She's wonderful – and full of surprises,' Kathy said, remembering last night's events. 'I'm so glad I've met her. But tell me about Dad – how is he?'

The slight pause before her mom spoke told Kathy all she needed to know.

'He's hanging in there,' Susan said. 'No sign of remission so far, but the doctors aren't giving up.'

Kathy felt she needed to say something to bridge the Atlantic-sized gap between them which had suddenly appeared. But nothing came.

'I need to be here, just now,' Kathy said eventually, which didn't come out quite right. 'I have to do this.'

'It's okay, honey,' Susan answered gently. 'I understand, you don't need to try and explain.'

But Kathy knew Susan didn't understand. Nor could she, without knowing everything. Kathy herself hardly understood what she was doing. She just knew that she had to find Amber, to discover the truth about the vampire, to unlock the cemetery's secrets. There was a resolution available, for everything. She could fix it all, if only she could find the truth.

After she'd hung up, Kathy took a deep breath and, after grabbing the bunch of keys from the kitchen, went down the thin wooden staircase at the back of the house. She knew there was no one to hear but stepped lightly down the heavy oak steps anyway, knowing what she was doing was wrong.

She tried five keys before finding the one that opened the door at the end of the passage. The handle turned and the door swung slowly open. She hadn't really known what to expect. Mummified vampires in bottles? Coffins hung from wires? A stuffed crocodile? Rows of sharp wooden stakes, maybe? But the room was filled with books, teetering piles of them, obscuring deep oak shelves groaning under the weight of ancient tomes. There was a desk in the middle of the room with yet more books piled on it. Kathy thought she recognized an armchair camouflaged by typewritten paper and magazines. She picked one up. *Gothic Quarterly*, dated Summer 2006, headline article: *Vampirecorp – Facebook for the Undead?*. She put the magazine back. A small fireplace was the only part of the room not covered with books, journals and loose paper. The remains of a log fire sat in the grate and she imagined her aunt here on long winter nights, poring over dusty papers, researching vampires, while the fire crackled gently. Over the fireplace was the only section of wall not hidden by bookshelves, and here was pinned a map of Europe and the Middle East. Kathy walked up and peered at the map; three red pins marked Jerusalem, London, and some unnamed part of what seemed to be Romania.

There was a book open at the desk. Kathy checked the

cover for the title. *Bloodlines of the Romanian Vampires*. She read half a page before giving up; the text was dense and meaningless. Who cared which of the Garic family was thought to be a vampire five hundred years ago? She needed to know who was a vampire now, in London. She looked through some of the other books. *A Vampire Chronology, Revenant Accounts in Austro-Hungary 1786–1856. A Vampire at Christ's Side?* She picked up this last. It was a comparatively recent book, published in 1973. She flicked through; it was badly-written and sensationalist, but the gist of the author's argument seemed to be that Jesus was served by a vampire at the last supper, who drank from the holy grail, symbolically drinking the blood of Christ himself, giving himself immense power.

As she read, Kathy thought she heard a creak from upstairs. She froze, but heard nothing further. Nonetheless she suddenly felt nervous about being there. She put things back the way she'd found them and left the room, locking it behind her. She ascended the stairs slowly, cautiously, but the ground floor was empty. The dissonant ticking of three or four clocks in various parts of the house was the only sound.

Kathy pottered around a bit, just enjoying being alone in the grand old house. Pleasant light floated in from the French doors at the back. She fixed herself a cool drink, took her laptop and sat out for a while, enjoying the birdsong. She relaxed into a comfortable garden chair and closed her eyes for a minute, clutching the laptop to her belly.

Kathy heard a noise and her eyes flicked open to see Amber, as a little girl, walking out from between a couple of mulberry bushes. She sat herself cross-legged on the grass opposite Kathy. The little girl frowned.

'I've phoned him,' Kathy said. 'I'm going to see him tonight.'

'Don't forget to take the book,' Amber said.

'You're so bossy,' Kathy said, laughing.

But then something changed. Suddenly Kathy felt the surge of power she'd felt on the dance floor at Marshall's party. She felt the fullness, the strength she associated with Amber's soul merging with hers.

'Are you in me?' Kathy asked. 'Are you part of me?'

But the girl only stared back, uncertainly.

Then Kathy was alone in the garden, blinking, awake again. What had happened there? It was like there were two Ambers, in conflict. One before her, one within. Her head buzzed and she squeezed her eyes shut as though this might let her block the confusion. Needing a distraction, she opened the laptop and punched in her password.

Logging on, Kathy typed *Vampirecorps* into the search engine and clicked on the first link. Vampirecorps was a social network site, set out like so many others, but with suitably Gothic lettering and gloomy graphics. She was invited to set up an account for herself but declined, simply browsing through the limited views she could access. It seemed to be mostly teens using the site, though she saw a few older users too. They were the sort of people who had been bullied at Kathy's school. The freaks, the Goths, the black-clad loners, wannabe vampires. No doubt some had been forced into the sub-culture by the bullying, others would have embraced it gladly, almost welcoming the inevitable attacks from the 'normals'. Part of Kathy felt sorry for them, but another part of her admired and wanted to join them. Isn't this what everyone wanted, really? To feel involved? To be a part of something bigger than oneself? There was a comfort in the thought of belonging to this collection of freaks and outsiders. After all, she was one of those herself, even if she didn't wear white foundation and fake fangs. She wondered if any of these people had ever encountered a real vampire, smelled the rank, intoxicating breath, felt the burn of the bite.

Had they ever been so close to real power?

Kathy shook her head to clear it of that last, unbidden thought. She searched again, this time adding *Gothic*

Quarterly to her search. Kathy clicked on the link to the magazine's website and opened the article about Vampirecorps. Maybe she needed to introduce Aunt Elizabeth to the wonders of the internet, she could probably clear out half the dead tree matter in her study and rediscover that old armchair.

> *John Bishop is an unusual man, at 54, he looks half his age as he sits himself opposite me. He wears a well-tailored, if old-fashioned, suit as uncreased as his pleasant, though forgettable face. John Bishop does not look like a rich man, nor does he act like one, with his modest London flat and last year's phone. But make no mistake, John Bishop is a very wealthy man, his social networking site, Vampirecorps.com, just floated on the NYSE, netting Bishop close to seventy million dollars, on paper at least.*

Kathy raised her eyebrows and skimmed further down the page.

> *'The traditional networking sites were aimed at the mainstream,' Bishop tells me, sipping his latte. 'Vampirecorps is the only major site which aims itself firmly at those who don't feel the world suits them. It's for people who feel they're looking for an alternative to*

*the crass, commercial modern world. Vampirecorps is
incredibly private, we don't take nearly so much
information about our users as the mainstream sites,
and we never, ever share what we do have.'*

*I ask how he expects to make money for his
shareholders if he won't sell things to his users and won't
allow anyone else to do so either.*

*'Users sell things to each other – they provide goods,
or services, we take a cut,' he says.*

*When I point out that too is a form of commercialism,
and that he's exploiting his users, Bishop disagrees with
a shake of the head and a small smile. I sense it's time
to move on. Bishop has a presence, there's something
about him that makes one anxious not to displease
him. He would not meet me in the day, this interview
had to be held at night. He is unusual, but he seems
like the kind of guy who could be your best friend, or
your worst enemy.*

Kathy looked up and checked the clock. Nearly time to
go. Bookmarking the magazine website, she checked the
bus routes again, then after watching the clock for ten
minutes, the excitement to know more about the book
just got too much and she decided it was time to go and
see this Oliver.

Kathy grabbed her bag and threw a thicker jumper in. Darker clouds were sweeping across London's sky and she didn't know how late she'd be. She packed Amber's book, checked she had some money and went to leave the house. But then she stopped, ran back upstairs and sprayed a little of her aunt's Chanel perfume behind her ears. She left the house for the second time that day.

Walking down Swain's Lane to the bus stop, Kathy had the feeling someone was following her and she turned to look three times, only to find no one there. The 214 bus turned up soon enough and she hopped on – after asking the driver if this was the right bus, he nodded. The bus pulled off with a tug and she found herself a seat at the back so she could keep an eye on the other passengers. She wanted to take the book out and examine it one last time alone, but she was nervous about being seen with it – and what was the point? She didn't even recognize the language it was written in. Hopefully Oliver would make sense of it all.

She arrived at the museum early and made her way through the tourists, mostly travelling in packs: Americans, Spanish and Japanese. She walked slowly through the gate, in through the gold-spiked railings and stood for a while in the plaza out the front, looking up in awe at the imposing stone building. Towering Greek columns, holding up a roof so massive it looked like it could squash the White House. Were those Doric columns? Or Corinthian? Kathy could never remember. She knew from looking on the internet that this was the museum of the British Empire. The Elgin marbles were here, plus a bunch of other stuff stolen from various other countries over the centuries when the Brits were striding around the planet like George Bush on angel dust. Kathy paid the recommended donation and wandered through an ante-room with a wide staircase. She passed into an enormous hall filled with white soft light that seemed to come from the heavens. Looking up she saw there was a glass ceiling, composed of hundreds of cells. She'd read about this. This used to be an interior courtyard, open to the elements, but it had been enclosed a few years ago. In the centre was a great round building like a shrine. Kathy walked around it and realized it was the gift shop – she grinned; the most sacred part of any museum. Kathy bought a couple of postcards for her mom and for Scarlet, then wandered back out into the hall.

Doors led off through each wall and Kathy picked one at random. She found herself in the Egyptian rooms and trailed through, drinking in the exquisite craftsmanship and the sheer age of the bronze cats and clay pots. It was busy in there and difficult to walk far without getting in someone's picture.

Passing through into a smaller, dark room, Kathy stopped to look at a mummy and found herself wondering if they ever came back to life, like in the movies. After all, she'd thought vampires were just camp-fire ghost stories too.

She wanted to take a picture. Photography was forbidden in this room, but she'd seen a couple of other people taking snaps on their cells, as though it didn't count on a phone. Still, she felt too nervous to do it when there were other people around. She could see a couple behind her, in the reflection of the glass. But other than that the room was clear. She waited for them to move on into the next room, then she took out her phone and took a picture of the mummy. She folded it quickly away and spun to find a man standing right behind her.

Kathy let out a little involuntary squeal of surprise.

'Sorry,' she said.

The man regarded her carefully, a faint smile playing on his lips, then walked on. *That was weird*, Kathy thought to herself. *I didn't see him reflected in the glass.* Something about the man seemed familiar to her. He looked to be in his early twenties maybe, brown hair, and very good-looking.

Kathy moved on. The man had disappeared. She walked along a corridor lined with vases and pots from Ancient Sumeria and headed towards the African rooms. She saw the man again, standing in front of a tableau featuring a Zulu warrior in the act of spearing a British soldier. He'd been joined by a friend, another young man, not so good-looking, but with the same air of confidence about him. Maybe they were brothers. As she looked over at them they both looked up in unison, catching her. She flung her eyes downward and marched on, going bright red. 'Leave him alone,' Kathy muttered to herself. 'He already thinks you're a lunatic, he'll call the guard.'

Kathy found herself enjoying the African rooms and had just thought to visit the rooms devoted to the Americas when she checked her phone and realized it was time for her appointment. She hurried back to the front desk and told them she had an appointment with Oliver Samson. The guard raised his eyebrows but tapped on his keypad and nodded.

'Take the lift over there to the fifth floor,' he said, pointing to an unobtrusive lift door in a quiet corner of the hall. 'I've activated it for you. Dr Samson's office is at the end of the hall – you'll see as you get out of the lift.'

'Thanks,' she said, and trotted over to the lift. As she crossed the entrance hall she saw the two men again. They were watching her this time. Suddenly she felt vulnerable and hurried along to the lift, clutching her bag tightly.

Kathy got in the lift and waited for the doors to close, the men watching her all the way. She tried to stare back but found her confidence had left her again. She had a sudden craving for a Puralex, but hadn't brought any.

The lift doors opened at five and Kathy stepped out into a long hallway lined on one side with modest doors, interspersed with marble vases. Along the other side were great windows, flooding the hall with evening light. She set off for the door at the end, some nine yards away. Her low heels clacked on the shiny marble floor. Her arrival would not be likely to take Oliver by surprise.

Upon reaching the door, Kathy took a deep breath and checked her hair in the reflection of a brass plaque on the door which read: *Dr Oliver Samson, Occult.* Then she knocked. 'Come in,' she heard faintly from inside and she pushed the door open.

In contrast to her aunt's study, Dr Samson's office was almost neat, though still packed with books. It was also larger, with a huge window overlooking Bloomsbury. Oliver sat at a great wooden desk, inlaid with some softer material for ease of writing. He looked up at her, his messy, short hair flopping forward over his balding forehead.

He looked exactly as Kathy had expected. What else would a professor of the occult look like? Leather patches on the elbow; thin-rimmed glasses; he was handsome; mid-forties. She immediately warmed to him.

Then he smiled. 'Forgive me,' he said, 'you look just like your sister.'

CHAPTER TEN

Jerusalem, 13th July 70A.D.

Antwain stood on the battlements, though this was forbidden. Everything was forbidden these days. Antwain ignored the proscriptions now he had powerful friends. What difference did it make anyway? They were all doomed. He'd come for visual confirmation of the news he held, though he had no reason to doubt it. He watched the tiny soldiers in the distance struggling to get a damaged catapult working again. Its neighbour was primed and being positioned. Smoke rose in plumes from a thousand fires dotted amongst the besieging Roman army. The Romans liked their fire. The catapult arm moved and he saw it slam forward against the rest. A small, smoking ball sailed lazily up from the scoop and headed towards him. Antwain watched it come, telling himself not to flinch.

It was impossible. The flaming ball, so tiny at first, grew larger and larger until it seemed to shadow the Earth itself and, despite his best efforts, Antwain ducked down, though it passed a dozen yards overhead and to his left. He felt the wind and heat from the burning pitch as the missile screamed past him and ploughed into an almost empty marketplace beyond the wall. He felt the ground shake as the ball bounced sluggishly and demolished a house. The market was empty because there was nothing to sell and nothing to buy. The city was starving.

This was the eighth month of the siege. Antwain, his heart racing, was hit by the foul stench of the burning pitch, temporarily masking the usual scent of battle-smoke, excrement and death which cloaked the city these days.

Antwain shielded his eyes against the glare of the mid-morning sun and squinted as he tried to see into the distance. His master would have been able to see easily and, one day, Antwain hoped he might too experience the sensory augmentation brought by Ascending. But today, even his human eyes were enough. There in the distance, to the east, he saw it. A plume of dust. A black smudge that could only be an advancing column. Another army.

He glanced up at the furnace-sun and realized he'd need to hurry. It would not do to keep his master waiting.

He ran down the steps and up the street where the merchants used to sell spice, the faint trace of the thousand exotic scents almost gone now, but still floating there, like a memory. Antwain darted up the temple steps, avoiding a drunk soldier who tried to grab him, and in through the main entrance.

Out of breath, Antwain stood with his back against the wooden door, sweat making his hemp robes itch. City smoke seeped underneath and through the gaps of the door. Antwain peered into the hazy gloom of the bustling temple chamber, waiting for his eyes to adjust. He could make out his master's form, standing at the far end of the temple, perfectly still while all about him was frantic activity. Antwain was unsure how to bring bad news to his master, for he knew it may mean his own destruction. Human slaves must always be sure to pick their moments, he'd seen too many a young vampire acolyte turned to dust before their time. Antwain took a deep breath to steady his nerve and began the long walk forward.

Aliza stood at the centre of the vampire temple, his long dark hair matted with sweat and smoke. He was bearded, an ironic homage to his one-time lord. He was dressed in dark-red leather armour accented by loose black robes that carried the golden symbols of his position. Antwain bowed his head and made his way to the foot of the altar. He did not look into his master's eyes, but addressed himself loudly, to the floor.

'The Romans have forged a treaty with the Muslim king, my Lord. It is known and it is true.' Antwain feared the slice of his master's sword, or worse.

'No matter, we are nearly done,' Aliza replied. Antwain was so surprised he nearly made the fatal mistake of looking up into his master's eyes.

'The truth will not be lost,' Aliza said, quietly.

This close, Antwain was awed by the almost physical presence of the ancient vampire. One of the other acolytes had told him Aliza had been at the Last Supper and had there received the blood of Jesus. Aliza had sat with Matthew, Mark, Luke and John and drank. Jesus had said to them, 'Most assuredly, I say to you, unless you eat the flesh of the Son of Man and drink His blood, you have no life in you. Whoever eats My flesh and drinks My blood has eternal life, and I will raise him up at the last day. For My flesh is food indeed and My blood is drink indeed. He who eats My flesh and drinks My blood abides in Me, and I in him.' That was before they betrayed him. Before they twisted his words for their own ends, eventually leading the so-called son of God into the hands of the Romans.

Aliza's voice was calm, almost soothing to the others,

despite the circumstances. 'Come, brothers. We must strike hard to save the truth.'

They all knew that with the coming sunrise they would all be destroyed; the city defences were on the verge of defeat. The rules of warfare dictated their fate. The population of a city that surrenders could expect mercy. A city which resisted would be sacked, the women raped and enslaved, the men slaughtered, tortured, impaled or crucified. They had to finish the text before the armies reached the Nest.

In the great chamber, under its fantastically painted gold ceiling, a hundred vampire scribes continued the work they had begun on the eve of the siege. They were charting vampire lore and legacy. From the dark times before the blood of Jesus, to their present and final legion. Writing with quill and ink in blood, under the orange light given from fat candles that spat angrily into the still temple air. With every hour that passed and with every completed page, each illustration and glyph, the book grew thicker, more complete. Aliza watched on as the scribes worked to document over a thousand years of vampire lore and religion.

More important than the lore was the magic itself. The rituals, the spells and teachings that would show mortal man the true path of God. A path that could lead man to a richer existence. One of intelligence and art, of heightened awareness and sophistication. This existence promised one more thing, if the path was followed to the full. It promised what all men craved. Immortality, as vampire. Heaven was immortality on Earth. The *true* path was not to be lost, not here, not now, not ever. The path for Antwain was one of slave to half-blood; he knew that to follow Aliza would lead to immortality, for that was the true gift to followers of the vampire religion.

Yet Aliza and the scribes knew that it was forbidden to write vampire magic down. For ever it had been taught or given to others only physically, through passed-on knowledge or through the drinking of the Lord's blood. Everyone in the temple knew the penalty for doing what they were doing would be a lingering and unpleasant death; but just now, Aliza and his kin had no other choice. He knew he and his hundred or so followers were the last of their kind. As the wolves closed in, as the last remaining vampire nest, they worked together through the night to preserve their culture, pass on their knowledge and to ensure their eternal survival. No matter the cost.

This was Aliza's last stand and the book would be his last testament. His eyes burned with rage – a rage brought on through the knowledge that he had lost and they had won. Since the crucifixion of his Lord Jesus Christ the other disciples had lied *en masse*, pulling more and more followers away from him. Mankind was falling for the lies, going over to the idea that heaven was not on earth. Now Aliza hated the weaknesses of mankind; he hated John, Mark and Luke; he hated them all.

'Please, sit,' Oliver said eventually, after remembering his manners. They'd been standing looking at each other like a pair of gateposts for an awkwardly long time. Kathy was stuck for words; again she suddenly felt like she was standing in her head teacher's office. For his part, Oliver seemed to be having trouble getting over how much she looked like her sister.

Kathy sat and rummaged in her bag, anxious to get the lecture started.

'Tea!' Oliver shouted suddenly. He bumbled to the desk and fumbled with the phone, pressing buttons and lifting, then replacing the receiver a few times. Eventually he got a line. 'Miss Finn?'

'Yes, Mr Samson,' a patient-sounding voice replied.

'Two teas, please.'

'Yes, Mr Samson.'

Oliver sat down back into his comfy chair, but then his features clouded over. 'You did want tea?'

Kathy had wanted coffee, as it happened. 'Tea's lovely,'

she said, then smiled. Oliver was the perfect archetypal English academic, tousle-haired and sexy in an absent-minded, mature way. By the looks of this office, he had the brains and ability to match. She could see why Amber trusted him.

'So,' he said, clapping his hands together. 'Vampires!' He pulled an 'OMG' face and Kathy laughed. 'I see you brought the book,' he continued, glancing at her lap.

She looked down – without thinking, she'd pulled the book out. She held it out towards him.

He looked back at her curiously. 'You trust me, then?'

Kathy blinked. 'Why wouldn't I trust you?' she asked.

Oliver looked down at his desk. 'I wasn't sure if . . . your sister had suggested I . . . might not be trustworthy?'

Kathy shook her head. 'No, just the opposite. She said I shouldn't trust anyone else.'

Oliver couldn't stop a smile appearing. 'It's just that . . . Well, I was surprised she didn't send the book to me, you know, when she thought she might be in trouble.'

Kathy thought about this. 'Well, maybe she was worried you might be in trouble too.'

Oliver nodded slowly, with his head slightly to one side, displaying doubt. 'I had considered that. It just seemed a little, well . . . unlikely. Why send the book to someone she'd only known as a baby, across an ocean, putting you at risk? It just didn't seem like Amber to take such a risk.'

Kathy paused for a moment, collecting her thoughts before she replied. 'Since I received the book, and even before, I've been having dreams and . . . urges. Something's been drawing me here. I think part of Amber is within me, guiding me. Does that sound insane?'

Oliver was staring deeply into her eyes as she spoke. His eyes were a rich chocolate, warm and experienced, and Kathy felt she was looking into the eyes of someone good – she felt safe and secure. But she felt a faint stirring, a pang in her tummy, a feeling of a family lost. Her emotions were now more active than ever, she was connecting at last with herself.

'It doesn't sound at all insane,' he replied. 'At least not when compared to some of the things I've seen during the two years since I met Amber.'

Kathy leaned forward. 'You've seen vampires?'

He nodded and was about to speak when the door opened. Miss Finn walked in, tall and slim, and carrying a tea tray. She looked like the prim librarian who'd turn so glam simply by releasing a few hair clips and removing her glasses. Kathy wondered if she and Oliver had ever . . . She blinked to remove the image. *What's up with me? This guy is old enough to be my father!* She brushed the thought away – Amber's mischievous influence inside her again?

'Anything else?' Miss Finn asked and Oliver smiled and told her no.

Once she'd gone, Oliver fussed over the tea for a while. 'It needs stewing a while,' he said. 'Do you mind if I have a quick look . . . ?' He held up the book.

'Go ahead. Do you mind if I admire the view?' Kathy asked.

'Not at all,' Oliver replied. 'I'll give you a little tour later on.' Then he opened the book eagerly and began reading, sliding his finger down the pages. 'There are two parts to the book,' Oliver said. 'Lore and Prophecies. It's the prophecies I'm interested in just now.'

Kathy wandered across the large, wood-panelled office. The clouds had passed and the sun was only just dipping below the buildings across the road – there was still half an hour's light. The afternoon sunlight poured through the glass thickly, like golden syrup. It splashed across her, warmed her. She saw stick figures down in the forum walking in groups, or standing alone.

She turned to watch Oliver for a while, engrossed in the book, nodding occasionally. His features were lit by a golden lamp on his massive oak desk. He'd forgotten about the tea and she stepped lightly to the tray, not wanting to disturb him. She poured two cups and he mumbled a quick thanks as she set it beside him.

Kathy walked back to the window and settled herself on the window seat, looking up and out, into the twilight of the London evening sky.

Oliver muttered aloud as he read.

'The final prison. The third prison? No, the three prisons. Take circle? What does that mean? Take. Have?'

He scribbled a note and looked up at the ceiling for a while, lost in thought, before sticking his nose back into the book.

Kathy's tea remained undrunk and had turned cold by the time Oliver stood. The sound of his chair being pushed back startled Kathy from her reverie and she turned to see him slam the book shut. He opened a drawer and pulled out a folded map which he hurriedly unfurled and laid on the desk.

Kathy wandered over to look. The map was of the cemetery, named graves dotted all across it. She recognized Swain's Lane in red, cutting north-south down the centre, and saw the many walking paths outlined in light blue, winding through each side of the cemetery.

'Found what you were looking for?' Kathy asked. Oliver jumped, not realizing she was right behind him.

Oliver took a ruler, checked the scale and measured a line south-east from the church at the top left corner. He then measured another line, this time from the pub. The two lines converged over a grave near the Circle of Lebanon. He leaned over to inspect the name on it, sliding a magnifying glass over the tiny writing.

'Not *take*,' he said, 'but *have*. Not *circle*, but *ring*! Havering!'

'What's Havering?' Kathy asked, peering curiously. But he didn't seem to hear.

'And that,' he muttered, 'is the very spot where the ley lines meet.' He grinned at her, looking like a schoolboy who'd just discovered where the Head kept confiscated sweets.

'So what's this all about?' Kathy asked, reckoning it was time for answers.

Oliver's face clouded over. 'How much do you know already?' he asked, guardedly.

'Plenty, but I want to know it all.'

Oliver frowned. 'Careful what you wish for, Kathy.'

'I know you want to protect me,' Kathy said. 'My aunt's the same. Look, I'm already in this up to my neck.' As she said this, she pulled down her scarf and ripped off the bandage to show him her wound.

Oliver stared. 'What am I supposed to be looking at?' he asked.

'This!' Kathy said, touching the wound. Her fingertips

felt nothing. She stood and rushed to the mirror. Her neck was smooth, pale and flawless. Kathy turned back to Oliver. 'I was bitten – a vampire – just yesterday. This is impossible.'

Oliver held up his hands in surrender, grinning. 'I believe you, I do. Like I said, I've seen a lot of weird stuff lately.'

'But how . . . ?' Kathy began.

'It's because of who you are,' Oliver said. 'Who Amber is.'

'Who am I?' Kathy said. She moved over to him, looking deep into his face, searching for answers there. 'My aunt won't tell me. Or else she gives half-answers that obscure more than they reveal. What am I?'

Oliver frowned. 'I think we'd better start at the beginning. Come on, sit.'

Kathy did as she was told.

'More tea?'

'You got anything stronger?'

Oliver walked to a cabinet and poured them both glasses of brandy. He handed one to Kathy and perched himself on the edge of his desk. He sipped the drink and grunted appreciatively. Then he set down the drink and picked up Amber's book.

'This book,' he began, 'is the *Word of Aliza* – the vampire we know as the Highgate Vampire.' Oliver held Amber's book clamped tight between his palms, as though he wished to hold its secrets safe for a while longer. 'He was born – a man – in Ancient Israel, around 24B.C. Which we think makes him the oldest surviving vampire. According to vampire lore, this makes him officially the head honcho.'

'The President of the Vampires?'

'The King of the Vampires,' Oliver corrected. 'Vampires are quite traditional. It is the goal of all vampires to find the king and worship him.'

'This sounds familiar,' Kathy said. 'My aunt told me the same thing.'

'Ah yes,' Oliver said, smiling warmly. 'How is Elizabeth?'

So Aunt Elizabeth does know who you are, Kathy thought. *Why did she lie?*

'She's well, thanks,' Kathy replied.

'Good,' Oliver said. 'Anyway, back to the lesson. We know Aliza was at the Last Supper and drank the blood of Christ. He then went to war with the other disciples—'

'What? Really?'

Oliver looked at Kathy, surprised by her surprise. 'Yes, that source is very strong.'

'But there were only twelve disciples.'

Oliver snorted with laughter, then looked mortified.

'Sorry, I didn't mean to be rude. How would you know? No, there were in fact many more disciples. Aliza, and quite a few others, were conveniently forgotten by the church soon after – you could say they were written out of history.'

'Now that *doesn't* surprise me,' Kathy said.

'Drinking Christ's blood seems to have infused Aliza with enormous power,' Oliver went on. He walked around the office as he spoke, still holding the book. 'We don't know if he was already a vampire at the time of Christ's death but it seems probable. What we do know is that he left Jerusalem around that time. Where he goes initially we're not sure, but there are hundreds, if not thousands of accounts of vampirism throughout Europe during the course of the next millennium; many of them follow a pattern familiar to accounts of Aliza.'

'And what would that be?' Kathy interjected.

'He appears as an immensely tall figure, cloaked, with glowing yellow eyes. He toys with his victims, entrancing them before murdering them savagely. Sometimes he kills without feeding. Sometimes he plays games.'

'Games?'

'Yes. Impaling them on spikes, hunting them in forests, tearing off their limbs and leaving them to die in agony.'

'Not sure I'd call those *games*, exactly,' Kathy began,

but Oliver was already continuing.

'It seems likely that he came to England during that period, first to a house in central London, then he was moved to Highgate itself. He also has help – followers,' Oliver said.

'Really?'

'Yes. You see *Vampire* is like a religion in itself, it has structure, you start at the bottom and work your way up, from slave to eventually being a vampire. Amber showed me a document containing part of the Prophecy, it refers to Aliza's *final* resting place, in Highgate, in the cemetery itself. I—' but then Oliver stopped suddenly and checked his watch. 'Ha,' he said. 'Museum's closed. Shall we go?'

'Where are we going?' she asked.

'For the tour,' Oliver said, grinning. 'There are a few things I want to show you.'

'So how do you know that's a vampire's coffin?' Kathy asked. A sarcophagus lay behind a glass panel in the Sumerian room. Kathy had passed this earlier, without thinking anything of it. The inscription simply read: *Sarcophagus, circa 150B.C.*

'We don't know for sure, but considering that the mechanism to open the thing is on the inside, we think that is a strong indication.'

154

'So why don't you write *Vampire's Coffin* on the inscription?' Kathy asked.

'Because vampires don't exist,' Oliver said.

Kathy turned to look at him. 'But you know they *do* exist.'

Oliver shrugged. 'I wrote a paper about it once, laying out all the evidence. Sent it to respected historical journals and the church. They thought it was a joke and published it on April Fool's Day. I spoke to the museum head about my research too, but she told me I needed to rest and sent me off on holiday.' Oliver sighed. 'When I got back it was made clear that I wasn't to discuss vampires with anyone. I gave up trying to convince people after that. I suppose Aliza did the same, no one would listen to him. I actually believe that once he was a good man, but he was turned against his mankind by our ignorance. At times I think I know how he felt.'

'But wasn't Dracula a real vampire?' Kathy asked. 'There are loads of old stories about vampires, surely there must be some historical interest?'

'Vlad the Impaler was said to drink his victims' blood,' Oliver said, indicating that they should move on. 'And yes, there have always been reports and accounts of vampirism, even in the earliest human histories. But there's no acceptance today that there has ever been anything supernatural about such accounts. If people drank one another's blood in the past then they did so out of religious or superstitious ignorance – according to *official* accounts, that is.'

'So it's the magical stuff people don't accept?' Kathy asked as they moved into the Ancient Israel room.

Oliver nodded. 'I'm suffered to write my papers on people's beliefs, but if I find any evidence of real, genuine magic, or any suggestion that vampires are a separate race, or a religion, living amongst us, then I'm expected to squirrel it away.'

They stopped in front of a display case filled with metal ornaments. 'So how does Amber enter the story?' Kathy asked.

'She came to me with some photocopied documents she'd found, but couldn't read. She didn't tell me where she got them, that she had the book itself. They were damned hard to decipher. But I figured them out and translated for her.'

Oliver grinned at Kathy, a mischievous look in his eye. 'I drew the process out a little, perhaps. I revealed the contents of the documents over a series of meetings. First coffee, then lunch, drinks after work.'

'You mean you tried to seduce my sister?' Kathy said with a cheeky smile.

'She is a very attractive woman, you cannot blame a man for trying,' Oliver said with a laugh. 'But I am too old and too wise to chase a woman half my age and way out of my league.'

'Some girls like experience.' Kathy almost kicked herself, Amber rising inside her again.

'Now here, we have a selection of glyphs,' Oliver said, ignoring her. 'These are like magical charms, they hold power over vampires.'

'I recognize that one,' Kathy said, pointing to one with a similar design to the carving over her aunt's door. 'That's a warding glyph.'

Oliver looked at her in surprise. 'Yes it is. How did you know that?'

Kathy tapped her nose. 'You're not the only one who does research.'

'That one there is a finding glyph,' Oliver said. 'If you hold it and walk purposelessly, it will supposedly lead you to your quarry.'

'And what's that one?' Kathy asked, pointing to a tarnished amulet with a pattern so intricate it made her eyes go crossed, like an M.C. Escher painting.

'That's a glyph of expulsion,' Oliver said. 'If you hold it face out towards a vampire and utter a power word, an invisible force will knock him backwards –

quite hard too, Harry tells me.'

'Harry's used these?' Kathy asked.

'Oh yes. Harry's Hunter blood is very strong. Like you.'

'And Aunt Elizabeth?' Kathy asked.

Oliver made a so-so hand gesture. 'Your aunt's mother, your grandmother, was a half-Hunter. Your aunt's father had no Hunter blood at all. He was a scholar, fascinated by vampires. He travelled to Romania in the Fifties. That's where he met your grandmother, Kasia.'

'What happened to them?' Kathy asked, intrigued that Oliver knew so much more than she did about her own family.

'Ah! There's a story,' Oliver said, staring through the glass at the glyphs. 'You see, your aunt's father was already married. The affair was torrid but brief, when he returned to England he took with him a tiny baby.'

'Elizabeth,' Kathy said, transfixed. 'Kasia sent her daughter away to live in another country?' The parallels with her own early life were striking.

'Yes, you must understand that Romania, in those days, was an impoverished country, and for a young woman to give birth outside wedlock was a heinous crime. Kasia did the best thing she could for her infant daughter.'

'And what happened to her, to Kasia?'

'She married your grandfather, a full-blood Hunter. They had three children. One survived. Magda, your mother.'

'So my mother was almost full-blood Hunter?'

'Yes, but according to Elizabeth, her blood was weak. It was your father, Draco, who passed his power on to you and Amber.'

'I think I know the rest of the story,' she said.

Kathy stood for a while lost in her thoughts, trying to control the tears welling. It was just too much, all this new information. She was finding her own history, this other world she'd repressed for so long. Oliver watched her carefully.

'Do they work then?' Kathy asked, trying to change the subject.

'What?'

'The glyphs, do they work?'

Oliver nodded. 'Well, to an extent. You see there are vampires, and vampires. They are intensely hierarchical. A recently converted vampire, or an acolyte who hasn't fed yet, is weak and lowly. He is stronger than a human and can perform basic magic, including flying sometimes. But compared to the older, more powerful vampires, he is nothing.'

'They gain power with age?'

'Yes, or at least they develop the potential for power with age. They must feed of course, or else they grow weak and senile. Followers of the vampire can imminently gain immortality – but that's not the real prize, the prize is when you couple immortality with power. Power over others.'

'You said they can become senile?'

'Yes. Take the Highgate Vampire, for example. He seems to feed every ten years, always in a year with a three in it. There have been attacks, and reports of missing people, animals drained of blood and so on, in 1943, 'sixty-three, 'seventy-three, 'eighty-three and so on. Harry tracked him down in 1983 and staked him. But he escaped and went to ground in the deepest depths of the graveyard. Since then there have been no reports of attacks that can definitely be attributed to him.'

'Thirty years? But I saw something,' Kathy said. 'And a cemetery tour guide told me she has recorded dozens of sightings more recently than that, credible ones too.'

'That could be his spectre,' Oliver said. 'Aliza is a supernatural being now, remember.'

'A ghost of a vampire,' Kathy said, remembering Becky's words in the pub.

'Yeah, something like that,' Oliver said. 'We think he's lying low in between the feed years, unwilling or unable to leave the cemetery, terrified of being discovered and destroyed. For twenty years he has had no nest, no support network, no followers. He's alone and feeds irregularly, if at all.'

'So he'll die, if we just leave him?' Kathy asked.

Oliver frowned. 'That's what we thought. But the sightings of his ghost have been growing more regular lately. He's hungry. And now Bishop's crew are looking for him too. Bishop and his own so-called *followers* are up to something. Something's afoot. If we can find him, then I'm convinced we can finish him off, or at least make sure he's properly contained.'

Oliver walked off out the door and Kathy, dry-mouthed, scurried to keep up with him. They passed a security guard in the corridor, who nodded at Oliver.

'So how do we find Aliza?'

Oliver beamed at her. 'Ah, well that's where it gets interesting. We knew that the cemetery sits astride two different ley lines. One runs east-south-east, under the church, towards the Holy Land. The second runs towards the east, under the Flask pub and off towards Romania.'

Kathy remembered the map in her aunt's study.

'Romania again,' she said.

Oliver carried on speaking as they walked. 'An account by a group of Hunters in the sixteenth century tells of a vampire who was holed up in a castle in Romania, disguised as a Templar Knight. The castle was besieged by Vlad the Impaler's troops and the vampire fled, but left behind a book which gave them some useful information about vampires and how to destroy them.'

'A book? Amber's book?'

Oliver turned to her and raised his eyebrows. 'It would seem so.'

'So you just look where the lines meet?' Kathy asked. 'That's where the vampire is?'

Oliver frowned and shook his head.

'Unfortunately the measurements are a bit vague. The tavern isn't in exactly the position it was a thousand years ago, and the church is big. The possible area covered is large. I needed the book to pinpoint the exact location of the Highgate Vampire's final resting place, according to the prophecies.'

The museum was silent now. If the guard was still walking around, he was too far to hear. Kathy stood and waited for Oliver to continue.

'Unfortunately Amber didn't photocopy the relevant page,' he said, looking down at his feet. 'She was due to bring me the next batch that same day she disappeared.'

'That was why she was so keen for me to bring you the book,' Kathy said. 'So what did you discover?'

Oliver gave a short bark of triumphant laughter.

'The book of prophecies gives the location of Aliza's final resting place,' he said. 'The relevant section reads as follows:

> *'The Lines of Power shall reveal the Tomb.*
> *The Tavern, the Church and the Daughter of Queens*
> *Have Rings to hold him.'*

'Okay,' Kathy said. 'But what does that all mean?'

'The lines of power are the ley lines, we knew that already. I was puzzled by the Daughter of Queens line … But then you opened your mouth and I recognized that Flushing accent.'

'That's me? I'm the Daughter of Queens?'

Oliver nodded, grinning. 'You are.'

'The final clue was the "Have Rings to hold him". It had me stumped for a while, I wondered if I'd got the translation wrong. But then I checked the map of the cemetery – I found a crypt with the name Havering, right where the ley lines meet. I'm convinced that's where we'll find Aliza.' He looked intensely at Kathy. 'You know what, Kathy? I really don't think I would have figured it out if it hadn't been you who'd brought me the book. You and your connection with Queens. I think there's a reason you're here. You're an essential part of this puzzle.' He waggled his eyebrows and strode off.

'But if this book was written two thousand years ago,' Kathy called after him, 'how could they have known about Queens? How could they know about me?'

'I told you,' Oliver said, not turning around. 'It's a book of prophecies. Visions. Given by God. The writers wouldn't have understood it themselves.'

After a moment, Kathy followed, her head spinning with it all.

They passed a collection of Victorian paintings showing ancient battles – dark, frantic canvases that unsettled Kathy; she hurried past. Then they were back in the Great Hall. Oliver waved to the guard behind the desk and led Kathy back to the lift. She was pleased he wasn't taking her to the doors, because that would have meant the end of the tour. The end of finding out more.

The lift arrived and the doors opened. 'So there's this book which tells us how to destroy vampires, yet London seems to be full of the damn things,' Kathy said.

Oliver shrugged. He hit a button marked *LG* and the lift lurched as it moved, down this time. 'There are a lot of vampires and few Hunters,' he said. 'And not all of the book has been translated. Yet. Like I said, Amber brought me pages one by one. She didn't want to show me the whole thing.'

'Why not?' Kathy asked as the doors began to open.

'She said it was because she didn't want to put me in harm's way.'

As he spoke his voice betrayed just a tiny amount of pain, the stiff upper-lip quivering slightly.

They stepped out into a basement with a high ceiling, almost lost in shadows. Wooden boxes were stacked neatly, row after row. Filing cabinets and great glass display cases lined the walls.

'What do you think has happened to her?' Kathy asked gently.

Oliver strode off down an avenue of packing crates, Kathy trotting to keep up. 'She got herself a job working as a dancer at Bishop's club, which we think is basically just a front for his nest. It was on her first full shift that she disappeared. I think she's still alive – I hope she is,' he said. Kathy thought of her dreams and nodded. 'The thing is,' he went on, 'you and Amber are both descended from the Hunter race. You have power of your own.'

'What sort of power?' Kathy asked. 'I've never had any power over anything. I have asthma.'

Oliver laughed. 'Nonetheless, it's in your blood. You're different to normal humans, that's why you were able to recover from the bite. A human would probably have died, or become a vampire herself.'

'But it was the salve that healed me,' Kathy protested. 'My aunt smeared some kind of cream on. *Morcana* they called it.'

'I'm sure that helped,' Oliver said. 'But your aunt would tell you the same thing as me, you recovered mostly because of your bloodline, and that bloodline, I believe, will keep Amber alive too.'

'We're not immortal though,' Kathy said as Oliver stopped at a rough wooden crate. He looked around for something.

'No,' he said. 'You're not immortal. Only full vampires are immortal, and even then only under certain circumstances. The reason I think Bishop will keep Amber alive is because he wants her to be a vampire. He will try to convert her. Bishop is a deluded fool of what was a man.' Oliver found what he was looking for, a crowbar. He prised open the top of the box, the shrieking of nails echoing around the great chamber.

'How can he convert her?' Kathy asked. 'By biting her?'

'He'll bite her first, but then she'll have to feed, drink human blood. If she does, she'll become a vampire.'

'And if she doesn't?'

Oliver looked at her, the top of the wooden box in his hands. 'Now that I'm not sure about. If she were human, she'd die unless she fed before the next full moon. As she

166

has Hunter blood . . .' He shrugged. 'I'm hoping she'll survive it.' He put the plywood outer box lid aside and opened the lid of a dark wooden chest within.

'Hoping?' Kathy asked. 'Is that all you're doing?'

'Not just that,' Oliver said, and lifted out a sharp wooden stake. 'I've been planning a little trip to Highgate Cemetery.'

Oliver emptied the box and laid everything out on the floor. A collection of wooden stakes, a mallet, some glyphs, a bottle with a clear liquid within, a claw hammer, two large crucifixes and two smaller. There was also a large pile of books.

'They won't let me display this stuff,' Oliver said. 'I don't see why not, it's an early-twentieth century vampire-hunter's kit.'

'Is that holy water in the bottle?' Kathy asked.

Oliver nodded. 'It won't work very well on more powerful vampires, it will repel followers and low-learned ones only,' he said. 'Just the acolytes and the weaker ones. Same with crucifixes. The glyphs work much better, because they're vampire magic.'

Kathy picked one up, the size of a large medal. Eldritch patterns curled and looped across its surface. It felt cool and heavy.

'A mix of lead and silver,' Oliver said. 'You keep that

one, it's a warding glyph. It'll stop you being attacked, at least give 'em pause to think.'

He sat on a crate and leafed through Amber's book. He held another glyph in his hand. Kathy's eye was caught by something and she turned her head quickly. Had something moved there, high in the shadows?

'Are there bats down here?' she asked.

'Hmm, bats? No, not down here.'

'I thought I saw something up there,' she said.

'Pigeon, maybe – sometimes they get in, God knows how. They crap over everything then find somewhere inaccessible to die.'

He'd found the page he was looking for and was reading intently, lips moving wordlessly as he translated.

'I read something in a magazine about John Bishop,' Kathy said, to break the silence. 'He's apparently an internet millionaire.'

'Yes,' Oliver said absently. 'The social network thing. Clever idea.'

'Lucrative idea.'

'Yes, but I mean useful for gathering a nest.'

'Is that what he's doing then?' Kathy said. 'Building his following?'

Oliver looked up at her from the book. 'Yes, that's exactly what he's doing. He's gathering vampires and would-be vampires. Gradually converting them, establishing a hierarchy, grooming captains and lieutenants.'

'Like the mafia,' Kathy said.

'Yes, very much like the mafia,' Oliver said, then shoved his nose back into the book.

'How did Bishop become a vampire?' Kathy wanted more.

'Bishop? He descends from a bloodline that's Eastern European in its origin – he's about four hundred years old from what we can gather. After following and then probably turning on another vampire, he founded his own nest here in London.' Oliver shifted, removing his glasses from his nose, giving them a wipe on his tie. 'You see, Aliza was forced into hiding by his own kind. He is a prize not only hunted by your ancestors but by other vampires too, other vampires that want to harness his power, his knowledge.'

'So where do vampires come from?' Kathy scratched her head, puzzling the questions; she was thinking out loud.

'As far as we know, Aliza was the first *organized* vampire, cultured if you like. He was the only one of his kind to feed on the blood of Jesus, the only one to receive the prophecies. For a time he brought vampires together – he founded their politics, their religion. Aliza gave vampires their structure, magic and beliefs – that was before he became the hunted, even by his own kind.'

As Oliver continued, a faint sound from somewhere to their left caught Kathy's attention. She stood and walked slowly towards the sound, peering into the shadows above.

'Ha!' Oliver said from behind her. 'It's a glyph of entrapment. Like Harry's prison glyphs.'

She turned to look. The glyph-pattern looked jagged and cruel.

'A bunch of these arranged around an area and the vampire becomes trapped,' Oliver said. Then his face grew thoughtful. 'Three prisons . . . It couldn't be so simple.' He began leafing through pages of the book again, intently.

'What about the three prisons?' Kathy asked, but she'd lost him now. She turned and wandered up the aisle. The crates were marked with numbers, offering no clues as to their contents. She turned a corner and walked along the wall, looking into the display cases. Row after row of insects were within, each stabbed with a tiny steel pin, holding it in place for ever. Here butterflies, there beetles, all looking pretty similar to her untrained eye. She shivered as she walked; it had suddenly grown cooler.

Another shout from Oliver stopped her.

'I've got it! Kathy, I've figured it out!'

She smiled and turned.

Behind her stood a vampire.

CHAPTER ELEVEN

Kathy's heart stopped. It was one of the men she'd seen when she'd arrived at the museum; he stood glaring at her, his mouth half open, showing the fangs, his eyes flashing yellow. Her skin shivered and puckered with icy fear. She wanted to scream for help, or to warn Oliver, but she couldn't move.

Then the vampire darted towards her and something, some instinct, gave her back her legs and she ducked out of the way. The vampire shot past her and she was away, back along the wall and into the aisle where she'd left Oliver. She could feel her limbs, her heart full of adrenaline. Oliver sat where she'd left him, still looking into his book, but behind him stood the second vampire, about to strike.

As she ran, Oliver looked up at her, surprised.

'Oli—' she called but it was too late. The vampire fell upon the academic and wrestled him on to the floor, twisting his head to expose the neck. Oliver fought back, turning his head so as to deny the vampire a clean strike. Kathy remembered the glyph and jammed a hand into her pocket as she ran. She didn't have time to stop and look behind her to see if the first vampire was still coming. With difficulty she managed to pull the bulky glyph out of her tight jeans pocket just as she reached Oliver and the vampire.

Without stopping, Kathy smashed the glyph into the side of the creature's head. It screeched and tumbled to one side, backing away hurriedly. She saw a red welt on its twisted features, like the one she'd seen in the cemetery, when Harry Viduc had saved her.

'Kathy!' Oliver shouted. She turned just in time to see the first vampire launch itself at her. She held up the glyph – but too late. The vampire's heavy body thumped into her, knocking her to the ground. Then almost instantly she felt herself being lifted up and she was sailing through the air, thrown by the vampire; a moment's balletic serenity as she spun, then crashed into a wooden crate, breaking it apart to expose a collection of tapestries, mercifully soft.

She looked up to see Oliver holding the two large crucifixes. The vampires stayed clear, snarling. 'Get the other stuff,' he called. Kathy picked herself up, ribs aching; her jeans were torn, the knee blood-soaked. She trotted over and collected up the holy water, stakes and glyphs. She tucked them into the leather pouch as the vampires watched her, balefully.

'They're not strong,' Oliver said. 'Recently turned.'

'Stronger than you,' the taller vampire said. 'Smarter than you.'

'We'll see,' Oliver said, and began backing away. Kathy looked forward, leading him back to the lift. The vampires followed, occasionally making darting rushes which Oliver would block with one or other of the crucifixes.

'Shouldn't we try to stake them?' Kathy whispered.

The vampires heard this somehow and howled with laughter.

'It's not as easy as it looks on telly,' Oliver said. 'Best done when they're asleep.'

Eventually they reached the lift and, ignoring the fury of their attackers, they closed the doors and went back up to the ground floor. 'There are security doors to the stairs, that should slow them down.'

'So how did they get down there in the first place?' Kathy asked. 'The lift didn't move when we were down there, we'd have heard it.'

Oliver didn't answer. The lift doors opened at the ground floor and he peered out carefully into the dim vestibule, waving a cross.

'And where are they now?' he said, grimly.

Coast apparently clear, they exited the lift and walked towards the desk.

'Cal?' Oliver called. 'Calum?' Then he stopped. Kathy looked around him to see what had made him halt. The security guard lay slumped in his chair, his throat a blackened mess of gore and gristle, the upper part of his uniform soaked with blood. His glassy eyes stared up towards a statue of Queen Victoria.

'Maybe we should just get the hell out of here?' Kathy said, pointing towards the main doors.

'Those are locked,' Oliver said. 'I have a code for the doors on the other side of the building. We have to go there.'

Kathy turned to look. In the north side of the vestibule a set of smaller doors led into the museum proper, where she'd walked earlier in the day. The rooms beyond were dark now.

'Great,' Kathy said.

10th October 1993, St Michael's Church, Highgate

Father Kennedy walked slowly down the central aisle of the church, candles flickering to either side. His feet ached. A long day when one started at five-thirty a.m. Just

175

one turn around the church to check everything was in order, that no one was lurking in the shadows, then he could lock up and head home, to his quiet room in the lodgings on the Highgate Road. It had been a difficult day too. There were so many troubled people these days. He didn't regret moving to this inner-city church, despite his great love for the Cumbrian countryside and the sweet village church he'd left. His calling was strong and firm. He knew he could make a difference to these troubled souls.

It was the drugs mostly, he thought as he glanced each way down the nave and moved on to the small chapel. Sometimes junkies would come in out of the cold and huddle up there, near the big old radiator. Though it pained him to do it, he had to turf them out on to the hard streets before he locked up. The government talked about a war on drugs. Heroin was the biggest problem apparently, but when city bankers and football stars were snorting coke off young ladies, he wondered if it wasn't society as a whole that suffered an addiction.

As Father Kennedy passed the door to the crypt, something made him stop and check the handle. He was surprised to find it unlocked. The crypt was hardly used. They stored stacking chairs and trestle tables down there but its echoing chambers were mostly empty. He clucked his tongue. It must have been one of the ladies who had organized the jumble sale at the weekend. They'd used the tables and must have left the door unlocked afterwards.

He pondered for a moment, then turned and walked away. It was too late to be walking down all these steps, his feet hurt too much. So what if there was a tramp down there? Let him rest in warmth and safety for one night. But then he stopped. Whatever impulse had made him try the handle spoke to him again. What if someone was down there and needed his help? He'd explored it fully once, with a local historian from the Highgate Society. Some of the brick walls that separated the crypt from the old bone yard catacombs had tumbled down. In fact they'd just received a letter from the society asking for permission to rebuild the walls. They'd offered to do it for free, as long as they could mount their insignia on the rebuilt walls. Father Kennedy was inclined to let them, but had sent the application off for approval.

The walls certainly needed repairing, it was only a matter of time before a tramp got himself lost in the catacombs. Those tunnels were unsafe and ran for miles, to goodness knows where, under this ancient part of the city. The thought of it tipped the balance.

'Okay,' he said wryly, looking up. 'You win, I'll go

down.' He flicked on the lights and began the long descent into the gloomy crypt.

The spiral staircase was lit periodically by wall lights, fizzing, as if in alarm at having been woken suddenly after days of dark rest. Father Kennedy stepped heavily down step after step, his belly bouncing over his belt. *Must cut down on the pie and chip suppers*, he thought.

Eventually he reached the bottom and peered out into the dimly lit crypt. A few naked bulbs shed insufficient light, the dirty old walls absorbing the yellow glow. It was cold. Too cold to make a good hiding place for a junkie. The trestle tables and chairs were stacked neatly to one side, scrambled footprints in the thick dust indicated how recently they'd been moved. One set of prints led off into the shadows.

'Hello?' the priest called. 'Is there someone down here?'

There was no answer. Father Kennedy stood still, listening.

'There's no one here,' he said to himself and turned to go.

Then he heard a noise. A click or a snap, perhaps. Like someone had stood on something made of plastic – or bone.

'Hello?' Kennedy called again, louder this time. 'Who's there?'

But again there was no answer. Kennedy shivered; it seemed to have grown even colder. Taking a deep breath, he walked off into the shadows, following the footprints. They led on through an archway into the next chamber. Kennedy stopped again to listen, his breath condensing in the chill.

There, again, the noise.

'Who's there?' he called. 'You can't stay here. You'll have to leave, come out!'

Again there was no answer. Father Kennedy carried on, towards the sound of the noise. Rounding a thick pillar he found himself at the arched entrance to a smaller damp chamber, cloaked in a velvet blackness. He looked for a light switch but found nothing. Was this one of the caverns with the broken walls? Was the cold air coming from within the catacombs beyond?

'I know you're in there,' he said, frightened now. The cold was intense, as though emanating from within this room. Father Kennedy wanted nothing more than to turn around and run back up the steps, locking the wooden door behind him at the top. If there was someone down here then damn them, they could be locked in overnight. He'd return in the morning with a torch. He turned to go and took a step.

But for a third time something spoke to him. Something

made him stop. Something made him turn back. Heart pounding, teeth chattering, Father Kennedy took a step towards the dark maw of the damp chamber. Then another.

Then he was inside, cloaked in an intense darkness that seemed almost physical. He turned to look at the entrance he'd just come through, even the dim light beyond seemed like a thousand suns compared to this . . . this utter blankness, this absence of light.

He turned back to see a pair of yellow eyes glaring at him.

Father Kennedy didn't even have time to shriek before something struck him in the chest, puncturing his ribcage and crushing the dense muscle of his heart as though it were jelly.

Lying on the stone floor, in the darkness, Father Kennedy slipped slowly away, glassy eyes searching for enlightenment as his attacker gorged itself on the soft organs within his chest cavity.

'Do you have your glyph?' Oliver said.

'Yes.'

'Take a cross too,' he said, handing her one.

'I'd rather have a stake.'

'Really,' he said. 'The cross is a better deal. We shouldn't try to fight them, just to escape them.'

'Why?'

'Because vampires are smart. A full-front attack is never a good idea. You have to always be one step ahead of them.'

Kathy rolled her eyes and felt a flush of annoyance. She wanted to fight. Then she shook her head, trying to clear it of the unfamiliar aggression surging through her. How had it come to this? Since when exactly had she become a vampire-killer? The old Kathy, lying on Gelion's couch, could never have anticipated any of this.

'This can't all be down to the Puralex,' she muttered.

'Hmm? What's that?' Oliver said as he knelt, studying the book.

'I said this isn't story time,' Kathy said. 'Maybe we could put the book away for a bit?'

'I need to find the abjuration,' Oliver said. 'Ah here. *Remulat*.'

'What's remulat?' Kathy said.

'It's the power word I need to announce when I show this glyph,' Oliver replied, indicating one of the patterned discs.

'What happens then?'

'If I've pronounced it right, they get knocked backwards by an invisible force.'

'If you pronounce it wrong?'

'We get our throats torn out.'

'Okay,' Kathy said. 'Good to know where we stand.'

The light had grown dim, wall lights the only source. The heavenly light Kathy had bathed in earlier had gone now. She looked up to the glass-celled ceiling. Night had fallen.

'What are we waiting for?' she asked, anxious to get on with it.

'I'm just wondering which is the best way to go,' Oliver said. 'They'll be waiting for us. Somewhere dark probably. Some small room or corridor.'

'Why do you think that?' Kathy asked.

'Because they don't like open spaces. They feel vulnerable. They'd never attack us in this great—' but his sentence was cut short by the sound of shattering glass directly overhead.

'Don't look up,' Oliver shouted, but it was too late. Kathy looked up to see a black shape dropping through the air towards her. Then she felt a sting as something sliced into her temple, and Oliver was pulling her away and through the high entrance portal towards the locked front doors. She heard a crash behind her as the vampire hit the ground, then a howl that sent freezing tendrils up her spine.

'This way,' Oliver panted, leading her up a wide flight

of stairs, lined with mosaics. These were the south stairs Kathy had passed and ignored earlier. 'Run.'

She sprinted up the stairs, hoping she didn't have an asthma attack now. She could hear the vampire behind, scrabbling on the slick floor.

As they reached the mezzanine and turned for the next flight Oliver stopped and held up the cross, but the vampire was coming too fast and barrelled into him. The entwined bodies thumped against the wall, into a mosaic which shattered, scattering thousands of coloured tiles across the floor and down the staircase. The cross went skittering across the floor. Kathy went for it but Oliver yelled, 'Leave it. Go!' and she ran lightly up the next flight of stairs.

She turned again to see Oliver on his back with the vampire over him, snarling and ready to lunge. But Kathy's heart surged as she saw Oliver slipping out the glass vial of holy water from his pocket. As the vampire ducked towards his throat, Oliver smashed the bottle against its temple.

The scream echoed around the stone walls and the vampire staggered backwards, stumbling and clutching its smoking head. Oliver was already up and sprinting up the stairs. 'Go!' he yelled and Kathy didn't wait to be told twice.

They sprinted through a room full of Greek pottery, the only sound the slapping of their trainers against the floor and the piston-pounding of their breath. Then it was Etruscan, then Roman, a thousand years of history in a dozen sprinted steps.

Oliver slid to a stop and held up an arm, halting Kathy, who skidded and went over on to her bottom, painfully.

'Sorry,' Oliver said and drag-led her into a side room. 'I just remembered there's another one.'

'They must have split up,' Kathy said, breathing shallowly.

'Shh,' he said. 'Let's listen.' They held their breath, with difficulty, for a few seconds but heard nothing.

'So what was all that about vampires not liking open spaces?' Kathy asked.

'I guess he was really thirsty,' Oliver said, shrugging. 'I suspect there's more to it, though. That was just the opening gambit.'

'This isn't a game of chess,' Kathy said.

'Oh yes it is,' Oliver replied. 'Come on.'

They crept out into the large room again and crept along, slowly and quietly this time, watching every shadow. Kathy still held her cross and her warding glyph. Oliver had a glyph in each hand.

'Is he dead?' Kathy whispered. 'The one chasing us.'

'No,' Oliver said. 'He won't be winning any beauty contests, he's only got half a face, but that won't stop him for long.'

They went across a narrow corridor and into another dimly lit room on the other side, *Europe 19th Century*, Kathy read as she ran past. A long room with half a dozen display cases on either side of a central aisle. Each cabinet was full of exquisite porcelain and delicate jasperware. *Susan would have loved this room*, Kathy thought.

'If we go through that door,' Oliver said pointing to the far wall, 'we can get to the north stairs, which will leave us close to the Montague entrance. We can get out of the building there.'

'Great,' Kathy said, 'so what's stopping us?'

'The knowledge that vampires can read maps too,' Oliver said, peering into the murky room.

'So do we just stand here, waiting?' Kathy asked. She looked behind them and shivered, each shadow seeming to be about the right size and shape to hide a man. Or a vampire.

She turned around to see Oliver had stepped into the long room. She followed behind, keeping close.

A few paces in and they heard a sweeping sound behind. They spun to see the heavy door swinging closed. It slammed, a huge noise in the silent museum, vibrations causing a fragile piece of pottery to tinkle in the case next to them. There was no one behind the door.

'Clever,' Oliver said, then turned around slowly. Kathy turned too and her breath caught in her throat as she saw a dark figure at the far door. She rushed to the closed door they'd come through and rattled the handle. Locked.

'Go left,' Oliver called. Kathy darted to the left-hand corner of the room as Oliver went right. She stepped slowly up the aisle at the side, peering around each case as she went. She couldn't hear the vampire.

'If you see it, hold up your cross,' Oliver called. 'Call out for me and I'll come.'

She passed the third case, then the fourth. Where was it? She saw Oliver at the other side of the room looking back at her down the aisle. Then the vampire slipped into view between them. It looked directly at her and snarled.

'Dive!' Oliver yelled, then he called something else and she saw something hit the vampire from behind, hurling it forwards, towards her. She rolled out of the way just in time as the creature crashed into the wall. Kathy fumbled with the cross and held it up as the vampire regained its footing.

'Back away,' Oliver called. Kathy did so, rounding the corner and backing up between two glass cases as the limping vampire followed, spitting and wincing at the sight of the cross, but coming after her nonetheless. Then suddenly the vampire hung back and seized hold of the case to her right. With a heave it toppled the whole thing towards her.

Kathy screamed and ducked as the glass panel shattered and a hundred tea-set pieces tumbled and smashed around her. She felt the pinpricks of the porcelain shards piercing the skin of her bruised arms. She held her breath so as not to ingest the dust. Then she felt something grab her and again she was hoisted off her feet and flying, smash, into a second case. A burning sensation as something sharp slashed across her back and she was huddled on the hard stone floor. She looked up to see the vampire walking slowly towards her, a twisted leg trailing behind. She couldn't tear her gaze from its vicious, hate-filled face, lips curled back.

'Kathy!' Oliver called. She looked over and he threw something to her. She caught it, fumbled, but then grabbed it again at the second attempt. It was the glyph.

The vampire realized the danger and hurried forward, but Kathy raised the glyph and spoke the word: 'Remulat!'

As she said it, she felt the power rush through her, the feeling that she'd felt in her dreams, when she'd thought Amber's spirit was inside her. It was a rush, drawing up through the floor into her feet, electrifying her legs, her belly, her heart, and finally the arm she held out towards the vampire. She felt and saw the force pound out of the glyph, catching the vampire full-square and hurling it backwards. The strength of the force seemed immensely greater than before, when Oliver had held the glyph. The vampire squealed like a child as it was hurled backwards, ploughing through three more cases before dropping out of view at the base of the last. Kathy saw a jagged shard of glass rammed into its back as it slid down.

Kathy slumped to the ground. Spent.

Oliver rushed to her.

'Are you okay?' he asked, concerned.

'I'm fine.' She nodded and got to her feet, painfully. Her cross was gone, but she still clutched the glyph. She gave it back to Oliver.

'I think you should keep it,' he said. 'You have real power, Kathy. Just like I told you.' His face seemed lit from within. He reached out a tender hand and brushed a strand of Kathy's hair away from her temple, inspecting a cut.

'I can't,' she said, and pushed the glyph on him, insistently. 'I have no strength left.'

Kathy was, in truth, a little frightened by the power. Part of her wanted to do it again, to feel that rush. But she sensed danger there too. She wasn't at all sure she could handle this.

Oliver nodded uncertainly and took the glyph back. He reached into his pouch and handed her a stake.

'If all else fails . . .' he said. Kathy tried to grin, but her heart was pounding too fast. The vestiges of the power rush still tingled within her and she felt shaky and weak. She nodded and they turned to go.

Creeping down the central aisle, crunching over the shattered treasures of nineteenth-century Europe, they peered about for their attacker, but it had crept away, perhaps to lick its own wounds. They reached the far door, open. Darkness beyond. Oliver turned and backed his way through while Kathy watched forwards. There was still the second vampire to deal with.

'Priceless,' Oliver tutted.

'Hmm? What's that?'

'The porcelain,' Oliver said. 'Those items we've just destroyed are worth more than some small European countries.'

'I won't say anything if you don't,' Kathy said.

They hurried through the Saxon room and through a door into a stairwell.

'Two flights down,' Oliver said at the top, then something smashed into him from behind and he was gone, tumbling down the marble staircase. A black shape flew out over the bannister, performed a somersault and landed neatly on the mezzanine. Then it leaped on to Oliver as he came to a rest at the bottom of the steps.

Kathy sprinted down to help. As she reached the bottom, the vampire looked up at her over the prone body of the academic. She could see the shard of glass still sticking out of its back.

'You bastard!' Kathy screamed as she ran, clutching the stake. The vampire stood and braced itself to meet her charge. Kathy didn't stop; she held the stake out before her and crashed into the vampire, knocking it over. They both slid across the slick floor, tangled limbs entwined. Kathy could smell the foetid stink of the creature's breath as it screeched in fury. It tried to grip her to stop her from raising herself up but one of its arms didn't seem to have any strength, perhaps the glass shard had severed something important.

Kathy pushed herself up and with quick hands rammed the stake into the vampire's chest. Its eyes opened wide, as if astonished that Kathy could have done such a thing. She rolled off the vampire and watched as it tried to pull the stake free, stamping its feet ineffectually and arching its back. She didn't stop to watch it die but instead turned to Oliver, whom she was relieved to see was moving. He groaned, hauled himself into a sitting position and peered over at the vampire in surprise.

'Like I said, this isn't a game,' Kathy said. 'And sometimes a full-frontal assault is *exactly* what's required.'

'Well done,' he said. He groaned again as she helped him to his feet. 'But there's still another one, remember?'

'So give me another stake,' Kathy said.

Oliver grinned and handed her another without protest.

They limped down the steps. They passed a doorway to an exhibition of Chinese jade. 'Can we take a short cut through there?' Kathy asked, peering at the map.

'No way,' he said, shaking his head. 'That jade is seven thousand years old and on loan from the Museum of Beijing.'

They carried on down the stairs and came out into an open-plan area. A couple of low-energy emergency lights suffused the chamber with an amber glow.

'Threatened Societies exhibition,' Oliver whispered.

Kathy saw cases filled with shields, carvings and implements from around the world. An Australian Aboriginal spear, an Amazonian Indian coracle, an Native American totem pole towered over them. Kathy looked up at dark, twisted shapes, carved from hardwood, disappearing into the shadowed ceiling.

As she turned, Kathy started in fright as she saw a figure standing against the far wall. But then she realized it was a model of a Maori warrior, spear held towards them, tongue out and skin lashed with cruel tattoos.

'The exit's through there,' Oliver said, more loudly, pointing to a doorway shrouded in darkness.

'Where's the other vampire, though?' Kathy said. She peered at him in the gloom, wondering why he'd abandoned the whisper.

'He'll be guarding the door, I suspect,' he said. And then Oliver winked at her. 'Let's go.'

Wondering why he was acting so oddly, Kathy turned towards the door, but then Oliver held out an arm and gently pressed her against the wall. Then he spun and ran to the totem pole, which he shoved hard. The pole rocked back, hit the wall and came back the other way, out into the centre of the room. Kathy stared in astonishment as she saw the wooden figure at the top of the pole seem to break and fall separately, then she realized it wasn't part of the pole. It was the vampire.

It hissed as it tumbled, seeming to take an age to reach the floor.

In fact the vampire never did hit the floor. Oliver had stepped back to give himself room and held out the glyph.

'*Remulat!*' he cried as the vampire sailed through the air. With a whump the forcefield hit the creature and fired it straight and true across the chamber, smashing into the Maori. Oliver followed it quickly, stake in hand. He didn't need it. As Kathy came cautiously forward, she saw the vampire thrashing, trying to free itself from the blood-smeared wooden spear which emerged from its ribcage.

'Bloody good shot,' Oliver said, admiring his handiwork. 'Played a bit of cricket at school in my days. Seems I haven't lost the timing.'

'Cricket?' Kathy said. 'That's a little like baseball, isn't it?'

Oliver shot her a dark look, then turned his attention back to the vampire. Half of its face was burned away from the holy water.

'Smarter than me?' Oliver said as the vampire hissed at the darkness encircling it, recognizing the sight of its own impending death. 'I doubt that. I got a First at Magdalene College, Oxford, my dear boy.'

They left through the Montague entrance. The air felt hot and close, like a thunderstorm might be approaching. Even so, Kathy breathed deeply, overjoyed just to smell fresh air again. Oliver rushed them over to his car as fast as he could with their various injuries. Kathy's back burned where a glass shard had slashed her and she limped, her left knee and calf soaked with blood.

Getting into a car seat felt so normal, so safe, after the fear and tension. Kathy almost sobbed with gratitude.

'Where are we going?' Kathy asked.

'I'm taking you home,' Oliver said.

He drove off quickly but soon got snarled in traffic. London's streets were busy. Oliver seemed nervous as he drove. He rubbed the side of his neck and looked up at the sky, dull orange from the reflected street lights.

'There's a storm coming,' he said.

'Are you okay?' Kathy asked as they waited at a red light.

He paused for a while before answering. A boisterous group of teenagers crossed the road before them, one shouted something at them then stopped to swig from a bottle.

'I've been bitten, I'm afraid,' he said.

'What? When?'

'On the staircase. Just before you saved me with your mad charge.'

'Oh God,' Kathy said. 'I'm sorry, I wasn't quick enough.'

Oliver looked over at her. The light had turned green and someone behind hit their horn. He smiled. 'You were wonderful, you did your family proud.'

'Come on, we need to get back to my aunt's house,' Kathy said. 'She has medicine that can save you.'

Oliver took off but he was shaking his head. 'I'm afraid not, Kathy. I'm not like you. I'm all human. Just an ordinary chap.'

'You're not ordinary.'

'Nonetheless, my body can't fight this infection,' he said. 'I am going to become a vampire myself.'

'But we can't just give up,' Kathy said. 'We could—'

'Look,' Oliver replied, cutting her off. 'There's something else I need to tell you.'

'What?' Kathy said, nearly in tears.

'You need to tell your aunt and her friend Harry. It's very important.'

'Okay, go on,' Kathy said, wiping her eyes.

'There's a mistranslation in Amber's notes. I think it's critical. There's another part of the prophecy. It reads *The Third Siege Shall Claim Him For Ever*. Harry thinks this means that the third time the vampire is trapped will be the final time.'

'Okay,' Kathy said.

'So Harry thinks the first siege was Jerusalem, when the vampire was trapped by the Romans. The second siege was in Carpathia in the twelfth century, when Vlad the Impaler besieged the Templar castle he hid in. And the third siege is now, in the Highgate Cemetery. In the Eighties Harry and others in the Highgate Society incorporated the entrapment glyph into their insignia, you'd call it a logo, and they put up plates all around the cemetery, trapping the vampire within.'

'But wasn't there an attack in 'ninety-three? A priest in the church?'

'Exactly. When the vampire struck again in 1993, Viduc was astonished. It took months of research before Draco, I mean, your father, discovered the truth, that the vampire's movements were only restricted, he was not trapped. It became clear he was travelling through the catacombs, crossing under Swain's Lane between the East and West cemeteries. Harry decided that although the vampire was restricted to the cemetery, it didn't count as a prison because he was free to roam the catacombs. So the Society surveyed the catacombs and set *another* ring of glyphs.'

'So that's why he hasn't been feeding since then?'

'That's what Harry thinks,' Oliver said, looking at her with large, earnest eyes. 'But he's wrong. Now I've seen the original document. The Ancient Sumerian word for "siege" is the same as for "prison", it translates better as "entrapment". And it doesn't suggest that the third time the vampire is trapped will be the final one. What it actually means is that the vampire must be trapped within *three* prisons. A prison, within a prison, within a prison.'

'So he's not trapped?'

'It doesn't seem so. The glyphs all around the perimeter of the cemetery, that's prison one.' He stopped to cough briefly, before drawing a deep breath and carrying on. Kathy saw a trickle of sweat run down his temple. 'The second ring of glyphs, in the catacombs, that's prison two.'

'And the third?'

'Well, that's where you come in, I guess,' Oliver said. He grinned, then coughed again. Kathy grimaced to see him rubbing the side of his neck vigorously. 'It itches,' he muttered, absently driving through a red light.

'Dickhead!' a pedestrian yelled as they swept by.

'What can I do?' Kathy asked, when he'd stopped rubbing for a moment.

He sighed. 'You'll have to convince them I'm right and Harry's wrong. You'll have to find the vampire and trap him for good.'

Oliver stopped speaking for a moment. The car crawled to a halt and he bowed his head slightly. Kathy reached out a hand, but he pulled away. 'I'm fine,' he said, and sped up again. Oliver was breathing more and more heavily. Kathy wanted to stop him, to tell him to rest, but she could see this was important, she needed to understand this and Oliver had little time left. He wound down the window and took a great lungful of the damp air. She could smell the sharp scent of the approaching storm. A fat droplet of rain splattered on the windscreen.

'How can we trap him though?' Kathy asked. 'A third ring?'

Oliver shrugged before replying, his voice slurred slightly. 'I guess so. I wonder though if there isn't a more permanent prison that can be constructed. Something more reliable.'

'The tour guide at the West Cemetery told me vandals keep trying to pinch the glyph-plates,' Kathy said.

'Probably Bishop's men, human slaves,' Oliver said. 'Actual vampires wouldn't be able to get close to those glyphs. Viduc keeps a close eye on things though, if plates get moved, they get replaced pretty quick.'

Kathy frowned. 'Honestly though, does it matter? He hasn't killed since 1993.'

Oliver frowned – he seemed a little better now. 'Maybe. Though of course it is possible he killed without the victims being found, he has become more careful in the last few decades. We just don't know. What if Bishop gets to him first?'

'So the race is on, we must find the tomb of Aliza before

Bishop.' Kathy realized her true quest.

The car crept up Highgate Road, red brake lights ahead of them. Kathy was thinking of the apparition she saw in the cemetery that day Becky let her in. Becky had suggested it was just the shade of the vampire, but what if it were the real thing? What if Bishop discovered him and restored him to power, here in London?

'Now you know which crypt he's hiding in we can put glyphs on that,' Kathy said.

Oliver nodded. His breath was ragged now and he rubbed the side of his neck feverishly. He noticed Kathy watching and looked over at her, grinning ruefully.

'It burns,' he said. 'It itches, and it burns. Quite interesting, from a research point of view.'

Kathy fought back the tears. More rain thudded on the windscreen.

'I'd write a paper, but no one would publish it,' Oliver said. 'Hey, maybe I'll turn up at work tomorrow as a vampire, that'll make 'em sit up and take notice.'

Kathy smiled weakly.

'Anyway,' he said as the car moved off again, 'you're right. You need to find his crypt. Find him. Harry will know what to do once you've got that far.'

'Surely we can just stake him?' she said.

'I told you, you can't kill the Highgate Vampire. He can

199

move from body to body. He's like the king on the chess set. You can't kill him, you have to trap him to win.'

'So where is he?' Kathy asked.

Oliver looked over. 'His resting place is in the Havering family crypt in the West Cemetery,' he said. 'You must remember that.'

'Havering . . . West,' Kathy said.

He nodded, then coughed. 'It's happening,' he said. 'We haven't much time.'

They'd reached Swain's Lane by now and Oliver pulled over, his shaking limbs making driving difficult.

Oliver looked over at Kathy and she saw his eyes had a glazed look, a clouding of gold. Oliver reached into the back seat and grabbed a stake. He handed it to Kathy, wordlessly.

'Really?' she asked, though she'd known all along what she would have to do.

'Do it now,' Oliver said. He tore open his shirt, revealing the muscled torso.

'Can't I wait?' she asked, the tears now flowing. 'Until you've gone, properly?'

Oliver coughed again; she saw fear in his eyes, but determination too. He shook his head and seized her hand, positioning the tip of the stake over his heart.

'I can't,' Kathy said. Thunder cracked outside; a second

later rain began drumming on the roof of the car, like signals of war.

But then Oliver snarled and the shock of it drove her hand forward. Oliver went rigid, then slumped against her; she held him as he quivered with the death throes. A passer-by might have taken them for a loving couple, entwined as they were. Kathy could feel his blood pumping out over her hands. 'Find Amber . . . Stop Bishop,' Oliver whispered as he went.

CHAPTER TWELVE

Amber came to her that night. Not as a small girl, but as a grown woman. The woman Kathy had seen on the Church website. She was transfixing, a more beautiful version of Kathy. She sat on the edge of Kathy's bed and smiled, her face alight, red hair and lips.

'I'm going to come and find you,' Kathy whispered.

'Bring the book,' Amber said.

Kathy nodded.

Amber was starting to fade away into the darkness of the bedroom.

'Wait. Tell me, where can I find you?' Kathy asked.

'I'm underground,' Amber said, her voice growing faint.

'Where underground?'

But her sister was gone and was immediately replaced by the black-suited man. Kathy recognized him now.

Bishop grinned his malicious grin at her and twirled his cane. They were in the darkened room again, but Kathy felt dead and cold.

'Lost someone?' Bishop asked, then cackled madly.

Kathy fought her way out of the dream and managed to wake herself. She lay in bed for a while, her mind dulled by sleep. There was something she needed to remember.

It took some time, but then it started to come back, in segments. She'd visited the museum. Vampires had attacked her, the journey back seemed a bit blurry. Had she taken a cab? It was a mess of hazy recollection; she tried to approach the memory from different angles but found it impenetrable, like when she'd tried to remember some of her own dreams. She dimly remembered staggering up to the house, drenched in the rain and her aunt's white face greeting her. Harry had been there, his strong arms lifting her and taking her into the sitting room. Then a soft towel and a hot drink. Harry had laid something on her head and the next thing she knew she was waking to the vision of Amber.

As she rose, she felt a faint ache in her back and a stiff knee. Looking in the mirror she could see a thin cut running right across her back. Her knee was bruised, patched up, bandaged; she squeezed it lightly and winced with the pain. How had she injured herself? She sat on the edge of the bed for a while, searching her memory in vain. Something was missing.

Coming downstairs, she came across her aunt on the telephone in the hallway. Elizabeth had her back to Kathy and didn't hear her approach on the carpeted stairs.

'Well I can pay if the ticket's not transferable. That's fine.'

There was a pause as Elizabeth listened. Then she spoke again.

'Yes, she's asleep at the moment, I'll tell her when she wakes. Okay, thanks, Susan. Good to speak with you, all right. Goodbye – and I hope he picks up soon.'

Kathy's heart was in her mouth as Elizabeth turned around. Her aunt started at the sight of her, then stood back, watching her niece with a calculating look.

'That was Mom?'

Elizabeth nodded. 'Your father is very poorly.'

'He's worse?'

Elizabeth didn't reply to this. 'Susan thinks you should go home. I agree.'

'Is he worse?' Kathy repeated.

'He's very unwell,' Elizabeth said sharply. 'Look, Kathy, I've loved having you, but maybe this isn't the best time for you to be here.'

'I can't leave now,' Kathy said. She sat on the stairs in the nightdress she'd borrowed. 'I haven't found Amber yet.'

'You've found plenty,' Elizabeth said. 'Leave this to me and Harry. It's too dangerous here for you.'

'Is that why you want me to go?' Kathy asked. 'To protect me?'

Elizabeth sighed. She came over to sit beside Kathy. A grandfather clock tocked loudly somewhere in the hall. No ticks, just tocks.

'I'm sorry I wasn't totally honest with you,' Elizabeth said. 'If I'd explained the dangers properly you might never have gone to see . . . the museum.'

As Elizabeth mentioned the museum, Kathy again tried to prod at the black hole in her memory. Someone else had been there. Someone important. But it wouldn't come.

'Your father fought the vampires, did you know?'

Kathy nodded. 'That's how he was killed.'

'You have his blood. You . . . we are descended from a race of people related to the vampires. The ancient enemies of the vampires. Our races have been fighting each other since the dawn of time. That's why we think Bishop took Amber. She's an important figure.'

'She's my sister,' Kathy said, simply.

'Anyway, I'm going to see about transferring your ticket so you can fly back tonight,' Elizabeth said. 'We need to get you home, where you belong.'

'Tomorrow,' Kathy said.

'What's that?'

'Can I fly home tomorrow instead?' Kathy said. 'It's Friday and I've arranged to meet Becky – I like her, she's the first real friend I have made in years.'

Elizabeth frowned. 'I'm not sure you should be leaving the house.'

'Oh please, Aunt Elizabeth. I won't be going far.'

Her aunt regarded her for a moment then relented, smiling. 'Okay, tomorrow. You can go out for a couple of hours but I want you home before dark. We can have a last supper together.'

Kathy thought of the last supper of Christ, of Aliza, of the history.

'Sounds great,' she said, already calculating.

Kathy walked up Swain's Lane, texting as she went. Though late in the day, the sun was still warm and the events of the previous evening seemed distant and more obscured by the minute.

FANCY A DRINK AT THE FLASK? Kathy texted. BRING YOUR VAMPIRE LOG BOOK, I HAVE A GOOD STORY TO TELL.

She looked up to see a man in a suit veering aside to avoid her. She laughed and apologized, feeling cheerful again. The cemetery looked bright and as welcoming as a bone yard could, foxglove and hollyhocks lining the path visible through the fence. Kathy's phone buzzed in her hand.

I'LL BE THERE IN TEN MINUTES. MINE'S A DRY WHITE WINE.

Kathy smiled. She wished she could stay in London longer, just a little longer. It scared her, the thought of going back to New York, to no friends, back to that hospital, with its buzzing strip lights and dark scent of impending death. Her cheeriness faded, to be replaced by mingled dread at the thought of return, and a sickening guilt that she wasn't yearning to see Dad one more time. What kind of monster was she?

Kathy slid through the throng of drinkers outside the pub, enjoying the Friday evening. She entered the pub, which was largely empty inside and ordered two glasses of wine at the bar. Modern folk music played quietly from discreet speakers.

'What do you think of Highgate then?' the landlady asked as she poured the Chablis, a middle-aged woman, who had the air of someone who'd always looked like this, someone born to be a landlady, in this very pub and who would seem out of place anywhere else.

Kathy looked at her, considering the question carefully, wanting to give the right answer. 'It feels like home,' she said. 'It really does feel like home.'

Becky was one minute early and arrived at the table looking flushed and excited. The girls hugged and Becky sat down and drank half her glass at once. She sighed happily and put the drink down.

'What a week!'

'Really? What's been going on in the exciting world of cemetery tours?' Kathy asked, grinning.

'Well, apart from your little visit,' Becky said, 'we had vandals on Wednesday night trying to take the Highgate Society plates off the fences, a fight broke out on this morning's tour and yesterday we found five dead foxes, their throats all ripped out.'

Kathy grimaced. 'What could have done that?' But it wasn't the foxes Kathy was thinking about. A half-memory tickled the back of her mind. Hadn't the tour guide at the West Cemetery mentioned something about people trying to steal the Highgate Society plates? She felt as if she should know why, but couldn't quite put her finger on the memory.

Becky raised her eyebrows. 'My boss says dogs, but personally, I think Satanists.'

'Not vampires then?' Kathy asked.

208

'Who can say?' Becky replied mysteriously, opening her eyes wide. She grinned and took another sip, smaller this time. 'So what's your story?' she said.

Kathy told her about the visit to the museum, how she'd looked around, then some men attacked her and she realized they were vampires. As she told the story, it seemed unreal. Like a film, and not a very good film either. She trailed off mid-sentence, frowning. Why had she been so sure this was a good story?

Becky stared at her, bemused. 'Didn't anybody else see?'

'No,' Kathy said. 'It was after hours, I was the only one there.'

'Um, why were you there after hours?'

Kathy looked back at her friend, her mind a blank.

'I . . . I don't know. I think I had an appointment . . .'

'Who with?'

Kathy tried to dig deeper into her memory, but came up against the black hole she'd discovered last night when she'd awoken. Suddenly, she felt the first, faint stirrings of a panic attack, not close, just there, but coming. Grey curtains at the perimeter of her vision, threatening to close. She slid a hand down on to her knee and squeezed. Pain. The pain was there. But had she imagined it?

'Kathy, are you okay?'

'I'm not sure,' Kathy replied. 'Look forget that, forget that.' She shook her head, trying to clear it of the confusion.

'Becky,' she said, trying again, 'remember we said we'd go to the Church tonight? You're still coming, right? There's someone there I want to meet.'

Becky looked doubtful. 'What's going on, Kathy? First you tell me this half-baked story about vampires in the British Museum, then you go all weird and want to go clubbing. Who do you want to meet there?'

'My sister,' Kathy said. 'I think my sister is there and I think she might be in trouble. I don't want to go alone.'

'Your sister?'

'It's a long story,' Kathy said. She looked at her friend, earnestly. 'Look I'm sorry, I'm not sure exactly what's going on. I know I'm being weird, but I think I'm on the verge of finding out something really important. I think there are people who want me to stay away. You're the only one I know I can trust – I'm asking you to come with me.'

Becky looked doubtful for a moment, but then her face softened.

'Okay, you mental American,' she said, grinning. 'But no more making up stories about vampires, okay?'

'Okay,' Kathy said, forcing a smile that didn't feel right.

The girls stayed for another drink, chatting about anything other than vampires. Becky told Kathy about her boyfriend, Jack, who sounded lovely. Kathy found herself wishing she lived here, working in the cemetery, dating Jack, or perhaps his brother. *Gotta stop trying to live vicariously*, she told herself. *One of these days you're going to have to find your own way, Kathy Bilic.*

The girls parted around seven-thirty p.m. with a hug and a promise to meet at the Church just after midnight, either in the queue or inside.

When she got home, her aunt was putting the finishing touches to a meal of rabbit casserole. The smell was delicious and Kathy realized she'd hardly eaten anything for the last two days. Two glasses of wine on an empty stomach had left her feeling light-headed.

'Sit, sit,' Elizabeth said, ushering Kathy to the dining room, where the table had been set for two.

'Harry not joining us?' Kathy asked.

'No, just us girls tonight,' her aunt said, bringing the food through.

Kathy declined more wine, feeling she'd reached her limit, but Elizabeth poured herself a full glass. They ate in silence for a few minutes, then Elizabeth spoke.

'I'm sorry you're leaving, Kathy,' she said. 'I've loved having you here. And if circumstances were different . . .

Well, you can visit again of course, after you've finished at college. Oh my dear, you mustn't look so sad.'

Kathy realized she was crying.

'Aunt Elizabeth,' she said, wiping a tear away. 'I came here for a reason. I came to find Amber. I haven't been able to do that.'

'Oh my darling . . .'

'I left Dad, when he was ill, Mom didn't understand, I spent all my money. And all for nothing.'

'It hasn't all been for nothing,' Elizabeth said. 'You and I have met, you've made friends, you've seen London. And I'm sure Amber will turn up eventually . . .'

'Are you?' Kathy said, a little sharply. 'Are you really sure? It seems no one really is taking this seriously. Everyone just thinks she'll turn up.' Kathy glared at her aunt, suddenly full of righteousness. 'Well, I'm *not* sure,' she finished.

Elizabeth stood and came around to Kathy's seat. She knelt down and took Kathy's hand. 'My dear,' she said, 'I promise you, we'll do everything we can to find your sister.'

Kathy nodded, and hugged her aunt. The women held each other tightly for a long time.

'Now,' Elizabeth said, releasing her niece, 'how about some chocolate pudding?'

Kathy smiled and nodded again, feeling a little embarrassed at her outburst.

They had coffee in the sitting room, watching the dusk creep over the skyline. Then Elizabeth turned on the television and they watched the news and a film. As Elizabeth's eyelids began to droop, Kathy padded off upstairs to prepare for the visit down the road to the Church. She texted Antwain to let him know she was coming and would see him inside. She sent a photo too, tousling her hair and pouting a little, trying to sex herself up. If he didn't like what he saw she'd just have to find another employee to pump for information.

Taking just her phone and jamming some money in her jeans pocket, Kathy sneaked down the stairs. She peeped around the door to the sitting room. Elizabeth snored lightly in her armchair; *The Day After Tomorrow* played quietly on the old television. Kathy opened the door carefully, slowly, and closed it gently behind her with a soft click. The night was mild and she could smell the cut grass and cow parsley from the cemetery across the road, floating across on a slight breeze. The background hum of the city soothed her, the bus roars from the Highgate Road mellow with distance.

She turned right and headed down the hill, towards

Swaingate. After a hundred yards she had to cross the road as the path was blocked by white-and-blue police tape, surrounding a parked car. She stopped to look at it for a while, almost recognizing the vehicle. A yellow sign had been erected.

> *Police are calling for witnesses to a stabbing in this location on the evening of 18th July 2012. Please call 0117 865765 if you have any information which may assist the police with their enquiries.*

She could see the hulking church as she approached, dark and shrouded by trees and the night's gloom. The church was big rather than beautiful. Fat, ancient and bloated, as though it had consumed a hundred generations of Highgate residents and held them still.

Reaching the door she found a line of dark city denizens who waited to get in, mostly teenagers, dressed extravagantly, perfectly, trying to look frosty but failing to suppress their nervous energy. This street, so peaceful during the day, had become a different world at the witching hour. Above the door a fanged viper's head looked down on a sign: *The Church*. Two giant bouncers flanked the door, sandwiching a silver-haired woman in a long gown, dressed to kill and appraising the would-be club goers. Like the Ancient Mariner, she stopped one in three. The rejects were quietly but firmly moved on by one or other of the bouncers.

Kathy took her place patiently at the back of the queue, looking around for Becky. She waited with her hands in her pockets. She now felt out of place, in her college T-shirt and jeans; the only thing right about her look was her long dark hair. But she couldn't go back to the house to change. She might wake Elizabeth and she didn't really have anything else anyway. She had to get in. She was sure she'd find Amber here, or at least a clue as to her whereabouts.

The queue moved slowly, drawing her into the viper's mouth. Eventually she was next in line. The silver-haired woman turned out to be a man in drag. He, she, looked her up and down with disdain. 'You need to try harder than that, love,' he said in an regional accent Kathy didn't recognize.

'I'm new in town,' Kathy protested.

'No shit. Well a nice girl like you would fit in better up at the Flask, a nice pint would be more your scene, love.'

Kathy heard titters from a couple of girls behind her. She realized the theatrical tone of the tranny's bitchy slants were all part of the club's show. This wasn't about the look so much as the attitude.

Come on, Amber, she thought, *I need your influence now. I need your power within me.*

'*Nice?*' Kathy said. 'I'll give you *nice*.' Kathy pulled off her T-shirt there and then in the street and took out the keys from her pocket. Standing in her black bra, within seconds she'd torn the T-shirt in half and removed its sleeves. She then took one of the sleeves and spun it into a bandanna around her head. Her dark hair flowed out of the top like a raining black fountain. Her tight midriff was now on show. She spun round to the tittering girls in the queue behind, plastered in oh-too-much dark Gothic make-up.

'Have you got any of that black lipstick I can borrow?' Kathy stuck her hand out sharply to one of the Goth girls, not really giving her a choice. 'Please?' The Goth chick quickly passed her a black lipstick from her leather jacket pocket. Kathy used the panel glass of her phone as a mirror as she applied the black lipstick, taking her time, not letting herself be rushed.

No one seemed to object to the length of the performance. As Kathy had realized, this was all part of the show now too.

'Now, how's that? Nasty enough for you?' Kathy turned, put her hand confidently on her hip and presented her new self to the door diva.

'My dear, it's a big yes from me,' the drag queen replied. Kathy didn't need a second invitation. As she entered the viper's mouth she could hear the crowds clapping behind her; one of the bouncers winked as she passed. She was in. She breathed a sigh of relief and wasn't surprised to find that as soon as she was inside the plush foyer, she felt weakened, as if a spirit had left her.

Thanks, Amber, she thought.

Kathy passed through velvet curtains into the main body of the church. This area had been converted into the coat-check area and the bathrooms. A large section of floor had been removed and a massive staircase led down into the crypt below. The staircase was lined with swaying freaks who watched her as she walked down. She felt violated by the looks, but at the same time part of her felt aroused by the outright lechery, as though here, suddenly it was acceptable and expected. She'd stepped over a threshold when she pushed aside the velvet curtain. Thrusting rock music pounded up from beneath, as though hell's residents had bought themselves some decks.

The noise increased as she reached the lower-ground floor. The central dance floor was dark and it smelled of patchouli oil, sweat, and stale beer: rock night. The crowds moved aside as Kathy made her way towards the bar. Behind the bar a short woman who had a face like the viper above the door stood on high platform boots. Even with her lifted boots she was no more than four feet tall and tattooed from the head down. As she waited for the dwarf to come over, Becky arrived, with a tall guy in tow, good-looking and dressed all in black. Kathy and Becky hugged, each saying something that the other couldn't hear through the music. It didn't matter.

'This is Jack,' Becky screamed into Kathy's ear. Kathy nodded and waved, grinning madly.

'That was some fast thinking out there,' Jack shouted.

'You saw that?' she said, embarrassed.

They nodded and Becky burst out laughing.

Jack and Becky had obviously anticipated the strict dress code and he wore nothing under his black leather jacket. Kathy felt herself looking a little too long at the olive-toned skin of his naked chest. Becky wore a lacy black top and a tiny leather skirt that left little to the imagination. She also had intense mascara on and looked eerily beautiful.

'Yeah, I'm not quite sure what came over me,' Kathy said, 'but it seemed to work.' She rolled her eyes flirtatiously, then looked up and tossed her hair from side to side. The girls laughed again as Jack leaned over the bar waving a fifty-pound note.

'Wow, he's hot,' Becky said, looking at someone over Kathy's shoulder. Kathy spun and saw Antwain dancing with a petite brunette. As she watched, he leaned her backwards and ran his hand up her body, seizing her throat and making as if to kiss her before setting her back on her feet gracefully and moving away towards the bar. The brunette stopped dancing to watch him go, her face a mix of lust and disappointment.

'He's coming this way,' Becky hissed in Kathy's ear, tickling her.

'Thanks, I can see that,' Kathy said.

Antwain walked right up to them, his tight T-shirt showing off his muscled torso. He was even more divine in person. Kathy felt her knees wobble a bit. The volume of the music dropped a little.

'Kathy,' he said. 'You are Kathy?'

Kathy nodded.

'Of course you are,' he said. 'And I, my Lady, am Antwain. At your service . . .' He took a graceful bow as if he was performing in a Shakespearian play. The girls laughed as the sour-faced dwarf behind the bar came over and gave Jack their order.

With drinks in hand, Antwain led the way as the group headed deeper into the club, carried on the waves of electronic music and the scent of perfumed bodies.

Heading down a further, shallow flight of stairs they pushed through heavy drapes separating the first dance floor from the next. They came out to a large cavernous room that already heaved with bodies as they moved, this time entranced by the swirling electronica, heavy four-on-the-floor beats thudding up through the sprung floor. Looking down on the crowd, a DJ with an illuminated head-dress bobbed as he slid one track into the next. Becky and Jack joined the dancing throng, Antwain took up a pose by a thick black pillar that supported the vaulted roof. Kathy wondered what to do, where to put herself; she suddenly felt out of her depth. *Don't fail me now*, she thought to herself – though whether she was addressing her sister or her own, faltering confidence, she couldn't be sure. Kathy took a sip of her drink and looked up to see the painted curtain behind the stage. The head of Bishop's silver-handled cane, the head of an eagle on a deep red canvas.

'Are you okay?' Antwain had stepped up behind her, his lips close to Kathy's left ear to overcome the din of the club. He hardly seemed to be raising his voice.

'I'm not here for dancing or posing,' Kathy said, stiffly, but Antwain had already taken her hand and spun her around on the dance floor. He pulled her back in, close to his chest. She flushed as she fell into his arms.

'I bet I can make you dance,' he said, looking deep into her eyes. For a moment Kathy heard nothing. No sense of what was going on around her. She was swallowed up by the other-worldly beauty of him and his intense, imminent maleness. His sharp cheekbones were cliffs and she wanted to jump off, to swim into the dark pools of his eyes.

'Dance.' It was a command that she could do nothing to resist. Her body became possessed by the rhythm of the music. Her senses returned in a rush, swamping her. The hairs on the back of her neck now stood on end, the music intensified in her ears, and the swooping lighting sent her mind into a trance. Becky and Jack came closer and the three of them danced together, touching each other, shifting from one to the other while Antwain, who had retreated from the floor, watched.

Kathy lost herself. She forgot about Amber, her father, the vampire, everything except the music and the movement. A weight had lifted from her slim shoulders; suddenly nothing mattered. She was where she needed to be, amongst friends, like-minded people.

She brushed against Jack and he seized and spun her towards Becky who laid her long arms over Kathy's shoulders and danced languorously against her friend, the music syncing into the movements. Jack moved up from behind and Kathy felt his hands on her hips and his breath in her ear. She closed her eyes, soaking up the pleasure, the ecstasy.

Kathy looked over to where Antwain stood with his back to the pillar. As Jack and Becky moved up and down her body she suddenly froze. Antwain had gone. In his place, watching her with a thin smile was Bishop, his dark hair wild and flowing over the shoulders of the dark suit. His long cuffs glittered with diamond links.

I like what I see. The man's words were unspoken but they rang out loud in her head. She spun back to the others as they danced, apparently oblivious to the man. She looked for Antwain, scanning the room of heaving bodies. As the man stepped forward towards her she turned and ran, putting the dancing crowd between her and him.

'Hey, where you going?' Kathy felt a hand grab her wrist and shrieked. When she turned, Antwain was standing there holding her.

'That man over there . . .' They both turned and looked back to the pillar. Bishop had gone.

'I'm sorry, I shouldn't have glamoured you like that.'

'Glamoured? What did you do to me? Did you spike my drink?'

'No, no, not at all. Come on, let's get some air.'

Becky winked as Antwain led her off across the dance

floor. Antwain walked through the crowd to a small doorway; a narrow, spiral staircase lay beyond. Antwain darted up, flight after flight, apparently tireless. Kathy followed behind, more slowly, panting a little with the effort.

Passing and ignoring a couple of doors on the way, Antwain took them to the top, out on to a roof terrace overlooking the cemetery. The night was a velvet blanket, hovering over a million lights of London, but the cemetery before them was a lightless hole. The terrace itself was lit by burning torches, under them stood groups of people smoking and chatting. Kathy brushed past a tall woman with pink hair talking to a smirking man dressed like a vampire, with a cape, painted white face and fitted fangs. The woman gave Kathy a look of disdain. Her confidence flip-flopped again; suddenly she felt as though she didn't belong here.

'Ignore them,' Antwain said. 'Wannabes, that's all.' Antwain pushed his way through to stand under one of the spitting torches. He reached into his pocket and lit a Lucky Strike cigarette. As the flame illuminated his face and the ringlets of his dark hair, Kathy watched as people in the crowd seemed to recognize him. As they did they moved away to give him space. Antwain looked up and others looked away.

'Do you know these people?' Kathy asked. A subtle breeze blew a strand of hair across her face and she left it there, wanting it to cover her.

'No. But most of them know me.'

Kathy knew she should be turned off by Antwain's swagger. He was the sort of boy who'd normally blank her, or bully her. But something about him had her hanging. Was it simply that he'd shown some interest in her? Was she that shallow?

'Are you in a band or something?' Kathy asked. 'Should I recognize you?'

Antwain laughed. 'No, not a band, I run a number of nights here. I organize a few parties, that's all.'

'Do you know a girl called Amber?' Kathy could see from his reaction that he did.

'I'd say everyone here knows Amber, she's a performer. A dancer, burlesque.'

'I think she's in danger, she's my sister.'

Antwain took a drag of his cigarette and shook his head. 'No, no way, she's not in danger,' he said. 'Amber is like a . . . special guest round here. She's friends with the owner.'

'Bishop?' Kathy asked. Antwain looked at her sharply.

'Yeah, that's his name. Amber is a favourite of Bishop's. He has a . . . like an inner circle.'

'She's his girlfriend?' Kathy asked, a hard lump in her stomach.

Antwain shrugged. 'Maybe, it's more than that, though. She's like a queen round here. There's a hierarchy. You know what I mean? If you're Amber's sister, then you're royalty too.' He grinned, the breeze ruffling his hair. She smelled the cemetery, comforting through the acrid scent of the cigarette. 'I knew there was something special about you when you pulled that trick at the door, it's just the sort of thing she'd do.'

'I need to find her, will you help me?' Kathy took his cigarette and took a drag, trying to look seductive. Fighting a cough, she handed it back to him. Antwain didn't answer, watching her suspiciously.

'Why don't you just call her?'

'Her phone always goes to voicemail. No one's seen her for weeks. When did you last see her?'

Antwain thought. 'Not sure. Maybe a couple of weeks ago? She seemed okay. Maybe she just doesn't want to talk to you. Why do you think she's in trouble?'

'I dream about her.'

'That's it?'

'No.' Kathy knew she was losing him. His suspicions were growing. She thought desperately . . . What could she tell him to get him onside? 'She sent me an old book.'

Antwain's mood shifted. He finished his smoke and walked to the edge of the roof terrace. Kathy followed him, already regretting mentioning it.

'What's this book about?'

'It has something to do with vampires. Well, there are pictures of them inside but I can't be sure. I don't understand the writing. I know it's very old.'

Antwain turned to her – his look was solid.

'I think you could be in danger too,' he said.

No shit, Kathy thought.

Antwain gave her a sideways look. 'Okay,' he said. 'I'll help you find Amber. But you have to do something for me in return.'

'What's that?' Kathy asked.

'Oh, nothing major, it's easier to show you than explain.'

Kathy shrugged. 'Okay,' she said.

Antwain smiled and Kathy melted inside.

CHAPTER THIRTEEN

Carpathia 1163

Vaclav looked up at the battlements. No flag flew and there were no signs of life. Overhead the full moon hovered, giving them a smooth light. The warped walls indicated this castle had been built long ago, probably by Magyars. He could see some attempts to improve and repair from the more recent occupiers, the Templars. It had been difficult to convince the prince to lay siege to this castle. Though the Templars were interlopers, they were at least Christian, supposedly allies in the everlasting battle against the Turks.

Vaclav looked towards the great double doors, two feet thick and reinforced with massive iron bands, forged in St Petersburg. The stones surrounding would be easier to smash through than those doors. The castle had held out for a surprisingly long time, resisting the month-long bombardments of firestones and diseased livestock. But a spy had indicated they were ready to surrender. A thousand soldiers crouched, half hidden by their shields for fear of archers. They waited, watching the doors. Prince Vlad had promised the knights safe passage out of the country, should they open the doors. Vaclav doubted this, having seen a hundred fresh wooden stakes being sharpened yesterday.

He didn't care. The fate of the Knights Templar was not his concern. He was interested in one whom he believed lurked beyond the castle walls. One who had more in common with Prince Vlad than with his compatriots. One who murdered and tortured. One who drank blood.

Then there was a creak and a roar from the soldiers and the doors swung open. Four brown-garbed servants pushed the great doors wide and stood, staring open-mouthed at their besiegers. Then someone shouted an order and the army sprang forward. The servants turned and tried to run but were cut down by the vanguard and trampled as the troops stormed into the castle.

Vaclav waited a few minutes, hearing the screams and clash of steel from within the keep. Then he unsheathed his own sword and followed the soldiers. He ignored the skirmishes going on in the courtyard and made his way into the living quarters as desperate defenders fought bravely but hopelessly. The knights were well-armoured, skilful and incredibly destructive, whirling maces and six-foot broadswords. Vlad's soldiers' bodies littered the cobbles but they were winning the battle through sheer weight of numbers. As Vaclav passed he saw a huge knight brought down by a slash to the ankle; once down, the soldiers piled on and he disappeared in a frenzy of stabbing short knives.

Vaclav's spy had told him where to go. He sprinted up four flights of a spiral staircase, having to sidle past a battle on the steps between a knight and three invaders. At the base of the final set of stairs, Vaclav paused and looked out of the window. This side of the castle looked out over nothing but a thousand-foot sheer drop to the shark's-tooth rocks of the Carpathian mountains. Many a poor soul had been cast over this cliff edge for the entertainment of whichever murderous megalomaniac this castle housed at the time. The present incumbent was no worse than many who'd lived here before. He was more dangerous though. Vaclav sheathed his sword, it was no use to him now. Reaching into his tunic, he pulled out a sharp wooden stake and a small, carved object. He mounted the final set of stairs and stood before the small wooden door at the top. With a kick he burst through and sprang into the room.

The man he sought stood at the window, dressed as a knight, though in chainmail rather than the full plate armour. His white tunic looked unwashed and grimy. The sounds of the battle raging below entered through the open slit-window.

'Aliza,' Vaclav said.

The vampire turned slowly. His eyes gleamed a soft yellow. His skin sallow and waxy, long hair unkempt. 'Your name is Vaclav,' Aliza said.

Vaclav swallowed, taken aback that the vampire knew him.

'You are a Hunter,' Aliza said. 'We thought there were no more of you.'

'You were mistaken,' Vaclav said. 'There are hundreds.' This was a lie. The Hunters numbered perhaps a dozen, and those were scattered to the winds.

'And you are here to kill me?' the vampire said. As he spoke, Vaclav noticed the yellow eyes flick over to a large book lying on a side table. It was just a flash, but enough for Vaclav.

He nodded.

Aliza laughed. 'Try, Hunter,' he said and shot out an arm.

An invisible *something* hit Vaclav in the chest, throwing him backwards and slamming him into the dusty bricks of the far wall. He slumped to the floor, winded. The vampire rushed him, one moment at the far side of the room, the next in his face, snarling. Vaclav felt the creature's hands gripping his shoulders and saw the fangs heading for his neck. He lifted a hand and thrust something into the vampire's face.

Aliza sprang backwards, howling, head in hands. Vaclav gripped the glyph tightly, showing its full face to the vampire. When Aliza's hands fell away, a bright red mark was imprinted on his cheek.

'Warding glyph,' Aliza hissed. 'Where did you get that?'

'Vampires aren't the only ones with lore,' Vaclav said, getting to his feet.

'But vampires are the only ones with magic,' Aliza replied and he screamed a word – no, not even a word: a sound, an abjuration. The volume was intense and did not end.

Vaclav stood stunned, the hideous cacophony carrying on, repeating, deafening and stunning him. He slumped to his knees and clamped his hands over his ears. But there was no respite from the noise, it clattered into him, arresting his heart and stopping his lungs.

But then it was over. It took Vaclav a moment but as his

breathing started up again and the room swam back into focus he realized a group of soldiers had entered, interrupting the spell. As Vaclav watched, stunned, the vampire lifted one soldier and slammed him against a wall, crushing his ribcage. Almost too quickly to see, the vampire turned and seized a second soldier by the throat. Turning him around, Vaclav clearly saw the soldier's face lit with horror as the vampire took hold of his upper jaw and serenely tore the top of his head away, leaving just the lower jaw, chin and a lolling tongue in its bowl of gore.

The point of a sword emerged from the vampire's belly, driven through by a soldier behind. The vampire twisted quickly; tearing the pommel from the soldier's grasp, the sword flew across the room, clattering against the stones. The soldier and his one surviving comrade stared in horror as Aliza raised his arms and screamed a spell. The soldiers slumped to their feet, clutching their throats and gasping for air.

Vaclav realized he had but a moment. He scrambled to his feet and grasped the stake in his favoured left hand. As the vampire was distracted, watching his victims' desperate fight for life, Vaclav lunged forward.

His aim was true. The sliver-sharp stake plunged easily inside the left shoulder blade, piercing the heart. Aliza screamed, a rattling, cavernous screech that seemed to emanate from the very depths of hell. Vaclav fell backwards, covering his battered ears again. Then silence – and the vampire slumped forward, dead.

Vaclav waited a moment or two before checking on the corpse. The face was already beginning to shrivel and crack. The Hunter breathed a sigh of relief. A faint haze seemed to have crept in from somewhere, marsh gas perhaps. It flowed across the floor towards one of the soldiers, whom Vaclav realized was still moving. Vaclav went to him.

'Are you okay?'

The soldier nodded, his face to the floor.

'Find your captain, tell him Vaclav got what he came for.'

The soldier nodded again.

Vaclav took the book, so small, yet heavy with knowledge. He knew what it contained. The written lore and magic of the vampires. Secrets that would lead to their utter destruction. Aliza had been a fool to allow this to be written.

Halfway down the first spiral staircase Vaclav heard a noise above and looked up. The soldier he'd left alive stood on the railings at the top. 'What are you doing?' Vaclav said, confused. But then the soldier jumped, and in the micro-second before the heavy boots smashed into

Vaclav's chest, he realized his mistake. Vaclav tumbled to the bottom of the staircase, still clutching the book to his belly, as though it might protect him. He lay, tangled in his own broken limbs, lungs struggling to take and keep breath within his smashed ribcage. The soldier trotted down the stairs, ducked down and thrust his face close to Vaclav's. The eyes flashed yellow.

'Transmigration,' Vaclav muttered.

The vampire grinned, showing the jagged canines of his new body's mouth.

Vaclav looked up, towards the window, where the moon shone as brilliantly as ever. He had one last act within him. Once more his aim must be true.

As the vampire's lips curled and he moved in for the kill, Vaclav shot out an arm and flung the book out through the open window. The vampire stared out after it and hissed. Then his head shot forward and for Vaclav it was all over.

They went back down the stairs but took a different door at the bottom: a service entrance into a corridor which Kathy judged ran behind the main stage. Doors led off it on both sides. The corridor was badly lit and littered with debris; the grimy walls covered in old posters and shabby painted plaster that hung from damp bricks.

'This is Amber's dressing room.' Antwain stood outside a heavy-looking door covered in thick black paint, a white pentagon star smeared across its panels. Antwain turned the handle. 'Locked. Dammit.'

Kathy stood with her arms folded, uncomfortable, not sure she could trust Antwain. Opposite Amber's dressing room was another door, this one open. Kathy craned her neck to look inside, curious. The room was empty apart from a few sledgehammers and a wheelie bin. The floor was dusty and littered with footprints. A hole had been knocked through in the far wall. As if they didn't have enough space down here already. Kathy remembered what her aunt had told her about the Roman catacombs in this part of London. What were they playing at?

As Antwain fumbled with the lock they saw a light waving up and down the corridor, shortly followed by heavy footsteps. Antwain suddenly pushed Kathy up against the door and held her in a tight embrace. As their bodies found each other they kissed and the footsteps passed by. Kathy closed her eyes with pleasure, her mistrust melting with the heat of the kiss.

'When you've done with her, get back inside,' a rough voice said. 'You know you're not allowed back here.'

Kathy hardly heard, lost as she was in Antwain's embrace. He broke off the kiss and they watched the bulky figure of a man wearing a grey robe.

'Security guard,' Antwain whispered. 'Thanks for not giving me away.' He was all business now. He turned his attention back to the lock.

Kathy leaned with her back against the grimy wall, her heart pounding. She touched her lips. As she took her fingers away and looked at them in the dim light, they were red with blood.

'I think you bit me,' she said.

'I had to make it look real. Right, stand back.' Antwain took no notice of Kathy, still examining her fingertips. Instead he ran at the black dressing-room door. He hit the door with leather, muscle and bone and it burst open, swallowing him. Kathy quickly followed.

'Close the door, or they'll find us.' Antwain was already at Amber's dressing table as Kathy closed the door.

'Who are *they*?' she asked, looking around.

'Vampires,' Antwain said, turning to look at her in surprise. 'Come on, Kathy, you know what you're getting into here. You don't have to play games with me.'

Kathy stared back, unsure how to respond. Antwain took a step towards her.

'You share Amber's blood and you have the book.'

Kathy shivered, suddenly realizing just how vulnerable she was.

236

'Are you a vampire?'

'Yes, no . . . I am just an acolyte, a half-blood,' he said, matter of factly, as though he'd just told her he was assistant manager at McDonald's. Kathy felt like she was back in school again. Outside. Unaware. Alone. Antwain had turned back and was pulling out drawers, rummaging through make-up and perfumes.

Why was she still here? This . . . creature had just told her he was a vampire, or as good as. She should be running, screaming. And yet something stopped her. Something inside her which told her not to be afraid. She needed Antwain. He was important, somehow, and not just in the hunt for Amber. Antwain had a role to play in this.

Kathy gazed around the room, wondering what exactly she was looking for. She walked to a rail of clothes and ran her hands along the fabrics, closing her eyes as the clothes released their menu of old scents. Her reverie was interrupted by a smashing noise and she looked over to see Antwain had knocked over a glass jar full of cotton balls.

'Antwain, stop for a moment,' Kathy said. 'You have to tell me what's going on. What do you mean when you say you're an acolyte?'

Antwain stopped and sighed. Then he turned a chair at

the table and sat down, facing her.

'I am a vampire, yes, but not how you think. I have not killed yet, it is forbidden for us to kill until our masters allow it. If I did kill I'd soon be destroyed myself. Until then I rise through the ranks from meat, to slave, to what I am today.'

Kathy stared at him, feeling sick.

'On the dance floor you said you glamoured me,' she said. 'What did you mean?'

Antwain grinned. 'Take what you know about vampires in the movies and then add what you know about witches and wizards. Combine it all together and you'll be close to what a real vampire is.'

'Vampires can cast spells?'

This was no surprise. Harry had suggested as much.

'Yes, and we have rituals too; it's more like a religion of blood. Being a vampire is about following a path of faith. A path that was laid down thousands of years ago.'

Just sounds like any other kooky religion, Kathy thought to herself. *If I hadn't seen the magic, felt the bite . . .*

'And Amber?' Kathy asked. 'She is on this . . . path too. That's what she's been trying to tell me.' *Everything's connected*, Kathy thought.

'Yeah, of course. In our nest she is a queen.'

'Then where do I find your queen?' Kathy walked

238

around the rack of clothes, as though Amber might be hidden behind there.

'You are here for a reason, Kathy,' Antwain said. 'If we find out that reason, we'll find your sister too.'

Kathy didn't reply. She opened a small chest in front of the mirror; inside she found costume jewellery, accessories and, at the bottom, a small photo frame. The frame held a faded picture of a woman in her late-thirties perhaps, holding a bundled baby, a thin smile on her pinched face. She looked a little like Kathy, more like Amber, though tired, so tired. Beside her stood a red-haired toddler. Kathy searched the picture; it was clearly her, Amber and their mother. She didn't know how she felt, seeing herself in this different world. The usual sense of disconnect held her at arm's length, like it was a different Kathy in that picture, one from an old movie perhaps. Just acting the part. But the photograph was a connection to her past, to her family. She knew it was important, even if she couldn't feel it. Kathy tucked it into a pocket and glanced up at Antwain, who was looking in the drawers again.

'There's nothing here,' he said. 'Don't worry. I have another idea.'

'We'd better get back to Jack and Becky,' Kathy said. 'They'll be worried.' She closed the lid on the box.

'Kathy,' Antwain said quietly.

Kathy spun to see the security guard in the doorway. He held a pistol.

'I knew you was up to something,' the man said. He spoke with a thick European accent and wore the robe of a clergyman. His bald head reflected the dim glow of the naked bulb overhead. His face was lined with age, his eyes wide with anticipation. 'Bishop will reward me for this. I always knew you was not to be trusted.'

Kathy looked over at Antwain, who looked pointedly at the hinged mirror Kathy stood beside. The security guard took a step into the room and lifted the gun, pointing it directly into Antwain's face. Kathy hit the top of the mirror, the bottom swung up sharply and cracked into the guard's elbow, knocking his arm upwards. The gun went off with a loud bang and a shower of dust rained down from the ceiling.

Then Antwain was on top of him and Kathy dashed for the door and raced down the corridor. The second crack of a gun shot rang out and she stopped. Fear held her from turning around until she heard footsteps approaching. Antwain was moving slowly, blood showed through his skinny jeans, he held the walls to steady himself.

'I'm okay,' he said. 'It's just a cut.'

'What about him?'

'He won't bother us again.'

'You killed him?'

'It was him or me.'

Kathy stared at him, aghast. Antwain scowled under her look.

'He was going to tell Bishop. You don't know what he's like. Bishop would have killed me – slowly. I'm serious, Kathy.'

She believed him. And after all, it was because of her he'd been caught down here in the first place. She got down on her knees and inspected the wound. It was more than a scratch but hard to see exactly what the damage was through the tight jeans. She unwrapped the bandanna and tied it around the wound, stemming the blood flow. 'That'll have to do,' she said.

'Thanks,' Antwain said, catching her eye.

Kathy swayed as she stood. The grey curtain wavered at the edges of her vision. Suddenly she felt a wave of concern. Not that they might be caught, but that she would have a panic attack.

Antwain took them through a different door to the one they'd come through. It led out behind the stage. Pausing to look through the red curtains and out on to the stage Kathy spotted Becky and Jack, still dancing. Moving from the flanks of the room she could see two more men in robes making their way to the club's backstage area. 'They know he's dead,' Antwain said. 'We have no choice, we have to go out this way.'

Kathy felt the grey curtains closing again. Her breathing sped up and she pulled back when Antwain tried to lead her on. He turned. 'What's wrong?' he asked.

But Kathy couldn't speak. She sank to her knees, panting now, fear gripping her insides with an icy claw.

Antwain knelt down and peered into her face. He muttered something: 'Muracha junaid.' And suddenly the panic attack was arrested. Kathy felt the claw release her and the grey curtains parted and swept themselves aside. Her breathing slowed and she looked up at Antwain in amazement.

'A trick like that could put my therapist out of business for ever,' she said.

'It's not a trick,' Antwain replied, a little haughtily. 'It's a glamour.'

Kathy nodded, impressed.

'Come on,' he said. 'We're wasting time.' He took her hand again and led her back to the curtain.

He waited till they had gone through the stage door and swung back the red curtain, leading Kathy on to the stage. The crowds below looked up as Kathy and Antwain ran towards the front of the stage. They leaped off and crashed into the throbbing throng of bodies below,

Antwain landing heavily and grunting with pain.

Still holding Kathy tightly by the hand, Antwain stumbled across the dance floor towards Becky. Kathy pulled hard on her jacket, bringing her close. 'We have to leave now, come on!' Becky had no chance to object as Kathy dragged her towards the staircase that led back down to the bar. Becky managed to grab hold of Jack too, dragging him with them.

The four of them jumped and pushed their way through the crowds and joined others leaving the club, out into the wet city street. The bouncers still stood by the door, uninterested in them. The drag queen had disappeared.

'We'll go back to my place and then we'll work out what to do,' Antwain said, still holding Kathy's arm, tightly. She pulled away.

'Actually, I think we'd better head home,' Becky said, seeing the uncertainty in Kathy's face.

Antwain looked to Kathy. 'If you want to see your sister again, I think you'd better come with me,' he said.

Jack stepped forward. 'Listen, Antwain, we've had a nice time, but we're all tired now, man, and—'

'Back off, little man,' Antwain said, dangerously. Jack bristled and raised himself to his not-inconsiderable full height.

Then the swing doors banged open and three cowled figures stood there, looking around, searching for something in the crowd. Antwain popped up his hoodie and, turning, walked resolutely down the street. After a moment, Kathy shrugged an apology at Becky and rushed after him.

'Wait!' Becky called. 'We're coming too.'

Kathy smiled in gratitude and Jack rolled his eyes but followed. The three friends chased after the limping Antwain into the darkness.

'I hope he's worth it, this boy,' Becky said.

'Have you seen his body?' Kathy replied, giggling, despite everything. She felt alive. She felt like she was part of something. Finally, the deadening bubble of anti-emotion had lifted. So she was still having the panic attacks, but better an occasional one of those than nothing at all. And if they could be cured with a glamour . . .

But then she saw that Antwain had stopped. The lights of a car approached from down the lane. Antwain turned and walked back to them. 'That's them, they're coming for you.'

'That's who?' Jack said, aggressive and sick of this foolishness.

'Vampires,' Antwain said. 'I can't be seen with you. Bishop will kill me.'

'What will he do to us?' Kathy asked.

Antwain stood, evidently torn. The car slowed to a crawl and a window wound down. Antwain looked up the street over Kathy's shoulder. 'Shit, more of them. Don't turn around.'

'We're trapped,' Kathy said.

'What the hell is all this about?' Jack said. Becky stood nervously, eyes flicking back between Kathy and Antwain.

'We've gotta run, Kathy,' Antwain said.

'But where?'

Antwain glanced into the East Cemetery by way of answer.

'In there?' Kathy said, looking into the depths.

'It's fine,' Antwain said. 'You're safe in there, with me.'

But Kathy wasn't scared. Not of the cemetery, despite what she knew must be in there. The cemetery was part of her now. And she part of it.

'Okay,' she said. And then Antwain spun her around, jammed his hands under her arms and suddenly she was flying through the air. They landed on the other side with a thump. Antwain had jumped, carrying her. She fell to the ground in shock, looking up at him. He smiled and leaped over the fence again. Through the bars Kathy saw the car doors had opened and dark-robed men were getting out, coming for Becky and Jack. Antwain seized

Becky as he had Kathy and leaped again. He seemed to spring almost without bending his legs, but it was a jump, he didn't fly, as such. He landed heavily again, spilling. They looked through the bars. Jack had stepped out into the light to meet the men from the cars.

'Jack, no!' Becky shouted.

'You guys wanna explain yourselves?' they heard him call out.

But the men did not wish to explain anything. Without pause, and with supernatural speed, two of the vampires swept into the tall man, bundling him over and on to the pavement, just as the three men from the club arrived. The five swamped Jack, hiding him from sight. He yelled, cursed and finally screamed.

Becky ran to the bars. 'Leave him alone, leave him alone!' But then Antwain was pulling her away.

'We have to go, *now*!' he hissed at Kathy. 'We can't help him,' he said to the struggling Becky, dragging her off through the gravestones.

Kathy looked back at the scene on the street; just one of Jack's legs was visible, stiff and quivering, poking out of the tangle of black robes as the vampires devoured him, a bloody feeding frenzy. One of the creatures looked up at Kathy through the bars and screamed in rage.

Kathy ran.

CHAPTER FOURTEEN

'Why didn't they jump the fence and follow us?' Kathy asked as they walked through wet grass in the darkness. Shrouded tombs lined their path on either side.

'They are full vampires. They can't enter the cemetery.'

'Why not?'

'It has glyphs all around it,' he said. 'Warding glyphs, to keep vampires out.'

'And in?'

'Depends on how strong they are.'

'But the glyphs don't affect you?'

'No,' he said. 'I told you, I've not killed to feed yet. I don't like glyphs, they make me feel funny, but I can pass them.'

At first, Becky had been shouting, ranting, begging them to go back and help Jack. Then Antwain had held her face in his hands and muttered some words, staring deep into her eyes. Since then she'd been calm and silent. She trotted along behind, impassive. Kathy periodically asked her if she was okay and she'd just nod quickly and carry on.

After what seemed like ages, they reached the far side of the East Cemetery. Antwain picked the lock of an old gate and they exited that way, Antwain looking up and down the street, watching for followers.

Antwain's flat was large and dark, situated on the top floor of a crumbling old office building overlooking a filthy canal. The windows were blacked out, hung with thick drapes and an upside-down Union Flag. And although it was a mess, it was strung with grand old antiques – a great chair here, an old cupboard there.

Becky sat on an old chest in a corner, staring straight ahead.

Kathy felt a gulf of darkness inside her. She was horrified over what had happened, but that old numbness had arisen again, enabling her to carry on.

'So who were those guys? Bishop's men?'

Antwain nodded. 'Higher-ranking vampires – his henchmen,' he said.

Antwain looked tired and thin. He walked unsteadily across the room and grabbed a bottle of Jack Daniels, taking a swig. Slamming the bottle back on the table, he dropped his blood-soaked jeans and Kathy looked away quickly, suddenly nervous like a schoolgirl. 'Can you check out the back?' he asked. Kathy looked back to see a gaping, deep wound in Antwain's right buttock and upper thigh. She turned away.

'That bad, huh?' he asked. She nodded. How could he still be walking? How could he have performed those jumps? She felt in awe of his power and suddenly she wanted him, more than she'd wanted anything ever before.

Antwain pulled up his jeans, wincing, and turned to her. 'Kathy,' he said, 'I need your help here.'

She nodded. *Anything.*

'I must feed if I am to heal,' he said softly, his eyes questioning. Kathy nodded, not really understanding.

'I told you before, I must not kill. My master would know.'

Kathy nodded.

'But I can feed, draw blood from a human. Or . . .'

'My blood is . . .'

Now it was Antwain who nodded. 'Yes, you have Hunter blood.'

'How much do you need?' Kathy asked.

'Not too much,' Antwain said, stepping towards her. Kathy leaned her head over, exposing her neck.

'No,' Antwain said. 'I must not bite you.'

He held up a curved dagger. Kathy gasped.

'The dagger is sharp,' he said gently. 'This will not hurt.'

Then Antwain ran the blade lightly across her wrist. A tiny sliver of pain made her gasp and blood, black in the shadows, ran across her white skin. Antwain ducked his head and wrapped his lips around her slim wrist. The sensation tickled and Kathy felt a little sick, like she'd felt the one time she tried to give blood, back at high school. She'd had a panic attack during the process and ripped out the needle, screaming and throwing herself on to the floor.

Today though she held herself tall and fought back the clouding grey shroud that warned her of an approaching attack. Antwain fed for a minute or so, then lifted his head and hissed loudly, his face just as pale; but life had returned to his expression and his eyes flashed yellow, just for a moment.

Kathy shivered slightly, at once terrified of his power, not knowing if she wanted to share it or destroy it.

Antwain turned and dropped his jeans again. 'How am I doing?' he asked, turning his head and grinning.

Kathy knew she shouldn't be surprised, having experienced something like it herself, but the speed at which the wound had begun to close up was astonishing. Like time-lapse cinematography, the skin seemed to grow and squeeze out the red flesh, blood evaporated and after a minute the wound had disappeared altogether.

'That's some strong blood you have there,' Antwain said.

Kathy flushed at the weird compliment and ducked her head. Antwain took off his shoes and socks and ripped away the tattered, blood-blackened jeans. Then he pulled his shirt over his head and stood before Kathy, naked. 'Gotta get some fresh clothes,' he said, watching her.

Kathy stood, staring back at him, trying not to let her gaze slip down. He walked over to the other side of the room, past the unresponsive Becky.

'I thought I was going to have another panic attack just then,' Kathy said. 'But I managed to fight it off.'

'I could put a permanent glamour on you, if you like?' Antwain asked. 'Stop the fear.'

Kathy paused before answering. 'Let me think about it, yeah?'

He grinned as he pulled on a pair of fresh jeans.

'By the way,' Antwain said, 'you do know you *already* have a permanent glamour over you?'

Kathy blinked. 'I do? What glamour?'

Antwain shrugged. 'It's powerful. Artfully crafted. Something to do with your past. Dampening memory and emotion. Not sure exactly – it's a complex one, not quite vampire.'

'How did it . . . ? I mean, who could have, glamoured me like that?' she asked.

Antwain pulled on a T-shirt and turned to look at her.

'Someone you trusted,' he said.

Antwain insisted they wait until dawn before leaving. He grabbed a bottle of Jack Daniels and invited Kathy to sit with him on his impressive four-poster bed.

'The vampires, they will not come out into the light,' he said.

'They die in sunlight?'

Antwain nodded. 'Direct sunlight, yes.'

'Bishop?' Kathy said. 'He's a full vampire?'

Antwain laughed. 'One of the fullest vampires in history, and now he wants to kill the king.'

'My aunt said he was two hundred years old, is that true?'

He nodded.

'Tell me more about him,' Kathy said.

Antwain seemed to think about it for a while, then shrugged his shoulders and began speaking.

'In 1812, a man, John Bishop, was born right here in Highgate. He had an uneventful childhood, but on coming of age he took a job with the East India Trading company. He travelled all over the world and developed an interest in the occult, in the arcane practices of what were then considered to be savages. Devil worship, voodoo, cannibalism. You know, the whole nine yards. Even human sacrifice. At first he just observed, claiming it was research, noting everything down in his leatherbound journal, the way old Imperialists did, to make themselves feel superior . . .'

Suddenly Antwain was on his feet and at the window. He lifted a corner of the old bed sheet that covered the glass and peered out. Satisfied, he came back and sat down.

'Thought I heard something,' he said, by way of explanation. 'Where was I?'

'Bishop was observing savage rituals . . .' Kathy prompted.

'Oh yeah, well the thing is he soon realized there was real power in some of these ceremonies. He began to understand, he had uncovered the path. He *joined*.'

Antwain stopped to swig from the bottle of Jack Daniels. He offered it to Kathy, who shook her head.

'Bishop married in 1835, a society beauty named

Maria. They had a daughter a year later. But she didn't understand his practices, she rejected the power it offered. She tried to leave him, with the baby. He tried to stop her and she died.'

Kathy stared at him, eyes narrowed. 'You mean he killed her?'

Antwain looked uncertain. 'Death is just a doorway,' he said, unconvincingly.

'How did this doorway open?' she asked.

'He stabbed her with a sacrificial knife,' Antwain said, after a pause. 'A maid saw Bishop kneeling over his wife's body. He had cut out her heart and was eating it.'

Kathy gagged.

'It's a way of binding the souls of the deceased and the living,' Antwain explained. 'Bishop was saving her soul.'

Kathy shook her head in astonishment. 'How can you follow this man?'

Antwain took another drink. 'You don't understand, Kathy. If you joined us you would understand.'

'I understand enough,' she said. 'What happened to the child?'

'The police were called and came to the house. Bishop barricaded the doors. It was a great stone house opposite the cemetery. The police decided to wait until he came out, wanting a peaceful resolution. The local townsfolk had other ideas; they set fire to the house.' Antwain sounded bitter now, as though Bishop was the victim here. 'The girl died, burned. They found her in her bedroom.'

'And Bishop?'

'No trace was found. Some think he had a secret tunnel underground – it was never found. The house collapsed soon after and was levelled.'

'A tunnel into the catacombs under the cemetery?'

'Perhaps,' Antwain said. 'Personally I think he used magic to escape.'

'He was already a vampire by then?'

'Yes.'

Kathy looked into Antwain's eyes, searching for understanding. 'Antwain, you must escape him. I don't believe you accept that what he did . . . what he does, is okay. I see a good person in you. You can't accept this murder, these atrocities.'

'All power comes at a price,' Antwain said. 'All strong societies require the punishment and sacrifice of those who refuse to accept the rules.'

Kathy screwed up her face. 'You're not thinking straight,' she said. 'You're brainwashed. The whole point of Bishop's websites, his businesses, is that they embrace those who don't fit in. Now you're saying people who don't follow the rules should be killed?'

Antwain looked uncertain, then angry. 'That's not what I said. Look, you just don't get it.'

'No, I don't,' she said. 'Look, Antwain. You told me earlier that you haven't killed yet – at least, not to feed.'

He nodded, looking sullen.

'Please don't,' she said. 'Please don't kill anyone else. Don't feed. You have the choice. You don't have to follow their rules.'

He said nothing. Still holding the bottle, he spun the loose cap around the lip.

'Just think about it, okay?' Kathy said.

He paused, then nodded.

They'd stayed up talking for a while, then Kathy must have dropped off. She woke on the bed, next to Becky. Antwain had gone, but returned a few minutes later with fresh bread, the glorious smell reviving Kathy's spirits. She fell on the still-warm rolls like a beast, tearing at the crust. Antwain crouched on his haunches, watching her, interested.

'I've forgotten what it's like, eating,' he said.

'So that's it?' Kathy asked, still munching. 'You'll never eat food again?'

He shook his head. 'Don't need food. Food sucks. You'll see.'

Kathy stopped eating. 'What do you mean, I'll see?'

Antwain paused for a minute, perhaps regretting what he'd said.

'Look,' he said, 'I see a lot of people come to the Church. People confused, people lonely. Outsiders, y'know?'

'And what? You . . . Bishop offers them something?'

He nodded, eyes flashing yellow, for a moment.

'We offer them companionship . . . family,' he said. 'But so much more than that, we offer them the possibility of eternal life.'

'Eternal life without bread,' Kathy said, frowning.

Antwain's face flashed with anger – suddenly Kathy had a glimpse of a demon's face – then it was gone.

'Amber didn't understand at first either. But Bishop brought her around.'

Kathy glared at him. 'So where is she then, if she's part of your big family? How come she's disappeared?'

Antwain shrugged. 'The procedure takes a little longer with some people.'

'Because they resist?'

Antwain stood and walked to the window again. He flicked back a drape momentarily; a beam of watery light flickered across the room, accentuating the grime on the walls and the mess on the floor. 'Time to go,' he said.

* * *

It was chilly in the early-morning air as they walked along the canal tow-path. Becky walked a few paces behind them, silent. Blank-faced.

Kathy turned to look at her friend. 'What will happen to her?' she asked.

'It'll wear off,' Antwain said. He wore dark glasses and a hoodie.

'And will she remember what happened?'

Antwain shook his head. 'Not unless she goes digging. Hypnotherapy and that shit.'

Something pulled inside Kathy's memory. Was this what *she* was doing? Digging?

'She should be allowed to mourn,' Kathy said.

Antwain ignored her, but in the early-dawn light she thought she saw a faint smile playing on his lips.

'Hey,' she said, suddenly realizing something. 'How come you can come out in the light? I thought you said vampires burned up in the sun.'

'I can't deal with direct sunlight,' he said. 'But we acolytes can handle a bit of light around dusk and dawn.'

Kathy remembered the two young vampires she'd encountered in the cemetery. Come to think of it, when she'd seen the Highgate Vampire, that had been during half-light as well. She hadn't thought about it at the time, but he was no acolyte.

'What do you know about the Highgate Vampire?' she asked.

Antwain flicked a look over to her. 'He is the King of the Vampires,' he said, his voice taking on a reverential tone. 'But he has not been seen for many years and his resting place is lost.'

Again the flash-sense of a lost memory prodded. Kathy now was sure there was something she needed to remember. When could this have happened? As they walked she went back over the events of the last few days. The attack in the cemetery, the tour, the trip to the museum. There was something missing, or someone missing. Someone important. But the memory wouldn't come.

Antwain stopped and turned to Becky.

'Take us to your home,' he said. Becky trotted on past them and took the next right. They followed her for a while longer until she came to a white stuccoed Victorian terraced house on a side street a few hundred yards off Swain's Lane.

'Go inside and go to bed,' Antwain said. 'When you wake, you will remember none of this.'

Becky walked off and Kathy watched her go. Her friend rummaged in her handbag for the key to the house and disappeared without looking back. Kathy blinked back the tears. If she started crying now, she'd never stop.

'Come on,' Antwain said, pulling her hand. She pulled back, surprising him.

'Is there no compassion in you?' she hissed. 'Is any part of you still human?'

Antwain came close and looked into her eyes. 'Did I not help you? Did I not save her life? I could have left you all to the pack.' They both suddenly became aware of a dog-walker approaching and there was an incongruous moment while they waited for her to pass. The dog, a mongrel, looked up at Antwain and growled as it passed.

Kathy eyed the acolyte suspiciously. 'How do I know you're not just intending to hand me over to Bishop yourself, me and my special blood?'

'Why would I do that?' he asked.

'Because that's what you do, isn't it? You acolytes – you do things for Bishop, hoping to gain his favour? Like he's the Godfather or something.'

Antwain stared her out. 'Do you not understand?' he said. 'If you want to find Amber, you'll need to see Bishop. He keeps her close.'

'So you *were* going to hand me over to him?' she asked, a bitter taste forming in her mouth. She backed away.

Antwain seized her wrist with extraordinary strength. He pulled her close. 'I can arrange a meeting between you and Bishop,' he said. 'If you want me to, that is. If you don't, then get the hell out of my town and get the hell out of my life. I do not need this shit.' Then he pushed her away and she stumbled on the uneven pavement and went over on her backside. He stood, watching her.

Could she trust him? Why was he helping her? That was the question. What was in it for him? But again, something inside Kathy spoke, without words, urging her to carry on. To accept his help. Maybe she couldn't trust him, but Antwain had a part to play, just like she did.

Kathy glared up at him. They stayed in their respective positions for what seemed like for ever, like grandmasters considering the next move. Then Kathy stood and brushed herself off.

'Please do arrange a meeting,' she said, stiffly. 'I want to see Bishop.'

Antwain nodded.

'Will . . . will you be there?' Kathy asked.

Antwain nodded, then said, 'I don't know. I hope so, but that's up to Bishop.'

There was an uncomfortably long pause. Kathy felt like she was at the end of a date that had started off well but ended badly. She felt maybe she'd had this feeling before, recently, with . . . who?

'Well I'm gonna head off, now,' she said, eventually.

He nodded. 'Want me to walk you home?'

'I don't think so,' Kathy said, stiffly.

'Okay, well, might see you around,' Antwain said. Suddenly he looked young. A child. Kathy's heart went out to him, what had he thrown away?

Antwain turned and walked off, Kathy watched him go. Then she too spun on her heels and headed back towards Swain's Lane. Upon reaching the house she walked heavily up the stairs, suddenly exhausted. The door swung open before she got there and her aunt stood in the doorway, managing to look simultaneously relieved and furious.

Elizabeth made as if to speak, but Kathy got there first.

'Why have you glamoured me?' she said.

CHAPTER FIFTEEN

Elizabeth set down a steaming cup on the old wooden table in front of Kathy.

'It wasn't me,' she said, sitting down opposite her niece. 'I'm not very good at that sort of thing, magic.'

'Harry?' Kathy asked. Elizabeth confirmed with a nod. 'Why?'

Elizabeth sighed but it was apparent she knew the game was up. 'You were attacked at the museum, someone was killed.'

Kathy's eyes widened. 'Who?'

Her aunt fixed her with an intent look, curious to see what would happen when she said the name. 'Oliver Samson.'

It took a moment, then something in Kathy's mind seemed to swirl, and the missing section of her memory was suddenly there; it swivelled and clicked back into place, like the last move on a Rubik's Cube. She gasped, not at the flood of memory, but the pain of loss, compounded by the guilt she felt through not having grieved. The darkness which had been locked away suddenly swamped her, choked her.

Elizabeth rushed around the table. 'Oh Kathy,' she said. 'I'm so sorry, we had to.'

'Sorry it happened?' Kathy asked, through the sudden rush of emotions. 'Or sorry you stopped me grieving a good man, a man who was just trying to help me?'

'Both,' Elizabeth said, laying a hand awkwardly across Kathy's shoulders. 'We did it to—'

'To protect me, yes, I know,' Kathy said, bitterly. 'Everyone's trying to protect me and everyone else ends up dead.'

'What? Who's dead?'

'Becky's boyfriend, Jack, he was killed last night. By Bishop's wolf pack.'

'More innocents,' Elizabeth said, grimly. 'Bishop must pay.'

'I don't care about Bishop,' Kathy said. 'I'm here to rescue Amber.'

'I think the two go hand in hand,' Elizabeth said.

'I'm not going back to New York until she's safe,' Kathy snapped, looking up at her aunt through steel eyes.

Elizabeth nodded. 'I know, Kathy. I know. For better or for worse, you're too far in now.'

'And no more glamouring,' Kathy said.

'No, Kathy. No more glamouring. But you must sleep.'

Kathy lay in bed for an hour, her mind racing. She tried to explore the recently-returned memories, replaying the terrifying chase through the museum, Oliver's faithful, old, yet handsome face, the dimple on his left cheek as he grinned at something she'd said. Then the slow, sickening journey home in the car as she realized what she had to do. Then their last conversation, his instructions to her, and the feel of the rough, splintered stake in her hands, the gush of blood warming her as he died in her arms.

What had he told her just before he'd died? The location of the tomb. No, the name on the tomb door. What was it? Having . . . Hattenstone . . . Hattersly? Something like that. An old family. She cursed her meddling old aunt and Harry too. Why had they damaged her like this? She thought of Becky, poor Becky, so alive, so cheerful before. Now a shell, a wreck. Not even able to grieve. This was the way of the vampire and the vampire-hunter? To destroy to protect. If so, she rejected it. The 'family' was a joke, the club nothing but a trap, the promise of power empty.

* * *

Kathy flew over London, delineated by a million lights and a black swooping swathe of the river. Looking up she saw Antwain's chiselled features. He held her tight, under her arms, as enormous, cruel-curved bat wings beat lazily, keeping them aloft. To her left Kathy saw Amber, similarly carried, by a winged Oliver. Amber looked across at her and smiled, as though this were a normal Saturday-night outing.

The carriers dropped suddenly, in formation, and Kathy blinked against the slipstream as they dived towards the blue ring of the Eye. The great wheel rushed towards them and Kathy felt sure they would crash into it when suddenly Antwain changed course, Oliver following, and they hurtled up the river, skimming the waves, lazily swerving to avoid river craft. They passed just to the right of a pleasure-boat, bright lights blazing, dance music leaping across the water. A girl holding a glass on the deck stood and watched them pass. Kathy felt like waving.

Following the curve of the river, they flew on; in a minute or two the white, floodlit canopy of the Millennium Dome appeared ahead. Their winged escorts slowed as they lifted up to the very top of the dome. As they approached, muffled music could be heard from below.

Antwain dropped Kathy lightly on to the tough canopy and went to open an access hatch. The volume of the music suddenly leaped by several orders of magnitude. He then picked Kathy up again, hovered over the hatch, then they dropped through.

Beneath, red and blue lights spun and waved madly as the music reached cacophonous levels. A swarming mass of dancing people juddered in time with the beat, like the vibrating cone of a boom box speaker. Antwain dropped neatly into a gap, attracting mild surprise from the entranced dancers nearby. Oliver and Amber dropped next to them, entwined. The escorts' wings folded rapidly and disappeared. Kathy watched Amber and Oliver, feeling awkward and outside as they began to dance. Then she was seized by Antwain, who spun her, gripped her and danced for the two of them. Leading her on, he showed her the moves by moving her body. She melted into him and melted into the song.

As he held her close, she asked, 'Is this real?'

She wanted it to be. So much.

'It could be,' Antwain whispered. 'If you want it to be.'

August 2003

Magda walked slowly up Swain's Lane, the way she always

walked these days, since Amber had left to go to college. There was nothing to hurry for any more. Elizabeth sometimes asked her to run errands, she knew her sister worried about her, that she never left the house, and when she did she spent too much time wandering around the cemetery.

Magda swung a carrier bag, bulky with bread and heavy with milk. The day was tired and the leaves trailing over the railings looked dusty and old before their time. She peered through the bars, seeing the tail end of a tour group disappear into the trees in the distance. So many tourists this time of year, the early nights drawing them in. Too late for wandering about today. She passed a section of wall, her view of the cemetery blocked momentarily. She didn't like being too far from the graveyard. Ever since she'd come to London she'd known that her place was here. Her family was connected with this soil now. An intimate bond that could not be broken and that stretched across the generations. She'd tried to escape once before, but had returned. She didn't believe in chance, the vagaries of the US Immigration Department were not to be blamed. The cemetery itself called her back, and Amber too.

She stopped as she heard something. A gentle singing, carried to her on the wind. A child's voice.

'Solomon Grundy, born on a Monday . . .'

She walked on, towards a section of railings.

'Grew up on Tuesday, married on Wednesday . . .'

Reaching the railings, she looked in. Then she gripped the bars tightly, her fingers whitening. Within the cemetery, a dozen yards from the fence, stood a child, maybe six or seven. The girl looked down at the path, sweeping the gravel with her sandal. She sang as she swept.

'Grew old on Thursday, died on Friday . . .'

Magda's heart pounded, the roar of blood in her ears drowning out everything. The child looked just like Amber, though it was not Amber.

'Kathy?' Magda whispered. There was no possibility the girl could have heard at that distance, but she looked up nonetheless and stared at Magda, through the bars. Then she turned and ran. Magda paused a moment, then something called her, something whispered, and she ran up the street, to the gate a couple of dozen yards away, the blue carrier bag left on the pavement behind her, contents spilling.

Magda paid at the entrance and entered the cemetery, trying to look calm, but her flushed face drawing inquisitive looks from the ticket-seller. She walked down the main path as slowly as she could stand to and turned right, back down the hill, losing herself in the trees; then she was running, something driving her on. It couldn't be Kathy, could it? Magda had never seen a photograph of her daughter, though she knew Elizabeth was in contact with the girl's foster mother in the US. It would have been too painful. Too much to bear.

As Magda alternately ran and walked through the woods, following the twisted path towards the area where the girl had disappeared, feverish thoughts crowded her skull. How could Kathy be here? A family holiday? Elizabeth would have known about it – had her friend been protecting her? She could believe that Kathy would be drawn to the cemetery, as they all were, but why would she be on her own? It didn't make sense. Was she in trouble? Magda choked in fear as she thought of her little girl, lost, alone, frightened.

Magda passed the end of a terrace of crypts and glanced down its long, grass-lined path. She saw the girl, walking away from her, halfway down.

'Kathy!' she called. The girl looked around then carried on, without hurrying. Magda ran after her, hot and sweating now. The girl reached the end and turned left at a junction. Magda called again. She reached the junction a few moments later and swung around just in time to see the flash of the girl's white dress as she

270

disappeared into the dark doorway of a crypt.

'Kathy, stop!' Magda shouted, scared now. She sprinted down the path and stopped before the tomb. *Gantry*, the inscription on the door read. The door was open a few inches, enough for a little girl to squeeze through. Magda pushed, and the door creaked and ground open a few more inches before becoming stuck. She thrust her head into the gap and looked around. Magda could see nothing in the darkness. With difficulty, she squeezed her way through and stood in the dank blackness, waiting for her eyes to adjust. Inside the tomb it was freezing, as though August hadn't managed to make it beyond the lintel. She heard a scuffling sound.

'Kathy? Are you in here?' Magda took a couple of steps forward, feeling she could make out a shape against the far wall.

Then a noise behind her made her spin. With horror she saw the door swing closed and, with a dull thud, it shut, plunging her into complete darkness. Suddenly swamped with terror she crouched down, unable to see where the threat might be coming from.

But then a hiss and a match was lit. Magda's eyes darted across to see a candlewick glowing. Its dim glow revealed the figure of a man by the back wall. She turned to see another figure by the doorway. Then another match was lit to her left and Magda saw two more figures: the girl and, standing by her, stroking her hair gently, a man in a dark suit, a man she recognized. She remained crouching, breathing shallowly, sweat trickling down her spine, despite the cold.

'I know you,' she said. 'Bishop.'

The man in the suit smiled. 'And I know you, Magda Bilic. And your husband.'

'You killed him.'

Bishop shook his head. 'Not I. It was another. One of great power.'

'You filthy vampires are all the same,' Magda replied. 'I don't care which of you killed him.'

'We are not all the same,' the man said quietly. Magda could tell she'd angered him.

'You like your ranks and divisions, don't you?' she said. 'You like to pretend you're important.'

His eyes flashed and he snarled.

Magda ignored him and looked at the girl. Up close, she could see it wasn't Kathy, she wondered how she could have thought that.

'Who's this?' she asked. 'Your daughter?'

'A waif, under my protection,' Bishop replied. 'But you're here to answer questions, not ask them.'

But Magda smiled broadly, staring him in the eye.

'I remember now. You killed your wife and left your daughter to the tender mercies of the mob.'

Bishop's nostrils flared in anger.

'They killed her,' he spat. 'By setting fire to the house. I was not responsible for her death.'

'She had a lucky escape, to die like that,' Magda replied, looking away. 'Not like this poor wretched replacement you've found. What kind of a life does she have? A half-life? Not even that.'

Bishop breathed hard, visibly trying to control himself. 'You will give me the answers I require,' he said, as calmly as he could manage.

Magda appraised him. He clearly thought she had valuable information for him, otherwise she'd be dead already. She hadn't believed there was any chance of her getting out of this alive. Her intention was to anger Bishop so much he'd kill her quickly, without attempting to turn her. If it hadn't been for Amber she'd have taken her own life long ago. Magda did not fear death. But if Bishop wanted information then maybe she could use this situation to the advantage of the Hunters.

'What do you want to know?' she asked.

Bishop paused a while. A candle spat and flickered briefly, before returning to its steady state.

'Where is your husband?'

Magda stared at his narrow face, golden in the candlelight, almost human. 'My husband is dead.'

He smiled thinly. 'Okay, where is your husband's body?'

Magda's eyes flicked nervously across to Bishop's companions and back. 'I don't know, he did not tell me or the others where he was going the night he left.'

'I don't believe you,' he said.

Magda laughed suddenly, having realized Bishop's purpose.

'You want to find your king. You think Draco found him first.'

Bishop said nothing, just watched, his eyes glowing yellow.

'Well, I tell you this,' Magda said. 'If Draco found him first, then you have no king any more. It's just you and your crew, you may as well give up now.'

Bishop continued to stare at her for some time. Magda had nothing more to say.

Eventually a new voice broke the silence. The little girl.

'She's telling the truth,' she said.

'I know,' Bishop replied.

'No one has seen our master for more than ten years,' the girl went on. Bishop held out a hand and touched a finger to her lips, gently quieting her.

'Why not let her speak?' Magda said.

'I'll speak for both of us,' Bishop said, a new edge to his voice.

'I see on the internet that your new nest calls itself a family,' Magda said. 'Is this how your family treats its children, stilling their tongues?'

Bishop shrugged. 'My children know their place.' He walked towards her and reached out a hand to gently touch her cheek. She turned away. 'Can you say the same for your own brood, old woman?'

Magda turned back, her eyes flashing in anger. 'You stay away from her,' she said.

'Her?' Bishop said, turning away. 'Don't you mean *them*?'

Magda felt sick.

'Perhaps you do not know where your husband is,' he went on. 'Women from your culture seldom do. But from what I hear of your daughters, they have inherited their father's intelligence and his curious nature.'

Bishop spun on his heel. 'They have his blood, you see,' he said. 'The blood of his race. Something which in you is diluted.'

Magda felt a cold root of fear worm its way up her spine. Bishop had had enough of her, and she could see the end game approaching. The vampires to her left and right shuffled closer, sniffing, hissing softly.

'I am not interested in your half-blood,' Bishop said, inspecting his fingernails. Then without looking up, he said, 'You may feed.'

The vampire to her right was quick but Magda quicker still. She turned and held out her palm. '*Horla!*' she cried. The vampire shrieked as a blue, crackling nimbus of energy shot from her palm. It fell to its knees, clutching long-fingered hands to its charred face.

Magda didn't stop to watch but rolled forward. She felt the second vampire brush past her as it lunged. Each of them regained their footing simultaneously and turned to face one another. The vampire rushed her again. This time Magda held out both arms. '*Remulat!*' she cried. The vampire flew backwards and hit the rear wall.

Bishop laughed.

'Not bad for common blood,' Magda said, panting with the effort. She felt drained, spent.

'Not bad for an old woman,' Bishop said. 'But now it ends.'

And Magda was frozen. Something, an invisible force, wrapped itself around her, crushing, tightening, restricting her breathing. A blow to the back of her knees sent her down into a kneeling position. She felt panic rise in her chest and then she saw the girl approaching. The vampire child bared her teeth, wicked teeth, glowing yellow in the candlelight.

Magda smelled the sweet-sick smell of the girl's breath and she closed her eyes, resigned.

CHAPTER SIXTEEN

Kathy was woken by the sound of the doorbell. She'd had a shower while Elizabeth prepared some food and phoned Harry. Elizabeth had told her to go to bed after she'd eaten but Kathy had refused, sure she'd never sleep again. She sat on the sofa and listened to Harry and her aunt discussing the latest developments. Despite her belief it couldn't ever happen again she must have drifted off, because when the doorbell went she was lying on the sofa, covered with a blanket. She could see street lights shining through the front windows. How long had she slept?

She heard her aunt's heavy footsteps coming up the stairs from her study.

'I'll get it,' Kathy called and skipped to the door.

'Kathy, wait!' Elizabeth called, but Kathy had already opened the door.

'Hello, Kathy,' Bishop said. 'We meet at last.'

Kathy couldn't speak. The man from her nightmares was here, in front of her, and she felt as trapped and frozen as she had when bound in sleep. A cold breeze tickled her hair.

'Aren't you going to invite me in?' Bishop said, pleasantly. He didn't look like a vampire. He wore a fedora and the suit of a dandy, a cream shirt underneath, open at the neck, the cuffs so long they obscured his hands. He still carried the silver-handled cane. Nonetheless, the look in his eye was the single most terrifying thing Kathy had ever seen, or imagined.

'Do you think we're that stupid?' Elizabeth said, coming up behind her niece. 'If Harry sees you he will strike you down in a heartbeat.'

'That would be a shame,' Bishop said calmly. 'For it would mean the end of your beloved Amber.' Kathy flinched at the sound of her sister's name. Bishop smiled at her. 'Yes, Kathy, if I don't return to the Church within an hour, Amber will die a slow and painful death. My cane sword is sharp. You are familiar with it, are you not?'

Kathy nodded.

'We're not interested in your mind games, Bishop,' Elizabeth said. 'You have come to bargain, I assume. What is your price?'

Kathy heard a noise behind them. Harry shouted

something in his own language and rushed towards Bishop, fumbling in the bag he always carried with him. Bishop hissed and Elizabeth turned to stop Harry – she fought to keep him under control. 'Harry, stop! He has Amber, we can't risk her life.'

Harry relented and backed off, growling.

'Keep your dog under control,' Bishop said.

'Just tell us why you're here,' Elizabeth replied.

'Simple,' Bishop said. 'Tell me where I can find the Highgate Vampire and I will release Amber.'

'We don't know where the damn vampire is,' Elizabeth said. 'If we did, we would have staked it long ago.'

Bishop looked at Kathy, a smile playing on his lips. 'But Kathy went to see your friend at the museum. He's clever. Sorry, *was* clever. I'm sure he managed to figure it out.'

Kathy shifted uncomfortably. *Haverill? Harving?*

'Kathy?'

'I . . . I might know,' she said.

'Delighted to hear it!' Bishop exclaimed. 'The deal's as good as done. Amber is as good as returned.' He gave a charming grin under evil eyes, but then a concerned look passed over his face. 'Of course, you may find she doesn't want to return to you. I can't speak for her.'

'What have you done to her?' Kathy said. 'Is she a vampire?'

Bishop shook his head. 'No. She has been bitten, but she refuses to feed. If she doesn't feed by the next full moon, she will die.'

'And if she does feed?' Kathy asked, but she knew the answer already. 'That's her choice? To die or to become like you – a monster?'

Bishop's eyes flashed yellow with anger, but he controlled himself. 'It is not her choice now; it is yours.'

'Kathy, there may be another way,' Elizabeth said. 'Harry knows more about vampires than anyone alive – or dead,' she said, glaring at Bishop, who smiled at her. 'There may be a way to help her.'

'I'm getting bored now,' Bishop said, looking out over the darkening street. 'Are you coming?' he asked Kathy.

'She's not going,' Elizabeth said. 'I am.'

Bishop shook his head. 'That's not the offer. Kathy can come, not you.'

'No deal,' Elizabeth said instantly. 'She's not going alone.'

Bishop thought it over. 'Tell you what, you can bring your dog.'

Elizabeth looked to Harry, who nodded.

'I need to grab my jacket,' Kathy said. She ran up the stairs to her room, then into the wardrobe. She grabbed her bag and rummaged in it till she found the red book.

The Amber of her dreams had told her to bring it. Kathy trotted down the stairs at the bottom; she saw Elizabeth talking to Bishop, still on the stairs, Harry glowering in the background, watching them. He turned to look at Kathy, his lined face unreadable.

Harry insisted Bishop walk on ahead.

'We follow,' he said.

Bishop rolled his eyes. 'So mistrustful,' he said, and walked off down the lane.

Elizabeth grabbed Kathy and, when Bishop's back was turned, thrust something cold and heavy into her hand. Kathy looked down to see.

'A glyph of warding,' Kathy said.

'It should offer you some protection at least,' Elizabeth said.

'You don't have a glyph of expulsion, by any chance?' Kathy asked.

Elizabeth blinked in surprise. 'I've never even seen one.'

Kathy closed her eyes and remembered the feeling of power that had run through her body, the intense, seductive almost-orgasm that had left her drained and terrified. She yearned for a repeat of that sensation.

'Come, let us do this,' Harry said. Elizabeth hugged

Kathy wordlessly and the young girl and the old man walked off down the hill. Bishop had stopped a hundred yards away and turned to watch. He waited for them to catch him up a little before walking off again.

'So where?' Harry asked.

'Hmm? Where what?' she asked.

'Where is the vampire?' Harry's eyes were fixed firmly ahead, as though he could see the end of his long quest.

'He's in a tomb, I think in the West Cemetery,' Kathy said. 'But I can't quite remember it exactly.'

Harry snorted angrily.

Kathy felt her own temperature rise. 'Well maybe if you hadn't ripped half my memory out I might have a little more recall.'

Harry nodded. 'Okay, sorry,' he said, gruffly. She let her mind drift. She was there, with Oliver, in the museum. What was the prophecy? Then it came, in a rush.

The Lines of Power shall reveal the Tomb.
The Tavern, the Church and the Daughter of Queens
Have Rings to hold him.

'Havering!' Kathy said. Her sense of relief was physical and she sighed deeply. 'It's Havering!'

'I know it. I know the grave,' Harry said. 'All the time stalking that cemetery.'

'Well, that's where he is,' Kathy said.

Harry reached into his bag and felt something there, as if reassuring himself.

Kathy looked up at the evening sky. A few tendrils of blue still scored through it, as though a planet-sized vampire had been clawing at it.

'Bishop cannot go out in sunlight,' she said, remembering Antwain's explanation, 'but acolytes can.'

Harry grunted in acknowledgement of this truth. 'The more stronger they are, the more older. The more they hate the sun. The more they hate the old magic.'

'It seems to me,' Kathy said, as they walked, with Bishop strolling on ahead of them, whistling, 'that in some ways, the more powerful the vampire, the more weaknesses it has.'

Harry nodded. 'In many ways that may be true, but to them, the balance seems worth it.'

Upon arrival at the Church, Bishop waited for them alongside a cowled acolyte, who held the door open. Kathy hesitated.

'Too late for that, my dear,' Bishop said. 'You're in now.'

Kathy walked into the dark interior first, pushing aside the heavy drape. The interior was dimly lit, quiet and empty. Kathy saw more cowled figures and the small girl vampire Millicent, who smiled a twisted smile at her, now flashing white fangs. Kathy shuddered and carried on. Harry followed her in, his eyes darting around, scanning for threats and escape routes. She was glad he was with her.

'Down the stairs, she's waiting for you on the main stage,' Bishop said. 'I think you know the way.'

As she walked down the steps, she wondered if he'd been aware of her presence when she'd been here before. She was aware of cowled figures in the gloom, waiting. Had Bishop been watching her? Then why not seize her then, why let her go through the farce with Antwain? Then it struck her. He was watching her, to see if she'd lead him to the grave. She, Antwain, they were just pawns on his board. Stamped for sacrifice.

Kathy walked past the dark bar and down the shallow stairs, through the drapes and into the main cavern. A single spotlight illuminated a silver cage in the centre of the stage, within it sat a red-haired girl. Kathy walked slowly towards the stage. The girl had her face turned slightly away, making her hard to recognize. But as Kathy approached she turned slowly and Kathy was struck simultaneously by her beauty but also by the intense sadness in her face.

Amber shook her head. 'You shouldn't have come,' she

said, her voice like delicate crystal in the vast space.

'I came for you, you called me here,' Kathy said.

Amber stood from the simple wooden chair which seemed to be the only item of furniture in the great cage. She wore a simple red dress, her fire-red hair spilled over her slim, porcelain shoulders.

'It's wonderful to see you, Kathy,' Amber said. 'You're so beautiful. But I'm dead, it's too late.' Amber looked over Kathy, into the darkness at the back of the room, where Bishop stood. 'Now he'll kill you too, or worse.'

Kathy shook her head. 'No, we have something he needs. We know where the king vampire is, the Highgate Vampire.'

Millicent giggled suddenly, then clamped her hand over her mouth as Bishop tutted at her.

Amber looked back at Kathy sharply. 'You must not tell him. If he finds the king, he will usurp his power, or attempt to. Either way, they will merge and become inexorable, indestructible. The vampire race would be reborn and destroy humans for ever.'

Bishop laughed. Kathy heard his footsteps on the sprung wooden floor as he approached. 'A nice tale: so dramatic, but your sister does like to exaggerate, Kathy,' he said. 'Firstly, I do not wish to usurp my Lord's throne. I intend only to worship him, to take my place at his side.

As your mother once told me, I am a Bishop, not a king.'

Amber gave a short, hollow laugh and turned away in disgust.

'Secondly, why on earth would vampires wish to destroy the human race? How would we feed?'

'You would have us enslaved!' Amber shouted, turning back to face him, clutching the bars.

'Such drama!' Bishop exclaimed, clapping his hands together.

'You should not have come,' Amber said, turning her attention back to Kathy.

'But you told me to come,' Kathy said. 'In my dreams. And you sent me the book.'

A great tear rolled slowly down her sister's face, reflecting the golden stage light. She shook her head.

'Oh,' Bishop said. He coughed gently. 'That just may have been me.'

Kathy turned to him. She was dimly aware of Viduc staring at her. 'You sent the book?'

Bishop laughed. 'A simple subterfuge,' he said. 'We couldn't unlock the code without your friend at the museum and he wouldn't reveal the code to anyone he didn't trust; you were necessary for our plans.'

Kathy swayed as the realization of what he said hit her.

'So all those dreams? Those visions?'

'All me,' Bishop said, taking a theatrical bow. 'And I sent Antwain here to . . . er, guide you in the right direction.'

Kathy only just managed to avoid gasping at the sound of the name. She flicked a glance at Antwain, hiding his face behind the cowl.

'I needed you, you see. Your sister wouldn't do as I asked. I needed a . . . bargaining tool, shall we say?'

'Bait,' Amber said, 'squirming on the hook. Sacrificed for your twisted ends.'

Bishop shook his head. 'Not necessarily. Once I have released the king I do not care what happens to you.'

'He's lying,' Amber said.

Kathy turned to her. 'What choice do we have?' She sensed Harry shifting slightly as she said this, balancing himself, ready to spring, should it be necessary. The shadowy figures circling the dance floor moved too, imposing themselves on her consciousness. It was her move.

'So, Kathy, what's it to be?' Bishop said.

She paused for a moment, though she'd already made up her mind. Why it was important for her to have them believe she was thinking this through she didn't know.

'I will take you to the crypt which holds the Highgate Vampire,' she said. Amber groaned behind her. 'But we

288

must all go. Amber, Harry and I will not enter the crypt; we will leave before you open the door.'

Bishop shook his head. 'Do you take me for a fool? I will not release any of you until I am sure I have found my king's resting place.'

'Then we will wait at the crypt door until this is confirmed, you can send one of your minions inside to check. Then we will go.'

Bishop considered this. Then nodded. 'Then let us go now,' he said. 'Antwain, open the cage.'

Kathy turned to see Antwain's cowled figure walk across the stage to the cage and unlock it. Amber followed Antwain across the stage and gracefully down the steps. She walked over to Kathy and the girls hugged.

'I'm so glad I've found you,' Kathy said, trying to hold back the wellspring of emotion bubbling up within her. She wasn't used to feeling so much. In her sister's presence, the dead cloak was lifted. If she started crying now she'd never stop. 'I'm sorry if I've done something stupid.'

'I'm glad you're here,' Amber said. 'Even though it *was* kind of stupid. I'm so happy my little sister came to save me.'

'Sorry,' Bishop called, 'but gotta cut this family reunion short, I'm afraid.'

Just before she released her sister, Amber whispered, 'So did you bring the book?'

'Yes,' Kathy whispered back.

'Great,' Amber said.

'What's so important about this book?' Kathy whispered as Amber pulled back.

'You'll see,' she said. Amber turned to Bishop. 'Let's roll.'

Kathy had expected Bishop to lead them back up to the surface, but he took them through the door to the dressing rooms, where she'd been with Antwain. They stopped at Amber's room and Kathy thought they were to go in there, when Bishop turned left instead and took them through the opposite door, the one Kathy had peered into while Antwain was trying to pick the lock of Amber's room. She recognized the dusty chamber within. The sledgehammers and wheelie bin were still there, and more work had been done on the wall. Now within the room, Kathy could see beyond, into the catacombs perhaps. A cold stream of damp air flowed from the hole.

'The church crypt has always been connected with the catacombs,' Bishop explained as they passed within. Millicent was eager to go first, but was held back by one of the acolytes. Harry flicked on a torch and Bishop sneered. 'I forgot your human eyes need such floods of light to see anything.'

As they passed the rubble from the demolished wall, Kathy looked down to see a broken glyph – one of entrapment, like the one in Amber's dressing room. She tapped Amber on the shoulder and pointed it out.

'The vampire killed a priest here in 1993,' Bishop said, noticing the interest and responding, like a tour guide. 'Someone put up entrapment glyphs, as though such a feeble prison would ever have stopped my king.'

'It stopped you,' Amber replied, shortly. 'You had to get your human slaves to knock it down for you.'

Bishop paused slightly, but chose to ignore this comment. He carried on walking, into the gloom.

They entered an arched tunnel and walked along, Harry's torch the only source of light. Bishop and one of the acolytes led the way, Millicent trailing them like a shadow. Antwain and one more cowled figure brought up the rear. Their footsteps sounded dull and muffled in the enclosed space. Kathy felt claustrophobic, the weight of thousands of years and thousands of graves pressing down on her. Bishop's words turned slowly in her mind. *Such a feeble prison* . . .

A prison, within a prison, within a prison, Kathy thought. Harry's ring of glyphs around the cemetery itself, a second set trapping him within the catacombs. Where is the third prison? What has been stopping the Highgate Vampire from rising?

'Your mouldy king has not been seen for twenty years,' Harry said after a minute or so. 'Seems to me he is stopped.'

Bishop hissed but carried on walking. 'He has been sighted many times in the last year; he stalks the cemetery.'

'His shade,' Harry said. 'Only his shade. His solid form is trapped. He hungers and will die soon.'

Bishop spun and was on Harry in a flash, but Harry had a stake in his hand and Bishop found the point pressing against his chest. The two stood there, face to face, vampire and Hunter, ancient enemies, glaring at one another. The acolytes ringed them, unsure how to proceed. But then Bishop released the old man and Harry stepped back.

'You be careful, old man,' Bishop said.

'*You* be careful, demon,' Viduc replied.

Bishop took them to a set of stone steps and led them up into darkness. At the top was a door which he opened with a muttered incantation and led them out into the cool night. Though there were no stars, the clouds reflected enough London light to reveal their surroundings. Kathy turned around, trying to get her bearings. 'I'm not sure where we are,' she said.

Bishop tutted, like an impatient child.

'I know,' Harry said. 'Follow me.'

The strange procession threaded its way through the jumbled graves, past weeping angels and down-turned torches on to a path. Nocturnal creatures rustled in the vegetation to either side, disturbed by the crunching of feet on the gravel path.

Harry took them up the hill to the Egyptian Avenue, leading up to the Circle of Lebanon. Black doors ran up and down the stuccoed walls on either side. Each had a name on a plate. Third from the end upon the right, Harry stopped and pointed to the door.

'Havering?' Bishop said, wondering. 'I knew them. John Havering was a fool, though a rich fool. The Highgate Vampire ate his grandson's heart in 1943, during an air raid.'

Bishop stopped, noticing the expression of disgust on Kathy's face. He stepped over to her and put his face close to hers. She tried not to flinch, unwilling to show him how much she wanted to run, to scream.

'Oh yes, Kathy Bilic,' he whispered, and suddenly she was back in the dark room of her dreams, bound and helpless. 'They all came crowding down into the catacombs, the wealthy, the grand. No one was exempt from Hitler's bombs, however powerful the family name.

So down they came. My master fed well that year.'

'Always a three in the year,' Kathy said.

Bishop eyed her carefully, then nodded. 'Yes, he learned a long time ago to hide. Ignorant humans and vicious Hunters sought him, even here, in his spiritual home.' Bishop glared at Viduc as he said this. 'He found young Millicent near here in 1883 and took her life, giving her immortality in return. It was then that I first learned of his existence. The locals lost their heads and rampaged through the cemetery, opening graves and staking corpses. My master was discovered and his corporeal form destroyed. Millicent escaped and has roamed the cemetery ever since. I bring her meat, do I not, my dear?'

Millicent crooned and rubbed her head against his hip, as though she were a cat.

Bishop pushed her away gently and walked to the door of the tomb and laid his palms against the cold Portland stone, reverentially. The moon was bright now and right overhead, flooding the row with cold light.

'But the townsfolk underestimated the power of Aliza, he merely transmigrated into the body of a young man from Highgate Village.'

Bishop's voice was mesmerizing. In the mild night air Kathy began to feel almost drowsy. She was revolted by the tale, but compelled to go on listening.

'He hid deep in the catacombs for all of ten years, waiting as long as he could. Then he struck again. He chose a different place to go to ground each time, emerging every ten years to feed.'

'Until I find him,' Harry said, breaking the spell somewhat. 'I gave him a good tap,' he said, miming hammering a stake home.

Bishop forced a laugh. 'You did well to find him. But you made the same mistake the villagers made a hundred years before. He transferred into the body of another young man, your assistant. You, the great vampire-hunter, fell for this simple trick. A sleight of hand.'

Harry bristled but Bishop had the power now.

'You didn't even notice he couldn't leave the cemetery. Your own glyphs stopped him in his tracks, but you had other things on your mind, didn't you?'

Harry spat at the ground before Bishop's feet, but said nothing.

'What was it, Harry?' he said, quietly, dangerously. 'Was it a woman? A local woman perhaps? Someone who'd seen the vampire herself, twenty years earlier? A convent girl who survived as her friend was taken by my master?'

Kathy's mouth opened in surprise as she realized whom Bishop was referring to.

295

Bishop turned to her and grinned a twisted grin.

'Yes Kathy, old Harry here has been harbouring unclean thoughts about your aunt.'

The schoolboy slur on Harry didn't concern Kathy. It was the realization that her aunt had been one of the convent girls who'd encountered the vampire way back in 1963. Elizabeth had been chasing this evil for fifty years.

'She felt bad, you see,' Bishop said, with mock empathy. 'She was unable to protect her friend. She has lived with the guilt ever after. But she hasn't seen him since. She is powerless, a joke.'

'Lies!' Harry shouted. 'She has trapped him. Together we trap him. This is the third prison. First Jerusalem, then Romania, now here, he will never leave. The third prison will trap him for ever.'

Bishop frowned, then shook his head.

'I know English isn't your first language, Harry,' he said, 'so that probably explains why you went wrong. But really, Elizabeth should have worked it out by now.'

'What are you taking about?' Kathy said, but she knew where this was heading. Oliver's words came back to her.

'It's not the third prison, or third siege, that will trap Aliza for ever,' Bishop said. 'But three prisons, at once.'

Kathy spoke, 'A prison, within a prison . . .'

'. . . within a prison,' Bishop finished. 'Very good, Kathy.' Then he turned to his acolytes. 'Open the door,' he said. Antwain and the other two revealed short crowbars from their sleeves and went to work on the door. Millicent looked up at Kathy calmly, innocently.

'We've shown you to your king,' Viduc said. 'Now you let us go.'

Bishop shook his head without looking at the old man.

'You've shown me a door, that's all. We check you are telling the truth, then we let you go.'

'Let the girls go, I come down with you,' Harry said.

Now Bishop did look over at Harry, ignoring the crack of stone as the acolytes broke the door.

Kathy saw Antwain flash her a quick look. He seemed worried, trying to tell her something with his eyes.

'We all go down,' Bishop said.

Harry made as if to reply when suddenly a voice cried out from down the slope.

'You there! Stop what you're doing!' A torchlight played across them as someone approached. *No*, Kathy thought. *Stay away.*

Bishop waited for the figure to come closer. Not a policeman, nor a security guard. The man wore the green fleece of the cemetery volunteers.

'What's going on?' the man said. He was young; Kathy

heard uncertainty in his voice, he'd probably thought it was kids, expecting them to run. He had no idea what he'd just walked into.

Bishop grinned and stepped towards the newcomer.

'Run!' Kathy said, finding her voice. The man looked at her, startled and just beginning to realize the danger. He even took a step backwards, but he was slow, too slow. Bishop was on him in half a second. The young man screamed and went down.

Then Kathy felt something knock her to one side and it was a moment before she realized it was Harry, stake in hand. He shoulder-charged Bishop, hunched over the man, and sent him sprawling.

Bishop hissed and sprang to his feet. Unsheathing the cane sword, he turned to meet the attack.

Millicent and the acolytes rushed to their master's aid, but he held up a hand to stop them.

'I've been waiting for this for fifty years,' Bishop snarled.

'Me too,' Viduc replied.

'Secure them,' Bishop said, indicating Kathy and Amber.

Antwain didn't move. The other two acolytes ducked forward and grabbed the girls' hands roughly, twisting them behind their backs.

Viduc lunged forward with the stake, Bishop flinched

away, holding up the sword in defence, respectful of his wily old adversary.

'You stink of garlic,' Bishop said, circling his opponent. 'You do know that garlic has no effect on vampires? It's an old wives' tale.'

'Very interesting,' Viduc said, reaching inside his shirt, fumbling for something. 'What about this, this an old wives' tale too?' He flung out an arm in a great sweeping motion, showering Bishop with a fine spray of liquid. Bishop turned away, protecting himself with an arm. It was difficult to make out detail in the blue light but Kathy thought she saw a few drops hit Bishop's hand and wrist. He hissed sharply, dropped the sword and shook his hand, like a baseball player hit on the hand by a line drive.

'Holy water!' Harry cried.

'You don't say,' Bishop hissed in response, nursing his burned limb.

Harry went to make another sweep but Bishop was too quick for him; he darted inside Harry's defence, collected the sword and slashed at the coiled arm holding the bottle – Kathy saw the glint of the steel in the moonlight then the bottle was flying and Harry had fallen away, backwards, clutching his injured arm. He regained his composure quickly though and turned to face the vampire before Bishop could press home the advantage. Harry backed away, breathing heavily, black drops falling from his sleeve. Millicent's mouth opened and a black tongue licked out, her nostrils flaring at the scent of the blood.

'Got anything else, old man?' Bishop asked, creeping forward, backing Harry up against a black crypt door on the opposite row of the terrace.

Harry shifted the stake to his injured hand and fumbled in the pack again. He pulled out a silver crucifix and held it up to the vampire's face. Bishop flinched again and took a step back.

'Don't like this, huh?' Harry said. 'The sign of Our Lord?'

'The sign of a fool,' Bishop replied. 'The poor, gullible fool. He gave us such power, offered us his blood, his flesh. We took it, we grew, we became stronger.'

'You killed him,' Viduc said, anger in his voice.

'No, we betrayed him,' Bishop replied. 'You humans killed him.'

'And yet he still has power over you,' Harry said, stepping forward and thrusting the crucifix forward.

But Bishop did not flinch again. He stood firm and slashed again with his sword. Kathy heard a *snick* as the sword sliced clean through the old man's wrist. Harry fell to his knees, groaning with pain. In the dim moonlight, Kathy could see a black cloud enveloping Harry's shirt as he held the bloody stump pressed tightly into his armpit. In the silence, a couple of seconds later, Kathy heard the tinny clatter of silver on stone as the crucifix fell to earth somewhere in the distant confusion of tombs.

'No!' Amber called, as Bishop took a step forward towards the defeated Viduc. Bishop looked up at her.

'You want me to show mercy to the man who swore to kill me?' he asked.

'I want you to keep your side of the bargain,' Amber said.

Bishop shook his head. 'He changed the bargain, when he attacked me.'

'So let's make a new bargain,' Amber said.

Bishop considered this. 'Go on,' he said.

'Let him go, and my sister, and I will . . . do what you want.'

Kathy gasped. 'No, Amber.'

'You will feed?' Bishop said.

'I will feed,' Amber said. 'And I will join you.'

Bishop stayed quiet for a while. 'It's a good move,' he said. 'I didn't expect it.'

'No, Amber,' Kathy repeated.

Amber turned to her. 'I'm dead anyway, Kathy,' she said. 'I'm lost to you, to everyone. And I hear now Oliver is dead also, is that true?'

Kathy nodded, tears in her eyes.

'The only thing to live for is you, and the only thing to die for is you,' Amber said.

'Then it is settled,' Bishop said. 'You will feed. You will feed now.' He seized one of the acolytes and dragged him forward, mewling. Bishop pushed the terrified acolyte down on to the path by Amber. Kathy could see the confusion and fear in his eyes. She stepped forward but her wrist was seized from behind; she looked back to see Antwain looking at her, shaking his head. Amber whispered something to him and leaned forward.

The acolyte turned his head, exposing his throat.

'No!' There came a roar and Kathy looked up to see Harry, stake in his lesser-injured hand. He sprang at Bishop, who leaped backwards, acrobatically. One of the acolytes darted forward to protect his master. Harry, finding his original target absent, rammed the stake deep into the acolyte's chest. The young vampire screamed and fell back against the tomb wall. He slid down the smooth stone, feet kicking and scrabbling to hold himself up as his body failed. Black blood pumped out over the exposed wooden stake. Harry had fallen to his knees again, spent with the effort.

Ignoring his stricken comrade, Bishop stepped forward, seeing the chance to end it.

Aware of the danger, Kathy yanked hard away from Antwain and pulled out the glyph from her pocket. She lurched forward awkwardly and thrust the amulet into Bishop's face. He recoiled as he realized what it was and shuffled backwards, genuine fear and hate in his eyes. But then Kathy felt a blow on her outstretched arm. It was Millicent, swinging a crowbar and knocking the glyph into a stand of nettles down the terrace. Kathy slumped to her knees, holding her throbbing wrist, sick with the pain.

'Children's magic,' Bishop sneered, confident now his ward had saved him. He shoved Kathy aside. She fell heavily against a tomb door, right beside the staked vampire, who was now screaming wordlessly as his struggles died away.

Bishop strode forward again.

'Harry!' Amber cried and tried to struggle to free herself. But Bishop ignored her; the sword flashed again as he slashed upwards, just once, but with immense speed and power, ripping through Harry's throat and snapping his head back. The body stayed in the kneeling position for some time, the jaw hanging disjointedly, windpipe exposed and bubbling with Harry Viduc's last, unconscious breaths. Then the corpse slumped forward, mercifully hiding the hideous death mask.

'Let's stop mucking about,' Bishop snarled. He grabbed

Amber and pushed her towards the door. 'Bring her,' he said to Antwain, who helped Kathy to her feet and led her along, refusing to look her in the eye.

CHAPTER SEVENTEEN

Down, down and down, the spiral steps led. Millicent led the way, with Amber and her acolyte following, then came Bishop and then Antwain and Kathy. The air felt dry and cold, so cold. Kathy felt her lips cracking. Antwain held her hand tightly, leading, rather than pulling her down. She could see little and soon enough they were in pitch darkness. But then ahead she saw a flare of blue light. Bishop's hand glowed with some unearthly phosphorescence. Too dark even for vampires, it seemed.

'These crypts were built deep, to join up with the catacombs,' Antwain whispered as they descended. 'They liked a lot of space, the Victorians.'

'Thanks for the history lesson,' Kathy said, coldly. 'What's going to happen to us? Same thing that happened to Harry?'

'I don't know,' Antwain replied. 'He's unpredictable.

Hard to read. He has a plan, some strategy.'

Not for the first time, Kathy wished Oliver were here. He'd know what to do.

'What about you?' Kathy whispered. 'Are you going to help us?'

Antwain paused before answering. 'I will do what I can, but . . .'

'But what? But not if it gets you in trouble with the boss?'

Antwain stopped and turned to her, furious. 'I have made my choice, Kathy Bilic. I know myself and my place in this world. You have yet to make that choice. When you do, then you may judge me and not before; I have seen more than you will ever know.'

'Antwain, do not dawdle!' Bishop called from below. Antwain glared at Kathy and pulled her on.

A few minutes later they reached the bottom. A large cavern, with four arched doorways set in each wall. One large sarcophagus lay in the centre of the room. On the far wall, above the door, a mosaic could be seen, an angel holding a downturned torch, to signify a life snuffed out. Whoever lay in the casket had died young. The six of them stood silently, looking around, even Bishop apparently awed by their surroundings.

'He's in there?' Kathy asked.

Bishop laid his hand on the sarcophagus and closed his eyes. He breathed deeply, nostrils flaring.

Then he shook his head. 'No. But he's close, I can sense him.'

Kathy looked to the gaping maw of the doorway closest to her. She shivered, suddenly realizing how cold it was down here. Then she heard something beyond the arch. A shuffle. Then a step.

Millicent walked to Bishop's side and he rested a hand on her shoulder. Antwain and the other acolyte each held tightly to Kathy's and Amber's wrists. The chamber glowed dully, illuminated only by the nimbus of light surrounding Bishop's hand.

Out of the darkness beyond the arched doorway came a figure. Amber gasped and Millicent shuffled backwards in a convincing display of fear. The figure was not tall. Not imposing in any way. It was a man of indeterminate age. It was obvious he'd once been handsome, but his face was pale and drawn, grey and lined with some hellish internal existence. To Kathy, his features seemed strangely familiar. He wore a simple checked shirt, stained almost black with accumulated dust and filth. His dark eyes stared back at the visitors impassively. The six stared back at the one.

Bishop laughed. Then stopped. He dropped his head to one side and looked incredulous.

'You?' he said. Then, 'But of course.'

'My God,' Amber breathed, softly.

'Who is he?' Kathy whispered.

Bishop heard and looked over to Kathy, grinning evilly.

'Kathy Bilic,' he said, 'meet Draco Bilic, your father.'

The room spun and Kathy slumped, panic rising. How could this be possible? The filthy man looked up at her, then over to Amber. He stared at them for what seemed like minutes, then suddenly, magically, his face softened and he smiled, briefly, his eyes lighting. Immediately he seemed more human.

Something inside Kathy broke at that moment. She slumped to the floor, Antwain releasing her. She burst into tears. She felt as though the blanket had been lifted off her. She'd felt a hint of this on the dance floor, when she'd found Amber. But that was as nothing compared to this – like the bubble surrounding her feelings, which had dulled her senses all her life, had burst in an instant. Whatever deep block had been crushing her, squashing her, stopping her feeling, suddenly was released and the emotion poured out, raw, like water from a broken dam. Her mother's death, her lost father, her dying adoptive-father, Becky, Oliver, Jack, all those lost or half lost. Suddenly she felt their pain, she felt her own pain. She could feel – and the most powerful emotion of all wasn't

308

grief, or regret, or anger. It was relief, relief that she was normal after all, she wasn't some kind of psychopath, unable to feel. She had a past – and a present.

Draco had taken a step towards her as she'd broken down, but Millicent stepped out and wagged a finger at him.

'It's okay, Daddy,' Amber said. 'Everything's going to be okay.'

'What the hell is going on?' Antwain said from behind Kathy.

Bishop shot him a furious look. 'Speak when you're spoken to,' he snapped. 'But in answer to your question, I think I might know.'

Bishop walked forward and stood directly before Draco, eyeing him closely.

'You see our old friend Harry Viduc thought he had my king trapped, within his double prison. It seems your father here knew better. Am I right, Draco?'

Draco said nothing, watching Bishop with a look of hatred on his dusty face.

'You knew, didn't you? You knew that to trap the king you needed not one, not two, but three prisons. A siege, within a siege, within a siege.'

Bishop turned his back on Draco and looked towards the girls. The ball of light lifted from his hand and floated up to the tiled ceiling, where it strengthened and cast a healthier glow over the assembly.

'Harry's glyphs provided the first prison. Then you added a second ring, within the catacombs. But what of the third?' Bishop said, a frown of mock puzzlement on his face. 'Draco found the answer. The third prison is . . . Draco himself.' Bishop turned to Kathy and pointed a long finger at the beaten man in the doorway.

'You see, my master has the ability to move from body to body. Human minds, he can easily control. Once he inhabits a body, he quickly takes over and the former inhabitant of that body is gradually crushed and destroyed. When he moves to a new host, the body will die, the former mind long since lost. However, your father is a Hunter, an entirely different breed. A lot tougher, mentally and physically too, by the looks of things.' Bishop patted Draco on the shoulder; the Hunter pulled away, slowly.

Kathy kneeled, gazing up at her father. She had controlled the tears, but felt exposed and vulnerable, exquisitely sensitive, as though she could be broken again by a harsh word.

'Your father broke into the tomb,' Bishop went on, 'sealing it up behind him. He descended, opened the sarcophagus and staked the body within. My master left that body and, having little choice, entered the body of your father. It seems Draco was able to maintain mastery of his own vessel. My king was unable to overcome his mind.'

Bishop gazed at Draco in admiration and fascination. 'What a titanic struggle it must have been,' he muttered. 'What a war has been fought behind those eyes.'

Draco looked away, showing the tiniest amount of pain at the memory.

'And he is still there, still within his cage,' Bishop said. 'Draco has been holding my king, entrapped, within his own mind for nearly twenty years.'

'How did you survive?' Amber asked. Her father looked over at her. Bishop waited for him to respond.

Draco opened his mouth, as though trying to remember how to speak. He croaked, then swallowed, then tried again.

'I have been drawing power from the ley line,' he said, in a thin, dry voice. 'I do not need food. No more than he would need. I turned the power of the graveyard itself to my advantage.' Draco stopped, seemingly exhausted by his marathon speech.

'And what do you do with your time down here?' Bishop asked with a jaunty grin. 'Poker nights with the dead? All-night parties with the cockroaches?'

Draco looked at him, oblivious to the sarcasm. 'I sleep,' he said. 'I dream.' Then he looked up at the girls and smiled warmly. Kathy felt the tears bubbling up again.

'Sounds awfully dull,' Bishop said. 'But never fear, old man, I'm here to release you from your self-imposed task.'

Draco shook his head, but Bishop had already placed a hand on his brow. Amber lunged forward but her acolyte grabbed her around the neck and forced her to her knees, next to Kathy. Antwain clamped a firm hand on Kathy's shoulder and squeezed gently, though whether to offer reassurance or a warning Kathy couldn't know. Kathy couldn't have moved anyway, she had no power in her body. Her limbs felt loose and useless. Empty and drained. All she could do was watch.

Bishop murmured quietly, still holding his hand over Draco, who also seemed frozen, or perhaps resigned, too weak from his self-imprisonment to resist. After a time, Kathy felt the temperature in the chamber drop further and she shivered as she saw a faint halo surround her father, a dusty cloud which seemed to ooze from his pores. Draco moaned softly and then slumped to his knees.

'It wasn't just Bishop,' Amber said, suddenly.

Kathy looked up. 'What do you mean?'

'Within you. He said that it was just him sending you the visions, encouraging you to come. I could sense what he was doing, he had to explore deep inside my mind to find out about you.'

'I felt you, I heard you,' Kathy said. 'At the party. You warned me. Then again in the garden at Aunt Elizabeth's. The little girl was Bishop, but you were there too, you were inside me.'

Amber nodded and smiled.

'Thank you,' Kathy said.

'You were riding on his power, my friend,' Bishop said, the incantation completed. 'He was keeping you alive, you should be grateful.' Draco looked anything but grateful. He tottered a little and Bishop shoved him over with a booted foot. The vampire looked down on the dusty old man. 'And maybe you kept him alive too,' he said, thoughtfully.

Kathy felt the tears come again but swallowed them down. She had half an eye on the dust cloud that was the Highgate Vampire. Bishop turned and bowed to the shimmering particles. 'Oh master, I have waited so long for this moment. I have brought a choice of new vessels for you.'

The dust cloud shifted, the bluish light of Bishop's nimbus reflecting a million particles, floating and forming themselves. It floated gently towards the kneeling girls and seemed to pause for a moment as if inspecting them for flaws. Then it moved firmly towards Amber.

CHAPTER EIGHTEEN

The cloud swept over Amber. Kathy heard her sister's sharp intake of breath as it flowed around her, then it was gone. Kathy looked at Amber, fearfully, waiting for the snarl and the yellow flash of eyes.

Amber looked back at her and shrugged. Then the girls heard a moan from behind. Turning, Kathy saw Amber's acolyte, holding his head in his hands. He sighed. Pulling his hands away, the acolyte stood up straight and his eyes flashed yellow. He opened his mouth, curling back full lips to reveal a new set of jagged teeth, the canines curving down wickedly.

'A wise choice,' Bishop said, nodding obsequiously. 'You must be hungry, my Lord. As you have seen, these girls are Hunters. They have Draco's blood.'

He walked towards his master, peering at him through the gloom. 'They are . . . resistant to our creed's rituals,' he said, regarding Amber. 'But their blood is rich and powerful. Perfect for breaking a fast.'

The Highgate Vampire stood still, perhaps getting used to its new home. Then it moved an arm, inspecting the hand. Kathy knew she should say something, plead for their lives. But she just didn't have the energy. It was like there was another type of vampire in the room, a psychic vampire, feeding on emotion, on reason.

'So this is the reason you wanted us both here,' Amber said. 'It wasn't about the location of the tomb. You wanted our blood, for him.'

'It was that too,' Bishop said, smiling gently. He could afford to be generous with his smiles now. He'd won the game. 'I knew what had happened some ten years ago, when I discovered your father had gone missing,' he said. 'I asked your mother about it, but she wasn't forthcoming.'

Kathy looked up at this; she felt a surge of anger, finally something to grip on to. She nursed the anger, goading herself, girding herself, as Bishop continued.

'Now your mother's blood? Not so good,' he said, grimacing. 'But it was more what she didn't say than what she did. I knew about the outer ring of glyphs, around the cemetery. We'd discovered another set, within the catacombs. I knew your father would have it figured out, even if that idiot Viduc hadn't. When it became obvious

315

that neither he nor your mother knew where Draco had disappeared to, I wondered if he'd come here and been killed. I had no idea he was capable of this. I have to say I actually admire him for that.'

Bishop waited.

Aliza shuffled behind Amber and she moved forward, away from him, but didn't take her eyes from Bishop. Ignoring the Death which stood behind her, sharpening its scythe.

Kathy was dimly aware that Antwain had retreated into the shadows, presumably out of respect for the ancient vampire.

Aliza stepped out into the light, blinking slightly, and slowly turned, looking around appraising each of them in turn. Everyone watched him, fascinated.

'Draco's was a noble sacrifice,' Bishop said, 'but futile. It was only a matter of time before we discovered the location. Besides, he couldn't have survived for ever. Somehow my master would have outlived him and, upon the death of Draco, Aliza would have been released, to find a new host.'

'And what now?' Amber asked.

'Now he feeds, now he grows stronger, now he has a nest to support him,' Bishop answered, inspecting his fingernails. 'The human members of our organization can remove the outer prison glyphs and my master will be able to roam the world once more.'

'With you at his right hand, I suppose?' Amber asked.

'I would not presume,' Bishop said, bowing his head.

Kathy felt sick. As Bishop's head ducked, Amber whispered to her, 'The book?'

Kathy glanced over at her sister, surprised that she might still be thinking of fighting back. She nodded.

'Give it to me,' Amber said.

Kathy jammed a hand into her satchel and pulled out the book. She handed it to Amber, just as Bishop lifted his head. He saw the exchange and the overhead light flickered slightly, suggesting a disturbance of his equanimity. But he made no move to stop them.

'That won't do you any good,' he said, with an indulgent grin. 'If there were something in that book that could hurt me, I'd never have sent it to you.'

He stepped forward and held out a hand. Amber clutched the closed book, toying with the binding.

'Now pass it over,' Bishop said, standing in front of Amber. 'The book holds many secrets, but not ones that can hurt me, not now.'

'No,' Amber said coldly. She tore the spine of the book away and pulled something out, about a hand's-length, and thin. 'But this can.'

With surprising speed, Amber lunged upwards and forwards at the same time, thrusting out the thin wooden shard she'd pulled from the book-binding. She seemed to punch his chest and leaped away to one side, executing a neat forward roll and ending up next to Draco. She didn't bother to turn back to see the result of her strike, but instead began muttering something into her father's ear.

Bishop stood, rocking back slightly on his heels, a look of astonishment on his face. Just half an inch of the thin stake jutted from his chest. His cream shirt grew a crimson rose, rapidly expanding. He looked at Kathy, as though asking her to explain just what had happened. 'What . . . ? What . . . ?' he said, Death already clutching at him, even as he stood.

'Checkmate,' Kathy said.

Then Bishop's face changed, crumpled. He seemed to take one last breath, then his head seemed to topple backwards and dissolve, as it became dust. Millicent screamed and ran past Kathy, heading for the stairs. Bishop's dark suit collapsed slowly to the floor of the chamber, supported by nothing. Kathy heard a faint clank as the cane head hit the stones. Then, with Bishop's death, the overhead light went out and they were plunged into darkness.

The darkness seemed to trigger something behind her

318

and she remembered the Highgate Vampire. Kathy found the strength to stand and turned, as she did, to see the flash of the yellow eyes, the vampire advancing, slowly, but inexorably. The eyes seemed to cast a faint light themselves. She saw a spindly arm reach out for her and she took a step back. Again the vampire advanced but it was still weak from its fast.

'Kathy?' She dimly heard Amber's voice from somewhere; it seemed a million miles away. Her throat was dry with fear, she could not speak to answer.

Kathy fumbled in her pockets and satchel. Empty. She had no crucifix. No glyph. Even the book was gone. Kathy felt her back hit the wall of the crypt. There was nowhere to run. The eyes approached. Kathy tried to scream, but the deadness, the blackness, the darkness cloaked her again, suffocating, smothering. The vampire was weak but its magic was growing stronger by the second.

Then there was a flash of light from somewhere to Kathy's right and the vampire grinned – or snarled – its teeth white and glistening.

'No,' Amber shouted, realizing what was happening. Kathy sensed her sister scrambling to her feet, but it was too late, the vampire was on her . . .

And then it wasn't, as another body charged out of the shadows and, with a thump and a tangle of limbs, took the vampire down. Antwain. The vampire screamed and cast the young acolyte aside, slamming him against the wall. The vampire got slowly to his feet and advanced on Kathy again.

This time it was Amber who moved to protect her sister. She rushed to the heap of dusty clothes which was all that was left of Bishop and searched amongst them.

'What are you doing?' Kathy gasped.

'Looking for this,' Amber replied, holding up the stake, but it was useless – only the half-inch which hadn't entered Bishop's chest remained, the rest burned away.

The vampire watched, amused; he was pulling in power. It laughed – at first wheezy, then an evil croaking cackle. Then it sprang forward like a cat and seized Amber. She shrieked and punched, but her strength was no match for that of Aliza. He seized her long red hair and pulled her head to one side, exposing the throat. Blood bulged through her veins.

Kathy ran, weaponless, and leaped on to the vampire's back. Instantly she found herself slumped against a wall, breathless. Kathy lay helpless, watching the vampire plunge its wicked teeth into Amber's flawless throat. Amber went rigid in his embrace, as though in ecstasy, her face contorted with exquisite agony.

Kathy closed her eyes, defeated; a light within her flickered and dimmed. It was over. The dead feeling within her had won the fight, as she knew it would. She had nothing more. Her body, bruised and exhausted, seemed almost to melt into the floor, so little strength remained within her. The sounds of the vampire mauling her sister sickened her, she wanted to stuff her ears and scream.

But Kathy heard another voice. 'The coffin. Look in the coffin.' It was Antwain. He lay face down, a few feet away, breathing shallowly. Obviously in pain. But his eyes were alert and earnest. Belatedly, she realized it was him casting the light. His finger pointed to the sarcophagus in the centre of the room.

Kathy got half a breath into her lungs and staggered to her feet. She dragged herself across the room, trying not to listen to the sounds of tearing gristle and ripping flesh. She reached the sarcophagus and hauled at the lid. It wouldn't move.

She closed her eyes, channelling. *Come on Amber, one more time,* Kathy thought to herself. *I need you, I need your strength.* And as Amber's lifeblood was drained, and her body jerked and shook in the tight embrace of the Highgate Vampire, something passed between the sisters. Something insubstantial, something beyond physics.

Kathy breathed in slowly, feeling the strength flood through her veins, like a drug, ice-cold and flame-hot at the same time. Then she opened her eyes, reborn, suddenly full of energy, alive and sharp-eyed. She heard Amber's body slump to the ground as the vampire finished feeding. It screamed, engorged with new-found and welcome strength – like Kathy.

Again Kathy hauled upwards on the coffin lid and, this time, she felt the faintest glimmer of movement, stone against stone. Encouraged, she tried again. Despite the flood of energy which now suffused her, she still found herself crying out with the strain, but she got what she wanted. The great stone lid went crashing down on to the far side. She saw instantly what Antwain had been referring to. Inside the sarcophagus lay a pile of dust, clothes and – jammed halfway through a denim jacket – a stout wooden stake. The stake her father had used to kill Viduc's assistant, or at least his body, the former vessel for the vampire.

She grabbed it and spun, to see the vampire approaching once more, its jaw and chest soaked with the red-black blood of her sister. Kathy stood firm, clutching the stake like a lifeline. Suddenly the light strengthened and the crackling nimbus descended from the ceiling, dropping between her and the vampire. From the corner of her eye

Kathy saw Antwain, on his feet, limping over to stand beside her.

The vampire flinched away from the bright light, scowling.

'Go,' Antwain said. 'Get out of here. I'll hold him off.'

Aliza stepped towards them and held out a hand, his laughter having ceased. Antwain stumbled and swayed to put himself between the vampire and Kathy, but Aliza swept his arm across and again knocked the teenage acolyte into the wall with a crunch of bone. Antwain fell to the floor and this time lay there, still.

Kathy held up the stake, but the vampire shook his head. He muttered a word, flicked a long finger, and the stake flew out of her hands and across the floor, into the shadows. Oliver's words came back to her. *It's best done when they're asleep.* Then the vampire was on her and Kathy felt herself lifted up for inspection.

Close up, Kathy could see the changes wrought by the vampire within the acolyte's body. The once-handsome, youthful face had twisted and changed, ageing a hundred years in minutes. The hair was lank and stank of foulness. The eyes were almond-shaped and bright yellow. Aliza opened his mouth, his foetid breath nearly causing Kathy to pass out.

'You have nothing left, Kathy Bilic,' the vampire growled,

reading her mind. 'No stake. No magic. No friends.'

'Maybe,' came a gravelly voice from behind the Highgate Vampire. The creature stiffened, its eyes opening in astonishment. 'She does have one thing though.'

Kathy looked down to see the point of a stake sticking out of the vampire's chest. As she watched, a drop of blood formed and fell from the tip, dropping in slo-mo down, down and down on to the dusty floor, between the vampire's feet.

'She has her family,' her father said, as she felt the arm holding her aloft lose its strength. She fell to the floor along with the vampire in an awkward tangle of limbs and ended up face to face with the creature. It screamed, a noisome blast of death across her face. She shut her eyes and felt someone pull her up and away.

Her father dragged her to safety and held her tight as the vampire died, howling, another vessel destroyed. Draco spoke words, an incantation. As the body of the Highgate Vampire's latest host dropped to the floor a glow of yellow appeared above it, now writhing in an unseen cage.

When Kathy opened her eyes all was quiet. It took her a moment, but then she realized the chamber was still lit.

'Is that your light?' she asked.

Draco shook his head. 'I have no light. Aliza – he is

held for now. Look, your friend is still alive.'

Kathy looked over to Antwain, lying in a pool of blood. His arm twitched and he shifted his head slightly, watching them and watching the vampire. Did she see a tear in his eye?

'Can we go now?' Kathy asked.

'You and your friend must leave,' Draco said. 'I must remain.'

'What?' Kathy asked, pulling herself up. She kneeled, looking into her father's face. She could see herself in his tired features, and Amber too. 'Why?'

Draco smiled weakly. 'So much like your mother,' he said, trailing a finger down her cheek. 'I must stay here to hold the vampire. He is not dead.'

'*You cannot kill the king,*' Oliver had said. '*You can only trap him.*'

'But I can't bear the thought of you being down here, on your own, in the dark,' Kathy said.

Antwain groaned as he pulled himself up on to hands and knees. He stayed in that position, head down, blood dripping into the pool beneath him.

'You must go now,' Draco said. 'Your friend needs a doctor.'

'I'm not leaving you,' Kathy said.

'You must, Kathy,' Draco said. He held her face in his

hands. 'This is our family's curse. We are enjoined to this place. Like the vampire himself. One of us must remain here always. But don't worry about me. I have seen my daughters now, and the memory of this moment will never leave me. It will shine bright in the darkness.'

'But Bishop said you couldn't survive for ever,' Kathy said. 'And when you die, the vampire will be released once more.'

'I'll hang on as long as I can,' Draco said, with a smile. 'Who knows, I might just outlive him, then it is I who will find my freedom. I may see you again.'

Kathy burst into tears and buried her face in his dusty chest, having run out of arguments. 'Poor you,' she said, 'poor Amber.'

'Amber is still alive,' Draco said. He touched her chest. 'She's in here, do you not feel her?' Kathy nodded. 'The two of you should never have been parted. Whilst apart, you were incomplete. Now you are together, for ever.'

As Kathy rested her head against her father's chest, she felt the rhythm of his breathing, of his life. He hugged her tightly and smelled her hair, then he muttered something. Words familiar to her. But in a language she didn't understand. Something changed, something inside her. Then she felt herself released. A curious and quite familiar detachment stole over her.

Remembering something, she reached into her pocket. 'Take this,' she said, handing him the framed photograph. The corners of his mouth twitched upwards as he recognized the picture, taken so long ago.

'Thank you – now go,' he said. He stood and walked over to the body of the acolyte. The shadowy haze was assembling itself again, above the prone figure. Draco turned one more time and smiled, then he turned back and held out his hand, to take back his burden.

Kathy sobbed and turned away. She stumbled as she rose and went to help Antwain, who was now standing, unsteadily. He looked disappointed, broken; she put an arm round him and they shuffled off towards the stairs.

Together they began to ascend, a step at a time.

Kathy didn't look back.

CHAPTER NINETEEN

Two bloodstained figures sat on the steps of an elegant town house in Highgate. A girl and a boy. The faintest traces of the new day could be seen over the distant city. The boy held an unlit cigarette in his mouth and patted his pockets. 'Fuck it,' he said, eventually. 'Lost my matches.'

The girl sat staring across the street, into the shadows from which they'd escaped. She replied after a delay.

'Those things'll kill you,' she muttered.

'Okay, Mom,' Antwain replied. 'What's the time?'

Kathy pulled out her phone. 'Ten to five,' she said.

Antwain sucked on the cold cigarette, then his cheeks let out and released the air slowly.

There was a long silence.

'What happened?' Kathy said. 'In there, just now?'

Antwain looked over at her, half surprised. Then he grinned wryly.

'Poor Kathy,' he said. 'Never allowed to remember nothing.'

She looked down at herself. A torn strip of T-shirt was wrapped around her wrist. 'I'm bleeding,' she said.

'You let me feed,' Antwain reminded her. 'I was injured. You saved me.'

Kathy looked at him. A lamp post a dozen yards up the hill lit his face with dashes of gold. 'I'm glad,' she said, and smiled.

'I gotta go now,' Antwain said. 'You gotta go too. Your aunt will be worried.'

Kathy nodded. 'What are you going to do now?' she asked.

Antwain looked back at the cemetery. At the darkness. He shook his head. 'First I'm gonna buy some matches. Then I'm going to think for a while. About what to do next. Y'know? Which way I'm going to go.'

'Up the hill, or down,' Kathy said quietly. 'Whatever you do, take it one step at a time, okay?'

'Yeah,' he said. 'One step at a time.'

Antwain leaned across. Kathy turned her head and they kissed. Not for long, but not without urgency.

'Thanks,' Antwain said.

Kathy smiled, and he was gone so fast she didn't see which way he turned out of the gate. Up, or down.

Kathy hauled her aching bones upright and up to the door. She rang the bell and, while she waited, looked up at the curious carving above the door.

The door opened cautiously and her aunt looked out. Elizabeth gasped to see Kathy's bloodstained, dishevelled appearance, then ushered her in and gave her a huge bear hug.

'Oh my darling Kathy,' Elizabeth said, pulling back to look at her niece. 'Are you hurt?'

Kathy shook her head. Her mind was full of cotton wool, but she felt safe here. Everything was going to be okay now, she knew.

'Is there anyone else?' Elizabeth asked, looking out down the street. Kathy stared at her blankly.

Elizabeth's face fell for a moment, but then she recovered. 'Come on dear, a hot bath for you, then sleep. We can talk about this tomorrow.'

As she followed her aunt upstairs, a flash of remembrance washed across her and, for a second, she was back there in the crypt, her sister's body crumpled on the floor, dusty clothes littering the stones, yellow dust. Her father standing, watching her go. Then it was gone. And Kathy felt a pang as the memories abandoned her, like everything else had abandoned her, leaving her with the blanket. The cloud, the muffled deadness of her own mind, shorn of its family.

In the morning what vestigial memory remained would be gone entirely. She would return to New York the same as she'd left. Having gained nothing. No truth, no strength, no history.

Kathy burst into tears. She cried silently throughout her bath, dressing in her nightdress, climbing into bed. By this stage she didn't know why she was crying, she didn't know what she'd lost. Her aunt left eventually, close to tears herself, and Kathy lay in bed as the morning light crept under the curtains, making urgent inquiries as to why she was going to bed at this time.

And just then, when all seemed lost, when Kathy found herself without hope, without even the pain of remembrance, when all she had to hope for was a quiet return home to her loving foster-mother, to find that her foster-father might still cling to life, something came to Kathy. Some*one* came to Kathy.

The now-familiar fluttering in her belly. A warmth, emanating from within. Burgeoning, blossoming inside her, like a time-lapse film of a flower bud in spring. Kathy took a sharp breath as the warmth spread, feeding her soul, opening her mind. It was like a second life had been begun in her belly, in her soul. A life richer and stronger than her own. As though she were merely the vessel for an altogether more worthy occupant.

'*Sleep now, sister,*' a voice whispered to her. '*We need strength.*'

'And what a sad day,' Elizabeth said to Kathy when she came down a few hours later. She felt content, and bright, full of life for once. She'd obviously needed a good night's sleep. The kitchen was warm. Soft light floated in through the French doors to the garden and birds chattered outside.

'But what a happy day too,' her aunt went on. 'Because today you go home, and your mother phoned this morning to say your father's condition has rather unexpectedly improved.'

'Oh my God, really?' Kathy asked, wide-eyed.

Elizabeth nodded, grinning. 'He's still under close observation, but the cancer is retreating, for now. He may even be able to return home soon.'

Kathy stared at her aunt, trying to take in this wonderful news. Then she rushed to her, giving her a hug. 'I knew today was going to be a good day,' Kathy said.

Elizabeth looked at her niece, searching for something in her eyes. She shook her head slightly, a thin smile on her lips.

'I'm so pleased for you,' she whispered. 'Now,

I'm making you scrambled eggs, go and sit down. I'll get the coffee.'

Kathy sat at the great wooden table and sighed happily. Elizabeth shuffled off into the kitchen, and if, as she went, she glanced at a picture which sat on the piano, a picture of a long-haired old man, it was only for half a second.

And Kathy didn't notice.

'Ladies and gentlemen, we will be taking off shortly. Please ensure tray tables are up and your seat is restored to its upright position. Please turn off mobile phones and electrical devices . . .'

Kathy reached into her pocket and pulled out her phone. Her eyelids already felt droopy. She'd thought about taking a Puralex before heading to the airport, to help deal with the stress of the check-in process, but as she stood at the bathroom mirror, staring at herself, she thought she noticed a slight disapproving expression on her own face.

'Okay,' she said and threw the packet of pills into the bin. The airport experience hadn't been that bad, apart from Elizabeth sniffing and wiping her eyes throughout. Eventually Kathy had had to pull her usual trick and run off after a quick hug.

'I love you,' she'd said. 'I'm glad I found you. I'm glad

I found what I came for.'

'And what was that?' her aunt asked, looking at her curiously.

'Family,' Kathy replied. 'Of course.'

And then she was gone, before Elizabeth could start on another speech about what a wonderful girl she had turned out to be.

Kathy unlocked the phone, so she could switch it off.

One missed call.

She tapped on the icon, unable to resist.

'Ma'am, could you please turn off your phone?'

Kathy nodded, otherwise ignoring the flight attendant. She stared at the screen, puzzled. *Who the hell is Antwain?* she thought to herself. *What kind of name is that, anyway?*

She tapped on the contact icon next to the name. A mobile phone number came up and a website address. *Vampirecorps.com.* The plane started to move.

'Miss, please turn that off now,' the flight attendant repeated, a little tetchy now. It was a long flight. She didn't need this.

'Okay,' Kathy said absently, 'okay.'

She switched the phone off and the flight attendant walked away.

Kathy pushed against the upright seat back, trying to get comfortable. She closed her eyes as the rumble of the engines became a roar and they headed off down the runway. Kathy gloried in the thought of the power thrusting her towards home. Towards her new life.

I'll check out that website when I get back, Kathy thought to herself. A few minutes later, as the plane headed west, over Oxford and still climbing, Kathy was asleep.

Two hundred miles behind the plane, twenty feet below the dank, black loam of Highgate Cemetery, a light flared, a struck match.

Draco used the flame to illuminate the photograph Kathy had given him. He stared at it for a long time, crying inside, but joyful at the strength it provided. It reminded him what he was struggling for. Kathy held all their hopes within her now.

The match burned his fingers and he snuffed it. Draco decided against lighting another. There were twelve left in the box he'd found on the floor. For now the image in his memory was bright enough. He could light another when it dimmed too much.

He'd cleared out the sarcophagus and laid Amber's body in it, gently. The dusty piles of clothes, he'd moved into an adjoining chamber, clearing up, removing all trace of the incursion, anxious to get back to his lonely vigil, free from distraction.

The vampire groaned inside him and began rattling the cage in one of its periodic and fruitless attempts to escape. Draco smiled grimly and clutched the matchbox and the photograph tightly to his chest, not quite alone in the dark after all.

MIST

The last shred of the mist swirled and drew back, and she saw where she was. She was very, very far from home.

Midnight: a mist-haunted wood with a bad reputation. A sweet sixteen party, and thirteen-year-old Nell is trying to keep her sister, spoilt birthday-girl Gwen, out of trouble. No chance. Trouble finds Gwen and drags her through the mist.

Only Nell guesses who's behind the kidnap - the boy she hoped was her friend, the gorgeous but mysterious Evan River.

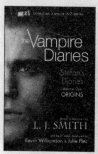 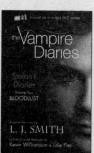 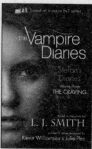 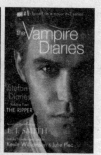
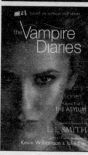 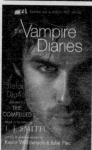

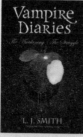
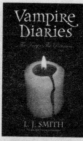

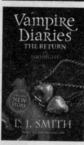
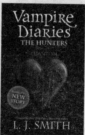